Command,
Control, and
The Common
Defense

Command, Control, and The Common Defense

C. Kenneth Allard

Lieutenant Colonel,

United States Army

Yale University Press ■ New Haven & London

Designed by Sonia L. Scanlon and set in Times Roman text and
Helvetica display type by The Composing Room of Michigan, Inc.,
Grand Rapids, Michigan.

Printed in the United States of America by Vail-Ballou Press,
Binghamton, N.Y.

Library of Congress Cataloging-in-Publication Data

Allard, C. Kenneth (Carl Kenneth), 1947–
     Command, control, and the common defense / C. Kenneth
Allard.
          p.   cm.
     Includes bibliographical references.
     ISBN 0-300-04360-0 (alk. paper)
     1. United States—Armed Forces—
Organization.   2. Command and control systems—United
States.   3. United States—Armed Forces—
Equipment.   I. Title.
UA23.A593   1990
355.3′3041′0973—dc20   89-25084
                                                   CIP

The paper in this book meets the guidelines for permanence and
durability of the Committee on Production Guidelines for Book
Longevity of the Council on Library Resources.

10 9 8 7 6 5 4 3 2 1

This book is respectfully dedicated to the memory of Congressman
Bill Nichols of Alabama—Soldier, statesman, patriot

The Romans said, "If you would have peace, you must be prepared for war."
And while we pray for peace, we can never forget that organization, no less
than a bayonet or an aircraft carrier, is a weapon of war. We owe it to our
soldiers, our sailors, our airmen, and our marines to ensure that this weapon is
lean enough, flexible enough, and tough enough to help them win if, God
forbid, that ever becomes necessary.

> From the opening statement by Congressman Nichols
> House Armed Services Committee
> Hearings on the Reorganization of the
>   Department of Defense
> February 19, 1986

Contents

Acknowledgments ix

List of Abbreviations xiii

1 Paradigms and Perspectives 1

2 The Roots of Service Autonomy, 1776–1850 21

3 Paradigms on Land and Sea, 1861–1921 47

4 The Quest for Unity of Command 88

5 Setting the Scene: Formative Influences on Modern

   Command and Control 123

6 Tactical Command and Control of American Armed

   Forces: Problems of Modernization 148

7 Building Joint Approaches: Of JINTACCS

   and JTIDS 189

8 Historical Linkages and Future Implications 241

Notes 265

Bibliography 293

Index 305

Acknowledgments

There is no way that a seven-year research effort can be completed without the help of many people, far too many than can be mentioned here. This book would not be complete, however, if I failed to thank those people whose contributions were essential. Professors Robert L. Pfaltzgraff, Jr., of the Fletcher School of Law and Diplomacy, Tufts University, and Professor Anthony G. Oettinger of the Harvard University Program on Information Resources Policy supervised the dissertation that eventually resulted in this book: both merit my heartfelt thanks for their professionalism, their sound guidance, and, most of all, their patience over a very long haul. Both the Harvard Program on Information Resources Policy and the Security Studies Program at Fletcher, then headed by Professor Uri Ra'anan, provided generous financial support, which is gratefully acknowledged.

The privilege of completing a combined degree program at two such distinguished institutions as the Kennedy School of Government at Harvard and the Fletcher School at Tufts would not have been possible for a serving Army officer without the sponsorship of a third distinguished institution: the United States Military Academy at West Point. It was a great honor to serve for three years as an assistant professor in the USMA Department of Social Sciences under Col. Lee D. Olvey: my debt to him and to all my colleagues in "The Department" is profound. The generous support of the Military Education Foundation is also acknowledged with appreciation. Brig. Gen. Roy K. Flint, dean of the Academic Board, deserves special thanks for his encouragement and the support provided by the USMA Science Research Laboratory during a 1985 fellowship at the National War College, Washington, D.C. Col. Roy Stafford, dean of the faculty at the National War College, extended every personal and professional courtesy during that fellowship; his generosity and encouragement helped to make the dissertation a reality. Gen. Robert T. Herres, United States Air Force, vice chairman of the Joint Chiefs of Staff, and Lt. Gen. C. E. McKnight, Jr., United States Army (Ret.), are two officers who served with great distinction during their respective tours of duty as the director, Command, Control, and Communications Systems Directorate, Office of the Joint Chiefs of Staff. Both General Herres and General McKnight made themselves and their staffs available during my frequent research visits; in 1984, they were equally generous in extending institutional support during a summer internship. Consequently, my respectful thanks are due both of these men, as well as the members of their directorate.

Paul Hammond of the University of Pittsburgh, Martin Van Creveld of the Hebrew University of Jerusalem, Frank Snyder of the Naval War College, and Lt. Gen. John H. Cushman, United States Army (Ret.), were kind enough to review the entire dissertation and to provide many comments and suggestions that made the task of editing and rewriting immeasurably easier. Two former assistant secretaries of defense who served with great distinction in the field of command and control, Gerald P. Dinneen and Donald C. Latham, reviewed the manuscript, and were similarly generous with their comments and encouragement. A special vote of thanks is due all six of these men for service "above and beyond the call of duty." The following military colleagues also reviewed the manuscript, either in whole or in part, and provided many helpful comments: Colonels Raoul H. Alcala and Rodger L. McElroy; Lieutenant Colonels Joseph Collins, William Culley, and William Beletsky; and Major Shelly Myers. Alan Sabrosky (formerly of the Army War College) also read the manuscript and provided some notably timely assistance on several occasions. Bert Hopkins, of the JTIDS Joint Program Office, has been an invaluable source of assistance and insight into the often arcane problem of interoperability, in both its electronic and bureaucratic manifestations.

I was fortunate enough in 1985 to be awarded a Congressional Fellowship by the American Political Science Association. Serving on Capitol Hill and participating in the events that ultimately led to the passage of the Goldwater-Nichols Act was an experience that would have been heady enough under any circumstances; but because it came at the same time that many of the ideas in this book were being formed, the fellowship provided a firsthand look at the problem of defense reorganization in a way that nothing else could have. Grateful thanks are due Congressmen Les Aspin (chairman of the House Armed Services Committee), Nicholas Mavroules, and John Kasich, as well as Kim Wincup, the committee's staff director. Dr. Arch Barrett, professional staff member of the House Armed Services Committee, deserves special mention for playing the interlocking roles of taskmaster, teacher, and friend. Mentors on the other side of the Hill include Senator John Warner, Les Brownlee, and James R. Locher III of the staff of the Senate Armed Services Committee. All these men will certainly recognize my debt to the late congressman Bill Nichols, to whose memory this book is respectfully dedicated.

His death in 1988 deprived the Congress and the country of a dedicated public servant who not only was a leader in the defense reorganization effort but was in a class by himself in his knowledge of politics and people.

It has been my privilege to be both personally and professionally acquainted with three distinguished soldiers who are known primarily for their lifelong records of outstanding service to their country: Major General Otto L. Nelson, Jr. (1902–85), General J. D. Nittle, USMC, and Dr. Lawrence H. Legere. Early in their careers, however, each of these gentlemen made contributions to the study of American defense organization that have had an enduring influence on each succeeding generation of students of the subject. While their works are liberally cited in the pages which follow, their advice and encouragement have been equally important. It is my hope that this book will in some small way repay their kindness and confidence.

No matter how helpful the assistance offered by everyone listed here, errors of fact or interpretation are of course my sole responsibility. The reader is also urged to remember that the views expressed throughout this work are the personal opinions of the author and do not necessarily reflect the official positions of the U.S. Army, the U.S. Department of Defense, or the government of the United States.

Finally, a special note of appreciation is due to the three ladies in my life: my wife, our daughter, and my mother. All three have helped in many ways, most of all by putting up with the countless inconveniences and personal shortcomings of someone who has seemed wedded not only to books and word processors but also to his uniform.

Abbreviations

AWACS	Airborne Warning and Control System
C2	Command and Control
C3	Command, Control, and Communications
C3I	Command, Control, Communications, and Intelligence
C4	Command, Control, Communications, and Computers
CINC	Commander in Chief (usually of a unified or specified command)
DA	Department of the Army
DOD	Department of Defense
HASC	House Armed Services Committee
OCMH	U.S. Army, Office of the Chief of Military History
OJCS	Organization of the Joint Chiefs of Staff
OSD	Office of the Secretary of Defense
JCS	Joint Chiefs of Staff
JTIDS	Joint Tactical Information Distribution System
NDU	National Defense University
NTDS	Naval Tactical Data System
SASC	Senate Armed Services Committee
USA	U.S. Army
USAF	U.S. Air Force
USMC	U.S. Marine Corps
USN	U.S. Navy
WWMCCS	Worldwide Military Command and Control System

1   Paradigms and Perspectives

On November 14, 1985, Secretary of Defense Caspar W. Weinberger appeared before the Senate Armed Services Committee at a hearing called to examine the organization of his department. At issue was a broadly crafted piece of legislation introduced by Senators Barry Goldwater and Sam Nunn to correct Pentagon organizational and command problems widely believed to have been at the heart of operational failures such as the 1980 Iranian hostage rescue attempt and the 1983 bombing of the Marine barracks in Beirut. Even the successful American invasion of Grenada two years before was included in this criticism, especially when allegations were made that the Army, Navy, Air Force, and Marine contingents deployed to the island had experienced difficulty communicating with one another and coordinating their movements. The most widely reported incident in that conflict was the apocryphal tale that an Army element, pinned down by enemy fire and unable to communicate with supporting ships and aircraft from the other services, had used the island's telephone system and one soldier's AT&T credit card to place a long-distance call to Fort Bragg in order to send a message.[1]

That this story was never subsequently confirmed and that the soldier in question was never produced did not prevent the incident from taking its place in popular mythology (a version of it even appeared in a 1986 movie, *Heartbreak Ridge,* which was loosely modeled on the Grenada operation). It was not particularly surprising that the senators' questioning of Secretary Weinberger would eventually turn to this issue. The *Washington Post* recorded the following exchange between Weinberger and Nunn:

> The defense secretary also clashed repeatedly with Sen. Sam Nunn . . . on whether inadequate radios hampered U.S. military forces during the invasion of Grenada in 1983.
>
> "They were not hampered significantly," Weinberger testified.
>
> "That is directly contradictory to your own Department of Defense report," Nunn said, holding up a thick, mostly

secret after-action report on the Grenada operation. "You are making unclassified statements that are completely rebutted by classified material."

"To say those communications problems interfered with the success of the operation is to fly in the face of the facts," Weinberger said.

"That's very crafty wording," Nunn snapped, his voice rising. "The operation was successful; therefore, nothing interfered with the success of the operation because it was successful. That's a ridiculous way to examine problems. . . . I congratulate you as a lawyer, but as a secretary of defense I don't think that's an appropriate method by which to proceed in solving problems."[2]

The asperity of this exchange turned out to be an unhappy harbinger of things to come. For the next eleven months, both the Senate and the House struggled with the issue of Pentagon reorganization, engaged at every step by representatives of the Office of the Secretary of Defense and the uniformed services who, despite their public protestations of support for the effort, feared that congressionally mandated reforms would upset relationships and procedures that had endured for more than a generation.

Their reservations are not hard to understand. For one thing, the Reagan administration had come into office pledged to build up the nation's defenses. During the preceding five years, modernization of nuclear and conventional forces, rather than structural modification of the defense establishment, had been one of the administration's main priorities. Altering that course threatened goals that were about to be realized, as well as raising difficult issues of stewardship sure to be exploited by the divided Ninety-ninth Congress. At a more profound level, the services sensed that the effort to reform the Pentagon had serious implications for the structure of command, that is, the system by which authority is distributed throughout a military organization. Each of the services has such a structure: it is a well-defined, hierarchical, top-to-bottom arrangement that precisely defines every layer of the organization, its relationship to every other activity, and—to a very large degree—the roles and functions of the people who make it up. The formal chain of command, the arrangement of "line-and-block charts," the perquisites of rank, and even the training of future leaders are all constituent parts of this system. Although command structures differ from service to service, they are at the heart of military life, exerting a common regulatory effect on the soldier, the sailor, the airman, and the marine.

The downside to this common heritage of service authority is that it is largely an internal mechanism and so, in a sense, stops at the water's edge.

Precisely because service command structures exert first claim on the loyalties of their members, command relationships *between* the services have been a persistent problem. In fact, it was largely because of the perception that there were such difficulties in these interservice, or joint, relationships, that the Ninety-ninth Congress eventually passed the Goldwater-Nichols Department of Defense Reorganization Act of 1986. Its provisions confirmed service suspicions, because the act represented a profound shift of power in favor of the joint institutions of the defense establishment. Among its major provisions:

- The commanders in chief (CINCs) of the unified and specified commands (who control American forces in the field) were given additional authority over their service components and assured of a larger role in defense resource planning.
- The chairman of the Joint Chiefs of Staff (JCS) was given additional authority over the services, including directive authority over the Joint Staff, a full-time four-star deputy empowered to act in his stead, and formal designation as the president's principal military adviser.
- Joint service experience was to be a legal prerequisite for any officer advancing to flag or general officer rank; also, a new joint specialty was created to groom future CINCs and chairmen of the JCS for performance in the joint arena.
- Service headquarters staffs were to be reorganized, the objectives being functional decentralization and personnel reductions of up to 15 percent.
- For the first time, the president was ordered to transmit to Congress an annual report detailing the "national security strategy of the United States," including not only an assessment of the nation's military capabilities but an analysis of how its political and economic powers might be brought to bear in support of American foreign policy goals.[3]

The phrase "landmark legislation" occurs commonly enough on Capitol Hill to encourage caution in applying it. Yet Goldwater-Nichols uniquely deserved this title and more: it was the most important single defense enactment since the National Security Act of 1947 created a permanent postwar military establishment.

Anomalies

It is interesting that the initial attention to the problems of command and control on Grenada did not result in more extended commentary in the ensuing hearings before the Armed Services committees of the House and the

Senate. Admittedly, there were other issues that were more easily understood and discussed in the open sessions that largely characterized these proceedings. But if the congressional purpose was to explore the problems of the military command structure of the United States and to address ways in which it might be improved, then the means by which that command is exercised might well have come in for greater attention. A notable exception occurred in the special staff report on defense organization prepared for the Senate Armed Services Committee by James R. Locher III. The report stated flatly that the reason command and control problems existed on Grenada was because "each Service continues to purchase its own communications equipment which all too frequently isn't compatible with the equipment of the other Services." It then quoted approvingly the following assessment by Gen. Wallace H. Nutting, the former commander in chief of the U.S. Readiness Command: "It is a function of the way we prepare for war and that is the fact that the law charges each military department to organize, train, and equip forces to operate in a particular environment for which it is responsible. That is too simple an answer, but that is where it begins: with the way we prepare for war."[4]

General Nutting's comment is intriguing. If each of the military departments is charged with the responsibility of organizing, training, and equipping forces for a particular operational environment, then it follows that service, rather than joint, command structures exercise the dominant influence over those forces. The communications media linking the service command structures simply reflect this basic organizational fact of life. Because they are directed toward the particular Army, Navy, Marine, and Air Force units taking part in an operation, an electronic confusion of tongues can result when these forces attempt to communicate with each other. It can easily be argued, as Secretary Weinberger did, that Grenada was a hastily conceived and executed operation, that such command and control difficulties as existed are understandable when seen in that context, and that, in any case, none of those problems interfered with the success of the invasion.

The counter to that argument, however, is that Grenada was hardly a fair test of the American military command and control system. Neither Soviet forces nor their surrogates were present in the numbers or with the capabilities that would be expected closer to the Eurasian land mass. Almost as important was the fact that electronic warfare was not a factor on Grenada as it certainly would be in any engagement with the Soviets, their major clients, or even the military regimes of many third world countries. Here the full measure of stress would be applied to American command and control links, including intelligence eavesdropping, active interference with radio transmissions, various forms of electronic "spoofing," and the use of the electromagnetic spectrum to identify and destroy high-value targets. Ironically, it is just those applications of modern warfare in which the American military machine, with its access to high-tech, state-of-the-art electronics, is thought to have an intrinsic advantage over its opponents. Writers such as retired Army Lt. Gen. John Cushman have stressed that the capabilities of modern command and control systems lend a qualitatively new dimension to the modern battlefield, breaking down artificial organizational barriers and rewarding those commanders who are swift and innovative enough to seize the opportunities thus offered. Other analysts have gone so far as to suggest the existence of an entirely new plane of combat, known as command and control warfare, in which the active use of one's own electronic information systems, together with protective command and control countermeasures, makes its possible to seize the tactical initiative, cripple the enemy's command and control system, and thereby defeat his forces.[5]

Whatever the facts contained in the classified reports brandished by Secretary Weinberger and Senator Nunn, American forces on Grenada had not, at the very least, displayed a conspicuous virtuosity in applying these new precepts to the invasion. Although it was little noticed at the time, further evidence on this point had surfaced just three weeks before the Senate hearings, when Navy Secretary John Lehman announced that he was terminating his service's separate role in a joint command and control project called JTIDS—for Joint Tactical Information Distribution System. Although the news that the Navy was now committing itself to the existing Army–Air Force version of JTIDS might have been welcome under other circumstances, the sad fact was that the Navy was taking this action only after having invested nine years of effort and at least $100 million in a stubborn effort to maintain a separate identity in what was supposedly a joint project. And even then, Secretary Lehman had canceled the project only after a restive House Armed Services Committee had questioned the wisdom of further investments in the increasingly high-risk approach taken by the Navy's JTIDS contractors.[6]

Again there were the predictable, plausible explanations: JTIDS was an experimental program in which the Navy had taken one alternative approach while the other services explored another; developmental technology was inherently risky and diverse; JTIDS was not really a single system but a family of systems; and so on.[7] Whatever the merits of those arguments, a larger pattern was emerging, which itself was suggestive of some underlying problems:

■ The JTIDS program, which continued through 1986 despite being billed in at least one newspaper article as a "Six Hundred Million Dollar Pentagon

Fiasco,"[8] seemed to demonstrate that the persistent problem of interservice rivalry would affect the evolution of command and control systems meant for use by American forces well into the twenty-first century. Interestingly, this development seemed to have taken place against the backdrop of a management structure that was resolutely "joint," the application of a technological approach that appeared all-embracing, and the expenditure of considerable amounts of the taxpayers' money—however much the exact figures may have varied.

■ The JTIDS experience seemed to confirm the earlier manifestations of interoperability problems seen in the service communications systems on Grenada. If the engineering of future command and control systems in the calmly deliberative atmosphere of the laboratory produced the same kinds of interservice difficulties seen in the heat and confusion of combat, then perhaps General Nutting had been correct in his assessment: maybe the root of the problem lay in the way the services were organized to prepare for war.

■ Finally, the most presumptive evidence of a larger pattern lay in the yearlong effort devoted by the Congress to passing the most comprehensive defense organization measure in a generation. Clearly this massive effort was driven by congressional perceptions that, to borrow a phrase often used during those debates, "the system was broke and it needed fixing." The system in question was nothing less than the structure of command, and in adjusting the relationship between the service and joint military institutions, the Congress made every effort to ensure that it had corrected the problems that had seemingly contributed to flawed operations in the field and ineffective functioning in the overall organization of the nation's defenses.

To put the point plainly, it had become clear that there was a larger pattern affecting the development of individual weapons systems and equipment (especially visible in command and control programs such as JTIDS), military organization (the way the services equip their forces and prepare them for war), and general command structure (the distribution of power within a military organization). The common thread linking the three is that the services, in preparing their forces for war, can have very different perspectives on war itself—if not on the nature of such conflicts, then certainly on the fundamental questions of service roles, missions, and capabilities that would be brought to bear. Historically, these service viewpoints feature the respective applications of land power, sea power, or air power as a first priority, generally stopping well short of a joint perspective in which the different elements of warfare are combined in pursuit of the nation's strategic goals. The JTIDS case points this up most vividly, if for no other reason than that it involved the application of computer technology to the combat operations of the three separate services—or four, if the Marines are counted. It may well be that Joseph Weizenbaum is correct in his assertion that there is something about the rules and operations of the computer that forces the user to be explicit about what might otherwise remain implicit.[9] Certainly there was something about putting JTIDS in the hands of the soldier, the sailor, the pilot, and the marine that forced their parent services to confront some fundamental differences that might otherwise have remained latent. Those differences were summed up in a classic statement by Gen. Paul X. Kelley, then Commandant of the Marine Corps, who, in reflecting on interservice rivalry and his own well-publicized opposition to the Pentagon reorganization effort, observed that "asking a man to be as loyal to the other services as he is to his own is like asking him to be as loyal to his girlfriends as he is to his wife."[10]

The subject of this book is precisely that tension between the traditions of service loyalty and the need to seek the often elusive synergy of joint combat power. The general question it addresses is this: What are the characteristics of the American military structure—its traditions, history, and organization—that affect the evolution of command and control in the information age? More specifically, what are the elements contributing to separate service identities, and how have those identities affected interservice relationships? How has the evolution of interservice relationships affected the structure of command and the operational employment of combatant forces? In what ways does the contemporary structure of command affect and influence the technological choices made in modernizing the command and control systems used by the armed forces of the United States?

The answers to these questions are subsumed in the thesis of this book, which is that the American military establishment embodies a tradition of service separatism, one that has been renewed and reinforced by patterns and paradigms of thought that stress the decisive effect of military force on the land, at sea, or in the air. Although these traditions, the natural result of historical circumstance and political choice, have on the whole served the nation well, they inevitably complicate the problem of command and control in an age of global missions and technological uncertainty. Increasingly, those missions and the forces required to carry them out have involved all the services. The need to seek unity of command over these joint forces, as well as the timeless effort to extend the span of control of military leaders and their civilian superiors, are parallel efforts that have inevitably collided with service roles, traditions, and prerogatives. Ultimately the problems of com-

mand, control, and organization—like every other aspect of joint endeavor—
are incapable of being solved without a redefinition of military professionalism that in its highest form places primary emphasis on the joint integration of
American combat power.[11]

Approaches

The question of service loyalties is not an unfamiliar one, usually
surfacing as "interservice rivalry," the pejorative of choice whenever a writer
wishes to characterize some aspect of military malfeasance or inefficiency
with the comforting outlines of stereotype. Although that appellation is certainly appropriate in some instances—including several discussed in this
book—it is probably more accurate to use the term *autonomy* to describe the
preferred or actual conditions governing the organizational life of the services. That word is variously defined by Webster's *New World Dictionary* as
"self-governing," "independent," or "functioning independently without control by others."[12] But none of those definitions quite captures the essence of
military organizations striking a constant balance between the requirements of
top-down control (including political control) and the need to delegate authority effectively enough to perform mission requirements, especially in remote
operational environments. It is equally important in applying this term to
appreciate that it suggests both a basic division of labor (separate land, sea,
and air forces) and a profound historical legacy. Each of the services is
responsible for producing the forces that ultimately defend American interests
in its particular operational environment, but each is also the repository of
powerful traditions and heritages embedded in the deepest roots of American
history. The Army, the Navy, the Air Force, and the Marines therefore need
to be understood not only as organizations engaged in the constant effort to
balance the pressures of centralization and decentralization but also as large,
well-established, and uniquely American institutions.

The strong self-concepts that characterize the services imply subtle degrees
of organizational difference that are sometimes overlooked. But the idea that
there are distinct service "personalities" or "styles" has received increasing
attention in recent years with the renewal of interest in defense reform. A 1986
best-seller, *The Straw Giant* by journalist Arthur T. Hadley, is a wide-ranging
critique not only of specific Pentagon problems but of the culture that helps
produce them. According to Hadley, it is a culture based on important intellectual and even psychological differences that affect each of the services and
can impede their ability to work together. These differences are rooted in the
operational conditions derived from specific service roles and missions.

Hadley offers this example: "The new-fledged Army lieutenant soon learns that he can make no movement without coordination. He cannot go right, left, backward, or forward without informing units on his right and left, artillery, tanks, supply trains, his superiors—all in detail. He is, for all his command authority, a rather restricted part of a whole. His unit's success, indeed its survival, rests on efforts not just of himself, but of outsiders."[13]

This picture is in stark contrast to the self-contained independence of a naval officer commanding a ship at sea: "The commander of a ship puts the wheel to the right, or commands a starboard turn, and, self-contained within the ship, all the paraphernalia of battle—ammunition, men, food, fuel—turn right also. There is no coordination necessary, no requesting permission, no letting people know. While the ship must return to base or conform to formation if maneuvering with a task force, it remains totally independent in ways no Army unit attains."[14]

Air Force officers, members of a service built around futuristic concepts and high technology, have equally different psychological profiles: "They are more apt to have a more passionate attachment to machinery and a very different sense of time. After all, an Air Force pilot can be in Moscow for lunch. An Army officer measures an hour's progress in yards, a naval officer in miles, an Air Force officer in continents."[15]

In a related article commenting on Goldwater-Nichols just prior to its enactment, Hadley made another important point: "These differences are, of course, inherently difficult to define or quantify. But they are often apparent to the most casual observer, and even seemingly simple questions of operations or tactics can elicit vastly different responses from officers who come from different service backgrounds. Taken together, these intellectual and psychological differences represent a key source of conflict and competition within our armed services. And until steps are taken to overcome them, it seems unlikely that any bureaucratic reorganization will greatly improve our defenses."[16]

Although Hadley's contention might seem self-evident to some, his negative view of service autonomy is not shared by all observers. Two articles in the July 1985 edition of the U.S. Naval Institute *Proceedings* are cases in point. In "A Separatist Case," Army Col. William G. Hanne argued that the Navy's historical tradition of technical competence and independence at sea explained its great reluctance to accept a strongly integrated, centralized command structure in which naval perspectives would be watered down (if that phrase may be used) to a least-common-denominator compromise influenced by the other services.[17] In reply, Navy Comdr. T. R. Fedyszyn set forth "A Maritime Perspective" which agreed with much of Hanne's formulation but argued that this was a good thing. "Specifically, the [Joint Chiefs of Staff, or JCS system] reflects the Navy's ideas of decentralization and unit autonomy, and its decidedly operational focus."[18] His argument was that the JCS system preserved the essential elements of service autonomy while promoting effective joint action and that it achieved this by encouraging a full airing of views which the nation's political leadership was free to accept or reject. Therefore, the JCS "symbolizes affiliation with a system designed to protect service loyalty, autonomy and competition while improving and rationalizing joint dialogue and planning."[19] Indeed, the system not only "resonates naturally with this maritime perspective" but also coincides with the democratic, pluralistic traditions of the American political culture.[20]

Interestingly enough, both sets of arguments implicitly accept the idea that autonomy is an important determinant of both the national command structure and service organization. Equally important is their acceptance of the idea that autonomy springs from underlying cultural differences—which are themselves grounded in the operational variances of combat on land, at sea, or in the air. Commander Fedyszyn also echoed a familiar point from American civil-military relations theory by his assertion that the nation's political values and beliefs exercise an important influence in determining the overall shape and characteristics of its military command structure. On the one hand, this observation may be sufficiently well understood as to be conventional wisdom. On the other, the effect of these varied influences in determining distinctive service personalities is, as Hadley pointed out, an exceedingly difficult thing to define or quantify.

Samuel P. Huntington's major works on civil-military relations, *The Soldier and the State* and *The Common Defense,* are the definitive chronicles of the rise of American military professionalism in the nineteenth and twentieth centuries. For the present inquiry, Huntington's contributions are particularly relevant not only for their historical insights but also for the light they shed on the development of the fundamental traditions and strategic principles associated with each of the services. In his view, "technicism, popularism, and professionalism are the three strands of the American military tradition."[21]

Technicism represents the practical and intellectual mastery the military man brings to his task, while popularism reflects the constant effort to win democratic and political support for military institutions. Professionalism embodies the concepts of both technical mastery and acceptance of the military's place in society; as such, it is the highest expression of the military's own aspirations. In tracing these principles and presenting their effects on the development of the Army and Navy, Huntington repeatedly calls attention to the doctrines that played important formulative roles in the growth of service professionalism and, eventually, in their respective cultures. For the Army, the writings of Baron Henri Jomini and Karl von Clausewitz were instrumental in the development of land power doctrine; the theories of sea power espoused by Alfred Thayer Mahan exercised a similar function for the Navy.[22]

Huntington's use of these strategic thinkers suggests the existence of separate service ideologies, which may help in understanding the impact of service autonomy on both interservice relationships and modern command and control. Looking for that common thread in the field of service-related ideologies calls to mind a classic work of contemporary strategy written in 1966 by Rear Adm. J. C. Wylie. In *Military Strategy: A General Theory of Power Control*, Admiral Wylie succinctly summarized the three major schools of strategic thought that have exercised a great influence over the American military establishment. They are:

- Continental or land power theory: Derived principally from Jomini, Clausewitz, and the record of American military practice over more than two centuries, its major tenets call for the destruction of the enemy army and effective control over the means required to bring this objective about.
- Maritime strategy: Heavily influenced by the writings of Alfred Thayer Mahan, classic maritime strategy aims for effective control of the sea by decisive defeat of the enemy's fleet. Once established, control of the sea also permits power to be projected onto the land.
- Air theory: Closely associated with the writings of Giulio Douhet and Billy Mitchell, the theory asserts the primacy of air power over every other form of combat because the inherently offensive nature of air power gives it a decisive edge over lesser, defensive weapons. Classically, this has meant the heavy bomber; in contemporary parlance, it is most closely associated with intercontinental ballistic missiles and nuclear warheads.[23]

Wylie's treatment of these strategic theories provides an important reference point for the present investigation. The three doctrines respectively correlate to the preferred theories of the Army, Navy, and Air Force. Each appears to contradict the others in a number of important respects, and, as Wylie noted as well, no general theory has yet been discovered that is capable of reconciling them.[24] Thus one can view these theories as the intellectual underpinnings of service autonomy, each one serving as a conceptual guidepost by which the service rationalizes its purposes, programs, and importance to the nation's security interests. Seen in this light, these sets of principles can also be conceptualized as "strategic paradigms," to borrow a phrase most closely associated with Thomas S. Kuhn. (Kuhn uses the term *paradigm* to designate a fundamental organizing concept, or "disciplinary matrix," that, once discovered, exerts a profound influence on its adherents.)[25]

Some more recent scholarship has also suggested the potential importance of the strategic paradigm as a heuristic device for assessing the impact of service perspectives on command and control problems, as well as a number of related concerns. Arnold Kanter's 1979 study *Defense Politics: A Budgetary Perspective* stressed "the importance of the military services as the predominant source of sanctions and the focus of organizational loyalty," despite the impact of unified combatant commands, defensewide agencies, and joint institutions such as the JCS. "Given an irreducible interdependence among the military services," Kanter wrote, "each service's efforts to stabilize its own organizational environment contain the seeds of unappeasable jurisdictional claims and insatiable demands for additional resources. In the absence of countervailing pressures, the interaction of these efforts will produce interservice rivalries over roles and missions as well as budget shares."[26] Consequently, defense policy outcomes do not so much represent conscious strategic choices as they reflect the results of bureaucratic bargains arrived at by quasi-independent service actors.

Rand Corporation analyst Carl Builder, in a 1987 report prepared for the Army, argued that the recognizable service differences observed by Huntington and Kanter are important in understanding that "the military services have acquired personalities of their own that are shaped by their experiences and which, in turn, shape their behavior." Builder suggested seven points of comparison to account for these differences, the most fundamental of which he described as "altars of worship"—basic service principles or cherished ideals. For the Navy, this altar is "independent command at sea," for the Air Force, the "inexhaustible fountain" of aerospace technology, and for the Army, its status as the nation's obedient servant: "If the Army worships at an altar, the object worshipped is the country; and the means of worship are service."[27] Builder merely repeated Wylie's original formulation in holding that service strategies result from these predispositions, especially with regard to the theories of air power derived by the Air Force from the writings of Douhet and Mitchell, as well as the sea power strategy first articulated by Mahan and now espoused by the Navy in latter-day form as the maritime strategy.[28]

The Army, however, operates at a comparative disadvantage in this realm: "The fact is that the Army does not have a theory which is the equivalent of the air or maritime strategy. It does have a theory of how it would prefer to fight— the Airland Battle doctrine—but not a concept for the selection of the means and ends of war, as do the Air Force and the Navy."[29] This would be a bold assertion under any circumstances, the more so in a report intended primarily for Army readers. Nevertheless, Builder cited Wylie as his authority for stating that "the Army does not have a strategic theory like the Air Force and Navy because its circumstances—its lack of control over terrain, engagement, and supporting resources—deny it the freedom to define war on its own terms."[30] The Army therefore is handicapped by a lack of coherence in the strategic planning process not only because its ideology lacks the hard, cogent outlines of sea power and air power theories but also because national commitments to use force do not always drive defense budgets, especially in matters relating to land power (such as airlift, sealift, fire support, and so on). Builder concluded that this very deficiency, however, may give the Army some future leverage in the renewed national commitment (both expressed and implied by the Goldwater-Nichols Act) to better joint planning and more disciplined strategic choices.[31]

Whatever the merits of that conclusion (and there were a number of internal Army audiences that doubtlessly found it persuasive), it is worth noting that Builder simply ignored classical land power theory: the standard works of Clausewitz and Jomini, for example, do not appear in his sources and are mentioned only briefly, if at all, in the text. This is in marked contrast to the approach taken by one of the more recently celebrated works in this field, *Strategy: The Logic of War and Peace,* by Edward N. Luttwak.[32] In the course of elaborating the paradoxical nature of strategy in war (a concept inspired by the Clausewitzian notion of friction), Luttwak delineated four levels of strategy (technical, tactical, operational, and theater) that are the underpinnings for the fifth and broadest level, or grand strategy. He placed great emphasis, however, on the theater level of strategy, which "governs the relationship between military strength and territory." In what amounts to a major restatement of continental theory, he analyzed this relationship almost entirely in terms of the relative strengths of competing ground forces that, together with their fire support, can be brought to bear within the confines of the theater itself.[33]

Lest anyone miss his point, Luttwak devoted an entire chapter to a debunking of the "nonstrategies" associated with sea power, air power, and nuclear weapons. His argument rested on two basic points. First, "it is not the medium of warfare that makes the difference (at the theater level), but rather the degree of mobility of the respective forces." Because ground forces are the decisive elements in any theater and have the greatest mobility limitations, they are a kind of least common denominator for evaluating force structures: "There is no basis for the conceptualization of distinct naval and air counterparts to theater strategy because it is the phenomena of ground warfare that are most important within that level."[34] Second, claims of autonomy for a single form of military power ultimately rest on the grounds "that it is decisive in itself." Yet Luttwak argued that both classical sea power and air power theories contain basic conceptual flaws (the relevance of maritime power against continental nations such as the Soviet Union, for example), and that their supposedly decisive effects have been exaggerated (such as the failure of conventional strategic bombing to overcome "the political and industrial resilience of its victims" during World War II).[35] The advent of nuclear weapons itself exerted a diminishing effect on traditional autonomy, even as it seemed to confirm in unexpected ways the tenets of the early prophets of air power. The catastrophic nature of nuclear weapons, however, as well as the operation of the perverse logic of strategy, seriously limited their operational utility, even as it led to extended military competition beneath the level of actual nuclear war.[36] Among other reasons, therefore, the need to think holistically about these instruments of actual or surrogate warfare drives the need for grand strategy and largely turns the notion of traditional autonomy into either irrelevance or anachronism.

Although they differ in their appreciation of the relative merits of traditional service paradigms, it can be argued that both Builder and Luttwak are correct: Builder in his realistic assessment of the bureaucratic utility of hard-edged service perspectives in making the incremental choices that are the daily bread of Pentagon life and Luttwak in his prescriptive call for greater attention to the demanding disciplines of grand strategy. On the one hand, the Army, the Navy, and the Air Force are not only the basic building blocks from which the combatant forces of the United States are formed; they are the institutional repositories of the military art as it relates to their particular missions. Applying this expertise to tough decisions on budget choices and weapons procurement is what they are expected to do, and it would be inconceivable for both the expertise and the applications not to have been shaped by fundamental notions of what is and is not important. Inevitably, these perspectives must shape the means (the armies, navies, and air forces, as well as their weapons, equipment, personnel, and doctrine) by which strategy at any level will be executed. On the other hand, there may be an important sense in which these fundamental service notions have been offset by the combined effects of a generation of defense unification, most recently augmented by the Goldwater-Nichols Act. A professor at the Naval War College has noted, for example, that "there is scant indication that the Navy today holds to the Mahanian view of strategy that exalts sea power over all other forms of military action, claims for navies an autonomous domain in the realm of warfare, and equates command of the sea with victory. . . . Mars, not Neptune, is again the god of war."[37]

Directions

The common ground between these perspectives may be suggested by an eminent student of military strategy, Peter Paret, who, in writing about Napoleon, noted that "each age has its own strategy."[38] Service autonomy is clearly an important part of the American military legacy, having been the primary organizational tool with which the nation's strategic needs were met for the better part of two centuries. Just as clearly, the search for more effective teamwork among the armed forces is likely to remain a dominant influence in the foreseeable future, as the nation's military and political establishment comes to grips with a new set of strategic challenges as we approach the twenty-first century. There is also much in the careful balance that must be struck between past legacy and future challenges that suggests various other constants: the timeless struggle between the tactical and the strategic, the operational and the bureaucratic, the decentralized and the centralized, or, for that matter, the rendering unto Caesar the things that are Caesar's. The trick in making these distinctions is to understand, first, that there are important differences of organizational perspective between those elements primarily charged with the nation's security and, second, that some of these differences are more important than others.[39]

Nowhere else are those differences less apparent but more real than in the field of command and control. To return for a moment to the Senate hearings that introduced this chapter, at least part of the reason for the particularly sharp questioning of Secretary Weinberger on the interoperability problems encountered during Grenada may have been a sense of incredulity (on Capitol Hill as well as among the public) that such a problem could even exist. After all, how could it be that forty years of joint experience were not enough to ensure that the armed forces could at least talk to one another? This was especially ironic since those armed forces represented a nation that had only recently triumphed over the trauma of the AT&T divestiture—an event that had carried some potential for a commercial interoperability problem of unprecedented magnitude. But here again was another example of the dichotomy noted earlier. It is the Army, the Navy, the Air Force, and the Marines who severally develop, procure, and field command and control systems (defending them at every step of the way, of course, before the civilian leadership of the Defense Department, the executive branch, and the Congress); so it is not particularly surprising that service perspectives should dominate this process. In contrast, it is the function of the joint military institutions (primarily the Joint Chiefs of Staff and the unified and specified commands) to weld these diverse service-procured systems into a coherent instrument of command that effectively controls all assigned combatant forces. The crux of the issue is the extent to which the JCS and the unified commanders are handicapped in achieving the level of cross-service integration required by the demands of combat.

It would also appear, however, that far more is involved here than matters of bureaucratic jurisdiction, however important the consequences. Consider, for example, the following definitions of three terms, *command, command and control,* and *command and control system,* as they are used in U.S. military parlance and throughout this book:

> *Command:* "The authority vested in an individual of the armed forces for the direction, coordination, and control of military forces."
>
> *Command and control:* "The exercise of authority and direction by a properly designated commander over assigned forces in the accomplishment of the mission. Command and control functions are performed through an arrangement of personnel, equipment, communications, facilities, and procedures which are employed by a commander in planning, directing, coordinating, and controlling forces and operations in the accomplishment of the mission."
>
> *Command and control system:* "The facilities, equipment, communications, procedures, and personnel essential to the commander for planning, directing, and controlling operations of assigned forces pursuant to the missions assigned."[40]

One of the most striking characteristics of these definitions is the extent to which they evoke the personal nature of command itself, especially the fact that it is vested in an individual who, being responsible for the "direction, coordination, and control of military forces," is then legally and professionally accountable for everything those forces do or fail to do. It is not hard to appreciate the extent to which service "personalities" can find their expression in characteristic command styles, such as the independence of command at sea noted by some observers.[41] At the very least, however, the focus of command, commanders, and command and control systems throughout the American defense establishment is on service components first, with joint or unified command as an important but still secondary priority.[42]

Given the fact that these service components are the nation's basic fighting forces (and that assignments to infantry battalions, destroyers, and fighter squadrons are obviously more exciting and rewarding than those involving joint or unified staff work), these priorities are understandable. They nevertheless create problems whenever command crosses service lines. In a Harvard syllabus prepared for use in command and control courses throughout the National Defense University system, Prof. Frank Snyder points out that "organizational decisions establish command and reporting relationships that, at a minimum, create requirements for communications . . . [not only] for the physical links themselves, but for staffs that share vocabularies and are dedicated to performing communications functions in the larger sense. . . . Organizational decisions shape the C3 [command-control-communications] system and commit C3 resources."[43] Modern communications technology, however, presents some important impediments: "As ideas move from the mind of one commander to the mind of another, the activities that are undertaken on the sending (transmitting) side have to be matched on the receiving side. . . . Everything that is done must be undone: every analog-to-digital conversion needs to be matched by a corresponding . . . conversion at the other end, every encryption by a decryption, and every modulation by a demodulation. . . . [Therefore] the dominant issue in establishing a telecommunications path is not its optimization but the standardization of the process. *More important than doing things the best way is doing them the same way"* (emphasis added).[44]

This perspective frames the major issue examined in this book: How do the pluralistic traditions of service autonomy which are a major part of the American military experience affect the way in which command is exercised over our combatant forces, now and in the future? This is an important question if one assumes that future military developments will increasingly demand a global view of American responsibilities, more coherent strategic choices (political and budgetary), and greater teamwork between the armed forces. It follows that command and control will be a linchpin in any such effort, not only because of its technological promise, but also because of its potential to transcend vastly different operational environments and equally diverse operational forces. The challenge, of course, involves the whole question of interoperability. Services organized and equipped on the basis of essential differences tend to do things the Army way, the Navy way, the Air Force way, or the Marine way—emphatically not the *same* way that Professor Snyder correctly emphasizes as a fundamental requirement of the modern telecommunications technology on which all command and control systems must ultimately depend.

This dual emphasis on organization and technology represents an organic view of command which assumes that its problems cannot be understood apart from the human institutions—governmental and military—that actually do the commanding and controlling. This viewpoint stands in some isolation from the usual discussions of command and control issues that appear in trade journals such as *Signal* magazine or *Defense Electronics* and are largely meant to inform a technically sophisticated audience of the latest projects, systems, or other developments in a fast-moving industry. Recently, however, the publishers of *Signal* have taken the lead in producing several volumes on conventional command and control issues, including naval and ground force applications.[45] Although both books are compilations of articles that appeared in *Signal* and other journals, they represent an important effort to establish broader linkages beyond the boundaries of system-specific problems. Another initiative by the same publisher produced Lt. Gen. John Cushman's book *Command and Control of Theater Forces: Adequacy,* which is a comprehensive analysis of the institutional, structural, and procedural problems confronting a unified commander.[46] The field of strategic command and control (which usually means nuclear command and control) is unusually complex and, because of its subject matter, presents major barriers to unclassified research. Yet it has recently been illuminated by the work of two men: Paul Bracken, in *The Command and Control of Nuclear Forces,* and Bruce G. Blair, in *Strategic Command and Control.*[47] Both volumes are remarkable for their authors' ability to look beyond specific weapons, warning systems, and command structures in examining the larger question of how American nuclear forces are commanded and controlled—and how well. Not only do these works demonstrate the merits of well-conceived organic approaches to this subject, but they also serve the further purpose of permitting this book to concentrate on those problems associated with the command and control of American conventional forces—those whose primary missions do not involve strategic nuclear retaliation.

Probably the most important contemporary work to treat the problem of command as a central focus is Martin Van Creveld's *Command in War.*[48] Viewing command as an "eternal function" of military organizations that is of surpassing importance, Van Creveld gives a brief summary of the nature of command and its functions in the "stone age" (that is, prior to effective long-distance communications) before examining at some length the evolution of command in modern warfare. That evolution, he asserts, is greatly affected by the technological improvements that make the exercise of command both more effective than ever before and yet more difficult to achieve. And, just as in modern economic theory, command in modern war is an activity in which everything depends on everything else: "Probably the most important point . . . is that command cannot be understood in isolation. The available data processing technology, and the nature of armaments in use; tactics and strategy; organizational structure and manpower systems; training, discipline, and what one might call the ethos of war; the political construction of states and the social makeup of armies—all these things and many more impinge on command in war and are in turn affected by it."[49]

In *Command in War,* as well as his more recent work, *Technology and War,* Van Creveld demonstrates the continuing importance of certain basic themes in military history: the competing demands of autonomy and integration, the similarly contradictory impulses of "rationalized" hierarchy versus the operational flexibility, and, above all, the ceaseless quest for military advantage through technology. Most recently, this quest has led to greater managerial efficiency through the use of automation, but with often pernicious side effects. Although there may be a cyclical quality to such apparently linear advances, Van Creveld observed a fundamental difference between the operational environments in which warfare is waged: "At sea and in the air, technology is required not merely in order to fight but for sheer survival. If only for this reason, and everything else being equal, *the simpler the environment, the greater the military benefit technological superiority can confer. By contrast, the terrestrial environment is much more complex,* including as it does terrain, lines of communication, obstacles natural or artificial, and every kind of clutter" (emphasis added).[50] Given the broad scope of his subject, as well as his primarily European focus, Van Creveld does not pursue the implications of this assertion in more depth. But an understanding that there is such a fundamental dichotomy in the operational environments of land, sea, and air warfare is the beginning of wisdom for any study of the unique requirements of the American military establishment. As such, that observation forms a point of departure for this book.

It is worth noting at this point that there is a downside in any effort to follow a broad-gauged approach to the study of command. Precisely because command and control issues affect so much that is critical to the nation's military establishment, there is a significant levels-of-analysis problem in any work such as this.[51] One could elevate the focus of the study to examine the issues of NATO command and control, encountering there an interoperability arena whose dimensions are the precise square of the American interservice problem; moreover, these sixteen nations are not only autonomous but sovereign. Similarly, one could focus the analysis beneath the level of the service, since intraservice loyalties can be almost as divisive as those encountered in the joint arena. The Navy is the classic example of three major communities wearing a single uniform: submarines, aviators, and surface warfare officers, as the captains of surface combatant ships are known, and even these classifications can easily be broken down still further. The justification for rejecting these alternative levels in order to focus on the services rests primarily on grounds of historical continuity: it is the Army, the Navy, and, more recently, the Air Force, rather than supranational alliances or shifting subordinate groupings, that have fought our wars. They also provide the most important continuous links to American societal values and therefore merit the closest attention in a study of this sort.

A final limitation is suggested by the need to keep the search for historical continuity within manageable proportions even while depicting its impact upon the evolution of modern command and control systems. For that reason, it is necessary to exclude detailed consideration of the defense reform debate that culminated in the passage of the 1986 Goldwater-Nichols Reorganization Act. Although that effort provides a backdrop for much of what follows, the scope of the legislative enactment and the extraordinary outpouring of literature that accompanied the debate dictate that it should be a boundary and not a focal point of this study. Clearly, that story and the impact the changes will have on the future evolution of command and control are topics richly deserving separate consideration.[52]

2　　The Roots of Service Autonomy, 1776–1850

During the first seventy-five years of their existence, the Army and the Navy fought the Revolutionary War, the War of 1812, and the Mexican War, as well as a host of what historians call lesser engagements. During each of these conflicts, the services confronted some profoundly challenging circumstances. Their response took on the hard outlines of precedence, especially when it came to their respective command structures and the basic norms those structures embodied. Gradually, the weight of precedence itself shaped basic organizational and even political directions for the future. This chapter explores those realities in terms of constitutional perspectives, the evolution of different command structures in each of the services, and the problems faced in tactical command and control during this period. The results of this evolutionary development will be seen in a brief review of the Mexican War.

Constitutional Imperatives

If the Revolutionary experience provided strong evidence of the latent American ability for self-defense, then the dismantling of the Continental Army and Navy under the Articles of Confederation provided an equally compelling counterpoint as those security arrangements proved inadequate to deal with British diplomatic intransigence and Indian problems on the frontier. The Constitutional Convention was thus forced to make a series of fundamentally important choices. In his classic work on American civil-military relations, *The Soldier and the State,* Samuel P. Huntington provided an eloquent summation of the mechanism set in place by the United States Constitution to ensure civilian control of the new military establishment:

> The Framers' concept of civilian control was to control the uses to which civilians might put military force rather than to control the military themselves. They were more afraid of military power in the hands of political officials than of political power in the hands of military officers. Unable to visual-

21

ize a distinct military class, they could not fear such a class. But there was need to fear the concentration of authority over the military in any single governmental institution. As conservatives, they wanted to divide power, including power over the armed forces.[1]

Huntington pointed out that the Constitutional Convention predated the rise of military professionalism that would characterize much of the history of warfare in the nineteenth century. The Framers turned to their own experiences as citizen-soldiers in the Revolutionary War in seeking an appropriate model for the future. The citizen-soldier was to be the Republic's unique substitute for a large standing army, the very idea of which was anathema. Control of the minimal defense establishment was to be divided between Congress and the president, as well as between the states and the federal government. In this division of power, Congress was given three principal responsibilities: "To declare War . . . To raise and support Armies . . . To provide and maintain a Navy." The president was made commander in chief of the Army and Navy of the United States, and the states were to exercise control over their militias until such time as they were called to federal service.[2]

This separation of powers implied from the outset that civilian control would always be compromised in part because the military would be forced to serve two masters. In delineating this view, Huntington set forth two models of civilian control: subjective and objective. Objective control isolates the military from society and sets limits on what it may and may not do. It assumes "the maximizing of military professionalism . . . [and] achieves its end by militarizing the military, making them the mirror of the state."[3] The Framers of the Constitution, however, adhered to the principle of subjective control, which presupposes the complete interpenetration of civil and military groups. Rather than standing apart from the civilian realm, the military is an integral part of it, fully participating in the give-and-take of a pluralistic, democratic society, civilian control being assured in large measure by the intimacy of this social embrace.[4]

Subjective control was a natural outgrowth of the reality the Framers perceived and incorporated into those constitutional provisions that would form the nexus of American civil-military relations. Since the military would function as an organic part of society, they would be forced to compete in the political arena along with other national elites and interest groups, forwarding their own agendas, seeking alliances, and advancing their claims for public support. The dual controls possessed by Congress and the presidency would reinforce the pluralistic nature of the system, ensuring that future generations of military leaders would be told not just what to do but, to a significant degree, how to do it.[5]

These competing models of objective and subjective control can be criticized as somewhat idealized, but their relevance for this analysis lies in the light they shed on the idea of service autonomy.[6] The concept of autonomy is implied in the language of the Constitution referred to earlier in which armies were to be "raised and supported," whereas navies were to be "provided and maintained." Implicit in this formula is the idea that the state militias and the citizen-soldiers who composed them were to be the decisive weapons used to repel any future invader, very much in the tradition of the Minutemen. Navies, by contrast, could hardly be called into existence with the same rapidity, so that it was necessary that they be "maintained" as a first line of defense for a country that increasingly looked to its maritime interests. Whatever permanent establishments were to be required for these two autonomous organizations—and opinions varied considerably in both the Constitutional Convention and in the state ratification conventions as to what those requirements should be—it was clear that questions of resources, missions, organization, and even personnel would be debated in an atmosphere characterized by considerable political scrutiny.

It was precisely the vitality of those controls that Alexander Hamilton, James Madison, and John Jay used as an argument in favor of the new Constitution. Hamilton, in particular, addressed himself to skeptical state legislatures (that of New York under Governor George Clinton being especially doubtful) by arguing that a small but permanent military force was essential not only to forestall pressures from neighboring British and Spanish colonies but also to perform the everyday task of manning garrisons on the western frontiers:

> These garrisons must either be furnished by occasional detachments
> from the militia, or by permanent corps in the pay of the government.
> The first is impracticable; and if practicable, would be pernicious. . . .
> The latter resource of permanent corps in the pay of the government
> amounts to a standing army in time of peace; a small one, indeed, but
> not the less real for being small. Here is a simple view of the subject that
> shows us at once the impropriety of a constitutional interdiction of such
> establishments, and the necessity of leaving the matter to the discretion
> and prudence of the legislature.[7]

Hamilton argued as well that the new Constitution contained safeguards sufficient to enable Congress to be both discreet and prudent in regulating whatever forces would be required in peace or war. Those provisions that assured legislative control of the purse strings would act to prevent any tendency to turn the Army into an agency of executive domination or a threat to American liberties.[8]

His defense of the Navy was couched in considerably less cathartic terms: "If we mean to be a commercial people, or even to be secure on our Atlantic side, we must endeavor, as soon as possible, to have a navy."[9] It is interesting to note that the twin points of his rationale for a navy—commercial expansion and national security—are a succinct statement of the primary and secondary missions the Navy would have for almost the first century of its existence. Madison developed the further point that a navy would become an essential adjunct of American diplomacy, thereby laying the ideological groundwork for a mission the Navy would acquire during the second century of its existence: projection of power.[10] Probably the most ingenious rationale for a navy, however, was written by Hamilton in Number 11 of *The Federalist* when he expanded the notion of maritime commerce to embrace the role each of the regions of the new Union could play in building and provisioning ships: "It happens, indeed, that different portions of confederated America possess each some peculiar advantage for this essential establishment." Southern wood could be a prime source of naval stores, the Middle States could produce iron for fixtures and weapons, and the sailors themselves could "chiefly be drawn from the Northern hive."[11] Although this view of the Navy as an agency of national integration can be taken at face value, one does not have to embrace Charles A. Beard's economic interpretation of the Constitution to read between Hamilton's well-crafted lines.[12] If a future navy was justifiable as a fundamental source of national security, then there was no reason a relatively permanent naval establishment should not also be an important source of economic strength throughout the states. Not only could a navy protect American commercial interests abroad, but its very existence would help promote them at home.

It is useful to summarize at this point the differences and similarities among these constitutional perspectives in relation to the question of service autonomy:

1. The language of the Constitution itself provided a basic division of labor that was fundamentally important for the subsequent organization of the armed forces of the United States. The Army and Navy were to be, almost from the outset, separate organizations set up to fulfill different functions. Although they were not well articulated at the time, both functions rested on a common set of strategic assumptions that emphasized America's insularity and its geographic isolation from powerful adversaries. Given the fac-

tors of insularity and isolation, it was expected by the Framers that the Navy would function as a kind of maritime police force in peace and a first line of defense in war. That first line was expected to capitalize on the factors of geography in order to allow sufficient time for the small constabulary garrison forces to be augmented by armies raised in the face of either war or national emergency. Although these armies would be disbanded once danger passed, there is no mistaking the Framers' clear understanding that political control of territory ultimately rested on the ability of ground forces to withstand threats from either Indians or colonial adversaries. If the Navy was to be the outward manifestation of American power, the Army was to be the essential instrument for maintaining continental security and facilitating expansion.

2. The difference of functions between the Army and the Navy led to a different assessment of the threat each posed to the fabric of American civil liberties. Precisely because the Navy was to have the bulk of its duties abroad, it does not seem to have been perceived as posing a threat comparable to that which was implicit in standing armies. Hamilton defended the necessity of a navy and some questioned the expense involved, but the only ideological cast to the debate seems to have come from spokesmen such as Patrick Henry, who considered all navies to be "instruments of imperial ambition."[13] In contrast, the Army's function was to exert territorial control at home, a capability that, if not fully guarded against, could easily become perverted by executive domination or personal ambition. These different functions led advocates such as Hamilton, Madison, and Jay to defend the military and naval establishments on different constitutional grounds. The unifying factor was, of course, that both services were to be completely subordinate to civil authority.[14]

3. Service functions were drawn with different views of commercial self-interest. The Navy's mission of protecting maritime commerce, its status in a seafaring nation where the line between commercial and naval establishments was often blurred, and the relative permanence of its shipyards and shore installations combined to give it a role that embraced the constitutional purposes both of the "Common Defense" and of the "General Welfare." The Army's functions were much narrower. Most of the time it was not to exist in any great numbers nor was it to be equipped with weapons requiring great public expenditures (harbor fortifications being the exception). It would usually comprise a series of isolated frontier garrison forces, which differed from the rest of pioneer society only by degree. Although the pork barrel would not be unknown in either service, the intimate relationship between

commercial and naval interests would often place nautical questions high on the political agenda.

Evolution of Command Structures: Heritage and Beginnings

The division of labor for national defense set forth by the Constitution over the next three-quarters of a century resulted in the creation of precedents that would contribute much to the historic traditions of the Army and the Navy. It was during this formative period as well that the services made a series of fundamental organizational choices that not only confirmed and advanced their separate identities but also revealed underlying differences in the way they viewed the essential military functions of command and staff. Those subtle but profound differences had an important effect on the way that each service confronted the problems brought about by the increasing complexity of warfare in their respective spheres. These responses in turn affected both the nature of their individual command structures and their overall relationship with each other.

It is ironic that many of these decisions seem to fit an evolutionary pattern as the services charted courses that were separate but roughly parallel. Indeed, they had begun that evolution in the same organizational cocoon, since Congress had created the War Department in 1789 and charged it with responsibility for both Army and Navy functions. This was due less to a perceived need for unified strategy than to the simple fact that the ships of the Revolutionary Navy had all been sunk, auctioned off, or otherwise disposed of. It was not until 1798, when the country stood on the brink of an undeclared naval war with France, that Congress created a separate Department of the Navy. By inaugurating these two agencies, Congress completed the first evolutionary step originally envisioned by Federalists such as Hamilton: executive authority concentrated in a single cabinet officer responsible for each department and that cabinet officer then being directly responsible to the president as commander in chief. By this legislative enactment, the constitutional precept of civilian control had now been welded into parallel chains of command that linked the nation's military and naval forces directly to civil authority.[15]

This was an organizational move of some significance, especially as it would affect the formation of corporate norms by which the Army and Navy would translate the overall value of autonomy. As a modern naval historian put it, the legislation ensured that "control of naval operations [would be] directly under the nation's Commander-in-Chief rather than through the War Department—thus providing some insurance against the adverse effects suffered by other nations when naval operations had been subordinated to land warfare and sea power objectives were ignored."[16]

The existence of the tradition of naval separatism can be traced back even further into American history, but the foundation of the Navy Department was clearly an important precedent. For the next century and a half (until the passage of the National Security Act of 1947) both services would have cabinet-level status. This was a position the Navy (as the above quotation implies) regarded as essential in pressing for the unique requirements of "providing and maintaining" naval forces. The Army does not seem to have taken as strong an ideological position on the same issue, probably because its status had already been secured not only through cabinet status but also by the constant necessity of providing forces on the frontier. By contrast, the Navy would look back on the period of subordination as a time of extreme weakness in the face of increasing provocation from a number of maritime foes, especially the British. The separate status achieved by the Navy by 1798 would indeed allow insufficient time for a recovery of maritime strength before the War of 1812 brought about a British naval blockade even more devastating than that of the Revolutionary War. It should be noted, however, that the creation of separate departments for War and Navy placed the president in his role as commander in chief in the position of being the sole officer of the government responsible for reconciling whatever different approaches these organizations might take in grappling with the problems of national security.

If the establishment of separate departments for the Army and Navy represented a victory for Hamiltonian concepts of administration, then these ideas stood in some contrast to another intellectual tradition of American life that had an equal or greater impact on military and naval organizations throughout much of the nineteenth century. Huntington summarized the key distinctions between Hamiltonian rationalism and the more democratic impulses of the Jeffersonian tradition: "Like other liberals, Jefferson had little interest in or use for regular military forces, and he had no recognition of the emerging character of professional military officership." Instead, military service was seen to be the universal obligation of a democratic society. When called to arms, the citizen-soldier would be led by a small cadre of officers who were essentially technical specialists in areas such as seamanship or engineering that were closely tied to the comparable civilian occupations of a developing frontier society—and not at all to a higher military science or concept of war. Although both the Jeffersonian and the Hamiltonian traditions represented idealized conceptions that were never entirely achieved, the influence of this "military technicism" would be a pervasive counterpoint to the growth of "military professionalism" throughout much of the nineteenth century.[17]

The matter of subordination also requires closer examination because it suggests certain differences in organizational strategies that would come to have a large impact on interservice relationships. There is probably no single organizational dynamic that is more powerful in describing any military structure than that of subordination. Armies and navies are fundamentally hierarchical in nature, and it is a common characteristic for both to have a well-established system of rank and organization designed to establish the lines of authority from highest to lowest. There is, however, a discernible difference between the Army and the Navy in the way that military and naval staffs evolved, although commanders in both services used organization as a basic tool to gain control over the increasing number of activities that were becoming adjuncts of modern warfare.

Whereas the naval staff would remain rudimentary well into the nineteenth century, the growth and sophistication of the military staff is a story that is deeply intertwined with the history of the U.S. Army as a whole. The Army shares this characteristic with the professional military establishments of most modern countries, a brotherhood that traces a common lineage back to the very beginnings of the profession of arms. In the opening to his history, *The Military Staff: Its History and Development,* Gen. J. D. Hittle stated, "When some unknown warrior chief asked for help or advice from one of his co-belligerents, military history saw the first functioning of the military staff."[18] This thought captures the essence of the military staff: the extension of the leader's span of control through officers who assist him in carrying out the functions of command. The translation of his intentions into actions, orders, and operations is a basic function of the military staff, so basic that it is known in most armies as the "staff action cycle." This cycle operates as a continuum, in which staff members gather the initial information on which the commander's decisions are based, write the plans that will carry out his orders, and supervise their eventual execution. In short, the military staff is one of the most basic methods for command and control, both as an organization embodying the personality of the commander and as an extension of the means by which his forces are to be controlled.[19]

Historically, three conditions, often related, have made it necessary for a commander's reach to be extended: the size of the force, its operational characteristics, and its functional complexity. The first is related to the idea of numbers: armies are essentially mass organizations of armed men who triumph in battle over other mass organizations of armed men. Although victory is not always a function of size, there is a strong presumption that more is better—or as Napoleon put it, "God is on the side of the bigger battalions." Obviously, larger numbers create larger problems for command and control in the melee of combat, and the standard solution has been to create subordinate echelons of control and a rank structure capable of handling them. One of the earliest recorded examples of this practice is that of Moses, who brought an army of some twelve thousand Israelites to battle against the Midianites. Although divine assistance was presumably assured, he found it necessary to set up "captains over thousands and captains over hundreds" in order to prevail.[20] Such systems were common throughout the history of warfare, and it often happened that the senior commanders as a group would become the sovereign's council-at-war, thereby arranging themselves into an informal kind of staff.[21]

The second condition has concerned the different operational characteristics of subordinate echelons. In the nineteenth and twentieth centuries the principle of combined arms was elevated into one of the hallmarks of modern warfare, but ancient armies incorporated the same idea with both heavy and light infantry formations, often in conjunction with archery and cavalry. These varied capabilities, however, created increased demands for the extension of personal control by the commander, and so his personal retinue sometimes shouldered these burdens in an elementary division of labor. The military system Alexander the Great inherited from Philip of Macedon was the most advanced of its day, with a staff that carried out hospital, commissary, and engineer functions. As various specialized activities became important to warfare—Alexander, for example, added an early form of *ballistae,* or missile-throwing catapults, to cover this river crossings—it was natural for staff form to follow function as trusted aides were given supervisory responsibility for them. Similarly, when a subordinate echelon had capabilities or a mission requiring it to operate independently—cavalry is an obvious example—it was accepted practice for the commander's most trusted subordinate to be placed in charge.[22]

The need to extend command authority brought about by force size and operational characteristics often contributed to the third factor: functional complexity. The larger the force and the more varied its units and operating characteristics, the more complex were the tasks of logistical support and operational employment. A fundamental tension arose from the need to achieve greater efficiency by delegating functions and the necessity to retain overall operational control. Since a division of labor could easily lead to a division of authority, the usual answer was for commanders to keep the reins of control in their own hands insofar as circumstances allowed. Like the ideas of concentration of forces and combined arms, the principle of unity of command was followed as an instinctive practice of land warfare long before its codification as a precept of modern strategy. Its contemporary importance, however, reflects the experience gained over the last three centuries as commanders were forced to extend their personal control to extraordinary lengths to accommodate the burgeoning needs of armies for logistical support brought about by the age of firearms. Although the ancient Egyptians, Assyrians, and Persians all developed rudimentary mechanisms for such support, the development of modern warfare created the most profound pressures for the growth of the military staff.[23]

By the end of the seventeenth century, the rise of the nation-state had resulted in the creation of armies numbering in the hundreds of thousands whose sheer size created logistical difficulties that simple plunder and pillage would not resolve.[24] The staff system pioneered by the Swedish king Gustavus Adolphus was one response to these unprecedented demands, but it was the genius of Frederick the Great that brought the military staff to an equally unprecedented level of efficiency. One of his most notable achievements, and an important step toward future organization, was the development of the quartermaster-general's office, a logistic post he expanded to embrace the functions of reconnaissance, intelligence, and operations. Although the post's evolution would not be completed under Frederick, the gathering of the three functions in a single staff officer eventually led to that position becoming institutionalized as "chief of staff," both in fact and in name. During the French Revolution, that nation became the first to create the office, and in the aftermath of the Napoleonic Wars, most European armies followed France's example. In this and other refinements of the staff system, Frederick the Great was a pioneer, striking a new balance between the continuing need for unity of command and the requirement to extend that authority throughout a military machine grown more complex than ever before.[25]

In a curious way, Frederick's innovations also imparted a structural foundation to the revolutionary army that was about to be born on another continent. This cross-cultural influence occurred primarily through the efforts of one man, Baron Friedrich von Steuben, who became Washington's inspector general and drillmaster to the Continental Army during the winter of 1777–78. Von Steuben was a product of the Frederickian system, having served in the Prussian army for more than twenty years in both field and staff assignments. His influence on the American military experience was to have a lasting impact; as Virgil Ney pointed out, he "established the disciplinary pattern for the U.S. Army which survives today."[26] He also organized Washington's headquarters, including the establishment of operations and intelligence sections, which he supervised directly during most of the war's campaigns. During the final campaign at Yorktown, his general orders for the siege (containing some fifty-five paragraphs) were a model of professionalism. Hittle's assessment of the baron's contribution is accurate: "Literally, and figuratively, Steuben was the first qualified staff officer of our army."[27]

Reflecting on these matters many years later, Washington wrote a remarkable letter to Secretary of War James McHenry which epitomizes the importance he had come to attach to the smooth functioning of a military staff and his concern that lessons learned in the Revolution not be forgotten by subsequent administrations. He went into some detail in discussing the duties of "the Inspector General, Quartermaster General, Adjutant General and officers commanding the corps of artillerists and engineers," who are important because of "the nature of their respective offices and from their being always about the Commander in Chief, who is obliged to intrust many things to them confidentially [so that] scarcely any movement can take place without their knowledge." His closing comment would become something of a legacy: "The appointment of general officers is *important,* but those of the general staff *all important.*"[28]

Although the general staff concept that Washington had in mind was far less ambitious than that which later prevailed in European armies, his advice was not without consequence. By 1798, the War Department's staff was organized along the functional lines suggested by Washington, eventually including departments of Quartermaster, Inspector General, Adjutant General, Paymaster General, and Surgeon General.[29] The early organization of the Army also reveals the extent to which it had internalized other instinctive principles of land warfare as well. Gen. Anthony Wayne was named to lead the field army that had been called into service in 1792 to deal with the Indians of the northwestern frontier. His appointment marked the second time Congress vested such authority in a single military leader, thus showing that the precedent by which Washington had exercised unity of command over the Continental Army had provided a model for the future. Eventually the service's senior general acceded to the title of commanding general of the army, an office that persisted into the twentieth century. Wayne's tenure was also remarkable for his efforts to convert the entire organization of the field army into a "legion," consisting of regiments of the three combat branches of infantry, cavalry, and artillery. Although the legion structure, which provided for the tactical integration of the three branches, would not long survive once the immediate crisis in the Northwest had been resolved, its establishment was significant. The importance of combined arms in land warfare had become a maxim transferred intact from the hands of von Steuben, however much its articulation as principle and doctrine awaited future developments.

Although the practices of combat at sea had some parallels with those on land, there was a striking absence of an organized body of doctrine at this stage in the development of the American Navy, if for no other reason than that the service was in its infancy. Of the six ships authorized for service against the Barbary pirates, only three were built, and the Navy suffered still more neglect under the administration of Thomas Jefferson. The War of 1812 was fought under the same approximate conditions of naval inferiority that had prevailed during the Revolution. Not even some spectacular victories in isolated ship-to-ship actions could mask the fact that the British naval blockade "annihilated our maritime commerce, all but paralyzed the economic life of the country, and laid the seaboard open to invasion."[30]

This is not to suggest that there were no parallels between the instinctive behavior of land and sea forces in terms of the three principles stated above which, as has been seen, placed a premium on the extension of the commander's control; but such parallels as existed were less important than some fundamental differences. At the most basic level, concentration of forces could not have much meaning when the entire American Navy consisted of fifteen seaworthy frigates, as it did at the start of the War of 1812. The British Navy was long accustomed to operating in flotillas and fleets, but American ships typically sailed alone or in a squadron of two or three vessels. There was consequently little need for an extensive naval command structure.[31]

The structure that did exist resided primarily in the person of the ship's captain, whose authority over his vessel and crew was absolute. One should not, however, casually equate this concept with the idea of unity of command as it existed on land. Whereas land warfare by now featured a military hierarchy in which the authority of the commander was disseminated through the staff and subordinate echelons, the Navy centralized authority at a much lower level: the ship's quarterdeck. Although shipboard organization commonly featured different departments for navigation, gunnery, and sailing, each of these functions took place under the firm control of the vessel's captain. There was also no counterpart to the concept of combined arms, although the existence of different ship types would later provide a sort of rough equivalence. Without the demands raised by large numbers and varied capabilities, it is not surprising that the naval command structure was uncomplicated.

The unitary command at ship level was mirrored in the rudimentary organization of the Navy ashore. Following the creation of the Navy Department in 1798, its civilian secretary entered upon an office that consisted almost entirely of himself and several clerks—a stark contrast to the General Staff already incorporated into the War Department. Mahan characterized this phase of American naval history as follows: "Until the close of the War of 1812, the Secretary in person . . . was the naval administration. He no doubt had assistants and obtained assistance, technical and military, from experts of both classes; but function had not yet differentiated into organization, and he not only was responsible [for], but had to give personal attention to various and trivial matters of most diverse character, which overburdened him by their mass, and prevented concentration of attention upon the really great matters of his office."[32]

The War of 1812 brought about changes in the organization of both the Navy and the War departments as the nation tried to cope with the demands of fighting what amounted to a second revolutionary war. The struggle was also the first real test of the military system set up by the Constitution, and the results were far from encouraging. Naval weakness was matched by the Regular Army which could not be quickly expanded from its peacetime strength of 6,700 men to the 35,000 authorized by Congress shortly before the outbreak of hostilities. The militia system would prove equally trouble-some, with the governors of Connecticut and Massachusetts initially refusing to provide their states' quotas of militia to augment the regular force.[33] No single event of that war, however, provided better proof of the military and naval weakness of the United States than the sacking of the nation's capital in 1814 by British forces who had landed with virtually no opposition and routed a hastily assembled force of American volunteers at the Battle of Bladens-burg. The battle was remarkable in that President James Monroe, Secretary of War John Armstrong, and other cabinet members directly involved themselves throughout the course of a thoroughly confused operation, ut-terly subverting whatever control could have been exercised by the local commander—a hapless brigadier named William Winder who had been chosen because he was a relative of the governor of Maryland and was therefore useful "in mitigating the opposition to the war."[34]

In response to these and other deficiencies, Congress took actions both during and shortly after the war to improve the organizational structures of the Army and the Navy. In 1813, Congress passed a law that strengthened the General Staff by setting up a Topographical Department and the departments of the Adjutant General, Inspector General, Surgeon General, and Apothe-cary General. Equally significant was the refinement of the secretary's power over these officers, including the authority to issue regulations to guide their functions and powers.[35] Congress would occasionally amend the charters of various General Staff agencies, but the enhancement of the secretary's powers would persist, especially during the tenure of John C. Calhoun from 1817 to 1825.

Calhoun secured congressional approval for additional staff agencies, such as the Subsistence Department, which gave him the technical advice needed to exert unified control of the Army's administration in accordance with his responsibilities as secretary. Eventually, this centralization of authority took on the structural form that became known as the Army's bureau system. Although it was an important milestone in the development of a professional Army, the bureau system contained an inherent weakness: it "meant dividing the management of the Army into specialized segments, with the General Staff not so much a coherent entity as a collection of varied experts. It also left unclear the relationship between the staff headquarters in Washington and the line officers in the military districts into which the country was divided."[36]

Other important changes brought about by Calhoun's administration included legislative recognition of the post of commanding general of the Army in 1821 and the retention of a force structure that enabled the Regular Army to maintain its peacetime strength at the unprecedented level of six to twelve thousand officers and men. The net effect of Calhoun's efforts was thus to give the Army a structural framework with which it would operate for the balance of the century, these refinements being a further indicator of the Army's instinctive preference for hierarchical organizational patterns.[37]

The Navy's organizational structure also underwent a significant change in the aftermath of the War of 1812 when a Board of Navy Commissioners was established by Congress in 1815. The board, consisting of three post captains—senior captains or those exercising major commands—was appointed by the president and attached to the secretary's office. The legislative objective was to "devolve technical detail with a measure of administrative responsibility on [these] selected officers, without at the same time relinquishing civilian control over policy."[38] As had been the case at the Battle of Bladensburg, civilian control could mean different things at different times to different people, for shortly after the board's creation, a dispute broke out between the secretary and the commissioners over the right to control fleet movements and naval personnel. The president eventually had to intervene, and thereafter the secretary's functions included the oversight of the operations and discipline of the Navy, while the commissioners confined themselves to providing technical advice regarding its civil functions, docks, shipyards, and the like. Although this seems an odd reversal of the usual civilian and military functions, it was both logical and an example of the Jeffersonian tradition noted earlier. Huntington pointed out that "the design, construction, and equipment of naval vessels and the operations of the Navy yards were jobs for experts. Compared to these, discipline, the assignment of personnel, and the employment of vessels were relatively simple matters. The man of affairs might still direct the latter; it was impossible for him to manage the former."[39]

This organizational initiative on the part of the Navy provides another contrast to the Army General Staff, which in the same period had progressed much further in bringing different functions into its top echelon of command, an integration that also permitted its top staff officers a wide degree of latitude in running their bureaus. The Navy pattern was altogether more austere: its three commissioners had no such differentiation in their responsibilities and their functions remained purely advisory in nature. A further contrast can be seen in the fact that, by the end of Calhoun's incumbency in 1825, the General Staff had achieved "a form so nearly definitive that no essential changes were needed, even to cope with the shock of the Civil War . . . and it long served as the model after which other departments were patterned."[40] By 1829, the Navy commissioners were confronting the tasks of protecting the rapid expansion of American maritime commerce and experimenting with steam-powered ships; in both numbers and complexity these new tasks were so demanding that the board soon found itself in danger of being—to use the appropriate nautical metaphor—swamped. The solution would have pleased von Steuben: the board was kept as before, but now its members subdivided their duties, "so that each member, giving particular attention to the branch confided to him, perform[ed] his own part in the most satisfactory manner."[41]

Although it is not clear that the Navy was consciously following the trail blazed by Army organizational growth—as Calhoun's biographer seemingly implied—by 1842 the maritime service had its own bureau system. Although differentiation of function had permitted the Navy commissioners to work somewhat more efficiently than before, Secretary of the Navy Abel P. Upshur entered upon his office in 1841 and promptly reported to Congress:

> I have had but a short experience in this department, but a short experience is enough to display its defects, even to the most superficial observation. It is, in truth, not organized at all. The labor to be performed must, under any circumstances, be great and onerous, but it is rendered doubly so by the want of a proper arrangement and distribution of duties. At present a multitude of duties are imposed upon the head of the department, which any one of its clerks could discharge as well as himself. . . . Hence, his whole time is occupied in trifling details, rendering it impossible for him to bestow the requisite attention upon more important subjects involving the great interests of the service.[42]

These lines, which could well have been written by George Washington prior to the arrival of von Steuben, eventually resulted in Upshur's recommending legislation to set up a bureau system within the Navy. Congress eventually approved five bureaus: Navy-Yards and Docks; Construction, Equipment, and Repair; Provisions and Clothing; Ordnance and Hydrography; and Medicine and Surgery.[43]

Congress did not, however, approve Upshur's recommendation that the bureau chiefs also be collectively constituted as a kind of corporate board of directors to the secretary. The lawmakers' reasoning on this point is not well covered in the standard naval histories, but the reorganization was part of a Whig naval program that had proposed the appropriation of the unheard-of sum of $8.5 million for the construction of new ships in the wake of the Anglo-American naval scare of 1840. The Whig program provoked a furor of sectional clashes, and the result, inevitably, was a compromise that fell somewhat short of the original proposal. Upshur's plan for the bureau chiefs to function as a rough kind of General Staff may have been one aspect of that compromise, possibly because Congress preferred to deal with the several bureau chiefs rather than with one collective whole, especially when any expansion of the Navy meant a burst of construction funds to be distributed through the nation's yards, docks, and constituencies. Commenting on the aftermath of this legislative fight, the Sprouts' history of naval policy states:

> A wide geographical distribution of naval patronage and other spoils was to become the established and accepted method of securing the majorities necessary to pass naval bills. Selecting naval personnel on a geographical basis, pouring public funds into superfluous or poorly located navy yards and other equipment, often paying exorbitant prices for inferior labor and materials, all for the purpose of promoting the political fortunes of Senators and Representatives, were to become distinguishing characteristics of naval legislation—characteristics which have persisted down to the present day.[44]

The Navy was left with an organizational structure that paralleled much of that of its sister service, but it stopped short of achieving the latent potential of such a system for functional integration. The Army's General Staff at this time also fell far short of that potential, but the failure of Upshur's recommendation to achieve legislative sanction was an important historical turning point. The bureaus would grow larger and become well established, eventually exerting an almost independent influence on policy determination. As the Sprouts noted, "The essence of this problem was how to combine the expert knowledge of the professional naval bureaucracy, the political leadership of the civilian executive, and the representative function and legislative power of Congress." The same problem also existed in the Army: service autonomy had now yielded a pair of separate but congruent Iron Triangles.[45]

Command and Control Perspectives
to the Mid-Nineteenth Century

The middle part of the nineteenth century was in many ways the classic age of command and control because the technology used to direct movements of forces on land and at sea had not materially changed since ancient times.[46] By the 1850s, the steamboat, the railroad, and especially the telegraph were ushering in a dimension of strategic control that would have profound effects on both service autonomy and the personal autonomy of commanders in the field. It is useful, therefore, to establish a baseline against which to compare the changes that will be addressed later.

Classical command and control can also be thought of as "restrictive command and control" because it typically represented the efforts of a single commander to extend his ability to control events on a battlefield, an ability that was subject to the physical limits of terrain, communications, and weaponry: "Napoleon's control of the course of battle at Borodino or Waterloo [1815] was scarcely greater, or less, than that of Marlborough at Blenheim, a century before, or that of Alexander at Arbela, twenty-one centuries earlier. Each commander, on each occasion, could see most of the battlefield."[47] If the commander's line of sight represented the prevailing reality of tactical command, then attempts to extend that line of sight have represented a large part of tactical control innovations throughout the history of warfare. Visual distance and the attempt to extend it were the common concerns of both military and naval commanders. Alexander's need to see the battlefield at Arbela (331 B.C.) was basic to the commitment of his reserves, and naval history records an even earlier example of the practice at the Battle of Salamis (450 B.C.) when Timon of Athens threw his cloak over the side of his flagship, thus signaling the Greek fleet to turn and ram the enemy.[48]

The visual signals used in land warfare down through the centuries were a tribute to human ingenuity. Raised weapons, personal pendants, battle flags, legion standards, signal torches, and distinctively colored uniforms were some of the most common devices. Terrain and the dust raised during battle, however, often limited visual range. (Ironically, the invention with the greatest potential for visual extension—the telescope—arrived on the scene at about the same time that black powder was clouding the battlefield more than ever.) Therefore, visual signals were usually augmented by audible signals, such as drums, trumpets, march cadences, and, later, signal cannons. Although these devices could extend the commander's ability to direct movements, they usually did not meet the basic communication requirement for an effective two-way flow of information. That task was most often the function of the courier or messenger, who could be used for effective tactical communication within the combat force and could bridge the gap to whatever strategic level existed. History's best-known example of the strategic use of a courier was the anonymous runner sent by Miltiades to Athens to inform the council of the Greek victory at Marathon.[49]

Visual signals were the prime medium used for the control of naval movements from antiquity through the nineteenth century. Bonfires, for example, served as beacons along the English coast to warn of the approach of the Spanish Armada, and Queen Elizabeth's naval commanders used the placement of the Cross of St. George on different masts as a signaling device at sea.[50] The flag signal system, incorporating a wide range of pendants and codes, would eventually become the primary communications system during the age of sail. Flags and pennants were repeated by each ship in the battle line, both to acknowledge receipt of a message and to pass it on to other ships farther away. This system was adequate for the generally slow pace of daily sailing, but far more problematic at night, in bad weather, or in the heat of battle when flags were obscured by cannon smoke. Naval commanders, then, shared the line-of-sight limitation of their land army counterparts, even though the line of sight on the ocean was likely to be greater than on land, owing to the absence of intervening terrain features.[51]

In the matter of strategic connectivity, naval forces presented an interesting contrast to armies. Although transportation by sea was faster than on land and it was often possible to use sailing ships as courier vessels, there were no reliable means of communication with a ship once it was out of sight of the shore. Oceans being vast and uninhabited, the only alternative was to rely on the ship's captain to carry out whatever sailing instructions and general orders he was given upon departure. Naturally, he was responsible for his own actions and those of his ship, always facing the possibility of later censure or even court-martial if his superiors found reason to question his actions. The essence of classical naval command and control can therefore be thought of as tactical autonomy tempered by subsequent strategic review.[52]

If the essential test of any command structure is how effectively it carries out the operational missions of the force that is to be commanded, then this quaintly decentralized system worked rather well. After the War of 1812, the Navy embarked upon a long period of gradual but sustained growth as it assisted in the opening of new markets to American commerce, patrolled the seas in search of pirates, slavers, and privateers, and in general began to fulfill the role that Hamilton and other Federalists had foreseen. These recurring missions in turn led to the formation of permanent squadrons, not only in

American home waters, but also in the Mediterranean (1815), the Pacific (1821), one each in the Gulf of Mexico and the Caribbean Sea (1822), and one in the South Atlantic (1826). As always, there was a downside. These widely scattered responsibilities could not be easily met by a Navy that was still small by European standards, and so most naval deployments consisted of either a single ship or a squadron of two to three vessels operating under the nominal command of the senior captain. The dispersion of ships was matched by the simplicity of naval administration ashore, which still lacked any semblance of a fleet organization, a deficiency that "unquestionably retarded the development of the Navy into a synchronized fighting machine. . . . In consequence, there was little opportunity for the larger group operations necessary to weld the individual ships into squadrons in fact as well as name."[53]

There is little to distinguish the command and control measures used by the American Army in both the Revolution and the War of 1812 from those commonly used by other armies of the period, the major difference lying in the difficulties of communication imposed upon land forces operating in what was still largely a wilderness with few well-maintained roads. The attendant limitations upon commanders' lines of sight tended to make extension of battlefield control problematic, so that engagements were mostly fought on relatively restricted frontages; at Germantown, for example, Washington fought the entire battle in an area less than five miles wide. Under these conditions, the use of couriers was the only realistic possibility, with long-distance communications being sent by water whenever possible.

The basic unit of control in the American Army was the battalion of five hundred to seven hundred men, which in both the Revolution and the War of 1812 fought with the linear tactics common in eighteenth-century warfare. These tactics resulted in largely set-piece engagements in which both sides had common formations: infantry in the center, cavalry on the flanks, and artillery and reserves in the rear. After an opening artillery exchange, the infantry would move forward in lines until the opposing forces faced each other by less than a hundred yards—a distance largely dictated by the maximum effective range of the smoothbore musket. Volleys would be exchanged between the opposing lines until one group or the other broke and ran, most often as the result of the reserves or the cavalry being committed at some critical juncture. The leveled bayonets of the victorious infantry formation would then add to the incentive for the losing side to flee the battlefield, turning defeat into rout. The problem of control, however, was no less a problem for the victorious side, since battle lines and communication with subordinate commanders would usually disappear once the forces closed with each other. Under those conditions, it is not hard to see why it was often difficult or impossible to achieve any sort of followup to exploit a tactical victory.[54]

Strategic control of the American Army was not an apparent problem during the Revolution, with a chain of command extending from the Continental Congress through its Board of War to the person of George Washington as commanding general. The physical proximity of the nation's political leadership to the theater of operations was a persistent problem for the survival of the new republic, but it greatly simplified the process by which Congress would direct the war, George Washington's correspondence being ample proof of the fact that he did not feel deprived of civilian control.

The War of 1812 provided extremes of strategic control, one pole of which could be seen in the presidential supervision of combat operations previously mentioned at the Battle of Bladensburg. Monroe's ability to intervene in this fashion was again a function, however unhappily, of his physical proximity to the scene of the action. At more extended ranges, strategic control over land forces was as disjointed as it was at sea. Just prior to the outbreak of war in 1812, Brig. Gen. William Hull was given command in the Northwest because he had been a dashing soldier during the Revolution, but, as the U.S. Army's official history notes, "by this time, age and its infirmities had made him cautious and timid."[55] Not knowing that war had been declared, he sent his military equipment to the West by ship, only to have it captured by the British who had known for two weeks that hostilities had commenced. The cause of the fiasco was that a letter dispatched to Hull by the War Department had been sent in care of the Cleveland postmaster, who had been tardy in forwarding it. After this inauspicious start, Hull continued to have control difficulties, withdrawing to Detroit when a letter that did arrive convinced him (erroneously) that the defenses of Fort Mulden, Canada, were formidable. In Detroit, he was quickly surrounded by the British and their Indian allies, and he thereupon sent out 350 scouts in search of reinforcements. He later reconsidered this action and recalled them: "They returned just in time to surrender with Hull's entire force."[56]

As severe as Hull's difficulties were, they are overshadowed by a better known example of the problem of strategic control at extended ranges—the Battle of New Orleans. Gen. Andrew Jackson won a brilliant victory there on January 8, 1815, some two weeks following the signing of the Treaty of Ghent which ended the war.[57]

The Army that presided over the next thirty years of peace nevertheless fought major engagements against the Seminoles in Florida as well as the Sac and Fox Indians under Chief Black Hawk. Indian fighting on the frontier, like other forms of irregular warfare, called for the greatest autonomy on the part of battlefield commanders like Jackson. In fact, the tactical autonomy of the field commander was such a well-established norm that Jackson complained bitterly to the president when, on one occasion, the headquarters secretariat bypassed the usual chain of command and reassigned one of his officers without prior notification.[58] Apart from dealing with major Indian uprisings, the Army was chiefly occupied with policing the frontier. Its strength in the years between the Treaty of Ghent and the outbreak of the Mexican War varied from a low of 5,702 in 1828 to a high of 12,330 during the Anglo-American crisis of 1840. In 1821, its structure had been cut to a total of seven regiments of infantry and four regiments of artillery, with the result that its experience with the integrated movement of mass formations (such as it was) would fall into disuse. As was the case with its sister service, peacetime functions would not contribute to wartime effectiveness.[59]

The following points summarize the similarities and differences affecting the command and control of the Army and Navy:

1. Tactical command and control measures generally were well adapted to the size and capabilities of armies fighting on battlefields that appear small by today's standards. The great limiting factor, both in America and elsewhere, was the commander's line of sight. Within that radius, existing means of control were reasonably effective; they were less so in direct proportion to the range at which visual control diminished. Within those limits, however, commanders had a wide range of options for affecting the outcomes of engagements *by personal intervention.* This intervention could be either indirect, such as committing a reserve formation to the battle, or direct, such as personally leading a formation into combat. Although line of sight was also the effective radius for tactical control in naval engagements, there was a clear difference that the embarked commander had to contend with:

> The complexity of naval command and control lies in the fact that *the naval commander has neither opportunity nor capability to interject his personality upon some specific segment of his command in combat.* It is not uncommon for a ground-force commander to visit one of his subordinate units during a moment of crisis. The naval commander, until a few years ago, carried his flag in one of the combat units of his battle line. . . . Once combat was joined, therefore, the naval commander was confined to that particular unit and shared its fortunes—his ability to control the action limited to signal communications.[60] (Emphasis added)

2. Strategic control during this period was a function of distance. The Army, having been constrained to fight some of its most critical engagements on its own soil in relative proximity to the seat of government, generally operated with a higher degree of effective civilian control (sometimes bordering on outright interference) than was the case with the Navy. Both because of its small size during this period and because there were no effective methods to extend strategic control over the horizon, the Navy developed an extremely decentralized pattern of command and control that can be characterized as tactical autonomy tempered by strategic review. A parallel can be seen, however, with Army elements fighting on the frontier; because they were operating across obstacles and at great distances, they were at least as remote as any naval force. They tended, therefore, to be equally autonomous in tactical decision making, yet quite as subject to subsequent strategic review of their actions.

3. The investiture of a significant degree of authority in the person of the on-scene commander was an essential feature of the classic age of command and control, extending across both naval and land forces. Given the factors of distance and the relative inability of prevailing communications to span that distance in a timely fashion, there was simply no other alternative except to work through the officers placed in tactical command. It was possible to relieve and censure the incompetent, and equally possible to second-guess the competent; but there was little opportunity for personal intervention upon command authority, and where the opportunity did exist and was taken, the results were not encouraging. Writing some years later about such a historical incident during the classic age of command and control, Alfred Thayer Mahan would speak for his brother officers in both services: "To interfere thus with the commander in the field or afloat is one of the most common temptations to the government in the cabinet, and is generally disastrous."[61] That sentiment obviously reflects a strictly military viewpoint which, even at the time, might well have been disputed; however, there is no better summation of the norm of tactical autonomy bequeathed by the classic era of command and control.

Meeting the Test: Command Structure in the Mexican War

Although the Mexican War of 1846–48 did not produce any major changes in the command structures the Army and Navy had set up earlier in the nineteenth century, it is a good example of how those structures functioned under the stress of combat. The outcome was a major triumph of American arms, enlarging the country's sovereignty by over one million square miles and thereby bringing about a continental dimension to the future tasks of national security. The war was the first not to be fought on native American soil, the first to feature an amphibious operation by the combined forces of the Army and the Navy, and the first to feature a successful invasion—which compelled the surrender of the enemy's national capital and led to the attainment of the war's original political objective. The war also showed that service autonomy had resulted in the growth of a more mature military establishment than the country had had before, one that was capable of putting into the field a force of over twenty thousand men and transporting it more than five hundred miles into enemy territory, while supplying it and providing strategic direction over its movements.

In this last regard, President James K. Polk played an active role, proving "that a President could run a war." If service autonomy had created strong but separate military and naval organizations, Polk showed that his constitutional and legal role as chief executive was competent to unify their efforts: "It had been demonstrated that a civilian commander in chief could and did function effectively as the single center for direction, authorization, coordination and in lesser degree for control of a larger military and naval effort. All lines concentrated in the White House. . . . Thus was achieved a genuine unity of command . . . that succeeded in keeping in coordination the various movements in the field."[62]

Polk achieved this unity of command by using his cabinet as an executive sounding board for all the important decisions of the war: "strategic plans, instructions to diplomats, blockade rules, choice of generals."[63] By involving the cabinet, he was also able to ensure that the separate perspectives of the Army and Navy were brought together at the highest level, an example of which occurred during a cabinet meeting on the eve of the amphibious landing at Vera Cruz in February 1847. Navy Secretary John Mason offhandedly admitted that the USS *Ohio* and some other ships had not yet arrived in the Gulf of Mexico to support the invasion. "The President remarked that he had supposed the Secretaries of War and Navy to be continuously in conference to coordinate the movements of their respective forces, and Secretary Mason, much mortified, left the room to hasten the movement of his ships."[64]

It is not at all clear just *how* the secretary proposed to bring about this haste, given the general difficulty of controlling naval movements and the specific problem of getting messages from the capital to the zone of operations—two to three weeks away by steamer. It is clear, however, that coordination at the top was inadequate. The Navy's bureaus were simply not chartered to act as a corporate body. The Army bureaus performed their assigned administrative functions well enough, but were similarly unable to come together to assist in the planning of strategy or operations; those responsibilities fell almost solely to Winfield Scott, then commanding general of the army. Although Scott was equal to the task, there was no institutional body below the level of the cabinet to translate political objectives into strategic plans or to coordinate the movements of the expeditionary forces. And when General Scott left Washington to command the invasion of Mexico in 1847, "a one-man general staff gave way to none at all" as the president, the secretary of war, and the bureau chiefs became the Army's "headquarters."[65]

Coordination in the field was much better: relations between the naval and ground force commanders were generally excellent although marred by some incidents that shed light on both the past and the future. The Navy, having concentrated one of the largest flotillas in its history, commanded the sea, cutting Mexico off from foreign suppliers and supporting the Army's movements ashore. The largest of these movements commenced with the amphibious landing at Vera Cruz referred to above. That operation, which took place under the watchful eyes of nearby British, French, and Spanish naval vessels, was unopposed by the Mexicans but still a brilliant success by any standard. Ten thousand troops were landed in four hours, debarked from the transporting ships by sixty-five heavy surf boats, which were then towed to shore by steamers. Once ashore, Scott found that his artillery was not adequate to reduce the walls of the town's fortress and requested that the flotilla commander, Commodore Matthew C. Perry, lend his heavier naval cannon to the effort. "Certainly, General," Perry is supposed to have replied, "but I must fight them." Naval crews then accompanied the six naval guns that were landed and dragged into position before the city walls. Service prestige thus assured, the bombardment soon commenced and the besieged garrison promptly surrendered.[66]

Similarly, in California, Commodore Robert F. Stockton commanded a flotilla operating under conditions quite as remote and decentralized as any in the service's history. Shortly after the war began, Stockton was instructed to seize control of the California coastline and as much of the interior of the territory as was practicable. At this moment, however, Capt. John C. Frémont entered Monterey at the head of an irregular force known as the California Battalion and became embroiled in a dispute with Stockton as to which of them would exercise overall command. An agreement was eventually reached that allowed Frémont to retain operational control over the Army contingent while Stockton exercised overall authority.[67]

This agreement was successful in that the two small forces were able to subdue most of the California territory (although the achievement was mitigated by the fact that resistance was light). It was less successful when Gen.

Stephen W. Kearny arrived with his Army of the West to take control of the occupation under the terms of a presidential directive, only to find that Stockton refused to recognize his authority. The situation was not resolved until the arrival of Stockton's replacement in 1847.[68]

Neither of these incidents, of course, affected the outcome of the war, and it is possible to ascribe both of them to personality differences, perhaps aggravated by the uncertainties of new situations. A closer look, however, suggests that whatever impact personalities may have had was almost certainly secondary to the accumulated effects of a half-century or more of service autonomy. Separate service organizations, first de facto and then de jure, had developed around a basic division of labor. Each service faced severe challenges in coping with its unique operational environment, and each developed a certain body of instinctive responses to those challenges. Not the least of the differences that naturally developed was a disparity in perspective regarding command relationships. The Army approach was built around the principles of mass, subordination, and concentration of force. It stressed a strictly hierarchical organization that distributed the commander's authority through the ranks and echelons in a pyramiding control structure that enabled him to intervene personally and directly as the tactical situation required. The Navy approach was, from the outset, far more federal in character, not only because of the relatively small number of ships to be controlled, but also because of the extremely limited means of controlling them. Equally significant was the relative inability of naval commanders to intervene with their subordinates as often or as effectively as their ground force counterparts did.

The organizations that had created General Scott and Commodore Perry, or General Kearny and Commodore Stockton, had also inculcated in them certain norms regarding command and expectations of what was appropriate and what was not in exercising the attendant means of control. The Navy under Perry was operating under conditions of strategic control much like what the Army had been accustomed to from the beginning: only several weeks separated the dispatch of messages from the seat of government from their arrival at the theater of operations. That fact, along with the strong coordination requirements imposed by President Polk, close observation by foreign rivals, and, above all, the presence of the enemy, worked to ensure that cooperation between Scott and Perry would be consistently strong—and that the only matter of contention would be trivial and quickly put behind them.

The ground forces under Frémont and Kearny were, in contrast, operating under conditions of strategic control that had almost always characterized naval operations: Kearny at San Diego was making decisions that were every bit as remote from White House supervision as those made by Preble, Bainbridge, and Decatur at Tripoli a generation earlier. With the two services thus operating under conditions of the most relaxed strategic control, it is not surprising that a conflict over command should have developed. It is interesting, not to say ironic, that the method chosen for resolving what was essentially a competition over the norms of subordination and control was a formula roughly corresponding to the arrangement characterizing today's unified and component commands. Given the Navy's ideas about subordination in general, it is also not surprising that even this agreement would come to an end when it appeared that naval forces would be subjected to the "unified command" of General Kearny. Without the pressure of a military threat, acrimony was predictable. Stockton and Kearny were, after all, the local representatives of two similar but autonomous organizations; those institutions shared a common purpose with respect to the nation's defense, but they were maturing under different political and operational conditions. Those differences would become more rather than less profound as the nation, following its triumphs in Mexico and California, drifted uneasily toward the Civil War.

3 Paradigms on Land and Sea, 1861–1921

The circumstances of warfare that required the services to work in concert were few in number during the first three-quarters of a century of the nation's existence, but increased markedly during the three major wars fought between 1861 and 1921. The Civil War, the Spanish-American War, and World War I eventually resulted in the adoption of the doctrine of mutual cooperation—a descriptive and prescriptive term for the proper exercise of operations whenever both services were involved. Equally significant during this period was the extension of command and control in both the tactical and strategic arenas as the telegraph and the wireless ushered in the age of telecommunications. The integration of these systems into the fighting apparatus of both services was one aspect of the attempt to gain control of the enormous complexities that technological change brought to warfare during the nineteenth century. Another was the growth of staffs which brought about during this period the Army General Staff and a comparable structure in the Office of the Chief of Naval Operations.

These developments took place against a backdrop of attempts to understand the principles of warfare, in both their articulation and their application, on land and sea. Strategic thought in the nineteenth century arose from the teachings of Antoine-Henri Jomini but would, in the development of its American approach, embrace two competing paradigms—that offered by Karl von Clausewitz with its prescriptions for land warfare and that of Alfred Thayer Mahan with his classic analysis of the importance of seapower. The final result of these developments—the extension of battlefield control, the development of sophisticated staff arrangements, and the existence of two related but different strategic paradigms—constituted the next stage in the growth of service autonomy, which would be increasingly challenged as the nature of warfare changed in the twentieth century.

Prologue: Toward a Paradigm of Land Warfare

Any discussion of nineteenth-century warfare must include an appreciation of the impact the writings of Antoine-Henri Jomini had on the generation of military leaders who applied—or misapplied—the teachings he derived from Napoleonic battlefields. Jomini, a Swiss native who attached himself to Napoleon's staff, lived to the age of ninety (1779–1869) and exercised a pervasive influence as the chronicler and interpreter of the emperor's campaigns. His *Précis de l'art de la guerre* was published in a complete edition in 1838, and was both a history of those Continental wars and an attempt to deduce from them certain immutable principles of strategy. His was the first modern work that attempted such a systematic approach. In it he set forth four basic maxims of strategic planning:

1. To throw by strategic movements the mass of an army, successively, upon the decisive points of a theater of war, and also upon the communications of the enemy as much as possible without compromising one's own.

2. To maneuver to engage fractions of the hostile army with the bulk of one's forces.

3. On the battle-field, to throw the mass of the forces upon the decisive point, or upon that portion of the hostile line which it is of the first importance to overthrow.

4. To so arrange that these masses shall not only be thrown upon the decisive point, but that they shall engage at the proper times and with energy.[1]

If the objective of warfare was the concentration of mass at the most critical point, then what determined where that point existed? Jomini argued that strategic points might be geographical, such as a mountain pass or the confluence of two rivers; they might be political centers; they might be established incidentally as armies maneuvered in relation to their lines of communication; or they might be sites that held a political significance for countries allied in a war. Capturing these critical points, or preventing the enemy from doing so, ought to be the objective of strategy. This, rather than the aimless maneuvers of eighteenth-century armies, was what, in Jomini's view, constituted the core of Napoleon's genius in making himself the master of Europe.[2]

Equally important to Jomini's formulation was the idea that the pursuit of these objectives should follow according to definite lines of operations that would optimize the direction of an advance while permitting movement by both interior and exterior lines. The exterior line of an advancing army would maintain overall direction, gain territory, and provide the shield for the interior lines, the chief functions of which were to provide communications and, most critically, to allow for the rapid shifting of forces brought to bear at strategic points. The emphasis on the acquisition of territory seemed to capture much of the essence of land warfare and for the first time to provide a methodology that was both theoretical and practical. "In his theory the campaign occupies the central and decisive position. The purpose of warfare is to occupy all or part of the enemy's territory. Such occupation is accomplished by the progressive domination of zones of occupation; and this domination is possible only if the campaign is planned carefully before the outbreak of hostilities. . . . The task of strategy is to make those preliminary plans."[3]

It is difficult to overstate the impact of Jomini's teachings on nineteenth-century military thought. Because Napoleon had emerged in the early years of that century as one of the great captains of history, it was natural that the articulator of his campaigns and methods should have enjoyed some measure of reflected glory. Jomini's influence in the United States was to be profound, accomplished chiefly through the work of two men: Dennis Hart Mahan and Henry Wager Halleck. Mahan graduated from the United States Military Academy first in his class in 1824 and, after studying in France, returned to West Point as a faculty member, a position he held from 1832 to 1871. Thoroughly conversant with Jomini's teachings, he was the professor who taught the principles of warfare to the generation of cadets who later became the leaders on both sides of the Civil War. One of his most prominent students was Henry Wager Halleck of the Class of 1839, who became a translator of Jomini's works, the author of *The Elements of Military Art and Science* in 1846, and chief of staff to Abraham Lincoln during the Civil War. His book is replete with Jominian precepts, stressing the offensive as the key to victory. That principle led in turn to his declaration that "the first and foremost rule of the offensive is, to keep your forces concentrated as much as possible. This will not only prevent misfortune, but secure victory since . . . you possess the power of throwing your whole force upon any exposed point of your enemy's position."[4] Concentration of force had thus achieved the status of a major precept of American military thought, a Jominian legacy that in many ways continues to the present day.

This legacy did not, however, extend to the American command structure or contribute very much to the development of the military staff as the agency for successfully combining arms on the battlefield while ensuring unity of command. This is not to say that those developments were not present in the military record of Napoleon or the writings of Jomini. The Imperial Headquarters under Napoleon's chief of staff Louis-Alexandre Berthier, for example, featured a well-developed general staff with permanent sections responsible for the major administrative functions: artillery supply, topography, military police, personnel. Similar staff sections made up the major field commands and corps headquarters. It is possible, however, that though Jomini's American readers paid lip service to his strictures concerning the importance of staff preparations, they were far more intrigued by the operational side of the Napoleonic staff. While Berthier supervised the administrative functions of the armies, operational matters were largely handled through the *Maison,* which reported directly to Napoleon. Small cells existed within the Maison that would roughly correspond to the operations and intelligence sections of a modern headquarters; but the most important components of the system were the aides-de-camp, trusted senior officers who were dispatched on special missions by the emperor as the situation demanded.[5]

These officers, usually brigadiers or major generals, were the means by which Napoleon injected his personal genius into diverse battlefield situations—much in the manner of a football coach sending in a play from the sidelines. The problem, of course, was that the system did not work as well without a Napoleon. The American staff system—if it can be called that—did not feature a well-organized arrangement of staffs within its tactical echelons until the twentieth century. Instead, Civil War commanders, although fascinated by Napoleon, tended to focus more on his tactics than on the prosaic but equally essential staff and administrative system that accompanied his operational genius. Their oversight is understandable. Napoleon's actions were conducted in a language of command and operations that was instinctively understood by, say, a captain of dragoons chasing Indians on the frontier. To the same officer, serving in an Army whose entire complement averaged between ten and fifteen thousand men in the years separating the Mexican and Civil wars, Berthier's elaborate staff system and the *grande armée* it administered must have seemed almost unimaginable.

Ironically, this inattention to staff development took place at precisely the time the technology of the Industrial Revolution had spawned four major advances whose application to land warfare would create unprecedented capabilities and challenges for the extension of command and control: the telegraph, the railroad, the steamship, and the rifled projectile. The most revolutionary of these capabilities was the electric telegraph invented by Samuel F. B. Morse, which, by 1844, had demonstrated its ability to transmit long-distance messages. Telegraph wires quickly linked the cities and regions of the country as private companies rushed to exploit the commercial potential of the new medium. By the time of the Civil War, both sides were able to make use of a well-developed communications infrastructure of land lines, telegraph stations, and trained operators. Although the military applications of the new technology were a matter for constant experimentation throughout the conflict, its utility had already been demonstrated by the British in the Crimean War in 1854 and by the French five years later in the Franco-Austrian War—the latter case showing that field telegraph lines could extend even to an army's front and flanks.[6]

The companion technology to the telegraph was the railroad; its advances in strategic mobility were as far-reaching as those of electronic signaling in strategic communications. The potential for the rapid movement of troops by rail fit well with Jomini's teachings concerning the concentration of force via interior lines, even as rail cars promised to resolve the immemorial problem of slow and ponderous logistical support. As Ernest Fisher pointed out, a horse-drawn "wagon could transport about 2 tons a distance of about 20 miles a day, while a train car could transport 10 tons perhaps 350 miles per day, an improvement factor on the order of about 100."[7] Army officers played a prominent role in scouting and defending railroad routes across the frontier, and many left the service to become railroad executives in their own right. The Union and Confederate armies would put this wealth of experience to good use in testing the military capabilities of the new technology under the stress of combat.[8]

The same principles by which steam was harnessed for railroad locomotives were applied to develop the steamship for use by navies. Under the leadership of Commodore Matthew C. Perry, the U.S. Navy was quick to realize the benefits of steam propulsion, although a building program for the new vessels was hampered by naval conservatism, fiscal constraints, and design flaws. For one thing, early steamships such as the *Fulton II* mounted paddle wheels on either side, a feature that made the vessel extremely vulnerable to gunfire and cut down on the number of cannon that could be mounted. Capt. John Ericsson's invention and perfection of the underwater screw propeller corrected both problems, however, and in 1842 the Navy launched two steam cruisers, the *Missouri* and the *Mississippi*. By 1861, the service had a complement of over ninety vessels, a dozen of which were steam cruisers— "first-class vessels armed with guns unsurpassed in any navy."[9] The chief implication of steam propulsion for command and control was that it made the movement of naval vessels far less susceptible to the vagaries of winds and currents, and more amenable to human direction. This increase in the regularity of ship movement and direction meant a corresponding increase in the speed and scope of naval communications, as packet vessels began to fill the same functions on sea as couriers did on land. And at least as significant was the fact that the increased use of steam vessels on rivers opened up greater possibilities for naval support of land operations, suggesting, however, a range of new problems for the command and control of joint forces.[10]

The fourth technology to have an impact on command and control was the rifled projectile, so called because of the rifling, or internal grooves, on the interior of a firearm's barrel that imparted a spin to the projectile as it left the muzzle, greatly increasing its accuracy. Some artillery of the Civil War was rifled, notably the Parrott gun, but most was not, and the twelve-pound Napoleon muzzle-loaded smoothbore became the most common fieldpiece. Naval artillery would undergo the same change in the later years of the century, an evolution foreseen by the Navy's foremost gunnery expert, Adm. John A. Dahlgren, in 1859. Union and Confederate ships, however, fought the war using eleven- and fifteen-inch smoothbore cannon as the weapons of choice.[11] The rifled projectile had its greatest effect on the Civil War infantry. Smoothbore muskets had not been accurate much beyond one hundred to two hundred yards, but the Springfield and Enfield rifles manufactured after 1855 were capable of effective ranges of four hundred to six hundred yards, with maximum ranges of almost a thousand yards. Although rifling was a technique long known to gunsmiths, much of the new effectiveness of weapons was due to the adoption of the minié ball, a conical projectile that expanded to meet the rifled grooves when the gun was fired. The tremendous striking power now placed in the hands of infantrymen would eventually spell the end of eighteenth-century linear warfare tactics, since concentrated battle lines invited concentrated slaughter. As battle lines spread out in response, the problem of command and control would become steadily more acute, for the advances in weaponry were not accompanied by corresponding changes in organization or technique. Tactical control would thus become the most intractable of the many problems on the extended battlefields of the Civil War.[12]

Each of these technological changes represented a vast potential for change, yet, as the Civil War was soon to show, change was not something the American military command structure was prepared for—however much its talent for improvisation might help overcome the effects of early ineptitude and lack of foresight. If the Army was largely unaware of the great strides in military organization made by the French under Berthier, it was blissfully ignorant of the even more comprehensive changes that had now made the Prussian general staff system the finest in Europe. This oversight again is somewhat understandable, given that the prevailing model was French and that Napoleon had beaten the Prussians so decisively at the Battle of Jena in 1806. What lessons could the losing side offer beyond the heuristic value of a bad example? It was precisely that defeat, however, that led to the reforms in the Prussian army made by Gerhard von Scharnhorst and August von

Gneisenau, improvements that resulted in Prussian victories over the Austrians in 1866 and the French in 1871. Those victories gave the Prussian system a credibility that made their systematic approach to warfare all the more appealing in light of the demonstrated failures of the American Army during the Civil War. Since the Prussian system became the model for many reformers in the American Army after the war, it is appropriate to review it here briefly.

In his book on the Prussian-German General Staff, Trevor Dupuy aptly characterizes that system as an attempt to "institutionalize genius—or at least try to perfect a system that could perpetuate military excellence through the vagaries of change."[13] Scharnhorst and the reformers recognized that the extension of the commander's control on the battlefield and the growing demands of military administration had resulted in the growth of staffs from regimental to corps and army levels. Their objective was to organize those staffs so they would serve as the central unifying influence to prepare the army in peacetime for its wartime functions and, when war came, to assist in meeting its operational objectives. The proponent agency for both tasks would be the General Staff, headed by a chief, whose function was to provide the king with military advice, thereby combining military excellence with the dynamics of political control.

Equally important were the educational establishments set up to train the officer corps in general and to select and groom prospective General Staff candidates. At the head of the system stood the *Kriegsakademie,* the central repository for theoretical investigations into the art of war and the principal agency for the final grooming of those selected for General Staff service. The system was especially well suited for the exploration of new ideas, primarily because of the lateral linkages established between the educational and operational sides of the General Staff. Because of those linkages, the Prussian army was quick to seize upon the potential of the telegraph after Morse's demonstration in 1844 and to investigate its military applications in a systematic way. Similarly impressive was its response to Germany's first railway, which opened in 1835; by 1837, the General Staff was studying its use in speeding the nation's mobilization for war.[14] And the same dynamism led the Prussian army to equip its infantry with breech-loading rifles during the period 1848–60, the first in the world to do so.

The contrast between the Prussian and American systems could not have been more stark. Where the one was organized and systematic, the other was either haphazard or nonexistent. Although bureau systems existed in both the U.S. Army and the Navy, there was nothing even approaching the careful organization of successive staff echelons that characterized the Prussian system. There is probably no better demonstration of the vast gulf between the systems than a mission on which three Army officers embarked in 1855. Led by Maj. Richard Delafield, the men were sent to Europe on an observation tour by Secretary of War Jefferson Davis, who was concerned that the Army be kept abreast of important military developments on the Continent. The officers returned two years later and, in 1861, published their findings in a volume entitled *The Art of War in Europe*. The book provided elaborate commentary and illustrations of weaponry, fortifications, even the organization of regimental stables—but it failed even to mention that there was such a thing as the Prussian General Staff. Even more interesting is the fact that one of those Army officers was Capt. George B. McClellan, who in due course was placed in command of the Union Army. His occasional difficulties in that position coupled with his tour of the Continent gave an ironic twist to this statement in his memoirs: "One of the greatest defects of our military system is the lack of a thoroughly instructed STAFF CORPS. . . . Perhaps the greatest difficulty that I encountered in creating the Army of the Potomac arose from the scarcity of thoroughly instructed staff officers, and I must frankly state that every day I myself felt the disadvantages under which I personally labored from the want of that thorough theoretical and practical education received by the officers of the German General Staff."[15]

The Prussian General Staff, then, was the model of operational art that the more perceptive thinkers in the Army turned to in the aftermath of the Civil War. If Jominian precepts, or more exactly the American interpretations of Jominian precepts, had not provided the answer to the riddle of Civil War strategy, they had at least created the beginnings of disciplined military thought and had provided an overall concept of what land warfare was all about. The paradigm would become sharper and yet more generalized as American military thought turned in the last quarter of the nineteenth century to the work of Karl von Clausewitz. Not translated into English until 1873, his book *Vom Kriege* (*On War*) became a classic of military thought and the dominant paradigm on the conduct of land warfare. As a twentieth-century writer put it, "A military writer who, after Clausewitz writes upon war, runs the risk of being likened to the poet who, after Goethe, attempts a Faust, or after Shakespeare, a Hamlet."[16]

What Clausewitz brought to his subject was an unparalleled breadth and clarity of vision that explained both the essence of warfare ("War is thus an act of force to compel our enemy to do our will")[17] and its appropriate context ("war is not a mere act of policy but . . . a continuation of political activity by other means. . . . The political object is the goal, war is the means of reaching it, and means can never be considered in isolation from their purpose").[18] Far more than Jomini, he emphasized the importance of the battle as the decisive factor in war, with the conquering of the enemy's forces rather than the mere occupation of his territory as the primary means for achieving victory. He was equally direct in his prescription for its accomplishment: "The best strategy is always to be very strong; first in general and then at the decisive point. . . . there is no higher and simpler law in strategy than that of keeping one's forces concentrated."[19] The composition of those forces ideally represent a mix of artillery and cavalry with strong infantry as the inevitable centerpiece so that "a combination of the three arms leads to a more complete use of all of them."[20] He was also concerned that the proliferation of subordinate echelons made necessary by these combinations not be allowed to interfere with unity of command. That advice fully reflected the limitations of the classical age of command and control and is not without contemporary significance as well:

> There is no denying that the supreme command of an army . . . is markedly simpler if orders only need to be given to three or four other men; yet a general has to pay dearly for that convenience in two ways. First, an order progressively loses speed, vigor and precision the longer the chain of command it has to travel, which is the case where there are corps commanders placed between the divisional commanders and the general. Second, a general's personal power and effectiveness diminishes in proportion to the increase in the sphere of action of his closest subordinates. A general can make his authority over 100,000 men felt more strongly if he commands by means of eight divisions than by means of three divisions.[21]

Clausewitz did not live to see the Prussian General Staff built into the institution that would help overcome the natural tendencies for subordinate echelons to subvert the control of the commander. Although he did not, therefore, deliver the same sort of definitive advice on its use and composition that he did on other aspects of the army, he indirectly suggested the General Staff's true function when discussing the property of military genius which is the critical element in the character of a military commander (Napoleon being the obvious example): "What we have to do is to bring under consideration every common tendency of the powers of the mind and soul towards the business of War, the whole of which common tendencies we may look upon as *the essence of military genius*. We say 'common,' for just therein consists military genius, that it is not one single quality bearing upon War . . . but that it is *an harmonious association of powers,* in which one or the other may predominate, but none must be in opposition."[22]

The General Staff was to be the agency for bringing about this harmonious association of the powers, reconciling the competing demands of administration and operations, optimizing the mix and employment of its combat branches, and, most important, amplifying rather than attenuating the commander's control through subordinate echelons.

This approach was complementary to the unity of view that Clausewitz maintained for all facets of the problem of land warfare, and as his teachings became the dominant theoretical model for armies as the nineteenth century drew to a close, the Prussian General Staff became the dominant practical model. Together they formed a paradigm for land warfare that was above all a prescription for the totality of war on land as the ultimate form of national expression. Jominian ideals would never entirely pass from the scene, but they were somewhat eclipsed by the hindsight of the American Civil War and the image it conveyed of the total mobilization of the nation's resources united in the attrition and destruction of the enemy force. For the U.S. Army, its organization, structure, and functions would eventually come to be measured against this paradigm. The precepts of concentration of force, employment of the combined arms, and the maintenance of unity of command had been elevated from casual instinct to prescriptive strategy, with all those factors displayed against a backdrop of technological development that, as the century drew to a close, the Army was anxious to exploit.

The American Civil War on Land and Sea

Despite the many developments in combat on land and sea brought about by the Civil War, its impact on the American command structure was minimal—at least in terms of forcing immediate and fundamental structural change. In many ways, the war even tended to support the belief that the mechanisms for strategic control of the Army and Navy, particularly those responsible for their administration, had worked rather well. Secretary of War Edwin M. Stanton had been primarily responsible for the smooth operation of the Army's bureau system, which had expanded to meet the needs of an Army that enrolled more than 2.5 million men between 1861 and 1865. Equally impressive was its consistently sustained logistical support for a force that eventually comprised some "1,696 regiments of infantry, 272 of cavalry and 78 of artillery," support that meant moving six hundred tons of supplies each day for each theater army from depots to encampments.[23]

Although it was necessary to create three assistant secretaries of war during the conflict, probably the most impressive achievement of all was the fact that "the organization of the existing staff departments or military bureaus was not materially altered during the period of the war, although their official and clerical force was augmented from time to time to perform the increased amount of work imposed upon them."[24] Somewhat more modification had to be made in the organization of the Navy Department, given the scope of its activities: "From 1861 to 1865 the number of ships increased from 90 to 670; of officers from 1300 to 6700; and of seamen, from 7500 to 51,500. The annual naval expenditures rose from $12,000,000 to $123,000,000."[25] Three bureaus were added in 1862: Navigation (which eventually and mysteriously became associated with personnel), Steam Engineering, and Equipment and Recruiting.[26] Coordinating the work of the eight bureaus and directing their activities toward wartime operations required that Gustavus V. Fox, a former naval officer, be appointed to the post of assistant secretary of the navy, a newly authorized office. A half-century later, Mahan gave this assessment of Fox's efforts: "Individual power and individual responsibility are the fundamental merits of the bureau system. Its defect is lack of coordination. Happily, this lucky country . . . in 1861 unwittingly introduced into naval administration a singularly fit man . . . [to] impart unity and direction to the eight distinct impulses under which naval expansion was advancing. . . . The activities of the establishment, of the Navy Department on its civil side, were thus harmonized with the requirements of the military situation."[27]

Although the creation of Fox's post was essentially a minor modification of an existing structure, it bore out the pattern of hierarchical control and consolidation noted elsewhere in this book: naval administration followed much the same path as military administration, but always later and always with a greater reluctance to create intervening echelons.

Assessing the impact of the Civil War on the norms of civilian control is somewhat more difficult. On the one hand, the structure of civilian control was not materially affected: the chain of command still ran from the president through the secretary of war to the commanding general of the army and through him to the various field commanders. Lincoln successfully used that mechanism to impose what is customarily regarded as a high degree of civilian control on Union forces throughout the conflict. His most notable achievement in that respect was his perseverance through a succession of field commanders who were tried and found wanting—although the painful process went on for almost three years before Ulysses S. Grant was brought from the West and placed in overall command of the Union Army. The ultimate triumph of both system and process, however, should not be allowed to overshadow the existence of a major problem in American civil-military relations.

Historian T. Harry Williams has pointed out that Lincoln became a far better strategist than most of his generals, but that he was unable to overcome their persistent tendency to see every Civil War tactical and strategic problem in Jominian terms—that is, to emphasize control of territory rather than the destruction of enemy forces. Probably the best—or worst—example was provided by General George G. Meade who congratulated his troops for having "expelled the enemy from our soil" at Gettysburg but failed to pursue the beaten Lee or to corner him against the flood-swollen Potomac River: "Weeks later the general came to Washington for conferences and during a conversation Lincoln said to him suddenly, 'Do you know, general, what your attitude toward Lee for a week after the battle reminded me of?' 'No, Mr. President, what is it?' asked Meade. 'I'll be hanged if I could think of anything else,' said Lincoln, 'than an old woman trying to shoo her geese across a creek.'"[28]

With Grant, Lincoln finally got a commanding general of the army who actually deserved his title, but any assessment of the eventual triumph of the command system must be counterbalanced by the enormous losses sustained as the system was made equal to the tasks of war. It is particularly hard to understand why a distinguished historian such as Williams would conclude that, by war's end, "the American system was superior to most command organizations then existing in Europe and was at least as good as the Prussian staff machine."[29] Such an assessment might, with qualifications, describe the working relationships that evolved among the president, the secretary of war, the general-in-chief, and the field commanders, but it ignores the fact that there was no institutionalized body available to provide the president with well-informed military advice on a regular basis. Nor was there a well-defined staff system that could have helped the Army deploy a field force fully ten times larger than that commanded by George Washington. What staffs there were in the field commands were small, haphazardly organized, and unevenly employed. At the end of the war, for example, Grant's entire staff consisted of a chief of staff (itself a major improvement), two military secretaries, seven aides-de-camp, two assistant adjutants general, one inspector general, one chief quartermaster, one commissary of subsistence, one chief engineer, one provost marshal, and several assistants.[30] Regimental commanders, who had to control ten companies and a total complement of five hundred to a thousand men, had a staff of seven officers and six noncommissioned officers.[31]

Staffs at all levels were organized primarily around administrative functions, which often overlapped with operational functions; staffs, being creatures of the units they served, were usually incapable of taking up the slack. McClellan was so poorly served by his own staff officers during the Peninsular Campaign that he blundered around for weeks trying to shift his base of operations from the York to the James River using a single road. Other parallel roads were there, but his staff knew nothing of their existence, despite the fact that elements of both his Third and his Fourth Corps had come across them by chance.[32] When the task at hand was purely operational, there were many instances in which the staff was simply incapable of extending either the control or the will of the commander. To return to the example of Meade at Gettysburg, there is little question that his recent assumption of command and the demands of three days of intense combat handicapped his ability to exploit the victory by pursuing the retreating Confederates. But "had Meade possessed a properly trained staff, orders for the pursuit would have been prepared and waiting only his word to put them into effect as soon as the Confederate withdrawal began. Largely because Meade lacked such a staff system, Lee was permitted to accomplish his southward movement and escape into Virginia without interference from the Northern forces."[33]

This last point is somewhat speculative; nevertheless, the difficulties of combat command undoubtedly were magnified not only by staff inadequacies but also by the lethal relationship that had sprung up between nineteenth-century technology and eighteenth-century tactics. The basic maneuvering unit of the Civil War was the regiment, which at the beginning of the war attacked in two lines, its companies packed shoulder-to-shoulder as they advanced. Here they faced the worst of two worlds: not only was rifle fire more accurate at extended ranges, but the rifle itself was loaded from the muzzle in a standing position. The only practical way for attacking infantry to maintain a volume of fire was to reload on the move, which meant advancing by ranks in the standing position. In reaction to the enormous losses of the early battles—over seven thousand casualties were sustained in little over an hour at the Battle of Cedar Mountain in 1862, for example—formations began to spread out and skirmishers were deployed in front of both offensive and defensive lines. Soon, brigades of three thousand infantrymen occupied a mile of front, a division might be spread across a distance of two or three miles, the corps area could range up to ten miles, and, depending on the number of corps attached to it, the field army's span of control could commonly encompass twenty to thirty miles.[34] Complicating the problem was the "enthusiasm and skill" with which average infantrymen used any available cover on the battlefield and their tendency to spread out when attacking. "Attacks started in close order, but troops often scattered for cover and concealment when they came under fire, and thereafter advanced by short rushes supported by fire from neighboring units. The generals attempted to combine frontal assaults with envelopments and flanking movements, but the difficulty of timing and coordinating the movements of such large bodies of men in broken terrain made intricate maneuvers very difficult."[35]

Although control remained a problem throughout the war, the improvements in tactical signaling and the adaptation of the telegraph for military use had far-reaching consequences. Both owed much to the initiative of Albert James Myer, who invented the "wig-wag" system of semaphore flags, spearheaded the drive to create a Signal Corps (the first such branch in any army), and became the chief signal officer of the Army in 1860. His system of semaphore flags and brevity codes represented an attempt to extend the range of visual control through a network of signal and observation posts. Aided by telescope and binoculars, soldiers manning these posts could provide a nearly instantaneous relay of information across a ten-mile distance, either from observation points sited on commanding terrain or from signal detachments stationed with units committed in actual combat. The Confederate Army was not slow to recognize the potential of the system, largely because Capt. Edward P. Alexander, formerly Myer's assistant, became its chief of signals. Alexander is credited with personally sending the message that alerted the Confederate force that its flank was being turned during the First Battle of Bull Run, a warning that led to the reinforcement by Jackson's Brigade (when it won for itself and its commander the appellation "Stonewall") and ultimate victory.[36]

Similar instances took place during the battles of Antietam, when Union signals gave a timely warning of the approach of Jackson's cavalry, and Gettysburg, when the Union observation post at Little Round Top helped provide Meade with information on the tactical dispositions of Lee's forces, including advance notification of Pickett's Charge. Although couriers continued their ubiquitous rounds on the battlefields of the Civil War, tactical signaling quickly established its own niche as commanders found that the speed with which information could be sent around the battlefield could often yield tactical advantage. Signalmen on both sides grew more sophisticated as time went on, and since ciphers were either simple or nonexistent, they learned to intercept and read each other's messages. One of the more famous instances of interception occurred when Grant's signalman wig-wagged the message to Admiral Porter that Vicksburg had fallen after a long siege. Southern observers saw the same signal and passed the news via their own relay system to the Confederate garrison commander at Port Hudson—who upon hearing the bad news promptly surrendered his entire force. "Northern newspapers hailed Grant's message as 'the most momentous signal in American history.'"[37]

The presence of signal centers at the corps and army levels created natural linkage points for the field telegraph, another of Myer's innovations. Like semaphore signaling, it was soon an integral feature of both the Union and Confederate armies. Armies on the move used a horse-drawn "telegraph train" which could not only receive messages while in transit but run out ten miles of wire in four hours.[38] The tactical system could thus be linked effectively with the much more extensive commercial networks, so that it was possible for messages from Washington to reach the most distant commands in a matter of hours. On the Union side alone, more than 6.5 million messages were sent during the war,[39] a clear indication that the Army would be either the beneficiary or the victim of the strategic control that now tied it directly to the seat of government. One action by Stanton that underscored the point was his ordering the terminus of the Army's telegraph wire moved from the headquarters of the Army of the Potomac into the War Department, where it was President Lincoln's custom to come from time to time to read dispatches—especially when a major engagement was brewing. Although this kind of long-range kibitzing was not an easy cross to bear for generals accustomed to a great degree of personal autonomy in their commands, the benefits of the telegraph in extending their control—in a situation where every other factor rose to constrain it—must have seemed worth the price. There is no other way to comprehend the praise that Grant, as hard-bitten a commander as American armies have ever had, paid in his memoirs to the military telegraph and its operators. He went so far as to say that the first thing the Army of the Potomac did with every change of position was to dig entrenchments; its second activity was to lay telegraph wire between each of its major subordinate elements. What had once been revolutionary was now an accepted practice, so much so that, in Grant's words, "no order ever had to be given to establish the telegraph."[40]

Signal communications were also an important aspect of joint operations between the Army and Navy during the Civil War. The Navy had turned down a proposal from Myer before the war for a semaphore system of its own, claiming that its existing system of flag hoists was adequate for the needs of the service. During the war, however, the Navy was required not only to blockade southern ports but to support Army operations on land. The usual practice, therefore, was for Army signalmen to be put aboard naval vessels whenever such ship-to-shore coordination was required. Such was indeed the case during the Battle of Mobile Bay in 1864, when Adm. David Farragut's flotilla attacked in cooperation with ground forces commanded by Gen. Edward Canby. Army Lt. J. C. Kinney handled signal liaison duties from Farragut's quarterdeck, narrowly missing being hit by an explosive shell and accidentally striking the admiral on the head with a flagstaff at one point, but successfully passing messages back and forth throughout the engagement.[41]

The Civil War tended to bear out the belief that the doctrine of mutual cooperation was a reasonable basis for Army-Navy relationships. There is a noticeable lack in the historical record of any but petty disagreements between commanders engaged in joint operations (although Gen. Benjamin "Beast" Butler, who became the military governor of New Orleans after the city capitulated to his and Farragut's forces, seems to have made it a point to offend not only naval colleagues but everyone else as well). Several factors appear to have minimized potential command problems. For one, the decentralized structure of the Navy placed a great deal of authority on squadron and flotilla commanders: there was no Navy equivalent to the commanding general of the army, nor was there, of course, a general staff of any description. Army forces operating in the West enjoyed, in the early years of the war at least, much the same sort of decentralized authority, primarily because of strategic confusion in Washington and the attendant problem with the Army of Northern Virginia. Commanders of both services, thrown on their own resources and at some distance from the national capital, found that common-sense solutions to mutual problems were attainable—especially when inconvenient questions of subordination were not involved. As Grant noted of his naval colleague at Vicksburg, Adm. David Porter, "I had no more authority to command Porter than he had to command me."[42]

In assessing that campaign, and by inference the performance of the Navy, Grant summed up the relations that had characterized the uniting in combat of two autonomous services: "The navy under Porter was all it could be, during the entire campaign. Without its assistance the campaign could not have been successfully made with twice the number of men engaged. It could not have been made at all . . . with any number of men without such assistance. The most perfect harmony reigned between the two arms of the service. There never was a request made, that I am aware of, either of the flag officer or any of his subordinates, that was not promptly complied with."[43]

This fulsome praise should not obscure the fact that all the joint operations of the Army and Navy during the Civil War were examples of "ad hockery writ large," in which success often was due not so much to goodwill and common sense as to chance. Nevertheless, both services clearly had learned a great deal about the art of what were then called combined (joint) operations, operations that became progressively more difficult as they were thrown against tougher Confederate defenses later in the war. If so much was accomplished from scratch, however, how much more might have been achieved had the services been better trained and prepared to work with one another—as indeed they might have been, given the example of the Vera Cruz landing during the Mexican War?

The question is not an idle one, especially given the strategic conditions of the Civil War which might well have called for the Union to have exploited its numerical superiority on land and sea in joint operations not confined to the periphery of the Confederacy. McClellan offered such a strategy late in 1861, just after taking over command of the Army from General Scott, whose Anaconda Plan aimed at doing little more than sealing the existing borders of the Confederacy. McClellan proposed a combined force of 273,000 men operating as a kind of amphibious invasion force, attacking port cities such as Charleston and Savannah and using rivers to capture strategic points located farther inland, such as Richmond. Lincoln rejected the plan, and historians ever since have derided it. Williams called it "as fantastic a proposal as Lincoln received from a military man, and he was to be the recipient of many." He also noted that the Union lacked the logistical resources, sea transport, and "staff organization to administer such a host," and concluded that it was fatally flawed in conception because "it made places rather than armies the objectives."[44]

That conventional wisdom was challenged by a 1978 book by Rowena Reed, *Combined Operations in the Civil War,* which, while it exhibits an undue admiration for McClellan and never quite comes to grips with the usual criticisms of his plan, provides a fresh perspective. Reed suggested that it would have provided a "flexible, water-based strategy" instead of the "plodding territorial invasion" that eventually ended the war after four years of slaughter.[45] There is something to that argument if one considers that the oceans and rivers surrounding and penetrating the Confederacy were indeed potential avenues of approach for an army and a navy able to exploit them; but this presumes both the availability of the physical means and the existence of the theoretical and practical knowledge necessary to bring them to bear. Neither the means nor the knowledge existed in the American command structure at that time. Although the vast industrial machine of the North might over time have provided the men and ships necessary to fulfill such a strategic conception, neither service possessed the command and staff capabilities necessary to have turned strategy into applied operational art. As it was, there were elements of truth in Scott's Anaconda Plan, McClellan's concept of waterborne mobility, and Grant's strategy of dogged attrition. Each might well have had its place in a grand strategic design that exploited northern strengths and southern weaknesses, but without a trained cadre of staff and operational experts, the Union was as capable of carrying out such combined strategic operations as it was of conducting space flight.

It is an exercise in historical hindsight to suggest that the Prussians might have done better, not only in applying a disciplined method to the study of likely strategic problems, but in designing the military means to deal with them. The American political experience, however, attaches great importance to the constitutional principles of separation of powers and civilian control of the military, values that resulted in the creation and maintenance of two largely autonomous service organizations united only by an informal and decentralized command structure. It was natural, therefore, that their early conceptual models should have favored the personalized improvisation of a Napoleon rather than the highly structured order of the Prussian General Staff.

The Civil War ended only after having created the conditions for profound changes in the internal conceptions of both services. The Army had deployed forces on a scale that could not previously have been imagined across a theater of operations of continental dimensions. Its campaigns involved a level of destruction that had far more in common with modern warfare than with anything that had gone before. The Navy had experienced the same kind of quantum leap in size, while acquiring invaluable lessons with the new technologies of steam and armored warships. But in the aftermath of the Civil War, these lessons, as well as their military and naval implications, were neglected. The Army returned to its favored occupation of fighting the Indians on the frontier, while the Navy reconstituted its foreign squadrons and resumed the prosaic task of "protecting maritime commerce." For a time, the Navy even experienced the throes of reaction to steam propulsion and ordered its captains not to use their boilers unless under emergency conditions. The Army, which had never developed a high-level planning body like that of the French or the Prussians, would with unconscious irony some years later describe the vast demobilization of the Grand Army of the Republic as the crowning achievement of the wartime "General Staff."[46] The nation, exhausted from the most terrible war in its history, was content to leave things much as they had been after Appomattox, perhaps even viewing the increasingly outmoded military and naval establishments with a certain nostalgic afterglow. Change, however, was to become a constant, and as the nineteenth century drew to a close, a naval paradigm was about to emerge.

Toward a Paradigm of Ocean Warfare

The writings of Alfred Thayer Mahan gave the U.S. Navy a strategic vision of itself and its role in the nation's defense so profound that it deserves to be called a paradigm. As had been the case with the Army and its reactions to the early theorists of nineteenth-century warfare, the Navy used Mahan's doctrines as both descriptive and prescriptive instruments around which to accomplish a major change in naval policy. The Navy's customary functions had always included protection of American maritime interests in peacetime and defense of the nation's harbors and coasts during war; a third mission would now be added which operated in both peace and war—projection of American power. It was no accident that Mahan's doctrines seized the temper of the times in such a way. The last Indians had been rounded up, the frontier was closed, and a burgeoning American industrial base was looking for new overseas markets. The traditional reliance of the Republic on a foreign policy that stressed isolation from all but hemispheric problems was gradually giving way to an acquired taste for foreign adventure.

There was also a matter of strategic choice that was being confronted even as Mahan's first great work, *The Influence of Sea Power upon History,* was being written. The old Civil War Navy, a polyglot collection of monitors, ironclads, and steam-and-sail cruisers, had to be replaced with the next generation of armored warships, a task the nation's new steel mills and shipyards eagerly anticipated—as, of course, did their elected representatives. Although Mahan's work failed to give particular answers to all the questions implied by these developments, it did succeed in formulating a theory of sea power that brought him international renown. As John Alger noted, "His thought precipitated and guided a revolution in American naval policy, provided a theoretical foundation for Great Britain's determination to remain the dominant sea power in the world, gave impetus to German naval development, and affected the character of naval thought and practice in France, Italy, Russia, Japan and among many of the lesser powers."[47] The theory itself, however, was not especially elaborate or even original: "His contribution lay rather in organizing into a coherent system, or philosophy, the strategic principles which the British Admiralty had been following more or less blindly for over two hundred years."[48]

That contribution began with a statement about the nature of the maritime environment: "The first and most obvious light in which the sea presents itself from the political and social point of view is that of a great highway; or better, perhaps, of a wide common over which men may pass in all directions, but on which some well-worn paths show that controlling reasons have led them to choose certain lines of travel rather than others. These lines of travel are called trade routes."[49]

This was an interesting conceptual reversal that was especially significant for a public long accustomed to thinking of oceans as barriers rather than as lines of communication. The factors influencing a country's ability to profit from those lines included geographical position, physical conformation, territorial size, population, national character, and type of government. Depending on the relative weight of those variables, three processes tended to occur. First, the dynamics of production necessarily involved a search for overseas trade in order to expand available markets. Second, trade led to the development of a national merchant marine, as "it is the wish of every nation that this shipping business should be done in its own vessels." Third, the necessity to secure lucrative trade led both to armed merchantmen (which eventually gave rise to naval fleets) and to overseas naval stations and outposts (which became colonies). In these three related activities—production, shipping, and colonial expansion—"is to be found the key to much of the history, as well as of the policy, of nations bordering upon the sea."[50]

The implications of Mahan's formulation for American naval policy did not obtain so much from these activities, however (since the United States possessed at that point neither colonies nor an especially large merchant marine), as much as from the necessity to protect the nation's productive base from blockade. This eventuality was made somewhat more likely by the impending construction of a canal across the Isthmus of Panama, which would have a transforming effect on the nation's geopolitical position: "The position of the United States with respect to this route will resemble that of England to the Channel, and of the Mediterranean countries to the Suez route." In other words, if the oceans were no longer a barrier to commerce, neither were they now a barrier against a determined naval opponent. Such an opponent, according to Mahan, could blockade the American coastline merely by staying out of sight of the shore and menacing the principal routes in and out of American ports. It is interesting that Mahan linked that idea to a basic change that had taken place in command and control technology: "It seems possible that, in these days of submarine telegraphs, that the blockading forces in-shore and off-shore, and from one port to another, might be in telegraphic communication with one another along the whole coast of the United States, readily giving mutual support; and if, by some fortunate military combination, one detachment were attacked in force, it could warn the others and retreat upon them."[51]

Although this argument presumes the rather far-fetched idea that an opposing force should have somehow been able to secure a foothold on American soil, Marconi's wireless became a reality just five years after *Sea Power* was published, allowing precisely this kind of over-the-horizon control to be exercised for the first time with naval forces.

It is true, as James L. Abrahamson has pointed out, that Mahan's most widely read book failed "to point unambiguously toward the need for an American naval resurgence or the creation of a battleship fleet"; nevertheless it provided the intellectual force behind the movement that resulted in both the resurgence and the fleet.[52] Even before *Sea Power* was published, its ideas were credited with having spurred the secretary of the navy in his annual report of 1889 to call for twenty armored battleships to act as a blockade-breaking force. That report led the House Naval Affairs Committee to approve construction the following year of three battleships that were to displace more than ten thousand tons and mount main batteries of eight-inch guns. These were formidable weapons, and with that decision Congress committed itself and the Navy to a process of naval expansion that future events would help sustain. The Spanish-American War of 1898 seemed to vindicate Mahan's precepts and served as well to heighten the support the Navy enjoyed in public opinion. The administration of Theodore Roosevelt and the building of the Panama Canal kept naval affairs at the forefront of the country's attention, with the "New Navy" coming to be seen as a symbol of national strength. The resulting pride of place and attendant political clout represented attributes the Navy would never again be entirely without.[53]

Mahan's ideological and political contributions to naval thought also prompted the development of naval doctrine and the creation of a new naval command structure. It is important in this regard to recall the reputation of his father, Dennis Hart Mahan, who was famous in his own right as the great interpreter of Jomini to the previous generation of American military leaders. It is a commonplace to say that Jomini's influence was equally strong upon the son, a fact the son often confirmed himself. The points of comparison are many, but none more important than the idea of concentration of force. This fundamental Jominian concept is expressed in one of the most frequently quoted passages from *Sea Power:* "It is not the taking of individual ships or convoys, be they few or many, that strikes down the money power of a nation; it is the possession of that overbearing power on the sea which drives the enemy's flag from it, or allows it to appear only as a fugitive; and which, by controlling the great common, closes the highways by which commerce moves to and from the enemy's shores. This overbearing power can only be exercised by great navies."[54]

One could note other Jominian influences as well: the Napoleonic zeal for the climactic battle and Mahan's teachings concerning the equally climactic central naval engagement; the Jominian formulation of interior and exterior lines and Mahan's equation of that principle to trade routes and strategic choke points; and both men's preferences for movement and offensive action.[55]

As important as those points are, however, they do not sum up Mahan's whole notion of command of the sea as well as does the idea of concentration of force. To a Navy long accustomed to single-ship engagements in war and peacetime patrolling in squadrons of two or three vessels, Mahan was now offering the revolutionary perspective that command of the sea meant destroying or neutralizing the enemy fleet en masse; this requirement in turn meant concentrating unprecedented numbers of ships and fighting them as parts of a coherent whole. Although the concept is akin to what Jomini had in mind for land battles, naval scholar Herbert Rosinski detected a difference; he contrasted the "indivisibility of the sea," which could not be fenced off, with the static nature of the land, which could be so divided between armies concentrated for the purpose:

> At sea . . . all the conditions that on land tend to strengthen the defense vis-à-vis the attack are absent. No common frontier enables the defender to establish and maintain contact; no accidents of ground help to canalise his opponent's advance into predictable lines, nor to support him in making his stand. On the contrary, once on the open sea, an attacker, thanks on the one hand to the mobility of ships and fleets, and on the other to the restricted range of vision and control . . . enjoys practically unlimited possibilities for evading the defender's forces. . . . Incertitude as to the opponent's dispositions and movements is thus the normal and characteristic condition of naval warfare.[56]

This essay, written shortly before Pearl Harbor, captures much of the essence of naval command in the era ushered in by Mahan: fleets must be concentrated, opponents must be crushed, and oceans must be controlled.[57]

The operational implications of this doctrine affected the naval command structure in ways that were reminiscent of the Army's coming to grips with the principles of extended battlefield control and combined arms integration a century before. Naval technology had now progressed to the point that armor was lighter and more extensive, gunfire more powerful and more accurate, steam propulsion both faster and more efficient. These changes in turn gave naval architects far more flexibility than they had had before and allowed the construction of different classes of ships capable of fulfilling a variety of roles in fleet formations. That development occurred just as the wireless gave ships a communications range of fifty to seventy-five miles from shore stations or other elements of the fleet. With its aid, cruisers could now operate beyond the visual range of the rest of the fleet, thereby extending the naval commander's effective range of control. The experimentation with different ship types continued apace, with fast-running torpedo boats being added and then countered by the advent of a new class, the torpedo boat destroyer, or as it became more widely known, the destroyer. The fast-moving destroyers effectively extended the fleet's defensive perimeter still farther.[58]

Sitting at the center of this perimeter, as ships were delivered from a construction program begun in 1907, were the first American dreadnoughts, twenty-thousand-ton battleships which featured a central system for integrated fire control of their eight twelve-inch guns, as well as their lesser batteries. Fire control officers, observers, range-finders, and guns were linked for the first time with a common set of calibrations and electrical communications. This integrated fire control system now enabled the dreadnought to have an effective radius of action of between six and eight miles, whereas naval engagements between wooden-hulled ships had usually taken place at ranges of less than a thousand yards.[59]

For American naval officers in the quarter-century between *Sea Power* and the outbreak of World War I, these new weapons systems meant that fleet command had at last been achieved in fact as well as name. Although large fleets of ships with varied classes had not been unknown elsewhere in the world, they simply had not existed in the U.S. Navy prior to Mahan—unless one counts as such Admiral Porter's rag-tag riverine force of ironclads and paddle-wheel steamers. The appearance of these American naval formations, however, also meant that a measure of tactical initiative had been taken away from the individual ship captain and given to the fleet commander. Whereas a squadron commander before had had little ability to project his influence beyond the limits of his own quarterdeck, the authority of the fleet commander now was consolidated and distributed throughout the tactical echelons assigned to him. He not only could "see" at greater ranges; he could effectively command there as well.

Mahan's unique exposition of philosophy and ideology represented one of those instances in history where an idea can be seen to have directly affected technological choices. His ideas shaped a political and strategic consensus that led to the revival of American sea power during an era in which sea power became synonymous with the revolution in shipbuilding that produced the dreadnought as the capital ship of an integrated fleet. The requirements of integration, in both the planning and the construction of these vessels, as well as in their utilization at sea, in turn led to a greater level of centralized control. The modification of the Navy's command structure to accommodate the results of these technological choices was not accomplished without the pain that attends most modernization cycles, and it is especially difficult for military or naval organizations. Yet the modernization of the administrative side of the Navy command structure proved to be an intractable problem: the admirals could experience a kind of operational gratification as the payoff for their efforts; the bureaucrats could only lose power and position.

It will be recalled that the Navy bureau system had been created in 1842 to replace the Board of Commissioners and that it had functioned without major changes ever since. It will also be recalled that Mahan delivered the classic comment on its character: "Individual power and individual responsibility are the fundamental merits of the bureau system. Its defect is lack of coordination."[60] Much the same thought was expressed by Paullin in his authoritative work on naval administration: "The bureaus are semi-independent principalities, whose obligations to their suzerain, the secretariat, are rather slight."[61] More recent scholarship has tended to support those assessments.[62] The bureau systems in both services provided hierarchies that carried out certain routine and well-understood functions, but this same division of labor made them inadequate mechanisms for comprehending activities that were not routine or that demanded a high degree of functional integration—war itself being the prime example. The Army's response to these pressures resulted in the formation and legislative sanctioning of a general staff (the principal topic of the following section).

The Navy's response was less dramatic, but in some ways more interesting: its highlights can be briefly summarized. In 1884, the Navy had established the Naval War College in Newport, Rhode Island, even as some prominent naval officers (such as the college's first president, Adm. Stephen B. Luce) were beginning to call for the formation of a naval general staff. During the Spanish-American War, the Naval War Board was formed to advise the Navy secretary on the conduct of operations, an initiative that led to the formation of a permanent General Board in 1900, an advisory body of senior officers headed until 1917 by Admiral of the Navy George Dewey. Pressure to create a true general staff was still being exerted by naval reformers, such as Comdr. William Sims and Adm. Bradley Fiske, and was just as steadfastly resisted by a coalition of bureau chiefs and congressmen. After several legislative initiatives were killed on Capitol Hill, President Taft's secretary of the navy G. V. L. Meyer ordered, on November 18, 1909, a reorganization of the Navy Department as far-reaching as was possible without further statutory enhancement.[63]

This plan, which became known as the aide system, created four principal divisions within the department for Operations, Personnel, Material, and Inspections, each headed by a senior line officer. Collectively, they would constitute an informal advisory body to the secretary, but, like the General Board, they would have no directive authority outside their respective jurisdictions. Under the leadership of Admiral Fiske, the aide for operations became a kind of primus inter pares until, on March 3, 1915, legislation was passed making the chief of naval operations (CNO) responsible for the deployment of the fleet and the preparation of war plans. Because of opposition by Secretary of the Navy Josephus Daniels—who denounced the plan as an attempt to "Prussianize the American Navy"—the CNO was denied authority to issue orders except through the secretary. This plan, of course, left the bureau system virtually intact, a condition that persisted until the eve of World War II.[64]

This marked the first time the pattern of Navy administration spun off in a direction different from that taken by the Army; to that point, the Navy had established many of the same kinds of structures set up to control the War Department, although usually after a delay of some years. Why the new tack? Part of the reason may have been the well-ingrained habit of personal responsibility in the bureau structures noted by Mahan. The Navy ashore and the Navy afloat stressed precisely this kind of unitary authority from the quarterdeck to the bureau chief; there was little room for the collective, coordinative ideals that usually characterized Army staff arrangements. The essence of the Prussian system was the General Staff—a body specifically chartered to span what would otherwise be gaps between the administrative and the operational, or between the tactical and the strategic. Such an arrangement would have been utterly alien to a system that had acquired its fundamental organizational values when it was small, decentralized, unitary, and highly personal.

Those attributes made the bureau chiefs the natural enemies of any system of coordinative authority, the degree of hostility being in direct proportion to the potential for loss of bureaucratic prerogatives. It was their political backing, however, that made their authority so formidable and that ultimately compelled the Navy to accept a compromise much less ambitious than what the reformers had hoped for. The previous chapter noted that the Navy from the outset was seen as an agency embodying the twin purposes of national defense and the promotion of commerce. Many of the critical battles over its maintenance and expansion had tended to be fought out in political terms. This is not surprising, since its largest yards were in such harbor cities as Norfolk, New York, and Boston, all of them well represented in Congress. These installations were commonly used for political patronage, an example of which occurred during the presidential election of 1888 when one thousand men were temporarily employed in the New York yard. The increasing technical sophistication of the Navy made inroads into the more flagrant applications of the spoils system, but even when a merit system was introduced at the New York yard in 1892, the superintendent found it expedient to keep a rough parity between Democrats and Republicans among the members of the work force.[65]

Given the additional monies spent on naval construction in the age of the dreadnoughts, the stakes for contracts, jobs, and effective political control had clearly escalated—and there was good reason to fear that a general staff–type organization might upset the cozy relationship that existed among the principal players. Paullin summed up their identities and roles:

> The two naval committees of Congress practically decide the amount of the annual appropriations for the navy, the uses to which this money shall be applied, and the numbers and types of new ships. . . . It is scarcely too much to say that the Secretary of the Navy, the chiefs of naval bureaus, the members of the General Board, the President of the United States, the Speaker of the House and the leading members of the two naval committees constitute a grand committee on naval legislation, whose members, by conference or otherwise, resolve differences, compromise conflicting interests, bring the legislature and executive to an understanding and reach an approximate agreement upon naval legislation.[66]

This is an accurate summary of the "grand committee" after the General Board had been created by the secretary of the navy in 1900 in response to the first wave of naval reform. It is interesting to note, however, that the other players regarded this most recent addition to the team with ill-disguised suspicion, a fact that became evident when Congress was asked to give legislative sanction to the General Board in 1904. The testimony of Assistant Secretary of the Navy Charles H. Darling was instructive, although he was compelled to mute his criticism of the board in deference to Admiral Dewey, the great naval hero who was its president. After noting its accomplishments, Darling said that the board's functions should nevertheless be restricted because of involvement with matters that did not properly concern it, especially the administration of navy yards. His muffled indictment was clearly meant as a warning to the senior membership of the inner circle: "These questions are entirely without military significance. It [the General Board] has undertaken to inform the department what legislation was needed. It has devoted much time and attention to the reorganization of the Navy Department, as well the civilian as the military side. It has prepared and circulated much literature advocating a general staff. In short, it has already invaded the province of civil administration and planted there the standard of conquest."[67]

The hint was taken: the Navy would never have a general staff in fact, despite the steady growth of the CNO's power. A basic difference in service responses to the dynamics of command and staff had now hardened into precedent and would come to play a large role in future interservice relations. The final point to be made here is that if Professor Huntington was correct in his assertion that both services were made subordinate to the norm of subjective civilian control, then the voluptuous intimacy of naval and political elites surely suggests that some services were more subjective than others.

The Spanish-American War and Its Aftermath

For a "splendid little war," the Spanish-American War had some rather large consequences, especially in its impact on the command structure of the Army. It also served as a demonstration of what could go wrong when two autonomous services were required to perform closely coordinated operations in wartime despite a lack of strategic planning ability in both organizations and the absence of any coordinative structure between them. The after-effects of the war, however, eventually produced the General Staff of the Army, the General Board of the Navy, and the Joint Board of the Army and Navy. The motivation behind Navy Department reform was based more on ideological grounds than on any wartime failure, because the Navy could look back upon its record during the war with much satisfaction. The renascence that had begun with naval reconstruction in the 1880s and attained ideological conviction with Mahan's writings in the early 1890s had, when the war broke out in 1898, produced spectacular if overrated victories, such as that by Admiral Dewey at Manila Bay.

Although the Army could take some comfort in victories such as that at San Juan Hill in Cuba, it was a recollection tarred by debacles in the mobilization, equipment, transportation, and direction of the expeditionary force. The War Department had not enjoyed the benefits of the national awakening that had paced naval developments. Following the Civil War and the disbanding of the great blue-clad forces, the Regular Army had settled back into the familiar routine of patrolling the frontier and subduing its remaining Indians. Administratively, Army line officers commanded seven territorially based departments under the supervision of the commanding general of the army, while the secretary of the army was nominally responsible for the twelve bureaus and boards that functionally controlled much of Army life. This great functional authority brought the bureaus into frequent conflict with line officers, compelling the secretary either to arbitrate or to remain aloof. The bureaus also maintained separate liaison with the relevant committees of Congress, spurred on by a promotion system that depended directly on the enlargement of their functional authority. The bureaus were, as a result, quasi-autonomous agencies in their own right and as naturally resistant to coordinative authority as were their naval counterparts.[68]

A few bright spots had existed in Army life since the Civil War, most notably in the person of Emory Upton, who had been one of the youngest major generals in the Union Army and had then gone on to become commandant of cadets and instructor of tactics at West Point. His work had been instrumental in the Army's coming to grips with the demands for extended control of battlefield formations, largely through the use of squads of four men which could maneuver on their own and as parts of platoons and companies. He was to be best known, however, for a work published posthumously, *The Military Policy of the United States since 1775,* which was an indictment both of the militia system and of the antiquated War Department staff. This book, a companion volume, *The Armies of Asia and Europe,* and the 1873 English translation of Clausewitz's *On War* helped focus the Army's intellectual leaders on the Prussian general staff system as an appropriate model for correcting the wrongs left by the long period of postwar neglect; Prussian victories over the Austrians and the French accelerated acceptance of the system toward the end of the century.[69] A significant effort had been made as well by William Tecumseh Sherman, who, as commanding general from 1869 to 1883, had been instrumental in establishing "schools of application" in the combat branches, enabling officers to receive organized higher instruction in their profession.

There was thus good reason to believe that the traditional fighting qualities of the officer corps had not atrophied over the years, but the outbreak of hostilities with Spain after the sinking of the battleship *Maine* soon proved that valor needed to be accompanied by efficiency. The bureaus would later be described as "a hydra-headed monster" by Army reformers, a metaphor that captured well their uncoordinated actions in response to war. One of those reformers, William Harding Carter, later wrote:

> At the outbreak of the war with Spain, the conditions in the War Department indicated to every officer who had given any study to the subject the absolute necessity for a General Staff. From the moment that it became apparent that a volunteer army was to be raised . . . the offices of the Secretary of War . . . and the corridors of the War Department were uncomfortably crowded with applicants for appointments or with Members of Congress presenting the claims of constituents for appointment to office. The Secretary of War and the Adjutant General could only attend to the proper functions of their offices in

guiding organization, equipment and mobilization of the great volunteer Army by secreting themselves for a few moments at a time, or during the night, when most of the real work of the department had to be conducted, to avoid the pressure from office seekers.[70]

Predictably, those efforts did not go well. The port of embarkation for the expeditionary force was Tampa, Florida, which had inadequate facilities for such a movement; this was fortunate, in a way, since initially there were not enough troop transports. Even after that embarrassment was sorted out, the entire force sat in port for over a week because of false rumors of Spanish cruisers. The force that finally arrived in Cuba was outfitted in wool uniforms and compelled to subsist on rations that became known in the subsequent public outcry as "embalmed beef."[71]

The operational command of the expeditionary force was no better. Maj. Gen. William R. Shafter was given a movement order for the assault on Cuba that was a masterpiece of ambiguity: "Land your force at such place east or west of that point [Santiago] as your judgment may dictate, under the protection of the Navy, and move it . . . as shall best enable you to capture or destroy the garrison there; and cover the Navy as it sends its men in small boats to remove torpedoes, or with the aid of the Navy capture or destroy the Spanish fleet now reported to be in Santiago Harbor."[72] Gen. Nelson Miles, then commanding general of the army, compounded the confusion by leaving for the field, surrendering effective control over the mobilization and Army-Navy coordination to the secretary of war and the bureau chiefs.

It was perhaps inevitable, given this lack of any effective working mechanism for interservice cooperation in Washington below the secretarial level, that confusion at the operational level should have persisted between the naval and expeditionary forces. Shafter's force and Adm. William Sampson's fleet wrangled bitterly over how they were jointly to overcome Cervera's fleet at Santiago and reduce the garrison holding the town. Communications were exchanged not only between the general and the admiral but also between their respective headquarters in Washington. The matter eventually reached the president, and Shafter was told, "The President directs that you confer with Admiral Sampson at once for cooperation in taking Santiago. After the fullest exchange of views, you will agree upon the time and manner of attack."[73] This high-level injunction was not enough to overcome service prerogatives: naval representatives were excluded from the Spanish garrison's surrender ceremony, and further acrimony over the disposition of Spanish vessels taken as prizes in the harbor was avoided only through the direct intervention of the secretary of war.

Interservice conflict during this brief war, as petty as it may appear on the surface, was the understandable outward manifestation of two organizations in the full flower of their own autonomy. The task at hand, however—a large-scale amphibious invasion—implied a coordination between ground and naval forces that was the first hint that the time-honored division of labor between land and sea might be breaking down and that interservice support based on occasional improvisations was a doctrine that was no longer appropriate. Although that realization lay far in the future, sober reflection in the aftermath of the war suggested that something ought to be done to improve mutual cooperation between the service sovereignties. It was in that spirit that a Joint Board was created in 1903 by the respective service secretaries, to be composed of four senior officers from the Army and Navy who would meet as often as necessary to discuss mutual matters of interest. Few such matters seemed to suggest themselves once the first rush of creationism had passed, and the board soon lapsed into functional disuse, not to be revived in a serious way until after World War I.[74]

Of more consequence as a reaction to the war was the movement that resulted in the creation of the Army General Staff in 1903. The appreciation for the advances made in the Prussian staff system, already apparent in some Army circles well before this, received another boost with the publication in 1895 of a book entitled *The Brain of an Army,* by Spenser Wilkinson, a prominent British analyst of military affairs. The book was the first detailed exposition of the Prussian system to appear in English, and it had a powerful impact on both sides of the Atlantic. In both the United States and Britain, whose own organizational deficiencies had been sharply highlighted by the Boer War, the book's clearly written, easily understandable prose helped focus public discussion on the model initiated by Scharnhorst and now brought to fruition under Helmuth von Moltke and Otto von Bismarck. The English parliamentary system, with its traditions of party discipline and collective cabinet responsibility, was able to accept the Prussian prescription without undue difficulty, and the Imperial General Staff became a reality. In the United States, however, its equally strong political tradition, which viewed with intense suspicion any concentration of uniformed authority, promised a far more difficult struggle against anything so "alien" as a system modeled on that possessed by a country whose government appeared synonymous with military autocracy.[75]

The outcome of that struggle might well have been different had it not been for the leadership of Elihu Root, who from 1899 to 1904 was one of the strongest and most able secretaries of war in the Army's history. Originally appointed by President William McKinley to direct the reforms following in the wake of the airing of the logistical debacles in Cuba, Root's political standing was enhanced not only by his own reputation for competence and probity but also by the enthusiastic support he received from Theodore Roosevelt following his accession to the presidency in 1901. As secretary, Root had the further benefit of an outstanding assistant, Maj. William Harding Carter, who had won the Medal of Honor during the Indian wars and provided much of the professional advice that proved critical in winning congressional support for reform. The cause of reform was aided as well by the political climate, which recognized that wartime deficiencies had made clear the need for improvement, especially in light of the widening demands of policing the territories now acquired from Spain. In the Philippines, for example, a native insurrection was already requiring a permanent Army garrison— necessitating a larger peacetime force than ever before to operate at an unprecedented distance from American shores.

Root developed three elements to deal with the larger problem of the Army's command structure. The first proved to be the easiest to accomplish. In 1901, he used his authority as secretary to create the Army War College, both to act as the capstone of the Army's professional development and educational system and to serve as an interim General Staff. This was a wise move, relying as it did on the precedents already established by Sherman's schools of application as well as the Naval War College set up seventeen years earlier. The second and third elements were more difficult. Root proposed in 1902 a formal legislative package that did away with the post of commanding general of the army, substituting a chief of staff of the army, with authority over both the line and staff departments. That authority he was to exercise on behalf of the secretary of war, and the agency by which he would exercise it was the General Staff of the Army. Rather than being permanent, General Staff officers (forty or fifty in number) were to be chosen from among the best of the regular line officers and detailed to the staff for up to four years.

In his letter of transmittal to the Senate, Root spoke directly to the main point at issue: "The General Staff scheme is not a new proposition, because officers of the Army have always been utilized to a certain extent in this business . . . but they have had no legal status. Neither law nor custom places the preparation of plans for national defense in the hands of any particular officer or body of officers, and what is everybody's business is nobody's business. . . . It has usually been because American character rises superior to system, or rather absence of system, that disaster has been avoided."[76]

The main point many Congressmen were likely to see at issue, however, was the effect that such a reorganization might have upon individual constituencies or on long-established working relationships. Any general staff scheme necessarily involved the redistribution of power away from the bureau chiefs with their direct linkages to Congress. Equally ticklish business of placing overall supervisory authority in the hands of the chief of staff, a move intended to resolve the ambiguous division of line and staff that had existed for over seventy-five years between the secretary and the commanding general of the army. The bureau chiefs stood to lose a great deal and, from his highly personal perspective, so did Gen. Nelson A. Miles, commanding general of the army and Medal of Honor recipient, whose confused campaign against the Spanish colonialists had not measured up to his previous gallantry against the Apaches.

The testimony by General Miles before the Senate was skillfully calculated to play upon the nostalgia of the many Civil War veterans in both houses:

> In my judgment, a system that is the fruit of the best thought of the most eminent patriots and ablest military men that this country has produced should not be destroyed by substituting one that is more adapted to the monarchies of the Old World. . . . Unlike our Presidents, the sovereigns of Spain, Italy, Austria, Turkey, Germany and Russia are trained from their earliest boyhood with a view to commanding armies when they arrive at the head of government; and a General Staff Corps such as suggested might be better adapted for those countries than for our Republic. The scheme is revolutionary, casts to the winds the lessons of experience, and abandons methods which successfully carried us through the most memorable epochs of our history.[77]

Although General Miles's testimony certainly assumed in his audience an uneven knowledge of comparative military systems at least equal to his own, opposition to the proposal was sufficiently strong that Root wisely did not press for the issue to be brought to a vote during that session. He acted instead upon a suggestion by Major Carter and arranged for a number of distinguished retired officers, such as Lt. Gen. John M. Schofield (himself a former commanding general of the army) and Maj. Gen. Wesley M. Merritt, to testify in favor of the bill later in the session.

Equally important in Root's campaign to educate the senators were the written statements by senior field commanders, such as Brig. Gen. George W. Davis, which strongly advocated the bill's adoption. One letter from the Army War College president, Maj. Gen. S. B. M. Young, went so far as to state that it was "a matter of conviction among all the older officers" that the position of commanding general was anomalous; similarly, it was the opinion "quite unanimous among the general officers of today" that the bureau system was unsatisfactory.[78] From the steadily accumulating weight of this evidence, as Carter said, "it will be seen that the members of the Senate Military Committee were being rapidly disabused of the idea that the Commanding General of the Army represented the advanced views of the Army on the subject of our military administration and command."[79] Although the final act did not include all the consolidations among the bureaus that had been requested, the bill creating the General Staff of the Army was passed by Congress on February 14, 1903. The General Staff officially came into existence on the fifteenth of August the same year, just one week after the retirement of General Miles.

Aside from his own retirement, the general's worst fears were not realized: the system created was far from being close to any of the autocratic models cited in his testimony. It was, above all, a distinctively American creation. Civilian control within the executive branch had actually been strengthened by realigning operational and administrative responsibilities and by giving the chief of staff an authority commensurate with that responsibility. In approving the new system on an experimental basis, Congress had recognized that civilian control by the legislature would be preserved, however much incremental gains and losses might affect individual interests. With the aid of hindsight, one can see that the volume of the debate on this point was significantly lower than might have been expected, especially when contrasted with the dire misgivings that had colored much of the constitutional ratification process. A century of experience had apparently given some confidence that the norm of civilian control was well established and a military dictatorship unlikely under the system proposed by Elihu Root. But how, then, to explain the congressional misgivings that occurred at about the same time when naval general staff advocates were accused of wanting to "Prussianize the Navy"— especially when the Army was traditionally the agency that in the popular imagination posed the greatest threat to civilian control? The difference may well have been a function of constituency interests: regular appropriations for ship construction concentrated in the large port cities during the Mahan-centered age of a "Navy second to none" represented a return on investment that ought not to be threatened by the uncertainty of a new and potentially powerful agency—therefore a naval general staff was rejected. The Army, by contrast, had only a marginal impact on a few constituencies scattered throughout the country: the General Staff could conceivably threaten a few of those interests, but both the stakes and their potential consequences were much less significant than those represented at the time by the Navy. Seen in this light, "civilian control" was simply a code word for the interests of the affected constituencies, their elected representatives, and their bureaucratic allies.

The General Staff was not, however, to be a panacea for all the Army's problems. Instead, as Richard Leopold pointed out, it was "burdened with unanticipated administrative duties and the old duplication of functions. . . . A constant flow of officers from the staff to the line and back was not always attained. A long period of building and experimentation lay ahead."[80] It would not be until 1912, for example, that a showdown between the adjutant general, Maj. Gen. Fred C. Ainsworth, and Secretary of War Henry L. Stimson would show that bureau autonomy had ended de facto as well as de jure. Congress, having created the General Staff, was disinclined to surrender its function of constitutional watchdog, and its scrutiny of the new group remained constant. The scrutiny reached an apex of sorts when isolationist sentiment in general and criticism of the Army and its General Staff in particular resulted in the National Defense Act of 1916, which reduced the General Staff complement to some twenty officers.

Despite these and subsequent difficulties, however, the creation of the General Staff was an important milestone. On the most obvious level, its very existence would be the structural steel underlying, reinforcing, and shaping later organizational changes. What was perhaps more profound was that the Army had taken a fundamental evolutionary step in its own organizational philosophy—one that directly affected its outlook toward command. In previous evolutionary stages, warfare had grown in complexity to the point that unity of command required separate agencies merely to cope with added functions. This functional authority had increased in scope and complexity to the point that rationality seemingly demanded tight control from the top. These were much the same organizational ideas that characterized American managerial thought at the time. Yet in the military context, centralization led paradoxically to inefficiency and even a loss of unity of command unless accompanied by steps to coordinate hierarchical authority at several levels— in effect a form of decentralization as the commander's authority was redistributed in nonhierarchical ways.

It is interesting, for example, that the writings of Carter, Fiske, and other reformers from both services are filled with references indicating their clear understanding that centralized authority in the bureaus was a form of industrial rationalism that had reached the effective limit of its military application unless accompanied by a corresponding increase in coordinative authority. They also appear to have understood that this coordinative authority, if it was to be effective in a military context, had to exist at several levels beginning at the top. Had the general staffs of both services been formed at about the same time and in the same way—as the reformers assumed they would be— coordinative authority might have had cross-service linkages from the beginning. That was not to be. The Army took the lead in forming staffs all the way down to brigade and battalion levels in ways that allowed its officers to be trained around a concept that they were extensions of a commander's authority and not a substitute for it. The test of efficiency for the staff would be twofold: first, the key divisions of labor (personnel, logistics, operations, and so on) must be competently handled and, second, there must be effective coordination between staff elements in areas of overlapping responsibility. The same principles would also be applied in coordination and liaison between staffs of subordinate or adjacent units. As a consequence, the staff became the preferred tool of action for an Army about to undergo the acceleration of warfare in the twentieth century. Much of its response was conditioned by a key lesson it had learned at the dawn of that century: staffs were the key to building an organization that could be both complex and efficient. The Prussian General Staff may have represented an attempt to institutionalize genius, but the General Staff of the U.S. Army was created with the more prosaic purpose of counteracting an uncoordinated process of bureaucratic centralization. The motivation for this effort, however, was the same as that which had generated the reforms of Gneisenau and Scharnhorst: a new balance was struck between centralization and decentralization—and between the need to manage more effectively the complexities of warfare while preserving and extending the unity of command.

World War I and Perspectives on Service Autonomy

World War I produced the first direct American involvement in a large-scale war on a foreign continent. Its significance for the Army and the Navy lay in the fact that the demands of raising, equipping, transporting, and supplying the combat forces in their most severe test to date did not, for once, result in an initial collapse of the command structure. Instead, the reforms in both departments that had taken place earlier in the century—the creation of the Army General Staff and the consolidation of staff responsibility in the Office of the Chief of Naval Operations—resulted in a highly creditable performance during the eighteen months that U.S. armed forces were in combat. Naturally enough, the test of war would suggest the need for some changes in these arrangements, but the changes that were made were essentially refinements of the earlier initiatives and did not represent fundamental realignments of the command structure of either service. Of more significance for the present analysis were the lessons learned, or at least suggested, during World War I concerning the future of twentieth-century warfare. The advent of new weapons systems, many of which came into embryonic existence during this war, would greatly complicate the problem of command and control. The most notable of these weapons was certainly the airplane, and its further development would eventually call into question the principles of service autonomy that had been developed over the previous century. A brief review of the effects of World War I is therefore in order.

For the Navy, the mission was twofold: reinforce a British navy that was in crisis owing to the depredations of submarine warfare and escort the transports carrying some two million American troops across the Atlantic to European battlefields. Both tasks resulted from the unexpected effectiveness of the German U-boat, which was carrying on a highly effective *guerre de course* against British shipping. In February 1917, for example, some three thousand Allied ships were spread out in search of no more than thirty U-boats, yet shipping losses for that month totaled 500,000 tons.[81] These figures certainly justified Mahan's analysis of the importance of command of the sea, but not his prescriptions for how to achieve that dominance. The battleships that were forming the backbone of the new American Navy would become less important than destroyers, which were originally intended as screening vessels for the battle line, but whose speed and flexibility now gave them a critical importance in convoy escort and antisubmarine warfare.

The naval command structure was forced to adapt to these far-reaching changes before having fully absorbed the impact of its own limited staff reforms. The legislation creating the billet authorized for the chief of naval operations (CNO) had just been passed in 1915, and then over the stringent objections of President Woodrow Wilson's secretary of the navy, Josephus Daniels. To both Wilson and Daniels, any form of strategic planning or strong central authority smacked of warmongering: "Daniels' intention when he first became Secretary was to convert the naval service from a military organization into a vast educational institution specializing in the inculcation of civic values and moral principles, not unlike a Boy Scout organization for adults."[82]

Nevertheless, under Adm. William S. Benson, the slow start was overcome as the rush of wartime operations propelled a steady consolidation of functions under the CNO. By the end of 1917, for example, that office had ten sections dealing with everything from general policy to ship movements and armed guards on merchant vessels. Logistics were the responsibility of a Division of Material, while coastal areas and ports were administered through a system of naval districts.[83]

The war at sea demanded both a concentration of force and the application of long-range strategic control unprecedented in naval history. The wireless radio, first developed for limited naval use only a little more than fifteen years before, had now assumed a critical combat role. Long-range naval communications stations on shore quickly grew into global networks as messages went to and from every class of naval vessel. So critical did the system become to ongoing operations that radio-direction finding, decoding of signals, and intelligence analysis became vital functions at naval shore stations: the results of their analysis would then be transmitted back to the forces at sea for operational exploitation. This was particularly important in antisubmarine warfare, in which the Navy rapidly became proficient. Convoy escort ships had push-button, five-channel radios, allowing far more flexibility in the coordinated control of screening operations. Additionally, radio direction-finding equipment on these ships allowed them to maintain better control of the convoy while also triangulating the transmissions of enemy submarines. Although these technological changes involved a far greater degree of long-distance control than had ever been tried before, the payoff was the operational success that characterized the use of destroyer screens around the all-important troop transports.[84]

For the Army, it soon became apparent that the development of the General Staff, beyond its basic organizational structure, was still embryonic. The Wilson administration, anxious to avoid any appearance of warlike provocation, had gone so far as to prohibit any detailed strategic planning for possible American involvement in the conflict. Equally disturbing was the situation in the five major service bureaus (Quartermaster, Medical, Engineer, Ordnance, and Signal) which, despite their nominal subordination to the General Staff, were still accustomed to operating with a pronounced degree of autonomy. Under the pressures of increased wartime procurement and logistical requirements, these bureaus struggled manfully to adjust, but they soon found themselves competing with each other for scarce resources: "When the Army went into the Nation's markets to buy the vast body of supplies needed for the war, it went not as a single agency, seeing the problem of supply as a whole, but as five separate bureaus competing with each other, as well as with the other great agencies of the Government and the Allies, for manufacturing articles, raw materials, industrial facilities, labor, fuel, power and transportation."[85]

Under fire, the War Department was forced to take immediate action. In early February 1918, the War Department General Staff was reorganized into five divisions: an Executive Office, War Plans, Operations, Purchase and Supply, and Storage and Traffic. Other measures consolidated General Staff control over logistical matters and centralized procurement within the headquarters of all but specialized items. The chief of staff, Gen. Peyton C. March—a hard-driving officer whose reputed "ruthlessness" was probably as necessary as that of Gen. George C. Marshall a generation later—was given additional authority "to carry out the Army program." With that mandate, he proceeded to eliminate weak performers in all areas of the staff and to create new agencies to deal with emergent technologies such as aviation and chemical warfare. Distinguished officers, such as Gen. George W. Goethals, were recalled from retirement to join the General Staff, as were prominent businessmen and industrialists, such as Benedict Crowell and George A. Scott. Coordination of national resources was further consolidated with the creation of the War Industries Board in March 1918; headed by Bernard Baruch, the board was given broad powers to control and regulate industrial output for national defense.[86]

These consolidations of authority were justified by the extreme urgency of a wartime situation made more difficult by a lack of foresight and planning, the very purpose for which the General Staff had supposedly been created. It was also evident, however, that the requirements of operating an expeditionary force on another continent demanded the grant of similarly wide-ranging authority to Gen. John J. Pershing, who had been selected commander of the American Expeditionary Force (AEF). That selection called to mind the old controversy between the commanding general of the army and the senior field commander. Since 1903 it had been clear that the chief of staff would not "command" per se. But how was the grant of functional autonomy to the senior field commander to be reconciled with the increasingly centralized authority now possessed by the chief of staff? The answer continued to be elusive, and a palpable tension characterized the relationship between March and Pershing throughout the war. Pershing, for example, was not at all reluctant to question March's instructions or to support his own staff in demanding modifications of weapons and equipment already in the production pipeline. His apparent high-handedness, from the chief of staff's perspective, even extended to back-channel communications to the secretary of war.

In defending Pershing's claim to virtually independent control of any overseas activity, Gen. James G. Harbord, formerly the AEF chief of staff, wrote some years afterward: "General Pershing commanded the AEF directly under the President and Secretary of War, as the President's *alter ego*. No military power or person was interposed between them. . . . No successful war has ever been fought commanded by a staff officer in a distant capital. . . . The organization effected in our War Department . . . scrupulously preserves the historic principle that *the line of authority runs directly from the highest in the land to the highest in the field*" (emphasis added).[87]

That principle was not as clear to some people as it apparently was to General Harbord, but his comment nevertheless represents an important lesson that emerged from the war. The matter of command would continue to be a source of controversy whenever American forces were to be deployed overseas, and troubling questions had to be faced regarding the extent of operational authority to be granted to the commander. A direct line of descent in the command philosophy articulated by Harbord extends from Pershing to Douglas MacArthur (who also had difficulty in submitting to anything less than a presidential directive and sometimes, to his eventual regret, not even then) and ultimately to the 1958 legislation that set up the system of unified and specified commands after World War II. Each of these commanders enjoys the same direct relationship to presidential authority originally posited by Harbord.

Otto L. Nelson pointed out that Harbord's statement was evocative of a deeper principle not only of command but of military organizations in general: "In this controversy over jurisdiction, there arose a principle quite as important as that of control—pride of position. Span of control tends to increase functional specialization and in so doing sets up of a necessity many rungs in the ladder of command and authority. Pride of position works to step over these subordinate rungs and insists that no coordinating or controlling restrictions emanate from any authority except the supreme heads, and only then from the chief in person."[88]

That distinction—between pride of position and span of control—was to be at the heart of a number of seemingly larger issues, and it would transcend both time and differing service positions.

However unsettling the problem of high command may have been, there was good reason for the Army to take pride in its accomplishments in World War I, especially in the refinement of battle staffs. Shortly after the AEF's arrival in France, Pershing organized his staff along the lines suggested by a close study of the staff systems prevailing in the British and French field armies. Under that organizational line-up the staff was broken down into four major functional groups, each headed by a principal staff officer known as an assistant chief of staff. Thus, the assistant chief of staff, G-1, handled personnel, G-2 had intelligence responsibilities, G-3 was the operations officer, and G-4 was the command logistician. That arrangement was replicated down through the division level; brigades and battalions had similar but smaller "S-level" staffs, arranged around the same numerical groupings. In slightly modified form, this system persists in the Army down to the present. Harbord summarized its operations as follows: "General Headquarters . . . concerned itself only with the broader phases of control. Under the supervision of the commander in chief, and pursuant to clearly determined policies, the assistant chiefs of staff . . . coordinated by the chief of staff, issued instructions and gave general direction to the great combat units and to services of supply, keeping always in touch with the manner and promptness of their fulfillment. *This system of direct responsibility contemplated secrecy in preparation, prompt decision in emergency and coordinated action in execution*" (emphasis added).[89] That is as succinct a statement of the proper functioning of a battle staff as has ever been produced by an American military writer.

The extension of battlefield control by electronic means was as much a feature of combat on land as at sea, the principal media being telegraph and telephone. The Army Signal Corps swelled to more than fifty-five thousand officers and men in order to keep up with the quantum leap in communications requirements caused by large frontages, increased numbers of troops, and the need for more precise tactical control on the remarkably lethal battlefields created by artillery and the machine gun. In the Meuse-Argonne offensive alone, for example, the two armies, twelve corps, and thirty-three divisions of the AEF required communicators to lay twenty-five hundred miles of field wire per week. Some idea of the ubiquity of the telephone and telegraph can be seen in the figures supplied by the Signal Corps at war's end. Nine thousand telephones were connected to permanent lines, 134 permanent telegraph offices were maintained, and 273 telephone exchanges established. The system handled approximately 12 million telegraph messages, 1.6 million long distance calls, and the staggering total of 47 million local telephone calls. And all of this in little more than six months of actual combat.[90]

Yet even this was not enough to meet the unprecedented demands for tactical flexibility caused by the primacy of the defense, arising from the machine gun's extension of the dominance of rifled musketry heralded by the Civil War. Although the field telephone was a great improvement over the telegraph, it could not begin to solve the control problems caused by the need for infantry to fight by dispersion and movement, primarily because the telephone was a fixed instrument. As convenient as it was for commanders to converse by telephone with superiors and subordinates, the onset of an engagement was accompanied by a loss of control—as indeed had been the situation in land combat through the ages. Wireless radio was far more useful at sea than on land at this stage, although some of the principal headquarters of the AEF were also connected by this means as well as by telegraph and telephone. The fast-growing dependence of commanders on both these means of communication, however, led to the first systematic efforts to derive intelligence from the use of the electromagnetic spectrum. Consequently, World War I is usually thought of as the starting point in the history of modern electronic warfare, as both sides sought to protect their own communications while exploiting those of the enemy.[91]

But the principal artifact of the First World War that would affect the future of service autonomy and the existence of separate command structures was not radio-telecommunications, but the airplane. Its use, first as an extended signal device and then as a weapon in its own right, meant that both services would take steps to incorporate the new capability into their respective force structures. That much was obvious from the outset. What was not so obvious was that the airplane would have a thoroughly subversive effect on the time-honored division of labor between land and sea forces. The air, it would later appear, was indivisible; so, therefore, was the need for air power and an air service to run it. Both the Army and the Navy would be forced to come to grips with that issue in fundamental ways. For the Navy, the airplane completed the picture that had begun to emerge with the maturation of the submarine as a weapon of war. Henceforth, the Navy would fight in three mediums of ocean combat: subsurface, surface, and above the surface. The Army faced an equally difficult problem integrating air power onto a battlefield already changed by the tank and the substitution of machine power for muscle power. The notion of the strategic use of air power in an Army accustomed to thinking in terms of divisional frontages had not yet arisen.

But air power and the problems of total war in the twentieth century were only distant thunder as World War I ended. The forces commanded by the Army and the Navy were at that moment the strongest in the nation's history, and the services themselves were enjoying the sense of completion that had been brought about by more than a century of autonomy. Autonomy had nurtured these organizations, had given them a character of their own, had established a tradition of victorious battlefield outcomes on land and sea, and had finally provided paradigms for the exercise of power in those operational environments. These were no mean achievements, and they would continue to exercise a formative role as the Army and the Navy turned increasingly toward the challenges of the future.

4   The Quest for Unity of Command

The aftermath of World War I was marked by a profound revulsion against the protracted slaughter that had taken millions of lives and unalterably changed the social and political order of Europe. Military strategy was not therefore a central focus of the immediate postwar period, but it experienced a kind of awakening as the proponents of the doctrine of air power—almost always capitalized as Air Power—preached a new gospel promising that aircraft technology would conquer the stalemate of warfare fought to the point of exhaustion by surface-bound armies and navies. Like the airplane itself, the new doctrine had important institutional and organizational implications. Its more extreme advocates openly suggested that control of the air made surface forces vulnerable whether on land or sea, and though traditionalists in both the Army and the Navy continued to dispute those claims in every way, there was a growing realization that the potency of air power was quickly coming to outstrip the capacity of either parent service to deal with it.

That realization generated pressures at two levels. First, each service sought to exploit the fast-developing capabilities of aviation to achieve new applications of the old principle of combined arms. For the Navy, this meant a greatly expanded command and control problem as it sought to adapt submarines and aircraft to the new imperatives of three-medium combat beneath and above the ocean, as well as on its surface. For the Army, the obvious ability of the airplane to support advances on the ground made it an attractive adjunct of traditional artillery bombardment; more troubling was the apparent potential of land-based aircraft for long-range strategic bombardment, a capability that, if fully exploited, threatened to alter long-established Army roles and missions beyond the point of recognition. As strong as these intraservice tensions were, the airplane would also generate fundamental conflict at the interservice level. Traditional service autonomy was based on a clear division of labor between land and sea forces: the airplane fit neither definition cleanly and appeared to transcend both. Where, then, did it fit in the service command structures—and if it did not fit, then where was its place?

These questions preoccupied the services during the interwar period, even as the proponents of air power developed both doctrines and a paradigm in support of their beliefs. Whereas Mahan had embodied the properties of both prophet and advocate in the building of the modern American Navy, advocacy of American air power was most closely identified with the public career of Brig. Gen. William ("Billy") Mitchell. World War II would force the services to come to terms with air power, as well as with other realities of true global combat—such as national mobilization and amphibious operations—which also transcended usual service definitions. The process by which that adaptation took place would change accepted notions of service autonomy; henceforth, the doctrine of "mutual cooperation" as the sine qua non of interservice relationships would be replaced by "unity of command" in the prosecution of the war. After the war, this new doctrine would be the basis for a redefinition of service autonomy, a process that culminated in the passage of the National Security Act of 1947 and the establishment of a centralized Department of Defense.

The Interwar Period: Toward a Paradigm of Air Warfare

One of the most frequently quoted passages of Brig. Gen. Billy Mitchell's memoirs concerns his reflections as commander of the First Army Air Service in the St. Mihiel salient in World War I: "One flight over the lines gave me a much clearer impression of how the armies were laid out than any amount of travelling around on the ground. A very significant thing to me was that we should cross the lines of these contending armies in a few minutes in our airplane, whereas the armies had been locked in the struggle, immovable, powerless to advance for three years. . . . It was as though they kept knocking their heads against a stone wall, until their brains were dashed out. They got nowhere, as far as ending the war was concerned."[1]

Mitchell, who had clashed repeatedly during the war with General Pershing, was to become the apostle of air power thereafter, arguing that air power was the solution to the strategic stalemate caused by the enormous increase in the defensive power of conventional weapons. In both speeches and magazine articles, as well as in two books, *Our Air Force: The Keystone of National Defense* and *Winged Defense: The Development and Possibilities of Modern Air Power, Economic and Military,* he put forward a vision of air power released from its shackles of tactical support and thrown against the "vital centers" of enemy military and economic power. Mitchell's unrelenting advocacy of the supremacy of air power was, of course, given additional weight by the famous demonstration he conducted in 1921, when his bombers sank the German battleship *Ostfriesland*, an exercise that clearly showed that unprotected capital ships were vulnerable to destruction from the air. As unsettling as that demonstration was to the Navy hierarchy, Mitchell's highly public calls for autonomy of the air arm were equally disturbing to his own service. When, in the aftermath of several air crashes in September 1925, he openly declared the leadership of the War and Navy departments to be guilty of negligence in the administration of their respective air arms, Mitchell was court-martialed, convicted, and allowed to resign from the service. Air power thus acquired a central place in public consciousness and a martyr of heroic proportions as well.[2]

To the public and political debate on air power, there was added by the 1930s the most comprehensive statement on air power yet to emerge. Giulio Douhet, through his book *The Command of the Air,* exercised a dominant influence on the development of air power, although his book had far more meaning for the fraternity of airmen in both the United States and Europe than for the public. Intrinsic to his writings was the common vision of airmen that a way had been found to break the stalemate resulting from the land paradigms of Jomini and Clausewitz, as well as the sea power prescriptions of Mahan: land warfare had become symbolized by the trenches of Flanders, while the meeting of the great navies at Jutland had proven not only that such engagements could be tactically inconclusive but also that Continental powers could withstand the effects of a naval blockade. For Douhet, the land and the sea were environmental barriers that lent themselves to the creation of "fortified lines of defense," which had reached a state of virtual impregnability prior to the advent of air power. Now these lines could be bypassed: "The airplane has complete freedom of action and direction; it can fly to and from any point of the compass in the shortest time—in a straight line—by any route deemed expedient. Nothing man can do on the surface of the earth can interfere with a plane in flight, moving freely in the third dimension. All the influences which have conditioned and characterized warfare from the beginning are powerless to affect aerial action."[3]

If there was no effective defense against aerial bombardment, it followed that the enemy's war-making potential was the proper target against which air forces should be directed. Once command of the air was achieved, however, only a portion of its true destructive potential need be employed in order to crush civilian morale and force a prompt end to the conflict. In its own way, air power therefore was envisioned as being more "humane," because it air power therefore was envisioned as being more "humane," because it would be a sudden and decisive substitute for the needlessly drawn-out slaughter between surface forces.[4]

Five prescriptive principles could be drawn from this formulation of the inherently offensive and decisive nature of air power.

1. An adequate national defense meant having effective command of the air.

2. Air power having obliterated the distinction between combatants and noncombatants, population and industrial centers, rather than military installations, should be the focal points for aerial bombardment.

3. Enemy air forces should be destroyed on the ground by attacking their airfields, support facilities, and aircraft production centers.

4. Surface forces should maintain a defensive stance along exposed fronts to stabilize the situation until the air forces had achieved decisive results.

5. The primary air force plane should be the biggest bomber with the longest range; only secondary attention need be given to specialized aircraft or one's own air defense.[5]

Applying these principles could give a country the means to achieve command of the air:

To have command of the air means to be in a position to wield offensive power so great it defies human imagination. It means to be able to cut an enemy's army and navy off from their bases of operation and nullify their chances of winning a war. It means complete protection of one's own country, the efficient operation of one's army and navy, and peace of mind to live and work in safety. In short it means to be in a position *to win*. *To be defeated* in the air, on the other hand, is finally to be defeated and to be at the mercy of the enemy, with no chance at all of defending oneself, compelled to accept whatever terms he sees fit to dictate. This is the meaning of the "command of the air." (Emphasis added)[6]

As revolutionary as Douhet and his proponents thought this doctrine to be, it of course owed important intellectual debts to earlier strategic paradigms. In a provocative book tracing the doctrinal impact of Douhet on Army Air Force planners after World War II, Perry M. Smith argued that Douhet's doctrines served the same purposes for the Air Force that Mahan's prescriptions had for the Navy a generation earlier: justification of service autonomy, funding for service-dominant "decisive" weapons systems, and recognition of those systems as "the nation's first line of defense." Similarly, Mahan had favored the concentrated offensive action of battleship-centered fleets as the key element in achieving command of the sea; Douhet's followers emphasized strategic bombardment by massed formations of heavy bombers as the key to penetrating enemy air defenses and achieving command of the air. This idea would become so fixed that Army Air Force "leaders and planners were reluctant to divert airpower to the close support of [ground] troops or to the defensive role of interception."[7] This adaptation of doctrines suggests that, unlike paradigms in other sciences, strategic paradigms did not wholly replace one another or render the preceding ideas obsolete. Instead, these developing perspectives of land, sea, and air combat tended to represent syntheses of old doctrines geared to new circumstances.

Nevertheless, the air paradigm continued to have important applications for service command structures during the interwar period. Army air power enthusiasts were at the forefront of efforts to create a separate department, hoping to achieve "autonomy for air" under a unitary command that would have coordinate status with the War and Navy departments. The lineage of this idea is not hard to discover. The Royal Air Force, with whom American partnership was closest, had been formed during the war; under Hugh Trenchard's leadership during this period, it continued to provide a model of development for American airmen. Douhet's thoughts on the matter were equally explicit, and he had the satisfaction of seeing the Italian government follow his advice in the 1920s, when it set up separate departments for the army, navy, and air force under a single defense ministry. In the United States, however, the Army's historical experience with complex command structures led in two directions with respect to air power. Traditionalists tended to view the air arm in much the same way they viewed other arms of combat power: its development might well include separate status as a combat branch, but its integration would take place within the outlines of the existing command structure. Therefore, the Army would accede to the establishment of a separate Army Air Corps in 1926 and would eventually include in its hierarchy a deputy chief of staff for air and an assistant secretary of war for air; it would, however, oppose until World War II the creation of a separate air force department.

Army aviators thus inherited both the Army staff tradition and the revolutionary perspectives of air power. In the delineation of staff structures that accompanied the growth of the Army Air Corps, the same principles of specialization, subordination, and coordinative authority guided the formation of the Air Staff in ways that were scarcely discernible from the pattern of Army General Staff development. For example, Army staffs were organized along the by now familiar lines of a G-1 for personnel, a G-2 for intelligence, and so on. The Air Staff was set up the same way, with the letter *A* substituted for *G*. It was in the strategic dimension of air power, however, that Army aviators most clearly showed their perception that aviation implied a combination of arms in a larger dimension than ever before. Appearing before the Morrow Board in 1925, Army aviator Maj. Horace M. Hickam provided a remarkably clear view of that perspective:

> Nothing short of a department of defense . . . with a new race of commanders, officers skilled in the operations of armies, navies, and air forces as our generals now operate infantry, cavalry and artillery, with the necessary staff—nothing short of that will meet the situation; . . . I believe we must develop a general staff who are skilled in the handling of armies, navies and air forces, and who are capable of laying out a campaign, and of using all these forces, either separately or with one another.[8]

The strategic concept of the Army's aviators was thus reinforced by both ideology and organizational vision. To these two factors should be added a third, which fit in neatly with the Army's traditional accommodation to the norm of strategic control. As aircraft technology was being pushed in the 1930s toward ever larger and more powerful airframes—in consonance with Douhet's doctrine of the big bomber—air-to-ground radios underwent a parallel growth in range and effectiveness. Large bomber fleets could thus be effectively controlled from the ground from the beginning of their existence. Strategic doctrine, an envisioned pattern of strategic organization and strategic control, provided mutually sustaining influences in the formative period of the American Air Force.

The air arm of the Navy developed in a much more contained way, so that it was kept firmly attached to the body of its parent service. The obvious potential of the airplane for naval reconnaissance and antisubmarine warfare, fully demonstrated during World War I, led to the creation of the Bureau of Aeronautics in 1921 under Rear Adm. William A. Moffett. Admiral Moffett was to head the bureau until his death in 1933, proving to be, as Robin Higham put it, a kind of Hyman Rickover of his day: skillfully using the inherent powers of a bureau chief, assiduously courting Congress and public opinion regarding the appeal of aviation, and constantly building aviation as a function of naval power rather than a substitute for it.[9] Moffett's political acumen enabled naval aviation not only to develop its own equipment and personnel but also to explore the new potential of the aircraft carrier, three of which had been added to the fleet by the end of the 1920s. Although the naval establishment was still dominated by battleship admirals—and therefore fleet doctrines and operations that stressed battleship supremacy—the traditional autonomy of naval bureaus and the support those bureaus enjoyed from Congress allowed naval aviation to develop in ways that would eventually create a new aristocracy of carrier admirals.[10]

While Army aviators continued their obsession with long-range strategic bombing during the interwar years—to the neglect of the close air support of ground troops that was being enthusiastically explored by the German Luftwaffe—the Navy developed carrier-based airplanes as an extension of the battle fleet's traditional role in securing command of the sea. Until Pearl Harbor, the guns of the battleship were considered the dominant naval weapon, but their 16-mile range was gradually augmented by torpedo planes which had an effective range of 150 miles from the main battle fleet. Carriers attached to the fleet provided the launching platform for these planes, as well as for the fighters providing air cover immediately over the battle line itself. Consequently, the carrier force often acted as a screening element to seek out and engage enemy forces while the battleships closed in for the knockout blow. Improvements in both the planes and the ordnance they carried would after 1942 turn this doctrine on its head. Equally significant, however, were the electronic advances that allowed the locus of control of the task force to be shifted from the battleship to the carrier. By the late 1930s, the marriage of shipborne radar and long-distance aviation radio had permitted an unprecedented degree of precision to be exercised in the control of aircraft, and it was the Navy, in the aftermath of its Midway victory, that would be the first to feel the resulting impact upon warfare at the tactical level.

Air power and its implications were the major elements dominating interservice relationships during the postwar period, evidenced by the deliberations of the Joint Board of the Army and the Navy, which had been reconstituted after World War I. Its members included the chief of staff of the Army and the chief of naval operations, their principal deputies, and the directors of their respective war planning divisions. The Joint Board's activities prior to World War I had been confined to little more than ceremonial matters, but the Treaty of Versailles had left Japan in a much strengthened territorial position which, with the advent of air power, threatened American possessions in the Pacific. The Pacific had long been considered by the Navy to be its own preserve, but the presence of an Army garrison in the Philippines demanded joint planning by the services. Throughout the interwar period Army and Navy planners worked under Joint Board aegis to come up with a common plan of defense. The effort resulted in War Plan ORANGE (for Japan), which however, never really reconciled differing service perceptions of what would be required in any war against the Japanese. As Legere characterized their outlooks, "The Navy's conception was that of a boldly offensive war carried to the enemy's part of the world, while the Army's conception was that of a war primarily to protect home territory and vital possessions within effective supporting distance of home territory." Even less was accomplished in planning a strategy that took into account the forces and logistical support likely to be available.[11]

The problems of protecting the Western Pacific or the Panama Canal were made even more difficult by the absence of any effective plan for the command of combatant forces if more than one service was involved—and with the advent of air arms in each service, those overlaps became ever more likely. The traditional doctrine was, of course, mutual cooperation, which in theory meant little more than the traditional separation of functions at the water's edge and the invocation of good fellowship and common sense in practice. The doctrine could not, however, resolve serious conflicts when separate service functions became intertwined, as had indeed been the case at Santiago de Cuba during the war with Spain. A possible solution was to select a leader such as General Pershing who would be placed in supreme command of all forces that might be assigned to an expeditionary force, but would exercise that authority through subordinate-level commanders. This was the principle of "unity of command," a concept so threatening to traditional service autonomy in the operational sphere that it acquired an almost pejorative meaning as it was thrashed out in Joint Board and Joint Chiefs of Staff proceedings for the next generation. At the first opportunity, for example, a planning committee of the Joint Board recommended against unity of command in favor of a new wrinkle on the old doctrine: "The committee is of the opinion that in joint Army and Navy operations the paramount interest of one or the other branch of the National forces will be evident, and in such cases intelligent and hearty cooperation . . . will give as effective results as would be obtained by the assignment of a commander for the joint operation, which assignment might cause jealousy and dissatisfaction."[12]

Nevertheless, by 1927, some progress had been made in interservice planning, as evidenced by the publication of a new edition of the Joint Board's guidelines, *Joint Action of the Army and the Navy,* and a revised ORANGE war plan. Now recognized were three principles for the coordination of armies and navies in pursuit of common objectives:

1. *Close cooperation:* when the mission could be accomplished by relatively independent action of the deployed forces. This was merely "mutual cooperation" under a slightly different name.
2. *Limited unity of command:* when it was determined that the objective

fell within the "paramount interest" of one service, and forces of the other were temporarily placed under the operational control of the service commander exercising paramount interest.

3. *Unity of command:* when the objective required the hierarchical subordination of all component forces under a single commander in those instances where such command was specifically authorized by the president.

Although an important doctrinal barrier had been breached, the next decade gave ample evidence of service reluctance to come to terms with the new theory. By 1938, a series of further changes to *Joint Action* recognized unity of command and mutual cooperation as equally valid principles of joint operations to be used as the situation dictated; this, of course, meant that mutual cooperation was both rule and reality. But far from being an effective tool for interservice planning, this philosophy was little more than a nonaggression pact concluded between the Army and Navy of the United States.[13]

The ability of the Army and Navy to plan joint operations, the movement for economy in government, and, most of all, the place of the air arm attracted consistent congressional attention throughout the mid-1920s—and virtually none at all thereafter, especially with the advent of the Great Depression. A high-water mark of a sort was reached in 1926 when Congress considered the bill that eventually resulted in legislative recognition of an Army Air Corps that was kept firmly within the traditional structure. While studying the bill, the House Military Affairs Committee published a report drawn up by the G-3 Division (Operations) of the War Department General Staff in what one can only assume, in light of its flat contradictions of official statements, was a sudden burst of candor:

It is believed that there are outstanding questions at issue today between the Army and Navy on which no agreement has been reached, or the agreement arrived at is in the nature of an inefficient compromise. Some of the most important are:

■ The question of unity of command in combined operations, maneuvers, or war plans.
■ The definition of the exact missions and functions of the two services in coast defense. . . .
■ The combined air programs of the two services. . . .
■ Mobilization of manpower and industrial resources.
■ Duplication and overlapping in procurement, supply and operating facilities.[14]

In light of subsequent events, this testimony ranks as a remarkably accurate assessment of the prevailing state of service autonomy and the often confused and confusing effects of the air power paradigm to that point in history.

These relationships would not change materially through the end of the 1930s, although controversies would persist at the intraservice and interservice levels as growing air power threatened existing hierarchies. For the junior officers who would later come to play key roles in the wartime and postwar services—including such men as H. H. Arnold, Jimmy Doolittle, Marc Mitscher, and Arthur Radford—these conflicts were a formative professional experience:

> These and many other officers, when they were later generals and admirals, never forgot the old animosities and the personal bitterness. These memories contributed to the intense nature of the struggle [for unification] when it erupted again in its full fury during and after World War II. . . . Never after the 1920's were the Navy men able to view any proposal for the re-organization of the armed forces as much more than a shrewd plot designed to enhance the size and prominence of some other military service at the Navy's expense. This suspicion was not infrequently justified, but it was present even when wholly unjustified.[15]

It was not therefore surprising that "unity of command" was never achieved in the interwar period or that "mutual cooperation" should have been the limited creature of service autonomy that it was.

The one place where the doctrine came together in combination with major installations of both services—complete with their respective air arms—was at Pearl Harbor. The writings of Roberta Wohlstetter (*Pearl Harbor: Warning and Decision*) and Gordon W. Prange (*At Dawn We Slept*) have explored in a wealth of detail the intelligence and operational failures that led to that disaster; both authors, however, place a primary emphasis on a more fundamental failure of command. Both Gen. Walter C. Short and Adm. H. E. Kimmel were all that might have been hoped for as commanders operating under "mutual cooperation." Conscientious and courteous with each other, they maintained a working relationship that was cordial if not intimate. Each conceded "paramount interest" to the other's sovereign areas, while "cooperation" was supposedly the rule in all areas of common concern. That cooperation did not extend, however, to such elemental concerns as all-around surveillance and reconnaissance of island approaches, the preparation of overlapping air defense plans, or comparative assessments of intelligence indicators. The commands were united only in a common failure to employ their air assets effectively: Kimmel left uncovered by long-range reconnaissance aircraft the precise quadrant used by Nagumo's carriers for their approach, while Short grouped all his aircraft together on the ground to avoid a chimerical threat from saboteurs, thereby exposing them to utter devastation from the air.[16]

That such mistakes could be made in the face of increasingly ominous diplomatic news and specific warnings from Washington is not so much evidence of individual failings by the on-scene commanders as a revelation of the end product of limited service perspectives. To paraphrase Elihu Root, who was also concerned with limited perspectives, cooperation was everybody's business and what was everybody's business was nobody's business. Cloaked in the mantle of organizational autonomy, the local representatives of the service sovereignties thus received an unfortunate but vivid object lesson in the deficiencies of the doctrine of mutual cooperation. Equally apparent was the vulnerability of surface forces to aerial attack: if Douhet would not be entirely vindicated by the end of World War II, Billy Mitchell certainly had been in the first hours of American involvement in the conflict. By demonstrating that the paradigm of air power had progressed from theory to reality, and by showing that the doctrine of mutual cooperation had foundered somewhere in the vicinity of Battleship Row, the attack on Pearl Harbor taught the services that they were no longer in business for themselves.

World War II and the Search for Unity of Command

More than fifty years after it began, World War II has an undiminished stature as a watershed event in human history. Among many other consequences, the demands of total war were to have a lasting impact upon the command structure of the armed forces. A complete recitation of those changes is well beyond the scope of this study, but their net effect was to bring about a radical transformation in the norms of traditional service autonomy. The services would evolve quickly from rather small, decentralized and utterly separate entities into well-developed hierarchies that deployed vast land, sea, and air forces in operational theaters encircling the globe. Presiding over a national mobilization which produced the planes, ships, tanks, and guns that eventually brought Allied victory, the services expanded their combined manpower from just over 1 million officers and men in 1940 to almost 12 million by war's end. When considering the difficulty of training, equipping, deploying, and supplying a force of this size, one can appreciate that this was an organizational feat of some magnitude in an age that did not yet know the computer. As impressive as these logistical feats were, the political objective of the war demanded the complete defeat in battle of geographically dispersed and fanatically determined enemies, an objective that presupposed the need to invade and occupy their territory.

The scope of these requirements led to contradictory demands. On the one hand, the need to conserve and allocate scarce resources among different theaters of operations, as well as the need to maintain overall policy and strategic control, argued for a greater centralization of authority in Washington than ever before. On the other hand, not even the remarkable advances in electronic communications would allow remote control of a global war that, in addition to its other precedent-shattering aspects, would feature an almost unimaginable increase in mobility. Therefore, a pressing need for operational flexibility required authority to be decentralized efficiently to commanders in the field. In striking the balance between centralization and decentralization, the services also had to come to grips with a new perspective of warfare itself, in which everything seemed to be related to everything else. In many ways, the operational art developed during the war appeared to justify the prophecies of early air power advocates such as Maj. Horace Hickam, in that land, sea, and air forces became a combined arms team at the level of grand strategy.

The predominant effect of the war on service command structures was thus the operation of the dynamic of functional integration at three levels: the high command, the unified and component commands that were set up in the theaters of operations, and, most of all, the operational forces themselves. Running through these levels was the common thread—or wire—of communications electronics, which came into its own as the technological tool that could tie diverse command echelons together, providing an extension of command authority that was, for once, equal to its assigned battlefield task. Although the age of telecommunications had begun with the Civil War telegraph and had developed still further with the addition of the telephone and wireless radio during World War I, World War II was the first conflict in which command and control assumed its modern electronic outlines. The marriage of organization and telecommunications consequently made possible the strategic and operational teamwork that brought victory, but it would create troubling questions for the perpetuation of service autonomy in the postwar world.

Integration of functions at the high command level came about as the services expanded their internal organizations to deal with a greatly expanded range of activities and as they put together joint planning bodies to coordinate those activities with each other and with the Allies. Here again, a contrast in approaches was in evidence. For the Army, always first to embrace hierarchical organizational principles, the General Staff set up in 1903 had proven not to be a panacea. The General Staff had never been able to overcome the institutional resistance of the long-established bureaus or the entrenched powers of the chiefs of the traditional Army branches (infantry, artillery, cavalry, and so on). Worse yet, the steady accumulation of functional areas coming under headquarters supervision had led during the interwar period to an excessive centralization that was now becoming unmanageable. The process recalled J. F. C. Fuller's classic warning on the subject: "The staff becomes an all-consuming bureaucracy, a paper octopus squirting ink into every corner. Unless pruned with an axe, it will grow like a fakir's mango tree, and the more it grows, the more it overshadows the general. It creates work, it creates officers, and above all it creates the rear spirit. No sooner is a war declared than the general-in-chief . . . finds himself a Gulliver in Lilliput, tied down to his office stool by the innumerable threads woven out of the brains of his staff."[17]

Shortly after being sworn in as Army chief of staff on September 1, 1939— the same day World War II began—Gen. George C. Marshall found that some sixty-one of his subordinate officers enjoyed the right of direct access to him; they included, for example, the chief of chaplains, the chief of the morale branch, the chiefs of the six combat arms branches, and the five assistant chiefs of staff from the General Staff directorates. Worse yet, even the most minor decisions had to be routed to Marshall or one of his principal deputies.[18]

Although not hesitant in making other reforms, Marshall was slow to tackle the problem of War Department reorganization. Yet as war drew nearer for the United States, his patience was running out. During a staff meeting in early November 1941, he found evidence that a shipment of bombs destined for the British garrison at Singapore had been delayed because of poor coordination. "We can have no more of this," he said. "This is the worst command post in the Army, and we must do something about it, although I do not yet know what we will do about it."[19] At the heart of the problem as well was the fact that the General Staff had grown by late 1941 to more than seven hundred officers. Those numbers alone were at variance with the classical concept of a general staff, which assumed some level of professional intimacy with the chief of staff. They contributed as well to the trivialization of the Army high command: the Army General Staff, created as a mechanism to cross-cut the bureaucracy, had now become part of the problem.[20]

Solving that problem became a priority after American entry into the war, and here two important influences converged that would affect the evolution of command structures not just in the Army but in all three services. A reorganization panel was appointed by Marshall and headed by Lt. Gen. Joseph T. McNarney, an aviator of broad experience. McNarney was assisted by Maj. Otto L. Nelson, Jr., a member of the History and Government Department at West Point, who had written his dissertation at Harvard in 1940 on the subject "The War Department General Staff: A Study in Organization and Administration." The dissertation was a description of General Staff evolution as well as an attempt to relate that history to both modern organizational theory and contemporary problems. As such, the manuscript was much in demand during the planning and implementation stages of the reorganization.[21]

While Nelson's manuscript provided an intellectual foundation for the project, a memorandum from Gen. Henry H. Arnold, deputy chief of staff for air, had far-reaching practical effects. Arnold's memorandum argued that "unity of command" should be the basis for both the reorganization of the War Department and the establishment of theater commands. After stating that "unity of command" was a fundamental concept "throughout all the strata of military organization" when "two or more integral forces are joined together for collaboration," Arnold continued, "This Unity of Command can be expressed only by a *superior* Commander, who is capable of viewing impartially the needs and capabilities of the ground forces and of the air forces. Only a superior commander can select the employment which will result in the maximum contribution of each force toward the National Objective. This kind of Unity of Command requires the establishment of a separate command agency; not the subordination of one member of the team to the other."[22]

This was to be the primary concept around which the reorganization of the War Department took place in March 1942. Three major commands were set up: Army Ground Forces, Army Air Forces, and Army Service Forces. These commands took over much of the burden of day-to-day operations, while the General Staff was refocused on strategic and long-range operational planning. The War Plans Division of the General Staff (soon renamed the Operations Division, or OPD) "was in itself a virtually complete general staff, tight-knit . . . and definitely oriented toward operations in the field."[23] The OPD was to be, therefore, the principal link between the headquarters and the theater commands.

It is important to summarize here three points that emerged from the reorganization. First, as Nelson pointed out, it was "the most drastic and fundamental change which the War Department had experienced since the establishment of the General Staff."[24] In essence, it took the General Staff another step forward toward more effective control. The Army's official history of this period says that this "rationalization of the department's structure . . . [substituted] the vertical pattern of military command for the tradi- tional horizontal patterns of coordination [which] paralleled similar develop- ments among leading industrial organizations."[25] What the reorganization actually did, of course, was to provide for both vertical and horizontal link- ages: this was the original purpose of the General Staff, and the 1942 reforms helped restore those functions.

The second point relates to the Air Force and was well summed up by Ray Cline: "The Army Air Forces . . . had [achieved] virtually complete control of the development of its [sic] own special weapon, the airplane. . . . It organized and supported the combat forces to be employed in theaters of operations. Finally, by advising the General Staff and participating in inter- service deliberations, General Arnold's headquarters was able materially to influence, though it could not control, both strategic and operational plan- ning."[26]

The de facto autonomy thus achieved by the Army Air Force influenced the final point to emerge from the reorganization. From the "unity of command" that had now created the Air Force as a virtually coequal branch with the ground forces, it was but a short logical step to a "unity of command" that embraced under a common command the forces of not only the Army and its high-flying stepchild but of the Navy as well. This was precisely the formula that was followed in some of the operational theaters of the war—and a considerable cause of interservice difficulty.

The Navy's adjustment to wartime demands was not as wrenching as that of the Army, if for no other reason than that the Navy did not have to absorb a thirtyfold increase in manpower (as the Army did in going from 269,023 officers and men in 1940 to 8,267,958 in 1945). Nevertheless, there were several adjustments in the Navy's command structure that are worth mention- ing. On March 12, 1942, at the same time that the Army was beginning its reorganization, the president signed Executive Order 9096 which combined in the Office of the Chief of Naval Operations (CNO) both increased power to direct the Navy's uniformed establishment as well as the authority to com- mand its forces through the creation of the dual office of Commander-in- Chief, United States Fleet (also known as COMINCH). The office of COMINCH was itself of recent vintage, since the previous practice of the Navy—in keeping with its decentralized tradition—was to vest command authority for all American naval forces in the three admirals who commanded the Atlantic, Pacific, and Asiatic fleets. "Provision was made whereby one of these three officers acted as Commander-in-Chief, U.S. Fleet, and in case two or more fleets operated together would exercise overall command and would coordinate their activities. On 7 December 1941, Admiral H. E. Kimmel,

Commander-in-Chief, Pacific Fleet, was also Commander-in-Chief, U.S. Fleet."[27]

As the Navy's official historian notes, the executive order creating the position of CNO-COMINCH (which was held throughout the war by Adm. Ernest J. King) contained a paragraph that largely went unnoticed but had great practical and historic consequences:

> Paragraph 4 of the Executive Order read that "as Chief of Naval Operations the officer holding the combined offices as herein provided shall be charged under the direction of the Secretary of the Navy with the preparation, readiness, and logistic support of the operating forces comprising the several fleets . . . and with the coordination and direction of effort to this end of the bureaus and offices of the Navy Department, except such offices (other than bureaus) as the Secretary of the Navy may exempt . . . " Thus, the CNO was given the legal authority for which the office had been striving since its establishment twenty-seven years before.[28]

Much of the Navy's strategic planning for the war was thus concentrated in the CNO office, while the bulk of operational matters was concentrated in the "dual-hatted" COMINCH headquarters. Together, these staffs were to experience a growth in function and numbers that was smaller than the Army's but still roughly comparable; the CNO's office alone, for example, employed over four hundred officers at one point during the war. The grant of authority to the CNO was not, however, a blank check. Several times during the war, Admiral King submitted reorganization plans that would have centralized his authority still further with the creation of a number of deputy CNO's, each supervising one of the office's major functional areas (aviation, personnel, material, and plans), but the scheme was rejected by President Franklin D. Roosevelt on grounds of civilian control. Roosevelt, a former assistant secretary of the navy, had a strong sense of its traditions and the limits they imposed upon reorganization, even in wartime.[29]

The formal chain of command in effect during World War II was essentially the same as it had been before: the president, acting as commander in chief, transmitted orders through the secretaries of the War and Navy departments for execution by the chief of staff of the Army and the chief of naval operations, respectively. Roosevelt also appointed Adm. William D. Leahy to be his personal chief of staff—a position similar to that which Halleck had occupied during the Civil War. The most important structure to emerge from World War II, however, was the office of the Joint Chiefs of Staff (JCS) which replaced the old Joint Board and provided the focal point for interservice planning and operations. The JCS was never formally sanctioned by Roosevelt, but grew out of the Arcadia Conference (December 1941) when a Combined Chiefs of Staff (CCS) secretariat was organized to coordinate British and American strategic planning. The JCS quickly became the agency for American representation in Allied councils of war, as well as the embodiment for the supreme command of all American forces. In addition to Admiral Leahy, JCS membership was to consist of Gen. George C. Marshall, Adm. Ernest J. King, and, interestingly, Gen. Henry H. Arnold, chief of the Army Air Force.

Each of the service chiefs played a critical role in the unified commands that were set up in cooperation with the Allies. The JCS acted collectively as the chief planning body for decisions on resources and grand strategy as they pertained to the unified commands. The work was carried on largely through what had become by the end of the war an elaborate structure of more or less permanent committees staffed by representatives from each service.[30] Transmission of orders, however, continued as before through the service hierarchies. The service with preponderant responsibilities for a given theater of operations would be designated by the JCS as its executive agent. The headquarters staffs of the Army, Navy, and (eventually) the Army Air Force then generated the orders to the theater commander carrying out the JCS directives. For example, the Navy Department staff would be used to generate orders to Admiral Nimitz for the Pacific Ocean Areas command, and the War Department General Staff would perform the same function for General MacArthur's Southwest Pacific Area command.[31] The concept of each service acting as executive agent for the JCS, a sensible approach to the new division of labor, was a logical outgrowth of the old idea of "paramount interest." Of equal importance were the "component commands" set up under the unified commands. Component commands were the building blocks of the unified command structure, each component comprising those elements of land, sea, or air forces assigned to the theater. Although they were part of the unified commands, components were still tied directly to their parent services for everything other than operational control. Consequently, this administrative linkage was maintained with a great deal of vigilance by the respective service staffs throughout the war.

Two fundamental tensions provided a backdrop to the functioning of the command structure, a system, it must be emphasized, that allowed the services to function under effective political control while defeating their enemies on every front. The first tension is directly traceable to the legacy of service autonomy. Roles and missions were clearly not a matter of indifference to services that had only recently embraced the concept of joint operations, especially when there was every reason to suspect that the inevitable postwar reorganization might lead to permanent structural changes. The war against Japan was divided, as noted above, between Army and Navy commanders in chief (CINCs) rather than being placed under a single unified command; the European theater of operations, in contrast, was placed under Gen. Dwight D. Eisenhower with the Navy playing a secondary role. Paul Y. Hammond has argued that interservice bargaining was the inevitable accompaniment of the resource decisions the JCS were called upon to make. In particular, the allocation of resources to the Pacific (and therefore the Navy) was surprisingly high in view of the absolute priority placed on the European theater, in which the Army was the dominant force.[32]

Hammond also noted that once the necessity for this coalition faded away after the defeat of Germany, the interservice coalition fell apart. Separate Army-, Air Force-, and Navy-dominated commands now prepared for the final struggle in the Pacific, so that it almost "seemed that all three services were to fight their own individual war with Japan."[33] That is precisely the correct point to be made when one recognizes that the scope of World War II combat was so vast that it allowed a relatively free rein not only for service interests but also for the paradigms of warfare which were the heart and soul of those interests. The disciples of Jomini, Clausewitz, Mahan, and Douhet would thereafter justify their postwar organizational claims on the basis that land, sea, or air power had been responsible for victory.

The second basic source of tension was not unrelated to the first: the role of air power as a component command. Not only did air power have important implications for both intra- and interservice relations; it was also a new implement of warfare, and much experimentation was required to see what did and did not work under combat conditions. The linkage between the parent services and their components helped keep this particular pot boiling, especially when the Army Air Force was involved in support of naval operations. One such instance occurred in 1942, when a memo, circulated among the Army staff, strongly criticized Navy "mistakes" in the handling of Army air assets during the just-concluded Battle of Midway. Not only were long-range bombers removed from the command of experienced Army airmen, the memo charged, but during the battle itself the planes were committed in an uncoordinated, piecemeal fashion. The moral of the story was that Army planes "whose striking powers either offensively or defensively are the strongest weapons available" should be commanded by Army Air Force officers.[34]

Whatever the merits of this specific instance, the more general truth is that many Army-Navy problems at the operational level revolved around differences in the use of the air arm. General Arnold, the Army Air Force chief throughout the war, revealed in his memoirs just how much Army-Navy rivalry was really Air Force–Navy rivalry:

> There were numerous things throughout the Pacific the Army did not like. One was the apparent fact that the Navy would do anything to keep control. They used higher-ranking officers than we had, and so normally retained command. While Naval officers could command an Army outfit, it was very seldom an Army officer ever commanded a Navy unit. A general impression existed that the Navy did not understand the technique of ground operations, nor the technique of our air operations. . . . Their plan of putting air units into operations and the way they had them distributed in depth, instead of using the mass of air units to destroy the Japanese Air Force, seemed poor to me—a waste of planes and trained airmen when we were so short of them. Our own doctrine was to use the mass of planes available to break the back of the enemy's Air Force as soon as possible.[35]

Doctrinal, organizational, and ideological differences would continue to divide Navy and Army aviators. For its part, the Navy was busily exploiting the capabilities of carrier-based aircraft and was rapidly centering the fleet around them. As wrenching a transition as this was—especially for battleship officers who now saw their beloved dreadnoughts reduced to the status of mobile antiaircraft and coastal bombardment platforms—the Navy nevertheless considered its organic air arm to be the key to survival of the surface fleet. It consequently greeted any attempt to share control of that air arm with another service with roughly the same enthusiasm with which it greeted the kamikaze.

The Navy was not alone in its difficulties with the Army Air Force: the Army itself shared many of these feelings. When American ground forces first took the field against the Germans during the North African campaign in 1943, control of tactical air operations was fragmented at both the tactical and the strategic levels. As Gen. William Momyer recalled, "The doctrine at that time . . . provided that an air support command was attached to an army formation and directed by that ground force commander who had the more important mission. Airpower, in other words, was adapted to the demands of the ground force commander fighting the battle."[36] The difficulty was that ground commanders were still trained to think of air power either as a kind of long-range artillery or as a levitational form of organic air defense. Far from being an element of combat power in its own right, the airplane was thought to be a mere supporting arm; given the usual pattern of the Army command structure, air assets were accordingly parceled out among the principal ground force commanders. German air forces, which operated under ground force control, but at a much higher level of centralization, were concentrated more effectively and were able to use the weight of numbers against the more dispersed Allied tactical air squadrons.

British Air Marshal Arthur Coningham and Air Chief Marshal Sir Arthur Tedder led the fight to reorganize while under fire. Tedder wrote, "Given centralized control of air forces, this flexibility brings with it an immense power of concentration which is unequalled in any other form of warfare."[37] Further setbacks in the campaign against Gen. Erwin Rommel, such as the Battle of the Kasserine Pass, helped to force changes. An air component was created within the structure of the Allied Expeditionary Force in North Africa, and under it were centralized the strategic, tactical, and transport aircraft assigned to the theater. This centralization indeed allowed the flexibility the airmen had been seeking, as bombers pounded enemy supply lines while fighters pursued their primary task of gaining air superiority. Once that superiority had been gained, close air support of troops on the ground could begin. This represented a radical shift in the Army's thinking, but under the pressure of war it was soon codified. Army Field Service Regulation 100-20, issued on July 21, 1943, was a watershed in air power doctrine. It began with the statement that "land power and air power are co-equal and interdependent forces; neither is an auxiliary of the other." It then set forth the approved doctrine for the command of air power:

> The inherent flexibility of air power is its greatest asset. This flexibility makes it possible to employ the whole weight of the available air power against selected areas in turn. . . . control of available air power must be centralized and command must be exercised through the air force commander if this inherent flexibility and ability to deliver a decisive blow are to be fully exploited. Therefore, the command of air and ground forces in a theater of operations will be vested in the superior commander charged with the actual conduct of operations in the theater, who will exercise command of air forces through the air force commander and command of ground forces through the ground force commander. The superior commander will not attach Army air forces to units of the ground force under his command except when [they] are operating independently or are isolated by distance or lack of communication.[38]

Further organizational refinements stemming from what soon proved to be an effective operational concept included a well-developed network in which the two chains of command were linked by air-ground liaison units that provided both the close air support the ground troops needed and the centralized control the airmen considered a prerequisite to all else.

The system reached its highest stage of development during the Normandy invasion and the subsequent campaign for the liberation of Europe. The Ninth Tactical Air Command, under Maj. Gen. Elwood Quesada, placed Air Support Parties in each of the armored divisions that were spearheading the breakout from the Normandy beachhead in July 1944, equipping them as well with radios that enabled effective two-way communications to be maintained between the fighter-bombers and ground commanders. This enabled both centralized control and decentralized execution of the operation. Intercepted German communications confirmed the effectiveness of the tactical air control system, as when Field Marshall Hans von Kluge, the German commander in France, was recorded as having said during the battle: "Whether the enemy can be stopped at this point is still questionable. The enemy air activity is terrific, and smothers almost every one of our movements. Every movement of the enemy, however, is prepared and protected by its air force. Losses in men and equipment are extraordinary. The morale of the troops has suffered heavily."[39]

The Normandy invasion thus represented a kind of high-water mark of service integration during World War II, not only in terms of the land, sea, and air forces welded together in the largest joint operation in history, but also in terms of results. As Caraley pointed out, that level of integration was only temporary, as the interservice coalitions shifted toward war's end. It is important to note, however, that these temporary alignments, as long as they lasted, provided a consistency of purpose that permitted the building of the most complex command structure that had ever been devised by American forces. Once mission and organization had been joined, complexity proved not to be an obstacle to operational effectiveness. Compare, for example, the wildly ambiguous instructions given the Army Expeditionary Force in Cuba, mentioned in chapter 3, with the crisp mission order Eisenhower received from the Combined Chiefs of Staff: "You will enter the continent of Europe, and, in conjunction with the other United Nations, undertake operations aimed at the heart of Germany and the destruction of her armed forces."[40] Hierarchical control had been consolidated by the services and extended down to the level of combatant command.

If command and control during World War II was dominated by organizational integration of land, sea, and air forces, integration within those forces in turn was driven by communications electronics. The use of the electromagnetic spectrum for voice communication, high-speed teletype, radar, and sonar allowed divergent forces to operate either in close proximity or at great ranges; it permitted commanders to receive advance warning of enemy dispositions while monitoring the location of their own forces; and it effectively combined previously separate systems for sensing and engaging targets. Above all, electronic communications provided an essential accompaniment to the revolution in mobility. As Walter Millis put it, "It was the teaming of the internal combustion engine in the air and on the surface, in order to take the traditional objectives of surface warfare which, together with the remarkable development of electronic communications, really determined the history of the Second World War."[41]

For the Army ground forces, mechanization was the answer to the enormous increase in the defensive power of firearms that had first been seen in the Civil War. Infantry, transported to battle in ships, planes, and armored vehicles, relied on individual firepower—the M-1 Garand rifle and the Browning automatic rifle—and dispersion to reach their objectives. With the basic building block of the twelve-man rifle squad, divisions were built around the concept of the task force so that infantry, armor, and supporting arms could be task-organized for specific tactical requirements. Mobility, complex command structures, and flexible employment doctrine each created demands upon tactical control: here telecommunications provided the answer. According to the Army's *Lineage Book,* "Five hand radios were included in a company's equipment. These and telephones knit companies tighter together than had been the case since the Civil War."[42] The key to this structure was, of course, the tank, with its inherent abilities for firepower and maneuver—capabilities that indeed made it the "arm of decision." Pioneered by the German general Heinz Guderian, the tank radio became the standard device for commanders to orchestrate armored sweeps in conjunction with infantry movements and supporting aerial and artillery fires. Because of the radio and the telephone, the means of control kept pace with the tactical complexity of the battlefield.[43]

For the Navy, telecommunications also allowed the integration of different combat capabilities centered around the carrier task force, as the evolution away from battleship dominance reached completion. The battle fleet was now a complex network of air wings and all manner of surface vessels, linked by an array of communications.[44] This equipment included shipboard and airborne search radars with a range of over a hundred miles; coded transponders for automatic identification of friendly aircraft; highly effective ship-to-shore, surface-to-surface, and air-to-surface radios; and sonar systems for detection of submarines.[45] The marriage of aircraft and electronics allowed surface fleets to operate at unprecedented ranges, the Battle of the Coral Sea in 1942 being the first naval engagement in history during which the surface combatants never saw one another. The speed of these engagements and the greatly expanded flow of data created their own problems, as naval commanders sought ways in which to turn combat information into combat decisions, as well as to coordinate fighters and antiaircraft defenses. These requirements led to the development of shipboard Combat Information Centers (CIC) that quickly rivaled the bridge as sources of decisions at sea. The CICs were, in effect, "sea-going versions of the Operations Room pioneered by the RAF. Manual or partly automated display plots integrated data from the ship's own radar with data from internal and external voice links."[46] Similarly, it became necessary to turn whole ships into floating command posts to deal with the control of amphibious landings, which, with their concentration of land, sea, and air assets, posed the greatest demands on timing and coordination. Some twenty-three amphibious command ships (AGC class) were built by the Navy during the war for service in all major theaters.[47]

The proliferation of electronic devices for improved command and control of highly mobile and dispersed weapons systems was a constant feature of technical innovation within the services throughout the war. As Adm. Sir Arthur Hezlet pointed out in his study, *Electronics and Sea Power,* not all the transformations that took place were caused by the electron's adaptation to modern combat, but most of them surely could not have taken place without it.[48] This is a proper way to view the services' first major exposure to the integrative potential of electronic command and control, because those services were organizations of human beings who could and did make choices that either exploited or limited that potential. The general point is that the services appear to have been most aggressive in pursuing electronic integration of the combat arms over which they exercised supervision, and less aggressive in fielding systems that had the primary purpose of integrating joint combat activities. Given the nature of residual service autonomy, this evolution could hardly have occurred in any other way.

Probably the best example of the limitations service autonomy could impose on the integrative influences of electronic command and control was the 1943 campaign against the German U-boat in the North Atlantic. By that time, airborne radar had progressed to the point that the microwave ASV Mark III transceiver fitted on four-engine, land-based bombers represented a significant advance in the technique of detecting and attacking submarines. The difficulty was that land-based bombers were under the control of the Army Air Force; the suggestion, therefore, that antisubmarine warfare could best be conducted by the joint operation of these bombers in conjunction with carrier-based airplanes immediately ran afoul of established service roles and missions. Worse yet, such a radical new approach conflicted with the Navy's preferred method of dealing with the submarine threat, which was by convoys under the escort of naval surface vessels—even though this method had not stopped the record number of sinkings of Allied merchant ships by the U-boat.

Although the convoy system was retained and ultimately prevailed over the U-boat—with the help of such purely naval electronics as sonar and sonobuoys—this incident illustrates that technology took second place to service prerogatives. Samuel Eliot Morison, the Navy's official historian, noted that the Navy's first thought on the problem was to acquire its own long-range bombers rather than utilize the Army Air Force assets already in existence. The problem was complicated by the existence of different service communications systems, as well as by a "deficient command organization"—although its deficiencies go unrecorded. The most telling reason is stated with admirable frankness: "Admiral King . . . had no intention of permanently sharing with the Army what he conceived to be a naval responsibility, the protection of shipping."[49]

Service autonomy, then, was far from extinguished, by either the integrative potential of electronics or the pressures of wartime cooperation. Technical modernization, with increasingly sophisticated command and control mechanisms, would continue after the war, its principal direction the same as before: intraservice rather than interservice. Although the shared experience of the services in responding to the pressures of mobilization and the consolidation of hierarchical control—to say nothing of the sanctification of unity of command as the principle that assured operational success—would seem to have ameliorated many of the organizational stumbling blocks in the creation of a postwar defense establishment, this commonality was more apparent than real. Instead, the services seemed to demonstrate the truth of the familiar Leninist axiom that holds that as the enemy retreats, the political struggle intensifies. With the end of the war against the Axis powers, the services positioned themselves to move from wartime unity of command to the postwar struggle for dominance. The quest for defense unification, which became known as the "Battle of the Potomac," was about to begin.

The National Security Act of 1947: Forging the New Confederacy

The National Security Act of 1947 was the most significant piece of defense legislation in the nation's history; only the Constitution is a more fundamental source of authority on the structure by which the government seeks to ensure the nation's security. The National Security Act's major provisions included:

- The establishment of a cabinet-level Department of National Defense, which two years later became, simply, the Department of Defense (DOD)
- The creation of the United States Air Force
- With the 1949 amendments to the act, the elimination of the War and Navy departments as cabinet-level agencies, their subordination to a common secretary, and their reduction to a coordinate status now shared with the Air Force
- The delineation of the principal functions of each of the armed services
- The legislative recognition of the Joint Chiefs of Staff, who were to coordinate, but not command, the armed forces
- The establishment of the Central Intelligence Agency and the National Security Council[50]

One might think that with the creation of the unified defense establishment that had been envisioned by reformers since the latter part of the nineteenth century, the troubling issues of service autonomy had been resolved and the entire issue reduced to one of purely historical interest. But consider Harry Howe Ransom's comment: "Since World War II, interservice rivalry has been the prime characteristic of the defense establishment. . . . With all of the reorganizations since World War II . . . the defense structure continues to resemble an alliance of semi-independent, sovereign units, often engaged in bitter jurisdictional warfare."[51] The answer to this seeming anomaly is that the existence of "characteristic" interservice rivalry was merely the outward manifestation of service autonomy that, although redirected by the National Security Act of 1947, was by no means eliminated. There is no question that the service organizations had undergone a radical transformation, largely brought about by the phenomenon of twentieth-century warfare and the pressures for centralization that accompanied it. But the centralization that had created the pressures for general unification of the defense establishment would also, paradoxically, create centers of institutional resistance grouped around service paradigms.

Those paradigms were much in evidence throughout the unification struggle, which began as early as November 3, 1943, when General Marshall proposed that the JCS endorse a scheme for postwar unification as a basis for future legislation. His plan, the features of which were embraced by the War Department throughout the controversy, suggested the establishment of a single department heading the ground, naval, and air forces; a unified logistical service; civilian under secretaries and a chief of staff heading each of these four departments; and a chief of staff to the president heading a U.S. General Staff, composed of himself and the four service chiefs.[52]

The Marshall proposal was opposed by Admiral King, with the result that the concept of a single military organization was merely studied throughout much of 1944, first by the Joint Strategic Survey Committee of the JCS and then by a special JCS committee headed by retired Adm. James O. Richardson.

More significant for the public debate were the hearings held in March through May 1944 by a select committee of the House of Representatives headed by Clifton A. Woodrum. The Woodrum committee hearings produced the first comprehensive airing of service views on unification and were important for two reasons. First, the Army presented its preferred scheme for postwar organization during the testimony of Lt. Gen. Joseph T. McNarney, the deputy chief of staff who had presided over the reorganization of the War Department General Staff in 1942. The McNarney Plan was virtually identical to Marshall's earlier proposal. It left deliberately vague, however, the key points on which the unification struggle would ultimately turn: consolidation of service air assets under the Air Force, the future status of the Marine Corps, and the nature of political control over the defense budget. The second reason the Woodrum committee hearings were significant was that they not only produced a well-defined Army position but also alerted the civilian leadership of the Navy and its congressional allies to the fact that this position threatened critical interests of the naval service. Partly because of the death of Navy Secretary Frank Knox at the end of April 1944, the Woodrum committee suspended its hearings and ultimately recommended that no further action on unification be taken until the war ended. This delay represented a tactical victory for the Navy, since it bought critical time for additional study and the development of other plans. Those alternatives began to emerge by mid-1945, when the report of the Richardson committee and the impending end of the war refocused attention on the unification problem. Before those alternatives are examined, however, it will be useful to summarize the objectives of the services as they approached the struggle.[53]

The objectives of the War Department "coalition" (which by 1945 included the Army, the Air Force, various congressional allies, and President Truman) in the reorganization proposals included the following: a unitary defense department headed by a single secretary administering a common budget; a JCS headed by a single chief of staff having control of the department budget and direct access to the president; a separate Air Force with control over all land-based aircraft, including those of the Navy; and the limitation of congressional authorization to broad organizational guidelines, with details being delegated to the executive branch.[54] Caraley has noted that these objectives were held by the Army against a backdrop of resentment carried forward from the interwar period when appropriations favored the Navy and thereby contributed to the Army's chronic lack of preparedness. His evidence on this point derives from a quote by Mark S. Watson, compiler of the Army's official history, *Chief of Staff: Prewar Plans and Preparations,* which confirms Army resentment at budgetary deprivations. Caraley's citation, however, omits the following passage which gives an important ideological context: "The Army was less favored, presumably because there was a continuing public confidence, shared by the White House and Congress, of oceans as a bulwark and a belief that the Navy could safely be thought of not merely as the traditional "first line of defense" but as the only really necessary line of defense for the time being. Even the growing reach of the airplane . . . was not exploited in military form to any such degree as it was in Europe and Japan."[55]

The position of the Navy as the first line of defense was most vigorously challenged by the airmen in the War Department coalition. Although Douhet's predictions regarding the efficacy of strategic bombing had not been entirely borne out by the massive but conventional campaigns of the Army Air Force over Europe and Japan, the use of atomic weapons at Hiroshima and Nagasaki suggested that the original air paradigm had been deficient only in its estimate of the bomb sizes required to achieve decisive results. With the atomic bomb, this deficiency had been corrected, and air power now replaced sea power as the nation's first line of defense. Army traditionalists did not counter these claims according to standard Clausewitzian or Jominian precepts of land warfare. Instead, ground force advocates insisted that the lessons of World War II demonstrated the importance of a combined arms approach to global warfare in which land, sea, and air forces were interdependent. Secretary of War Robert P. Patterson's testimony before the Senate in 1945 stated the matter directly: "The elementary lesson which we have learned from the hard experience of World War II is that there must be single direction of the Nation's land, sea and air forces. While the foundation of our organization is three coordinate arms—air, land and sea—these arms must operate as a single team under single direction, which has responsibility and final power of decision over all."[56] This was not only a reasonable inference to draw from the actual conduct of the war but also an acknowledgment of the Army's new dependence on the Navy and the Air Force for strategic and tactical mobility.

In his free-ranging critique of the general staff system, John C. Ries has pointed out that the War Department proposals were entirely consistent with hierarchical organizational principles regarding unity of command, span of control, staff coordination, and integration of specialized activities.[57] As shown in chapters 2 and 3, these organizational principles were the touchstones of the Army's rise to institutional professionalism, as well as its habitual response to the problems of modernization. In the testimony of its leaders— Patterson, Marshall, and McNarney, among others—there is the consistently expressed need for a single military decision maker, a chief of staff, presumably supported by an all-service general staff with directive authority, although there is an equally consistent and perhaps deliberate vagueness on this point. Caraley linked this organizational pattern to the Army's "general theory of decision-making" which assumed the existence of an optimum solution that maximized military effectiveness and was therefore in the "real interest of all the services." By advocating what was in effect a national general staff system, the Army was seeking to transfer the results of its own historical experience to the problem of the postwar defense establishment.[58]

The Navy approach to that problem similarly reflected the results of its own historical experience. The tradition of decentralized control that characterized both the operations of the Navy at sea and its organizational philosophy ashore had provided a formative experience not entirely overcome by the catharsis of World War II. Hammond pointed out that the Navy command structure still rested on a philosophy that emphasized the precepts of horizontal organizational structure linked by voluntary cooperation. "Horizontal structure was the major characteristic of the old Navy Department organization that had miraculously worked in World War I, but required substantial reconstruction in World War II. It assumed that people responsible for only segments could produce a whole. . . . In contradiction to Army tenets, it asserted that program formulation and direction could be achieved by an organization without a unified command structure at the center."[59] Navy spokesmen throughout the unification controversy persisted in arguments that reflected their inherent distrust of the subordination characteristic of the development of Army staffs, and in so doing, they adopted a phraseology that seemed at times to suggest constitutional arguments concerning the concentration and separation of powers. In arguing against the Army's single chief of staff concept, for example, Admiral King testified that it was "potentially, the 'man on horseback.' It is allegedly based on the premise that unity of military command in Washington is necessary to insure unity of effort in the field. . . . Although unity of command is well suited to the latter, there are positive dangers in a single command at the highest military level. I consider this fact the most potent argument against the concept of a single department."[60]

Nor had the experience of the war reduced the Navy's faith in its ideological underpinnings: "Navy leaders still considered axiomatic the Mahan thesis that a strong navy and command of the sea were indispensable elements in maintaining overall combat effectiveness and national security."[61] Having gone through the painful experience of adapting the surface fleet to the demands of three-medium combat, the Navy was not about to surrender control over the elements it deemed organic to its new combat power. A familiar jibe has it that "the navy is already a unified service. It has its own Navy, of course; but it also has its own Air Force, the naval air arm, as well as its own Army, otherwise known as the Marines." This was the essence of the naval self-image as it developed during and after World War II: a complete sea-air-land team that could be rapidly concentrated "in support of" military operations and just as rapidly moved elsewhere to strike whatever blows might be required by a national command structure that was "coordinated," but not necessarily "unified."

In comparison with War Department objectives, the Navy was playing for the status quo, while the Army and its allies were, in a manner of speaking, revisionists. Two Navy goals were especially critical.[62] First, the JCS decision-making process, in which unanimity was a prerequisite for action, was an important legacy of service autonomy. Fleet Adm. William F. Halsey, whose gift for idiom surpassed that of any sailor of his era, considered the alternative unacceptable: "The single direction which would direct the planning and control the expenditures would be the Chiefs of Staff of the Army, the Army Air Corps and the Navy. If this would not give the Army control over the Navy's budget, then I've forgotten my arithmetic. . . . I, for one, am unwilling to have the Chief of the Army Air Forces pass on the question of whether or not the Navy should have funds for building and maintaining a balanced fleet. One might just as well ask a committee composed of a Protestant, a Catholic, and a Jew to save our national souls by recommending a national church or creed."[63]

The second critical Navy objective was civilian control, the most important aspect of which was the direct access to Congress that had been a hallmark of naval support since 1798. Admiral King's testimony subtly reminded his listeners that control over naval appropriations would be a casualty of the Army reorganization scheme: "Under the Constitution, it is the duty of the Congress to 'provide and maintain a Navy.' . . . the Congress is entitled to full and public examination of all considerations which have a bearing on the question. The needs of the Navy should not be subject to review by individuals who do not have informed responsibility in these premises."[64]

The objectives of the War and Navy departments clashed most sharply during the Senate hearings on unification held from October 17 to December 17, 1945. The Army had resubmitted its proposal in a slightly modified form that incorporated the findings of the Richardson committee report of the previous spring; the new plan was presented at the start of the hearings by Gen. J. Lawton Collins. This time, however, the Army plan was countered by a comprehensive alternative developed for the Navy by Ferdinand Eberstadt, a close friend of Navy Secretary James Forrestal. The recommendations of the Eberstadt Plan incorporated traditional Navy preferences for the coordinative approach:

- "Organization of the military forces into three coordinate departments," all of them with cabinet-level secretaries.
- Creation of the National Security Council and Central Intelligence Agency as coordinative agencies for policy and intelligence, respectively.
- Continuation of the JCS as the agency responsible for strategic direction of the armed forces, but with statutory limits imposed to ensure that it would be coordinative in nature.
- Creation of an elaborate set of coordinating committees for mobilization, research and development, military training, and so on.[65]

With the development of two clear alternatives, the Senate hearings took on what at times became a no-holds-barred atmosphere. With the ink barely dry on the Japanese surrender document, service advocates were not shy in assuming the lion's share of credit for victory. Their statements usually began with a ritualistic bow to the team concept of "unity of command"; decorum then having been satisfied, unrestrained candor often ensued. Lt. Gen. James Doolittle, hero of the Tokyo raid and Medal of Honor recipient, stated that "no single service won the war" but then, almost in the same breath, added, "The Navy had the transport to make the invasion of Japan possible; the Ground Forces the power to make it successful; and the B-29 made it unnecessary." The senators, who knew good copy when they heard it, then goaded the general into expounding his theory of aircraft carriers: "The carrier has two attributes. One attribute is that it can move about; the other attribute is that it can be sunk. As soon as airplanes are developed with sufficient range . . . there will be no further use for aircraft carriers."[66]

Predictably, the Navy also waxed lyrical in describing its war at sea, especially in the Pacific. Admiral Halsey, never one for understatement, declared: "The tide of war changed with the ebb and flow of sea power. . . . Almost every landing, every amphibious operation, every campaign of the all-out offensive was spearheaded by carrier aviation backed by the mighty power of the big guns of the United States Fleet. . . . Yes, without our Navy, and its carrier aviation, we could not have won the war. In the kind of warfare that the vast expanses of the Pacific impose, a strong fleet is indispensable."[67]

Not to be outdone, the Army sent Gen. Dwight D. Eisenhower, who began his testimony by declaring, "At one time, I was an infantryman but I have long since forgotten that fact under the responsibility of commanding combined arms." He then added that sailors and airmen had come to regard him as "one of their own services, rather than of an opposing one." In summarizing his argument for a "single executive department to preside over three coequal and autonomous fighing teams," the future president said, "There is no such thing as a separate land sea or air war; therefore we must now recognize this fact by establishing a single department of the armed forces to govern us all."[68]

Just after the Senate hearings ended in December 1945, President Harry Truman addressed a message to Congress that endorsed the need for a unified defense department built along the lines suggested by the Collins Plan. By this point, however, the Navy and its allies were committed to what they increasingly saw as a fight for survival. The incautious rhetoric, especially from air advocates, escalated. Caraley cites the example of a goodwill dinner given by Norfolk, Va., businessmen for some seventy high-ranking Army and Navy officers, at which an Army Air Force brigadier spoke:

> You gentlemen had better understand that the Army Air Force is tired of being a subordinate outfit. . . . The Army Air Force is going to run the show. You, the Navy, are not going to have anything but a couple of carriers which are ineffective anyway, and they will probably be sunk in the first battle. Now as for the Marines, you know what the Marines are, a small, bitched-up army talking Navy lingo. We are going to put those Marines in the Regular Army and make efficient soldiers out of them. . . . We know this is a Navy town, and a Navy hang-out, but Army Air is still going to stay, and we are going to take over, too.[69]

Remarks like these could hardly have been more upsetting had the speaker also chosen to cast aspersions on the virtue of Navy wives. But with powerful congressional allies such as Representative Carl Vinson and Senator David Walsh, the Navy was able to use the Eberstadt Plan as an alternative to Army consolidation. With a quick resolution of the unification question thus denied, the conflict dragged on throughout 1946, but moved inevitably in the direction of a compromise between the two service positions.

Even as the services were grappling publicly with the shape of the postwar defense establishment, privately they were still at odds with each other over the peacetime structure of unified commands. Caraley stated that "unified command in the field . . . in 1945 was not opposed by anyone"; this reflected not only the public stance of service leaders but their acceptance of unity of command in principle.[70] Applying that principle, however, was something else. Throughout most of 1946, the JCS sought to find a solution for the problem of divided Army and Navy commands in the Pacific; equally difficult was the determination of which service would exercise unified command over the other theaters in which the rapidly demobilizing American forces were still deployed. In the midst of this controversy, a declassified memorandum by the Army General Staff highlighted the basic differences in the service positions on the meaning of unified commands:

a. The Army and the Navy do not have a meeting of the minds on unified command. . . . the Navy is unwilling in fact to place what is called "a fleet" under other than a naval commander. This stand means that there cannot be true unified command of the three services unless the joint commander is a naval officer. The Navy are [sic] willing to assign certain naval forces to other than a naval commander, but fleet units operate in support, that is by cooperation. Furthermore, there does not appear to be a clear meeting of the minds on the Army concept that an officer assigned unified command is above service and is a true joint commander.

b. There appears to be a difference in concept as to the nature of "commands," especially in peacetime. The Navy concept appears to be one of service sovereignty or ownership of an area. The Army concept recognizes the subordinate and limited role of the military, particularly in peacetime. . . . therefore what we have are commanders with certain assigned forces and assigned missions.[71]

These differences led General Eisenhower, by then the Army chief of staff, to propose what eventually became the Unified Command Plan. Under this document, theater commanders would be appointed who were responsible to the JCS, which in turn would have the responsibility for strategic direction of the armed forces assigned to the unified command. This responsibility would be exercised through the unified commander, assisted by a joint staff composed of representatives from all assigned component commands. The component commands, as had been the case in World War II, would deal directly with their respective service headquarters in Washington on all matters not directly linked to joint operations, especially logistics, training, and administration. President Truman approved the plan on December 14, 1946, and with it, the establishment of the following commands: Far East, Pacific, Alaskan, Northeast (Newfoundland, Greenland, and Labrador), the Atlantic Fleet (subsequently changed to Atlantic Command), Caribbean, and European. Finally, the plan also included the establishment of the Strategic Air Command under the direct supervision of the JCS.[72]

Even while these matters were being hammered out, another legislative battle in the unification struggle ended without resolution. Senate Bill S. 2044 was introduced in April; it followed closely the lines suggested by Truman's message of the previous December (which had generally favored the Collins Plan) but incorporated as well several of Eberstadt's provisions for policy coordination. The bill generated hearings that again created a forum for Army proponents to argue the case for the economy and efficiency of unification. The Navy, however, was shrewd enough to base its case on the grounds that unification would hurt the Navy and possibly eliminate the Marine Corps. Given the residual goodwill the naval service enjoyed in the aftermath of the war and the congressional committee structure that allowed its allies virtually unlimited opportunities for delay, obstruction, or modification once their critical interests were threatened, it was not surprising that the Senate adjourned without taking action on S. 2044. This outcome represented a legislative stalemate: the War Department coalition was strong enough to raise the unification issue and keep it on the public agenda, while the Navy Department and its allies were sufficiently well entrenched that they could prevent passage of any bill that threatened their coalition objectives.[73]

The impasse placed the ball back squarely in Truman's court, and the president, having other legislative and political problems to deal with, became anxious to resolve the issue. Shortly after the congressional adjournment, Truman pressured Forrestal and Patterson to come up with a proposal that was jointly acceptable and would form the basis for legislation. One of the first concessions the president made was the abandonment of the principle of a military chief of staff and acceptance of the JCS as an advisory body with statutorily limited responsibilities. Throughout the summer and fall of 1946, the differences were slowly overcome and the outlines of a compromise emerged: a single cabinet-level department, three coordinate services, and policy coordination much along the lines suggested by the Eberstadt Plan. The status of naval aviation and the Marine Crops remained problematical. There was no doubt at all, however, that congressional prerogatives for oversight and budgetary control would be a feature of any organizational proposal.[74]

The countdown to the final agreement came when, on January 16, 1947, Patterson and Forrestal reported to the president that they had reached agreement on all outstanding issues between their departments affecting unification. The bulk of the concessions had clearly been made by the Army. The defense establishment would rest upon coordinative lines: not only were the three services to be coequal, but the authority of the JCS and the "Secretary of National Defense" would be carefully limited. Above all, the essential autonomy of the services, as well as their roles and missions, would continue much as they had emerged during World War II, including the retention of naval aviation and the Marine Corps. Final approval of the National Security Act came at last on July 26, 1947, when President Truman signed it into law. As passed, the act contained language that made explicit congressional intent regarding unification of the services: it was to "provide for their authoritative coordination and unified direction under civilian control but not to merge them." As the official history of the Office of Secretary of Defense points out, "Because the military departments . . . retained the status of 'individual executive departments,' they were still largely autonomous organizations, with nearly full control over their internal affairs. In fact, all powers and duties not specifically conferred upon the Secretary of Defense became part of the authority of each respective departmental secretary. Furthermore, any service secretary, after informing the Secretary of Defense, could appeal any decision relating to his department."[75]

The JCS was given what appeared to be far-reaching powers, including three principal duties: (1) to prepare strategic plans and to provide for the strategic direction of the military forces; (2) to establish unified commands in strategic areas when such unified commands were in the interests of national security (which was itself an interesting qualification!); and (3) to act as the principal military advisers to the president and the secretary of defense.[76] The Joint Staff, however, was limited by the same title to no more than one hundred officers, drawn from all the services. These numbers, the establishment of the JCS as an officially collaborative, coordinative body, and the preservation of its pattern of unanimous decision making all represented a return to the status quo ante. However far-reaching its legislative charter, the JCS would remain a collective entity, its authority and ability to carry out the mission entrusted to it a subject for nearly constant debate and controversy.

The picture that thus emerged from the unification struggle was one in which service autonomy was only slightly altered. Congress had been presented with three paradigms of warfare loosely grouped around two competing coalitions and, in the aftermath of the nation's greatest military triumph, was asked to choose between them. It was unable to do so, particularly when that choice involved the possibility of offending popular constituencies and disrupting long-established political and administrative relationships. Undoubtedly, the Air Force side of the War Department coalition represented a kind of messianic zeal and a strategic vision that was attractive to some—and deeply troubling to others. The Navy represented a countervailing conservatism in the unification struggle as it had on other occasions as well. Henry L. Stimson, secretary of war under two presidents, included in his memoirs, written with McGeorge Bundy, a classic reminiscence:

But some of the Army-Navy troubles, in Stimson's view, grew from the peculiar psychology of the Navy Department, which frequently seemed to retire from the realm of logic into a dim religious world in which Neptune was God, Mahan his prophet, and the United States Navy the only true Church. The high priests of this group were a group of men to whom Stimson always referred as "the Admirals." These gentlemen were to him both anonymous and continuous. . . . in 1940 and afterwards he found them still active and still uncontrolled by either their Secretary or the President. This was not Knox's fault, or the President's, as Stimson saw it. It was simply that the Navy Department had never had an Elihu Root. "The Admirals" had never been given their comeuppance.[77]

Giving "the Admirals" their long-awaited comeuppance was a task that too many Army and Army Air Force officers set for themselves at the outset of the unification struggle, when mutual cooperation, or at least common civility, might have achieved better results. And in the end, having been asked to approve what could be variously described as a merger or a hostile takeover, Congress simply shrugged and gave its blessing to a limited-liability partnership.

5   Setting the Scene
Formative Influences on Modern
Command and Control

In assessing the impact of autonomy in the century and a half that preceded the birth of the modern era in command and control, it is important to begin at the micro level and to look in particular at the differences in the sociology of service command. One of the most basic distinctions involves command "style"—the manner in which command was traditionally exercised. As Rear Adm. Julius Furer noted, the hallmark of naval command has always been the undivided and unchallenged authority of the ship's captain. Command in the Navy was indeed an indivisible entity during much of this period not only because of the relatively small numbers of ships in the American fleet throughout most of the nineteenth century but also because those limited numbers dictated a deployment pattern that emphasized single ships or, at most, a squadron of two or three vessels. The indivisibility of naval command in such a setting was reinforced by the absence of any physical means for naval commanders to extend their influence beyond their own quarterdecks or, until the invention of the wireless, to exert any sort of control over ships that were not literally within their line of sight.[1]

Those norms stood in stark contrast to those of land warfare, which from the founding of the Republic emphasized the standard practice of achieving battlefield success through the application of mass at the decisive point. The necessity to achieve these concentrations and to promote the contributions of the various arms of land combat power made the division of authority axiomatic. Unity of command, under these circumstances, reflected the essential balance of land warfare: controlling large numbers through the use of subordinate echelons and commanders while preserving tactical flexibility and the power of overall decision. Although battlefields prior to World War I were largely subject to the same line-of-sight limitations that characterized naval engagements, land warfare offered more reliable ways for the extension of tactical control by

123

military commanders, including their ability to intervene personally when a subordinate echelon was threatened. Similarly, strategic control could be exercised in indirect but occasionally decisive ways. These
environmental characteristics reinforced the tendency for Army officers and
those who directed them to be comfortable with the notion that authority
could be divided without prejudice to command prerogatives or operational
effectiveness; indeed, victory on the battlefield positively demanded this
practice.

These micro differences are also discernible at the macro level of service
organizational development. It is a short step from divisible authority patterns
to a reliance upon staffs, and much of the Army's history, particularly as seen
in chapters 2 and 3, is linked to its attempt to extend control by the expanded
use of staffs. Initially formed as repositories of functional and administrative
responsibility at service headquarters, the Army staff gradually became an
adjunct of battlefield control that was indispensable in overcoming the complexities of warfare in an industrial age. The Navy also used a headquarters
staff to divide the labor of "providing and maintaining a Navy"; but its
experience with battle staffs was limited until well into the twentieth century.
It is thus possible to conceive of the Army as having embraced a tradition of
centralization brought about by the sheer force of numbers, while the Navy
remained committed to a decentralized model of organization in which administration on shore reflected its command preference at sea. In assessing the
outcomes of the defense unification struggle, Paul Y. Hammond echoed
Samuel P. Huntington's delineation of the "Hamiltonian" and "Jeffersonian"
traditions referred to in chapter 2. He saw the Army's organizational philosophy as the embodiment of Hamiltonian principles of administration: structure
based on function and a clear line of authority from top to bottom. The apex of
this development, which Hammond termed "neo-Hamiltonianism," took
place in the Root reforms and emphasized centralization of authority, accountability, and policy control along hierarchical lines. In his formulation,
the Navy represents a more decentralized model, one that is Jeffersonian in its
inherent distrust of concentrated authority, subordination, and structures built
along other than federal lines. Both philosophies, anchored in the bedrock of
the American political-military tradition, have shown a remarkable resilience
over the course of two centuries.[2]

Whatever the conceptual tools used to define the respective service organizational philosophies, there is no question that they shared a common commitment to individual autonomy. It is difficult from a modern perspective to
appreciate just how far-reaching this separation was prior to World War II.
Testifying during the Senate's 1945 hearings on unification, former Navy

secretary Josephus Daniels (who, despite his Jeffersonian leanings, was an ardent and articulate supporter of unification) delivered an unforgettable anecdote that captured the essence of traditional autonomy:

> Early in my administration as Secretary of the Navy . . . I proposed some tentative arrangements that would prevent duplication and promote economy to my good friend Judge Garrison, Secretary of War, and suggested further study by Navy and Army officers to effect the reforms and closer cooperation I envisioned. Judge Garrison, barely looking at the plan outlined, said, "Joe, I don't care a damn about the Navy and you don't care a damn about the Army. You run your machine and I will run mine. I am glad if anybody can convince me I am wrong, but I am damn sure nobody lives who can do it. I am an individualist and am not cut out for cooperative effort. I will let you go your way, and I will go my way.[3]

This powerful tradition remained long after the burdens of mobilization, global combat, and a permanent postwar military establishment had transformed the services into huge bureaucratic complexes which, in scale and scope, resembled each other more than their respective organizational antecedents.

All the standard histories of the postwar period document the rise of centralization in the three services whose autonomy had been confirmed by the National Security Act of 1947. Ray Cline, writing the official history of the Operations Division of the Army General Staff, showed just how quickly the principal staff directorates moved to reestablish the authority they had been forced to delegate during the war. Although couched in language stressing the need for the "principle of decentralization," the 1946 reorganization resulted in a more centralized and complex structure than had been in place at the start of the war (when Marshall, it will be recalled, termed his own staff headquarters "the worst command post in the Army") and included twenty-nine individual elements with the right of direct access to the chief of staff.[4]

The pattern of consolidation was the same in the Navy as well, and as the process of demobilization was halted and reversed by the onset of the cold war, the services found that this consolidation was the key to continued control over their own budgets. Since their respective shares of the defense budget were a function of approved roles and missions, these became the subject of a bitter controversy that did not end with the passage of the National Security Act. Instead, the "corollary functions" of each service (in reality, a polite code word for the always troublesome question of organic air assets, now complicated by the issue of nuclear weapons) required constant redefinition. So bitter did these disputes become that the new secretary of national defense, James Forrestal (who had argued so persuasively as Navy secretary to limit the powers of the office he would later hold), had to intervene and, at conferences held at Key West, Florida, and Newport, Rhode Island, in 1948, to negotiate service agreements on roles and missions that were eventually codified by executive order.[5] Troubles also arose from the fact that the services each had de facto proponency for a portion of the unified commands while maintaining direct ties with "their" components in other unified commands. Part of the postwar consolidation was the gradual extension and formalization of these ties, the result of which, it can be argued, was to enhance the power of the components at the expense of the unified commander. Eventually these service guidelines were published by the JCS under the title *Unified Action Armed Forces,* a document written with all the precision of a well-crafted union contract.[6]

Controversies such as these were ample proof that service autonomy was alive and well in the postwar world. That it should have been so is plain enough not only from the language of the National Security Act but from the events that surrounded its passage. The temperament of the Seventy-ninth and Eightieth Congresses, which wrestled with this legislation, was entirely consistent with that of the Continental Congress and the Constitutional Convention: in all cases, concentration of power in any official or in any agency was viewed with deep suspicion. Not only was the putative chief of staff of the armed forces proposed by the Army pilloried as a "man on horseback," but there was also a surprising amount of discussion asserting that the secretary of national defense and whatever assistants he hired might turn out to be the dreaded Prussian General Staff in mufti. Accordingly, the secretary's powers were limited to "general direction, authority, and control" over the services, and he was authorized to hire a maximum of three special assistants, each to "receive compensation at the rate of $10,000 a year" (Sect. 202, Title II, P.L. 253).

The quaintness of that language is itself testimony to subsequent events that took place over almost four decades. From three underpaid assistants in 1947, the Office of Secretary of Defense (OSD) has grown to encompass a deputy secretary, two under secretaries, a comptroller, an inspector general, a general counsel, and eleven assistant secretaries, as well as almost 100,000 civilian and military personnel counting the employees of the OSD-supervised defense agencies and field activities, such as the Defense Communications and Defense Mapping agencies.[7] A full recitation of the steps leading to a staff of that size is beyond the scope of this book. But briefly, the enhancement of secretarial powers took place in three legislative increments:

- *Amendments of 1949:* These broadened the secretary's powers to include "direction, authority and control over the Department of Defense," which was now fully established as an executive agency while the military departments were not. The role of the secretary in preparation and review of the defense budget was broadened by Title IV of the act. These amendments also created the position of chairman of the JCS and increased the Joint Staff to 210.

- *Reorganization Plan 6 of 1953:* President Eisenhower submitted this plan for reorganization of the Defense Department for congressional approval; the plan, not being overturned by either the House or the Senate, became law on June 30, 1953. Its provisions further increased the size of the OSD by transferring to it several of the Eberstadt-inspired coordinating committees and adding six assistant secretaries and a general counsel.

- *Amendments of 1958:* These further solidified the secretary's control over the military departments, which were to be "separately organized" with each department functioning under the direction of the secretary. The chain of command was redefined with the president and the secretary of defense exercising direct command of the unified and specified commands, the JCS empowered, as before, to act as their principal advisers, and the individual service chiefs removed from that chain of command. The Joint Staff was increased to four hundred officers, but was limited in scope by personnel assignment restrictions and an express prohibition against its functioning as an armed forces general staff.[8]

In the passage of the 1947 National Security Act as well as in these incremental changes, Congress consistently stipulated that power in the Defense Department be consolidated in civilian rather than military hands. This preference was the product of the most deeply rooted national values. Suspicious of any concentration of power, Americans are doubly so whenever that concentration involves *military* power. But it is the task of the nation's political leadership to apply those values to specific situations, and here one can observe an uncritical interpretation of the norm of civilian control. Huntington's model of subjective civilian control, which assumes the greatest level of political-military interaction, suggests that political direction may involve some spillover into what otherwise might be purely military functions. Seen in this light, civilian control as applied to the Defense Department was not limited to the careful positioning of civilians at the apex of its hierarchy, or even to the linkage of those leaders to the executive and legislative branches of government. Instead, OSD became the agency of horizontal and vertical integration within the Defense Department. Its growth was fueled by the demands for a tightly coordinated security policy that was essential in coping with an international environment that was itself undergoing a fundamental transformation. Like the National Security Council, which grew in power and influence because it was an essential coordinator of divergent governmental policies, OSD performed the vital function of integrating the work of three otherwise autonomous military services.

This was a task that the services were unable or unwilling to do for themselves. By design, the consensual, collaborative nature of the JCS was not the kind of military staff structure that could have unified service efforts and acted as a counterweight to the dominance that OSD eventually imposed. It is of course questionable whether Congress would ever have allowed an armed forces general staff even if the services had advocated one and even if it had been convinced that such a body would remain tightly controlled by the civilian leadership of the Defense Department—although such an outcome had at times appeared likely at the outset of the unification struggle. Having made its decision, however, Congress found it easier to acquiesce in the creation of additional bureaucratic development within OSD. But in a particularly perverse way, this process tended to generate its own multiplier effect as the services tried to keep pace with the inroads that were being made into their own organizations. The phenomenon was nowhere better illustrated than when Robert McNamara seized upon the powers that had been gradually built into the secretary's office and used cost analysis as a tool to evaluate service acquisition and development programs. The creation of the Program Analysis and Evaluation Office within the OSD structure soon spawned similar offices within the service staffs. Thus, a good-faith effort to enhance precision in defense budgeting had the unintended consequence of contributing to bureaucratic proliferation: the creation of one office generated three others.

This is not to suggest that the integration of service planning was not a proper goal of the civilian leadership of the Defense Department, but merely to point out that the mechanism chosen to bring about that integration had costs as well as benefits. With the passage of the 1958 amendments, for example, the secretary of defense became the immediate superior of the generals and admirals heading the unified and specified commands, while the service chiefs—the Joint Chiefs themselves wearing their other "hats"—were reduced to being the "providers and maintainers" of those forces. Yet that initiative represented a nearly complete reversal of a principle that had prevailed at the time the National Security Act was passed: namely, that those responsible for carrying out a policy should have a voice in framing it. That principle was at the heart of the coordinative philosophy of Ferdinand Eberstadt which had won out over attempts to subordinate the service chiefs to the dictates of a superior staff. Now, however, the JCS would give advice (when asked) while the unified and specified commanders, who were by definition in the field and not at the seat of government, were responsible for executing whatever military decision was reached. If policy formation and policy execution were now separate, an even wider gulf separated the unified commanders from the procurement process, which would remain, as before, within the purview of the services. In theory, the needs of the unified commands would be solicited by both the services and OSD. In practice, however, the unified commands and OSD would find that there were limits on the ability of a civilian staff to achieve control over the budgets that were still, in spite of McNamara's initiatives, largely administered by the services.[9]

The command structure that emerged, therefore, by the beginning of the modern age of command and control featured a decidedly mixed bag of integration and autonomy. One of the most important aspects of service autonomy continued to be the effective control the Army, the Navy, and the Air Force exercised over their budgets and programs. However much secretaries of defense such as Robert McNamara scrutinized the defense budget or forced critical cuts on selected programs, the bottom line always was that it was the generals and admirals who not only drew up the basic document but defended and justified it throughout each phase of the congressional appropriations process. This fact of life was to become especially important in the development of command and control systems because each one of them would be developed by one service or the other—not the Joint Staff, which had no procurement funds whatever, nor the unified and specified commanders, despite their responsibilities for commanding and controlling the combatant forces of the United States.

The second implication of service autonomy for command and control development is related to the first: the development of those systems would primarily take place along service-directed lines. The extraordinary use of the electromagnetic spectrum to enhance combat integration during World War II continued apace thereafter as the services pursued their aggressive search for more and better ways to control such new weaponry as the jet fighter, the intercontinental bomber, the helicopter, and the nuclear submarine. Most of those developments would, naturally enough, be built around the major combat systems that were being fielded. Consequently, it became standard practice for command and control systems to be chosen with technical characteristics that best suited each parent service's perception of its tactical requirements, a view formed by reliance on military, naval, or aerospace doctrine. Often, however, the weapons and their command and control systems were considered in isolation from their most likely employment in a joint operational setting. Because of the nature of service autonomy, it was not uncommon for command and control systems that would operate in a joint environment to take second place in the procurement process to systems that controlled the favored weapons wielded by the Army, the Navy, or the Air Force.

Thus the maintenance of service control over budgets and an emphasis on service-related command and control systems over joint systems were two of the primary ways in which autonomy would affect the future. But there was another influence emanating from the historical experience of military staffs and their effect upon military organizations. It is perhaps easiest to summarize this point in terms of a paradox: centralization was essential to decentralization. Although staffs and organizations grew as they did because of the increasing complexity of warfare, size alone did not adequately address the problems. This is another way of saying that a balance always had to be struck between elements that were so critical they had to be managed centrally and those so diverse they had to be left to commanders at progressively lower echelons. The trick, of course, was to know the difference, and it was here that the military staff played an important role in sorting matters out. The best example in American military history is that of Pershing organizing his command with a General Staff centralized along functional lines, while effective decentralization was achieved through similar staff structures set up through subordinate echelons. Precisely because there was a unanimity achieved through centralization of some matters, others could be decentralized—and the staff was the agency that spanned the gap. In more contemporary parlance, the staff was an interface not only between echelons but occasionally between divergent systems as well.

Centralization versus Autonomy in the Defense Department

The 1958 amendments to the National Security Act became the legislative backdrop to the building of centralized civilian power within the Defense Department. Although not entirely overcoming the residual forces of service autonomy, these amendments cleared the way for the secretary of defense, heretofore something of a final arbiter of competing interests, to become a strong executive in his own right, making and enforcing his own policies. When Robert McNamara assumed that office in 1961, he seemed to personify the new philosophy, both in the analytical tools he brought with him from the business world and in the aggressive personal style he used to consolidate his power over the Pentagon bureaucracy. His weapon of choice in gaining control over defense policy was the planning, programming, and budgeting system (PPBS), a method of analysis developed at the Rand Corporation by Charles Hitch and Alain Enthoven—both of whom were brought to Washington by McNamara to establish a Systems Analysis Office under the defense comptroller. The PPBS approach allowed McNamara to evaluate the programs of the military services through the use of systems analysis—comparing weapons and support systems with the objectives and missions they were intended to fulfill. The results of this evaluation were then used to determine which of these systems and projects would be supported by the secretary's budget requests—and which would be eliminated. In a bureaucratic system in which "dollars equal policy," there was no more effective tool to achieve central control than the budgetary whip wielded by McNamara. Thus, defense centralization had been achieved without creating the Prussian General Staff long feared in congressional lore: what had emerged instead was a kind of civilian general staff, the key members of which would vary from administration to administration, but whose institutional viewpoints would come to dominate Pentagon councils.[10]

This is not to say that this control was absolute under either Robert McNamara or his successors. Defense Department management would always be something of a contest involving OSD, the services, and (more often than not) Congress, with winners and losers varying from issue to issue. The rationalization of competing nuclear strategies, for example, was an issue that demanded McNamara's attention from the first days of his incumbency. Given his strong backing within the new administration (Kennedy had campaigned against the "massive retaliation" strategy of the Eisenhower-Nixon years in 1960) together with his domineering administrative style, McNamara was able to inaugurate "flexible response" as the centerpiece of American nuclear strategy. The services, each of which had its preferred plans for nuclear war–fighting that complemented organic missions and functions, now had to accept the role delineated for them in the Single Integrated Operations Plan (SIOP), which for the first time linked the national strategy to a coordinated employment doctrine based on known capabilities.[11]

But if the creation of the SIOP was a victory for the "pipe-smoking, tree-full-of-owls type of so-called professional defense intellectuals," as a former Air Force chief of staff termed the new OSD staff, then the case of the TFX (for tactical fighter, experimental) showed their limitations.[12] This case had its origins in the late 1950s, when both the Air Force and the Navy were experimenting with new designs for the next generation of fighter-bombers. The introduction of the swing-wing, pioneered by NASA, made it appear to the new administration that a single airframe could meet the varied needs of both services. Although the services had some experience with limited adaptation of common airframes (the F-4 Phantom, for example), neither the Air Force nor the Navy welcomed the idea of their premier future aircraft being a single plane designed and built by a contractor in thrall to OSD. Yet this was exactly what appeared to happen, when McNamara arrogated the contract decision to himself and then, against the recommendations of both services, awarded it to the team of General Dynamics–Grumman. The criteria for the award were vintage McNamara: the General Dynamics bid was higher than that of its competitor, Boeing, but cost-analysis was used to justify it as being more realistic. Further, General Dynamics offered a commonality factor between the Air Force and Navy models that was 20 percent higher than Boeing's and thus brought it closer to McNamara's guidance. Consequently, the TFX emerged as the showpiece for commonality and cost-effectiveness under the new regime at OSD. The Air Force, however reluctantly it approached the project, was gratified to find that General Dynamics, a favored Air Force contractor, had been chosen. This factor, plus the greater number of planes planned for the total Air Force "buy," placed that service in the driver's seat in administering the contract. Development of the plane went well: a prototype flew in 1964, and by 1968, the first production models of the Air Force version of the TFX, now christened the F-111A, entered combat service in Vietnam.[13]

The Navy, however, had no intention of being forced to accept a plane that was the product of its "shotgun marriage" to the Air Force. Consequently, it dragged out development of its "B" version of the F-111 by a combination of tactics that altered the airframe, degraded its handling performance, and also added weight to the point that the plane would not be suitable for carrier use. By 1967, the Navy had played for time so effectively that it was able to use the appearance of a new generation of Soviet fighters to argue that the program should be scrapped. In a stunning reversal, Grumman—although it had been the General Dynamics partner in representing the Navy side of F-111 development—now came forward with an allegedly "unsolicited proposal" for an alternative to its own aircraft. In November 1967, McNamara announced his intention to resign from OSD the following February in order to accept the presidency of the World Bank, thus setting the stage for the final act. In April 1968, with a procurement decision about to be made by the Senate Armed Services Committee, Navy officials delayed carrier trials of the F-111B prototype because of "small difficulties with the aircraft and bad weather." With McNamara gone and the public distracted by such tumultuous events as President Johnson's renunciation of his reelection candidacy and, several days later, the assassination of Martin Luther King, the Navy and its Senate allies were able to cancel the F-111B with a minimum of fuss. In its place, the Senate added the funds for development of the Grumman alternative, which eventually became better known as the F-14 Tomcat.[14]

The TFX episode is an instructive lesson in the interaction between central direction by civilian officials in OSD and the residual impact of service autonomy. Neither held absolute sway: OSD had unquestioned legal authority but the services had considerable discretion over the pace and extent of policy implementation. Moreover, both relied upon political alliances that extended throughout the government. Robert F. Coulam's analysis of the TFX decision noted also that the Navy feared centralization because civilian officials might not appreciate the unique requirements of sea power, but he added that, even beyond this, "commonality itself was a sufficient threat to arouse Navy antipathy." The reasons? Not only are the definition of requirements and the development of combat systems primary functions of the services, but the decisions throughout this process are made on the basis of military combat experience and service doctrine. Therefore, these are operational decisions intimately linked to basic service roles and missions, so much so that even the common procurement of minor items becomes a controversial de facto challenge to the technical expertise of the services, their respective jurisdictions, and even their relationship to their civilian masters. The TFX case is a succinct reminder of the limits to commonality in weapons procurement and an object lesson well worth remembering in appreciating the problem of joint command and control.[15]

While the OSD under Robert McNamara came to play an increasingly dominant if not unchallenged role in the defense bureaucracy, the pressure of events and the accumulation of technological choices combined to extend the influence of the new civilian elites into areas in which American military commanders were accustomed to exercising considerable operational sway. Although every major crisis since the end of the Second World War had been handled with the tight politico-military coordination necessitated by the implicit threat of nuclear escalation, the marriage of satellites, communications, and computers from the 1960s onward gave Washington-based decision makers an increasing ability to intervene in the conduct of crisis operations across great distances. During the 1962 Cuban missile crisis, for example, President Kennedy's personal direction of the naval task force sent to intercept Soviet freighters was considered to be unprecedented, but understandable in light of the stakes involved and the relative ease of communicating with a fleet that was operating in close proximity to home waters. Consequently, "government leaders had both the capability and the incentive to reach out beyond the traditional limits of their control."[16]

This extension of political control over operational autonomy was not accomplished, however, without overriding some deeply held feelings by professional military officers concerning the extent and propriety of civilian intervention. According to Adm. Thomas Moorer's recollection of the Pentagon command post during the missile crisis:

> Mr. McNamara came into the Navy Flag Plot, took a hurried look at the situation and demanded that a picket ship be moved to a different area. The Chief of Naval Operations objected, telling him the ship was in the correct area and, furthermore, that it could not get to the point where the Secretary wanted it in time to be effective. There was a heated argument—an uninformed, inexperienced civilian telling the Chief of Naval Operations how a picket ship should be deployed. [Later, Secretary McNamara] came into the Navy Operations Center and began to give commands at the level of a single destroyer. He insisted on talking to the captain of the destroyer by telephone because he was interested in the expression on the face of the Soviet merchant ship commander when the destroyer pulled along-side."[17]

But given the facts that the Cuban missile crisis was resolved on terms so distinctly favorable to the United States and that the chief of naval operations, Adm. George W. Anderson, who had clashed so bitterly with McNamara was shortly thereafter retired and shipped off to become ambassador to Portugal, it was not surprising that military commanders would eventually come to accept these interventions as a new set of obligations to which they, as professionals, would have to adjust as best they could.

The pace of those adjustments increased during the 1960s, as advances in communications technology made instantaneous global command and control a reality—and thereby enabled the secretary of defense to become as much a commander in fact as he already was in law. In a sense, these advances represented nothing more than the familiar example of military commanders seeking to extend their span of control; only now, with the fielding of the strategic nuclear triad of bombers, missiles, and submarines, the requirement was to produce an integrated system of sensors, command centers, and reliable communications that would ensure that the United States would never be subject to a "nuclear Pearl Harbor."[18] The extension of real-time control over the nation's strategic nuclear forces was matched in the conventional forces as well. Long-distance radio and telephone communications were enhanced by the addition of single-sideband wavelengths and microwave relays in the 1950s. By the 1960s, military communications were making use of the first satellite relays, a development that permitted the use of ultra-high frequency (UHF) links that carried greater quantities of message traffic more cheaply and reliably than ever before. Of equal significance was the wide expansion of computer applications for military purposes. This innovation spawned computer-to-computer networks joined by data links that were increasingly carried by satellites: Anthony G. Oettinger termed the process "compunications."[19]

These improvements, together with the increasingly demanding requirements for what has since become known as the "strategic connectivity" of the nation's nuclear and conventional forces, led to several initiatives. One was the establishment in 1960 of the Defense Communications Agency, which was placed under JCS control and given responsibility for long-distance military communications, especially those from the seat of government to the combatant commands around the world. Another was the issuance of DOD Directive S-5100.30 in October 1962, which was titled "Concept of Operations of the Worldwide Military Command and Control Systems" (WWMCCS, pronounced "wim-ex"). This directive set overall policies for the integration of the various command and control elements that were rapidly coming into being, stressing five essential system characteristics: survivability, flexibility, compatibility, standardization, and economy.[20] The general guidance of the directive was supplemented over the next two years with three others that attempted to translate overall objectives into specific criteria to be followed by the services in designing their command and control systems. However, WWMCCS evolution was not influenced as strongly by any of these directives as it was by the episodic availability of both technology and resources to meet individual requirements of the unified and specified commands. These requirements, however, were seldom viewed as related components of a single system, and given the diversity and institutional interests of the services, WWMCCS was "more a federation of self-contained sub-systems than an integrated set of capabilities."[21]

These diverse subsystems were apparently responsible for several well-publicized failures of command and control during the latter part of the 1960s. During the outbreak of hostilities between Israel and Egypt in June 1967, the USS *Liberty,* a naval reconnaissance ship operating under control of the European Command, was ordered by the JCS to move farther away from the coastlines of the belligerents. Five high-priority messages to that effect were sent to the *Liberty* by the various headquarters involved, but none arrived for more than thirteen hours—at which point the ship was the victim of an apparently mistaken attack by Israeli aircraft and patrol boats that killed thirty-four officers and men, wounded seventy-five more, and damaged the vessel so severely it was subsequently scrapped. In the words of the resulting congressional investigation, "The circumstances surrounding the misrouting, loss and delays of those messages constitute one of the most incredible failures of communications in the history of the Department of Defense."[22] Similar problems were blamed for the communications and procedural breakdowns that attended two subsequent incidents involving hostile actions by the North Koreans: the seizure of the USS *Pueblo* in January 1968 and the downing of a Navy EC-121 reconnaissance aircraft in April 1969. The congressional report stated that the heart of the problem was a DOD communications management structure that was "confused, overlapping and fragmented."[23]

The result, predictably, was a growth in the centralized, high-level management of WWMCCS. Under the direction of Deputy Secretary of Defense David Packard, twenty-seven command centers were equipped with standard Honeywell 6000 computers and common programs, which not only represented an economy of procurement but also allowed the rapid exchange of information among the command centers. An assistant secretary of defense for telecommunications was established within OSD, and, with the 1971 revision of DOD Directive S-5100.30, he was given primary staff responsibility for all WWMCCS-related systems. The directive also designated the JCS chairman as the official responsible for the operation of the WWMCCS, including the power to coordinate the WWMCCS requirements of the unified and specified commands. These changes accompanied another jump in the technical sophistication of long-range command and control: plexiglas boards and grease pencils were replaced by computer consoles, electronic displays, and other forms of executive aids. Those devices were nowhere more concentrated or advanced than in the Pentagon's National Military Command Center or the situation room in the west wing of the White House, where they were used to control crises in which the stakes were much lower and the distances far greater than those in the Cuban missile crisis. Even more pronounced was the propensity for the regular chain of command to be bypassed in the relay of orders from the seat of government to on-scene commanders. Secretary of Defense Donald Rumsfeld is said to have even used such a crisis communications link to speak directly with a naval coxswain operating an amphibious landing craft during the 1976 evacuation of American nationals from Lebanon. The practice became so commonplace it soon was enshrined in the regular military lexicon as "skip-echeloning."[24]

As efficient as the system undoubtedly became as the tool of skip-echeloning crisis managers, more questions arose toward the end of the 1970s when an acrimonious dispute over WWMCCS system management broke out between DOD and the General Accounting Office. The controversy centered around congressional criticism that DOD management of the WWMCCS was still divided among a number of agencies.[25] More troubling were persistent press reports about WWMCCS "breakdowns," the most notorious of which was a power outage during the Jonestown, Guyana, evacuation in November 1978, which apparently interrupted communications between Pentagon officials and their site control team for more than an hour. Other stories asserted that the problem of computer nonavailability was chronic. In a 1977 exercise, for example, it was reported that several of the major commands experienced failure rates of 70 to 80 percent. The Pentagon repeatedly denied these reports or maintained they were exaggerated, Gerald P. Dinneen (Carter administration assistant secretary of defense for what was then called communications, command, control, and intelligence) calling the criticism on one occasion "a bum rap."[26]

While some writers have expressed concern over what happens when the computer fails to work, other have pointed out the consequences of too much information inundating the high command. John Fialka reported that during a mobilization exercise in late 1980, one participant stated that "WWMCCS just fell flat on its ass." Although a computer malfunction locked Army planners out of the network for twelve hours, the main problem was information overload. Rather than focusing on basic strategic problems that required decisions, the command structure found itself nearly capsized by waves of computerized trivia. According to the Army chief of staff at the time, Gen. E. C. Meyer, "There is more information than we need. We must discipline ourselves to only get at the level of data needed to cause decisions to happen. . . . Clearly we are passing too much data back and forth. If there is one thing I want to charge the staff with, it is to decide what are the elemental bits of data we need to make the decisions."[27]

The problem, of course, was that the organizational preferences leading to centralization had also created a highly efficient electronic system that not only mirrored those preferences but magnified them. Only in the aftermath of the Iranian hostage disaster in 1980 (which had featured real-time communications with the White House) was there any reversal of the trend toward electronically enhanced centralization. The Reagan administration, as a deliberate act of policy, stressed a greater need to rely upon the judgment of the professional military and especially on that of the on-scene commander. There was a resulting increase in the degree of local tactical control noted during small-scale operations, such as those in the Gulf of Sidra in 1981 (when a Libyan jet fighter was shot down by Navy F-14s), as well as those involving considerably more military force, such as the 1983 invasion of Grenada. Lest it be thought, however, that good old autonomy had displaced bad new centralization or that strategic connectivity had been superseded, direct White House control over the October 1985 interception of the *Achille Lauro* hijackers provided dramatic proof to the contrary.[28] Defense centralization as well as its electronic extension into the domain of service and operational autonomy is likely to be a constant, differing only in degree from one set of political decision makers to the next. This basic fact of contemporary military life was perhaps best summed up in the anonymous comment of one much-decorated and high-ranking officer: "There may be some times when our crisis management communications system breaks down, but there aren't many. Most of the time, the damned thing works *too* well."

New Battlefield Technologies

While the pressures of autonomy and centralization provide their familiar historical counterpoints, an appreciation of the pivotal role of technology is critical in understanding the significance of contemporary command and control developments. Three battlefield technologies summarized here emerged in the 1970s and continue to play an important role in the strategic and tactical calculations of the services: electronic warfare (EW), combat intelligence and battlefield automation, and precision-guided munitions (PGM). Strictly speaking, none of these technologies is completely new. As was seen in chapters 3 and 4, EW initially came into play in World War I with the development of wireless radio and reached maturity during the "combat in the fourth dimension" that characterized World War II operations. Intelligence, of course, is one of the fundamental ingredients of warfare; however, it too acquired additional importance when an American intelligence establishment developed virtually from scratch during the war and acquired full institutional status with the creation of the Central Intelligence Agency in 1947. In its modern usage, the term PGM refers to the ability of a munition to be guided in its flight to the target by a human or robotic controller, thereby achieving great accuracy and pinpoint target destruction. Although World War II combat produced at least one example of the PGM in the form of the kamikaze suicide bomber, most Americans got their first exposure to these weapons in April 1986, when camera footage was released that showed "smart bombs" dropped from Air Force F-111s destroying Libyan transport aircraft during U.S. retaliatory strikes against the Quaddafi regime.

These technologies have been closely related throughout their development—to the point that, like triplets, it is not easy to discuss the one without bringing up the other two. The key to their closeness lies in the destructive capacity of the PGM, which was demonstrated by the appearance of unpowered but laser-guided bombs during the final phases of the air campaign over North Vietnam in 1972. Laser "designators" on an attacking aircraft simply pointed out and "illuminated" their targets. Receptors on the bomb homed in on this reflected energy and turned the steerable front fins so that the projectile followed a devastatingly precise trajectory. Because there are very few battlefield targets that could survive the impact of a five-hundred- or two-thousand-pound bomb delivered within twenty feet, it was not long before PGMs could be found throughout the inventories of all three services. The Navy, for example, was equipped not only with the Phoenix air-to-air missile but also with the Harpoon antiship missile, which had a range in excess of fifty miles. The Army added the TOW antitank missile, which could destroy the largest armored vehicles with a single hit at three thousand meters.[29]

The key to applying PGMs was to "acquire" targets at extended ranges and then guide the missiles toward their final destination. This requirement led directly to the need to field intelligence and electronic warfare systems that could identify and pinpoint those targets while denying enemy forces the same advantage. In this, the Air Force and the Navy had an advantage in the initial stages of development, since both services by this point had a long history of exploiting the electromagnetic spectrum to permit combat surveillance of their operational environments. That history was itself the product of the laws of physics that render the sea and sky susceptible to electronic penetration to a far greater extent than is the case in land warfare.

With the advent of effective guided ordnance systems, naval combat entered an era in which the radius of surface action of the carrier-centered task force now approached five hundred miles. Carriers routinely operated with aircraft that had specific EW missions, the two stalwarts being the A-6 Intruder/Prowler, developed for electronic countermeasures (ECM), and the E-2C Hawkeye, which carries a radar system for both early warning and air control. Carrier aircraft and surface ships carried sensor suites that helped maintain this umbrella of coverage, the force being tied together by the Naval Tactical Data System (NTDS), an electronic digital data link that allowed information to be shared by all components. All NTDS-equipped ships or aircraft thus became part of an integrated information network, each member drawing upon the data reported by any of the electronic, acoustic, or optical sensors possessed by the group, individually or collectively. Because of the need to organize this information, both to track incoming threats and to assign weapons to deal with them, "automated data processing has become a basic element of naval combat."[30]

The carrier task force had now become the focal point for what became known in the Navy as composite warfare doctrine, which stressed the "layered threat" to the battle group from coordinated attacks by enemy air, surface, and subsurface forces firing a variety of PGMs. It was around this concept that the Aegis cruisers were developed during the 1970s, the first of the class, the USS *Ticonderoga,* being commissioned in early 1983. Aegis cruisers are equipped with advanced sonar, the AN/SPY-1A omnidirectional radar, and an extremely sophisticated computer that will automatically and simultaneously track subsurface, surface, and airborne threats and assign appropriate weapons systems to deal with them. Indeed, the Aegis is so important to the composite warfare concept and to the Navy's vision of future ocean combat that it is discussed in some detail in the following chapter. It is sufficient to note here that, operating in conjunction with the carrier, its planes, and escorting vessels, Aegis enables the Navy to counter the "layered threat" with a "layered defense."[31]

The use by the Air Force of PGMs has already been mentioned, but it is important to note that its use of EW and electronic intelligence in general reflects a heritage that stems directly from its coming of age in World War II. Both its bombers and fighters depended for a large part of their effectiveness on the radar, ECM, and even ECCM (electronic counter-countermeasures) that marked aerial combat throughout that war, particularly the air campaigns over Germany. Technology that had been undreamed of months or even weeks before it was developed and rushed into combat—the "bending" of German radar beams, for example—became accepted as commonplace when American airmen joined their British counterparts from mid-1942 onward.[32] This "war in the ether" became an integral part of Air Force history, but many of these same lessons had to be relearned during the air war over North Vietnam from 1965 to 1972. While American policymakers dawdled during the escalation of U.S. involvement, the North Vietnamese received Russian help in constructing an air defense system that produced the heaviest concentrations of antiaircraft artillery (AAA) fire ever seen in warfare. Augmenting the AAA concentrations were belts of surface-to-air missiles (SAM), which grew in numbers and complexity until "during the eleven-day offensive in 1972 . . . more than 1,000 SAMs were fired with the resulting loss of 15 B-52s and three other aircraft."[33] Under these circumstances, every technique of EW was used: jamming, confusing enemy radars with chaff, or false signals, and employing specially equipped "Wild Weasel" aircraft that locked on to enemy radars and fired missiles that tracked the beam back to its source. Measure and countermeasure followed one another until the end of American involvement in the war. The Air Force maintained air superiority throughout and retained the ability to strike at any target approved by Washington-based decision makers.

The Air Force emerged from the war impressed by the vitality of Soviet-directed air defenses and the losses they could inflict upon attacking aircraft. By the end of the 1970s, the Air Force was taking the first deliveries of the aircraft that would be the linchpin in its efforts to turn airborne intelligence and electronic warfare into a decisive multiplier of combat power against the Soviets or their proxies. This system was the Boeing E-3A Sentry, better known by its acronym AWACS (for Airborne Warning and Control System), consisting of a Boeing 707 four-engine jet aircraft mounting, among other things, a Westinghouse APY-1 radar with a radius of coverage of over two hundred nautical miles. Sophisticated computer consoles on board the aircraft provide real-time displays (including air, sea, and surface targets) for the crew, as well as a link to ground controllers. The fact that the AWACS is an aerial system also gives it a true "look-down" capability, countering the ability of attacking aircraft to evade detection by slipping under ground-based radar "envelopes." The use of the AWACS in conjunction with first-line fighters such as the F-15 Eagle and F-16 Fighting Falcon, both of which carry advanced avionics of their own, has held out the promise of a qualitative edge to offset the expected Soviet advantage in numbers. Meanwhile, development continues on ever more sophisticated airborne PGMs for use against enemy air defenses, airfields, and other high-value point targets.[34]

The reaction of the U.S. Army to these battlefield technologies is an interesting study in the mechanics of organizational modernization, especially in relation to the development of military intelligence, first as a discipline and later as a combat support branch of the Regular Army.[35] The creation of a G-2, or intelligence, section for Pershing's staff in World War I was an insufficient precedent to ensure that the integration of intelligence and operations would be effective during either training or wartime service. For one thing, the G-3, or operations officer, tended to dominate the rest of the staff, and the G-3 office continued to attract the most capable and ambitious officers, who regarded themselves as the heart and soul of the command staff and earmarked for greater things. This tendency eventually caused problems the next time Americans found themselves at war. Gen. Omar Bradley's memoirs contain a passage recalling the situation at the start of World War II: "The American Army's long neglect of intelligence training was soon reflected by the ineptness of our initial undertakings. . . . In some stations the G-2 became the dumping ground for officers ill-suited for command. I recall how scrupulously I avoided the branding that came with an intelligence assignment in my own career. Had it not been for the uniquely qualified reservists who so capably filled many of our intelligence jobs throughout the war, the Army would have been pressed."[36]

The record of just how crucial intelligence was to Allied victory in the war was not revealed until the publication in 1974 of a remarkable little book, *The Ultra Secret*. Its author, F. W. Winterbotham, disclosed for the first time that British cryptographers had broken the German high command code early in the war, so that virtually all radio communications from Hitler to his generals, and from them to their subordinate commands, had reached British intelligence almost at the same time the messages arrived at their intended destinations. That revelation, as well as those that followed as historians and other scholars took up the trail, showed that many of the victories of celebrated Allied tactical commanders had depended directly on this precise intelligence. This hitherto unsuspected factor was to overturn, or at the very least, alter much of what had been written of the history of the war.[37]

Although the Army's top leaders were well aware of the extent of that contribution long before it became public, military intelligence continued to be looked on in many of the same ways as before. Army officers were still not systematically trained in the use of tactical intelligence; counterintelligence and signal intelligence units were strategic assets remote from the control or use of combat commanders; and there was no "corporate identity" for the discipline as a whole until the creation of the Military Intelligence branch in 1964. Traditionally, one of the best ways for a tactical commander to gain intelligence—assuming that he wanted it—had been to engage in active operations in the best Jominian tradition and observe enemy reactions and dispositions. Yet the generals picked to command combat units in Vietnam found that, although their training had prepared them well for the efficient employment of overwhelming tactical force backed by elaborate support mechanisms, their chief problem now consisted of locating a highly elusive enemy. Worse yet, this enemy was virtually indistinguishable from his surroundings and emerged to fight only when he enjoyed a decisive advantage. One general officer commented on these perplexities: "I knew that finding the enemy would be one of our toughest jobs. It occurred to me that perhaps we would be able to identify the guerrilla, a farmer by day and a fighter by night, by the dark circles under his eyes. As it turned out, our surveillance was just about that sophisticated."[38]

The response to these difficulties was primarily technological, as were so many other features of the American experience in Vietnam. To the traditional fields of signals intelligence (SIGINT), counterintelligence/human intelligence (HUMINT), and imagery intelligence (IMINT), an entirely new array of sensors was added. Battlefield radars, new types of reconnaissance aircraft, unattended ground sensors, and infrared photography all provided an increasingly technical base to the development of intelligence. Other airborne sensors sought out enemy radio signals and flashed the location of the sending unit back to artillery units on the ground. The HUMINT teams sought out the enemy infrastructure through computer-assisted pattern analysis and, in some cases, directed infantry units to the targets thus developed. Almost overnight, military intelligence had become an important part of the target acquisition process and an increasingly visible part of operational planning. Military intelligence units, however, were not as a regular thing particularly well integrated into tactical line units; rather, they tended to be held as strategic assets and detached to lower echelons for specific purposes. Although that procedure worked well enough in the highly irregular arrangements of a guerrilla campaign, it left open the question of the permanent place of military intelligence in the peacetime Army.[39]

The lessons from the guerrilla war in Vietnam had not been fully absorbed when the 1973 Arab-Israeli War provided an important object lesson on the impact of modern technology on more conventional battlefield outcomes. Adding to the significance of the observations made possible by the conflict was the fact that, more than in previous Middle East wars, there was a direct face-off between protagonists wielding top-of-the-line U.S. and Soviet equipment. This was also the first mid-intensity conflict in which electronic warfare had such demonstrable results on ground combat, as Soviet-supplied air defense radars operated with deadly effect against Israeli planes, limiting the ability of that arm to redress the traditional numerical superiority of Arab armies. Equally impressive were the results of a variety of PGMs that were able through either improved optical tracking or terminal guidance systems to exact a much higher "probability-of-hit" ratio than had ever been seen in modern combat. Largely for that reason, there was an unprecedented attrition of forces on both sides that for a time threatened the ability of both superpowers to effect timely resupply of their client states.[40]

The parallels with a putative war between the Warsaw Pact and NATO armies in Central Europe were obvious and, given the close-run nature of the Israeli victory, more than a little disturbing. The numerous debriefings, special studies, and analyses in the aftermath of the 1973 war resulted in a sweeping revision of the Army's tactical doctrine and the publication of a new field manual on operations, FM 100-5. This document, "the capstone of the Army's system of field manuals," was intended to open a new chapter in the way the Army went about the business of preparing for war and to put commanders at all echelons on notice that a new era had begun: "The war in the Middle East in 1973 might well portend the nature of modern battle. Arabs and Israelis were armed with the latest weapons, and the conflict approached a destructiveness once attributed only to nuclear weapons. . . . In clashes of massed armor such as the world has not witnessed for 30 years, both sides sustained devastating combat losses, *approaching 50 per cent in less than two weeks of combat.* These statistics are of serious import for U.S. Army commanders" (emphasis in the original).[41]

The manual went on to analyze the changes in land combat, the most significant of which was the tank. Because of improvements in armor, firepower, and maneuverability, "the capabilities of modern tanks have been extended to as far as the tanker can see. What he can see, he can hit. What he can hit, he can kill."[42] Interestingly, the manual also noted that antitank PGMs (the Sagger AT-3 for the Soviets and the TOW missile for the United States) had made the battlefield into a more deadly place than ever, with 90 percent hit probabilities being registered at ranges of up to three thousand meters. Both conventional and mechanized infantry formations were equipped with PGMs, giving them the ability to defeat armored targets at extended ranges. Artillery rounds using laser designators similarly made point destruction of individual targets possible by indirect fire. This acquisition of targets at such extended ranges was impossible without precise intelligence, so commanders were now told unequivocally of their new responsibilities for the effective management (through their G-2 officers) of the three major intelligence disciplines: human intelligence, signals intelligence, and imagery intelligence. Making the three work together would allow the commander to "see" his adversary on the battlefield, to pinpoint the location of his main forces, and to engage them at long ranges, thereby reducing the numbers that would survive to attack American front-line units. This concept became known as the modern application of the old doctrine of attrition: electronic warfare, battlefield intelligence, and PGMs were the new technological realities the doctrine sought to exploit.[43]

This would not be the first time, however, that doctrine and organization failed to mesh. An Intelligence Organization and Stationing Study completed in 1974, at the direction of Army Chief of Staff Gen. Creighton W. Abrams, was a virtual indictment of the system that prevailed at the time. It found that military intelligence units were not properly organized to support the tactical mission and, indeed, were in most cases beyond the control of tactical commanders because of their strategic responsibilities. Given the fact that many military intelligence units existed under functionally separate chains of command and reported to different national-level agencies, the study concluded that, at least in the tactical commands, "the integration of intelligence from all sources into a single product was largely a myth."[44]

These findings were the genesis of a new tactical structure known as the CEWI battalion (for Combat Electronic Warfare and Intelligence, pronounced "see-we"), first developed at Fort Hood, Texas, in 1976–77. Despite its uninspiring name—which, like the "Boy Named Sue," proved impossible to change later on—the CEWI battalion was a rather daring innovation that originally incorporated sections for ground surveillance (battlefield radars and ground sensors), electronic warfare, operations security, imagery intelligence, and interrogation. At its heart was the "all-source production section," whose sole mission was the integration and production of tactical intelligence. The existence of battlefield intelligence presupposed battlefield automation, because a U.S. Army Corps–level intelligence system would typically be expected to track some thirty-five thousand "movers, shooters, and emitters" (fire and maneuver elements) in an opposing Soviet force. As an article in *Army* magazine pointed out, "Automation must be the savior, for only through a carefully designed automation architecture can one hope to search, sense, sort, sift and select the right set of equipment or targets from the mass of 35,000. The human mind is a wonderful mechanism, but 35,000 is more than it can manage."[45] Statements like this seemed visionary at the time the first CEWI battalions were formed: after all, how did this new branch expect to join a field Army while carrying fragile, bulky, and troublesome computers? The answer became clearer now with the advent of briefcase or lap-top computers with fold-down LED displays and built-in printers: like it or not, the computer's place was every place. The CEWI battalion, therefore, became an accepted part of the tactical structure of the Army, even though the process of experimentation with its different sections and missions would provide continuing challenges for the new breed of tactical intelligence officers.

The battlefield technologies of electronic warfare, intelligence, and battlefield automation as well as precision-guided munitions thus generated responses in each of the services: Aegis for the Navy, AWACS for the Air Force, and CEWI for the Army. In some cases this meant far-reaching changes that went to the heart of service organizations, doctrines, and procedures. What, for example, were the implications for the tradition of independent command at sea of the Navy's growing reliance on extended command and control? How would the AWACS—the quintessential airborne system—affect the cardinal principle of air control exercised from the ground? How would the Air Force and the Army handle the delicate but critical matter of sharing intelligence at the theater level or, for that matter, at the tactical level? These questions were important, but they were possibly less significant than the fact that all of them stemmed directly from the efforts of each service to come to terms with fundamental changes affecting its particular warfare environment. They were part of the cycle of change and renewal that has been a constant of American military history.

Now, however, something else was about to change, and it involved the traditional role of the services as the primary repositories of operational expertise and arbiters of technological choice in the development of weapons systems. The choices customarily made in this arena, to the extent that they involved interservice conflict, were normally resolved somewhere in the defense budget process, as individual dollar amounts and programs were subjected to the inevitable scrutiny and trade-offs. But now command and control systems did not simply reflect individual program choices as the services exercised their usual stewardship in these matters. Instead, the very systems the services were procuring—usually in hopes of securing a tech-nological edge on an increasingly capable Soviet adversary—were raising larger problems. How would these systems work together in any environment involving more than one service? What higher authority would be in charge of referring and resolving likely conflicts? And in the event of tough decisions, who would make them, and who would pay the bill?

The discussion of the legacy of service autonomy that introduced this chapter allows a quick summation of its potential impact on command and control. The American political system, the norms of civilian control, and the reluctance of the Republic to centralize power in either civilian or military hands produced services that over time represented an effective balance be-tween those traditions and the requirements of military efficiency. Pluralism and the norms of autonomy were somewhat altered by the events of World War II and the defense unification struggle, but the services were left as the embodiments of their respective institutional wisdom, with primary respon-sibilities for the development and procurement of the tanks, warships, and airplanes that were the muscles and sinews of the combatant forces. This tradition of separatism, however, was less effective when it came to the problem of putting together command and control systems—the nervous system of those forces, whose composition transcended service lines. In a nutshell, the issue was this: the services had institutional expertise and pro-curement responsibility (that is, programs and money) for command and control systems, but only a secondary interest in systems that crossed service lines; the JCS had primary interest in joint command and control, but neither the responsibility nor the money for procurement of such systems; the unified and specified commands had all the responsibility for the nation's combatant forces (and arguably much of the expertise as well), but no money either to procure new items or to fine-tune what was in place; finally, OSD had none of the operational expertise and only incomplete control over procurement, but complete responsibility for anything that anyone did or failed to do anywhere in the system. The search for sound policy under these conditions is the focus of the remainder of this book.

6 Tactical Command and Control of American Armed Forces
Problems of Modernization

The decade of the 1970s can with some accuracy be thought of as the dawning of the modern era in command and control. The major influences in this process highlighted in the previous chapter—the advent of battleworthy precision-guided munitions, the higher plateaus reached by electronic warfare in close association with new methods for tactical intelligence, surveillance, and target acquisition, and the development of a global system for controlling U.S. strategic and tactical forces—all implied great changes for the combatant forces and the command structure itself. All too often, the pace of modernization appeared to outrun the capacity to understand what was taking place. The writings by experts in the new discipline of command and control often seemed to consist of a myriad of technical details unrelated to any larger context. Worse yet, their prose could be an impenetrable thicket of buzzwords, jargon, and obscure usages. Pondering this problem, Gerald P. Dinneen, appointed by the Carter administration as the first assistant secretary of defense for communications, command, control, and intelligence, said in a 1979 speech: "We go to Congress and tell them that our WWMCCS has got to have a BMEWS upgrade, and our fuzzy sevens have to be replaced by PAVE PAWS, we want to keep PARCS and DEW in operation, we have to harden the NEACP, and we have to improve our MEECN with more TACAMO and begin planning to replace AFSATCOM with Triple-S. And then we wonder why no one understands."[1]

If command and control defied easy explanation by an assistant secretary of defense, still less did it carry unambiguous implications for the military organizations that were in the forefront of the rush to modernization. For example, even as the Army brought smaller and more powerful computers into its tactical units, one of its leading professional journals quoted an unnamed NCO who damned the new machines as "a monster that could destroy us all."[2]

148

Another generalized concern as computers became steadily smaller and more ubiquitous throughout the armed forces was the issue of their survivability. Not only were the new techniques of electronic warfare an obvious threat to the functioning of computer networks, but the presence of nuclear and chemical munitions in superpower arsenals implied that the integrated battlefields of the future would be particularly inhospitable places for complex and delicate equipment of any kind. And if there was a reasonable presumption that computers might fail at the very moment when they were needed most, was it sensible to make the vast investments of time and money that would be required to achieve even a minimal level of tactical automation?[3]

These were not easy questions to answer, particularly when there were few intellectual reference points that could serve to guide the thinking about a discipline that was as old as warfare itself and as new as the information revolution of which it was a part. Inevitably, a few hardy souls ventured to offer conceptual models of the command and control process that were useful jumping-off points; the following section briefly surveys several of them. But this chapter is primarily about the effects of high-technology command and control systems on the services, all of which faced problems in coming to terms with the changes demanded by these new technologies. The Navy is presented here as an example of a technically sophisticated but essentially autonomous command and control structure. The Army and the Air Force, though separate services since 1947, have never been closer than in their recent efforts to determine how their respective forces can best achieve the synergy required in modern theater warfare. But even with the best of intentions, the problem of ground and air integration is difficult, especially so in relation to the Army's new doctrine of the "Airland Battle." Inevitably, the different organizational structures of these two services present some interesting conflicts in their approach to modernization, as well as in their understanding of what it is that command and control seeks to accomplish, especially when ground and air component commanders work together. If there is a single point to be made here, it is that organizational realities exert an influence on command and control development that is both pervasive and, in some cases, decisive. Or to put it another way, electrons cross service boundaries with far greater ease than is apparently the case with humans.

Some Conceptual Models of Command and Control

It is not difficult to find conceptual models of command and control systems. The field's trade journals, such as *Signal* and *Defense Electronics,* devote considerable space to articles on the technical parameters of communications or computer systems that are on contractor drawing boards or in some stage of the defense procurement process. Although these articles address the issue of how such systems fit into the organizations they are meant to serve, the larger question of command and control as a process is more elusive. An elegantly simple baseline for that discussion is provided by I. B. Holley, Jr., who conceives of *command* as a process by which the commander perceives and decides both the "ends and objectives to be sought," as well as the "means to achieve them." *Control* is basically everything else: "the communication of the commander's decision to his subordinate echelons, followed by continuous monitoring." Overall, command is to control what a pilot is to an autopilot.[4]

A number of other thoughtful analysts have also wrestled with the conceptual outlines of the command and control process. Three of them are presented here: John Boyd, a former Air Force colonel active both as a civilian consultant and as a staff analyst in the Office of the Secretary of Defense, and Dr. Joel S. Lawson, who retired from the Naval Electronic Systems Command, where he was known as "the guru of Navy C3I." Gen. Paul Gorman, now retired after a distinguished Army career, is not a command and control "modeler" in the same sense as Boyd and Lawson, but his writings have shed important light on key service differences with respect to command and control. These three perspectives suggest something of the universal aspects of command in the information age, balanced as always by fundamental organizational differences.

John Boyd's model of command and control is the simplest and probably the best known theoretical treatment of this problem. Figure 6.1 depicts what is essentially a four-step process of observation, orientation, decision, and action which he views as basic to the command and control process—so much so that he abbreviates it simply as the O-O-D-A link. Each of these steps is part of the tactical decision loop, the idea being that success in battle often depends on which commander can complete the loop faster. By "turning inside" his opponent's decision cycle—that is, thinking more quickly and coherently—a commander not only can react rapidly to events but can control them. He can then progressively complicate his opponent's decision cycle, so that eventually the adversary's command and control system collapses and his forces are defeated. Like the fighter pilot he once was, Boyd clearly envisions combat as a dogfight in which victory depends upon lightning speed, instinctive reflexes, and, most of all, positional advantage. Or, as Chuck Yeager might have put it, "Get on the other guy's tail and hammer him!"

The O-O-D-A link is intrinsic to the "maneuver warfare" school of thought espoused by Boyd, Pierre Sprey, Steven Canby, and William S. Lind. Their

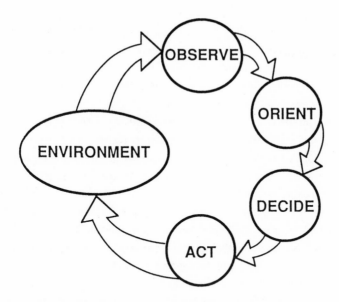

Figure 6.1   The Observation-Orientation-Decision-Action (O-O-D-A) Cycle
Source: Author (after John Boyd)

critique of the traditional American style of attrition warfare will be outlined later in this chapter, but it is enough to observe here that the essence of maneuver is the Jominian concentration of superior force against an opponent's vulnerable points so as to bring about his defeat. Boyd's decision loop provides a coherent conceptual underpinning for modern maneuver warfare theory because it focuses primarily on the enemy command structure and, more specifically, on the mind of the opposing commander: that, rather than the enemy force, should be the object of maneuver. Rather than engaging the main body of the opposing force, for example, an operation should bring pressure against vulnerable points in its control mechanisms (headquarters, command posts, communications nodes, and so on) in order to sow confusion, create panic, and bring about defeat.[5]

It follows that Boyd's approach to command and control is both ideological and conceptual, primarily resulting from a common mind-set between leaders and subordinates. This shared view, which is developed and reinforced by years of training, personal relationships, and common experiences, colors both perceptions of and reactions to combat situations. Rather than relying on a wealth of electronic communications, leaders control through the use of *Auftragstaktik* (literally, "mission-type orders"): previous conditioning and a specified but general objective are the primary means used to govern the actions of subordinates. Accordingly, Boyd's "organic design for command and control" relies heavily on "implicit orientation" rather than "explicit internal arrangements"—that is, on general leadership and direction rather than micromanagement aided by high-technology electronics. Therefore, command and control is itself a rather suspect concept, which ought largely to be replaced by "leadership and monitoring."[6]

Boyd's model was criticized in a 1983 Air Force study by Maj. George E. Orr, *Combat Operations C3I: Fundamentals and Interactions*. Orr's main contention is that Boyd's function blocks require a "substantial expansion and clarification" in order to provide an acceptable "combat operations process" model. Far more satisfactory from his point of view is the conceptual model offered by Joel S. Lawson, shown in figure 6.2. While noting the "clear relationship" between the Boyd and Lawson models (the final two steps, DECIDE and ACT, are identical in both), Orr argues that Lawson's five functional steps yield a clearer understanding of the role of intelligence in command decisions.[7] Lawson can be defended also on the grounds that his basic model fits in well with his larger concept of command and control. This view treats command and control, or simply "command control," as a *process* in which different components have different roles while operating as parts of a larger system. Lawson asserts that "to talk about a completely integrated C3I system is ridiculous. Its various parts must be pretty much self-contained and perform definable and separable functions so that we can change one 'module' without affecting all the others." It then follows that "the purpose of the command control process is to either maintain or change the equilibrium state of the environment, as determined by a higher authority."[8]

The four-step SENSE-COMPARE-DECIDE-ACT basic model thus becomes a component in the more detailed model of the process (also shown in figure 6.2), in which external data are processed, compared to the desired state, and acted upon with the help of decision aids. When one's own forces are added to the environment, they are then capable of influencing that environment: the results of those interactions in turn become part of the data chain. Lawson calls this his thermodynamic model of the command control process in order to connote its interaction with, and effect upon, the surrounding environment. Both that formulation and the basic model provide a convenient way of thinking about the command and control process. Thus the final box of figure 6.2 shows the Lawson model nested three deep and applied to a notional naval task force so as to illustrate both the functional differences applied to that process by each command level and their conceptual similarity.[9]

Both of these models are, after the nature of models, capable of illuminating some things while obscuring others, the test of effectiveness being largely

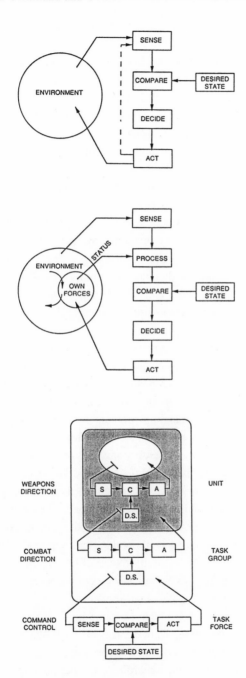

Figure 6.2   Lawson's Models of Command and Control

Source: AFCEA Press

in the eye of the beholder. The Boyd model is the simpler but carries inherent implications that go far beyond its immediate prescriptions for command and control. Lawson's model is slightly more complex, but provides a more precise sense of how environment affects various levels of the command and control process. One could as well select other models and expand the four or five discrete steps highlighted by Boyd and Lawson to a very large number, depending on the task being highlighted (in the same way that a military commander chooses large-, medium-, or small-scale maps on the basis of mission and geographical area). The most important thing about these models may be their essential similarity in viewing command as a *process,* one that is, moreover, repeated over and over in recognizable ways. In addition to the congruence of the individual analytical elements observed earlier, both models suggest a certain unanimity of both form and function that transcends service lines.

This tendency is particularly noteworthy in Lawson's work, and it is easy to see why his basic process and nested models have made an important contribution to the study of command and control. The models themselves are analytically crisp and, without being unduly busy, tend to clarify the essential processes that characterize many systems. At least part of this attractive simplicity may stem from the fact that most of Lawson's professional experience comes from his work as a naval command and control analyst. As he freely admits, naval command and control is at once the most technically sophisticated yet least demanding problem faced by any of the services. Defining a total of seventy-seven thousand warships, merchantmen, and military or civilian aircraft as the entire universe of items of potential naval interest, he notes that this is the "whole Navy world." In contrast, "the Army or the Marines face a very different problem because their targets are different. They have to deal with a much larger number of objects on a not-very-large battlefield because their 'objects' turn out to be individual radios or tanks or field pieces. In the Navy, these things are aggregated into one hull so that we have a smaller number of discrete objects with which to deal. Therefore, understanding and solving the Navy's command-control problem may be much easier than solving the other Services'."[10]

Gen. Paul Gorman made much the same point during a conference on defense reform hosted by the United States Military Academy in 1982. Addressing the subject of interservice differences in military operations, he put forward the idea of "movable subordinate entities"—ships, planes, tanks, battalions, or similar groupings of personnel and matériel—which would be commanded by a three-star general or admiral from the several services. The Navy vice admiral would logically expect to command 10 to 100 ships, planes, and submarines in a typical carrier battle group at any given time. His Air Force counterpart, a three-star wing commander, however, would have a command and control problem at the next order of magnitude, typically 100 to 1,000 aircraft of all types, in addition to ground reporting and controlling stations. But the Marine and Army Corps commanders would have the most complex problem of all: their squads, platoons, companies, battalions, and higher formations typically entail 1,000 to 100,000 *or more* movable subordinate entities:

> These numbers are tyrannical, but probably les so than the communications systems and command mechanisms that would be available to each. The navy commander would have the most assured communications, the army commander the least. The navy commander would be dealing on the average with relatively high-ranking officers, and the average rank of subordinate leaders . . . would decline as one proceeded from navy to air force to marines to army. The navy commander's information regarding his subordinates would be quite precise and real-time, that of the army leader vague and slow-arriving. The navy commander would have . . . the greatest tactical flexibility, the army commander the least. The navy command principle would be centralization, while that of the army commander would perforce be decentralization. The air force would be much closer to the navy in all these respects, the marines closer to the army.[11]

Figure 6.3 highlights these points by Gorman. Although it is not a conceptual model per se, it can be argued that his observation is of critical importance in understanding the interservice differences that form the settings in which command and control systems exist.

The initial chapters of this book examined the respective strategic paradigms underlying service approaches to the problem of command in war. Gorman's view is a powerful reminder that those verities and the operational realities giving rise to them continue to be important. This is a valuable perspective since it suggests something of the context in which the universal and the particular meet and define one another. Another element of that context not mentioned by Gorman is that of the different service operating environments. In exactly the same sense that the land and sea presented dissimilar challenges to both strategic connectivity and tactical command in the nineteenth century, today these same operational mediums (to which the complicating factor of the aerospace environment has also been added) present very different opportunities and obstacles to command and control. Consider, for example, the relative transparency of the air, sea, and space en-

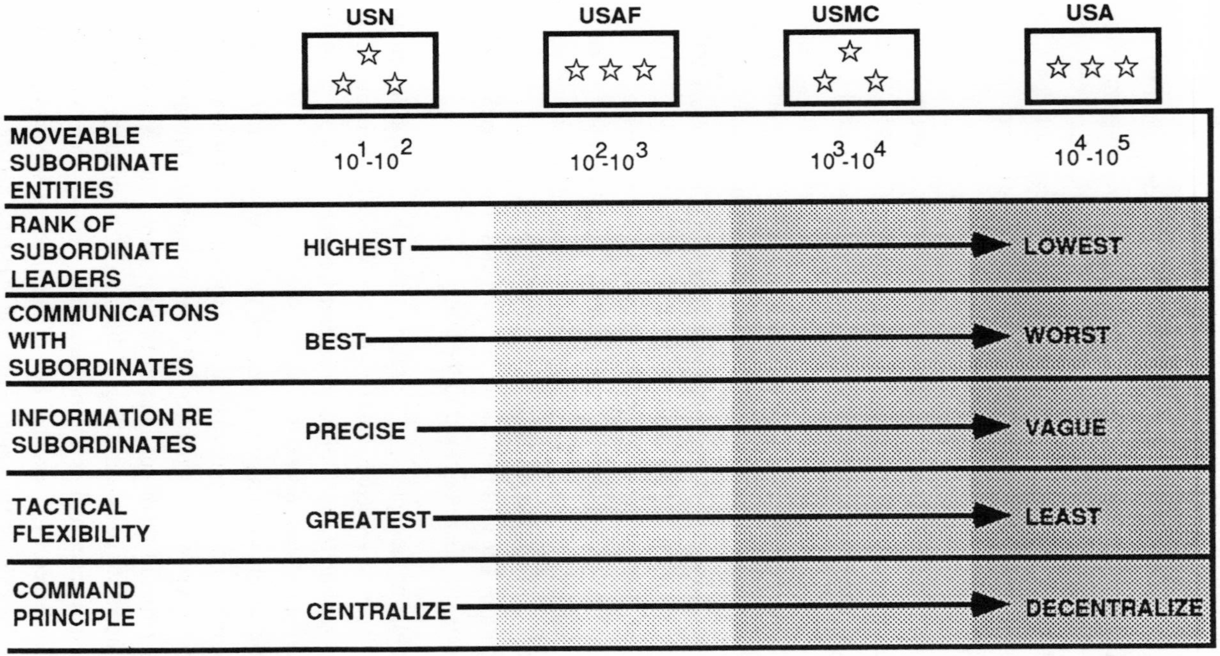

	USN	USAF	USMC	USA
MOVEABLE SUBORDINATE ENTITIES	$10^1 - 10^2$	$10^2 - 10^3$	$10^3 - 10^4$	$10^4 - 10^5$
RANK OF SUBORDINATE LEADERS	HIGHEST			LOWEST
COMMUNICATONS WITH SUBORDINATES	BEST			WORST
INFORMATION RE SUBORDINATES	PRECISE			VAGUE
TACTICAL FLEXIBILITY	GREATEST			LEAST
COMMAND PRINCIPLE	CENTRALIZE			DECENTRALIZE

Figure 6.3 Service Organizational Differences: Relevance to Command and Control

Source: Author (after Gen. Paul Gorman)

vironments which renders them vulnerable to penetration by optical, electronic, and acoustic sensors and communications systems. Compare those environments with that of the earth and add the additional limitations on long-range surveillance imposed by surface terrain features: jungles, forests, mountain ranges, buildings, and cities, among other things. It becomes apparent not only that land warfare encompasses far more "moveable subordinate entities" than either air or sea combat but that the laws of physics make this operational environment far more difficult to monitor than the others.

The heart of modern command and control is therefore something of a paradox: no matter what far-reaching changes have been brought about by science and technology, differing service approaches persist and indeed flourish in the modern era. Although the strong arms of tradition and history that reinforce the norms of service autonomy can never be dismissed, it is interesting that many of these differences are also the product of basic environmental dissimilarities. As will be shown in this and the following chapter, differences in the number and character of forces, as well as their respective operational environments, help account for the persistence of interservice command and control problems in the face of some extraordinarily integrative technologies.

Global Reach: An Overview of Navy Command and Control

In a 1979 article, Rear Adm. Frederick C. Johnson summarized the approach of his service to command and control as follows: "The naval commander through the ages has sought to attain target detection at the maximum practicable range in order to provide sufficient distance and time for decision-making and preliminary actions, and . . . to provide weapons systems with the quality and quantity of data needed to acquire the target for timely engagement and kill. The compression of time, the vastness of the aerospace atmosphere above and expanding operational volume below the surface of the sea necessitates that this range now be extended to dimensions which are beyond the wildest dreams of even the most farsighted of our predecessors."[12]

The time compression and range extension of which the admiral wrote are themselves functions of the marriage of the precision-guided munitions and supersonic airframes previously outlined. Coming to terms with these fast-paced changes in naval warfare has increasingly meant coming to grips with the computer in shore-based command centers, in combat information centers aboard ships at sea, and even as integral parts of individual weapons systems. From the mid-1950s onward, the Navy correctly considered these adaptations critical to its combat effectiveness and tactical survival; ships and aircraft, for example, were being controlled through digital data flows after the Naval Tactical Data System (NTDS) became operational in the early 1960s. It is thus startling to realize that, almost unnoticed, the Navy has acquired a generation of experience in the technological modernization of its command and control systems.

The results of that experience are helpful in gaining the perspective of a more "mature" view of a process the Army and Air Force are contending with as well. And, as has so often occurred in the past, the modernization strategies of the services offer a useful contrast for study. The Army has concentrated its efforts on the development of a tactical architecture from the ground up, while the Navy experience stresses the importance of a top-down approach. The Army has a discernible tendency toward the creation of theater-specific command and control networks, even as the Navy remains firmly wedded to the concept of global systems that can reach the fleet upon whatever seas it is deployed at the moment. Naturally, this reflects basic differences in the operational character of the services as well as in their specific missions.

Since World War II, the Navy has again laid claim to the strategic mission it occupied throughout the nineteenth and early part of the twentieth centuries. Despite its fears that its traditional role would be largely taken over by the Air Force in the postwar reorganization, the nuclear era dealt the Navy a surprisingly strong hand. For one thing, nuclear weapons were gradually introduced into the fleet not only as munitions to be delivered by carrier jets but as warheads for use in submarine warfare, antisubmarine warfare, and air defense. This made the carrier strike force into a "nuclear strike force" with a role in the deterrence mission, as well as a "mobile air force for regional conventional wars" and a diplomatic signaling device providing a "visible demonstration of national interests."[13] The deployment of ballistic missile submarines in the 1960s meant the gradual eclipse of a primary carrier role in strategic nuclear bombardment, even as it guaranteed a permanent Navy place in the nuclear triad. The diplomacy of the nuclear era, however, made naval forces into a favored instrument both of power projection and of crisis management. The standard study of this use of American armed forces, *Force without War* by Blechman and Kaplan, notes the utility of moving fleets to a crisis area. By confining a carrier battle group's presence to international waters and its activities to innocuous patrols, a leader can demonstrate the American potential for power and support "coercive diplomacy"—often without firing a shot. The decision by the Reagan administration in 1987 to reflag Kuwaiti oil tankers and place a large naval task force on escort duty in the Persian Gulf was consistent with this use of sea power.[14] As events there and in the Mediterranean have demonstrated throughout the 1980s, these front-line forces are also capable of carrying out or supporting actual combat missions in response to fast-breaking changes in the international situation.

All these missions necessitated the development of a global approach to naval command and control, despite the clear preference of that service for decentralized operations. The Navy has attempted to bridge the gap between the requirements of an efficient global command network and the demands of tactical autonomy by embracing the concept of modularity outlined above. The idea is very close to the federalist model of organization the Navy embraced on so many occasions in its history. The concept thus represents a basic naval philosophy, as well as a preference for a command and control system that, insofar as possible, will be "all things to all men," spanning the complete range of activities and operations that naval units worldwide might be engaged in. This ideal is often attenuated by reality, however, for reasons that are partly technical, partly financial, and partly organizational. The modular units that compose naval command and control perform functions that vary greatly depending on the tactical environment, although all of them will, as Lawson puts it, SENSE, PROCESS, COMPARE, DECIDE, and ACT. A global system takes account of this diversity by permitting component systems to be interdependent, but not necessarily congruent.[15]

This point is perhaps more easily understood in its organizational context. The Navy is deployed in four fleets that traverse the world's great oceans— itself a powerful factor encouraging diversity—and is composed of surface forces (ships), subsurface forces (submarines), and air forces (carrier as well as land-based aircraft). The marriage of precision ordnance and electronic fire control has affected all these platforms: guided missiles now constitute both their principal offensive weapons and the principal tactical threats they are meant to counter. These systems come in a variety of forms: antiship missiles, surface-to-air missiles (SAMs), air-to-surface missiles, and even antisubmarine rockets or missiles. Submarines themselves are capable of launching maneuverable torpedoes, SAMs, or antiship cruise missiles such as the Tomahawk.[16]

Each of these naval force components controls and is controlled by systems of communications that are peculiar to that platform. Ships, for example, carry their own complements of sensors and communications gear, primarily radio and radar, that must be linked to the larger task force. Complicating the matter is the fact that most task forces are built around aircraft carriers that must not only coordinate ship movements but control air operations as well. No single system of communications could easily accommodate such a melange of different frequencies and technical characteristics, especially when different task force elements must be added or detached to meet changing mission requirements—hence the need for interactive communications modules.

One of the other characteristics of the naval command and control system is its increasing ability to expand the range of tactical engagements at sea. As noted in chapter 5, the organic assets of the carrier battle group (the E2C Hawkeye advanced early warning aircraft and the Aegis class cruiser, among others) give it an effective surveillance umbrella of approximately five hundred miles. Shore-based command and control links can presently extend that range in some geographical areas, and even those capabilities are being improved to the point that it will be possible by the 1990s for battle groups to conduct tactical reconnaissance over entire oceans.[17] The major technological factors speeding the development of ocean area tactical integration are advanced satellite systems, including NAVSTAR (global precision positioning), FLTSATCOM (high-speed data links), and reconnaissance platforms using high-resolution radar and infrared scanning.[18] The use of satellites for sensing and data relay has been accompanied by the development of more capable earth-based sensors: SURTASS (a large, towed-array sonar system), improved and rapidly deployable sonobuoys, as well as the Air Force AWACS, with its great utility for support of maritime missions. With the data from these sensors, the instantaneous relay of information from high-speed communications links, and advanced signal processing of the next generation of supercomputers, ocean area tactical integration is a near-term possibility. And what will be the payoff for gathering and analyzing all this data? "A cruise missile utilizing this type of ocean area targeting grid can have an effective range of two or three thousand miles without any basic changes in engine or airframe technology."[19]

Meanwhile, the expansion of tactical operating ranges is an everyday problem in today's Navy. To understand this, one must appreciate how much modern naval forces differ from earlier ones. A comparative study published in 1983 showed that the weight of offensive airborne firepower has remained much the same in carrier task forces from World War II to the present. But, because of the great improvements in munitions, ships, and aircraft over the last forty years, the same firepower can be delivered more effectively using only *10 percent* of the ships and aircraft that typically operated in World War II carrier task forces.[20] Because there are fewer of these ships, and because each represents a heavy investment of dollars and capabilities, they are naturally high-priority targets for any opposing force.

Because of the increased lethality of precision-guided munitions, as well as the ever-present threat of nuclear weapons, the ships of the task force typically operate as far apart as possible. Escort vessels for the carrier will have primary antiair warfare (AAW) or antisubmarine warfare (ASW) functions, but will also act as command and control relay points to maintain the 300-to-500-mile umbrella surrounding the carrier. A two-carrier task force, such as that which operated against the Libyans in the Gulf of Sidra in April 1986, would typically cover some 56,000 square miles. If such an area were superimposed upon a map of the eastern United States, it would show a task force centered around Washington with carriers deployed in Richmond, Virginia, and Baltimore, Maryland, AAW ships spread from Norfolk, Virginia, to Trenton, New Jersey, and airborne interceptors operating from Boston, Massachusetts, to Charleston, South Carolina. It would be capable of mounting air strikes as far away as Chicago, Illinois, Indianapolis, Indiana, St. Louis, Missouri, and Atlanta, Georgia.[21]

These ranges obviously present a challenge for command and control systems within the fleet. Moreover, the threats they must contend with have increased with the expansion of the Soviet navy from a coastal defense force into a deep-water fleet whose surface and subsurface combatants are capable of interdicting American sea lines of communication. The huge (14,000 tons) OSCAR submarine, for example, carries twenty-four nuclear-capable SS-N-19 antiship cruise missiles, each with a range of over three hundred miles. Even more widely known are the three Kiev-class aircraft carriers added to the fleet since 1975 (a fourth aircraft carrier of a new design is under construction). The sea-going combatants are supported by long-range naval aviation, whose capabilities are being augmented by the continuing production run of the TU-22 Backfire bomber. Its estimated speed and range (Mach 2.3 and 3,500-mile combat radius) make it a direct threat to U.S. surface ships almost anywhere in the world.[22]

A naval confrontation, therefore, between the United States and the Soviet Union or some of its better-equipped client states would likely involve a barrage of Russian missiles fired from aircraft, surface ships, and submarines, all coordinated to arrive at the same time from many directions so as to overwhelm any possible defense.[23] To counter such attacks, the fleet relies first upon its early warning aircraft, which send fighters to engage the attacking aircraft, ships, or submarines before they can launch their missiles. At the fleet's perimeter, any missiles that are launched by the survivors are detected by shipboard radars of the escort vessels, who then engage them with antiaircraft missiles. Final point defense against any remaining "leakers" (that is, penetrating aircraft) is provided by the defensive systems aboard each ship—chaff, decoys, and fast-firing Phalanx guns, meant either to deceive the missile or to shoot it down.[24]

Because of the speed at which these missiles close with their targets, naval command and control is directed at buying time for the officer in tactical command to identify specific threats and take appropriate action. It does this in several ways. First, it extends the range of the sensor suites available to tactical commanders at sea. Since there are limits to the range of sensors organic to the fleet, extending them has increasingly meant having real-time access to national-level systems and shore-based command and information centers. This linkage takes place largely through Fleet Command Centers which represent the land-based side of naval command and control and are also the focal points for the transmission of up-to-date intelligence to the fleet, gleaned from both national systems and Navy sensors. The system is an extension of the Navy's experiences in World War II, in which (as recent scholarship has demonstrated) shore stations were the key elements in the production of the naval intelligence that produced victories such as that at Midway. [25]

The second major function of the naval command and control system is to improve the ranges and data-handling capabilities of the on-board systems used by commanders at sea to make operational decisions. Highlighting the potential deadliness of naval combat have been the Navy's recent experiences in the Persian Gulf—the accidental attack on the USS *Stark* (struck by an Iraqi-fired Exocet missile in May 1987) and the tragic downing of the Iranian airbus by the USS *Vincennes* in July 1988. The heavy investment in the Aegis-class cruisers, of which the *Vincennes* is one, is itself an excellent demonstration of how seriously the Navy regards the threat from highly accurate, fast-moving missiles. Its experience with digital data and its global mission have made imperative the improvement of its principal fleet command and control system, both to counter Soviet-style missile barrages and to deal with the proliferation of similar weapons in the third world. Antiair warfare (AAW) was a particular problem for the Navy prior to the arrival of Aegis, not only because of the growing Soviet threat, but also because older AAW platforms—primarily the Leahy-class cruisers—could track only four radar targets at once. Other ships had even less capacity, so that a small number of enemy missiles could saturate the system. Making the matter more urgent after 1982 was the object lesson of the British experience in the Falkland Islands war, which demonstrated that even a relatively unsophisticated opponent could produce devastating results with far fewer missiles than the Soviets would be expected to launch. [26] Worse yet, the Naval Tactical Data System (NTDS), largely the offspring of first-generation data-processing equipment, now faced a problem for which its original design had few answers. How, for example, would separate NTDS modules and their human controllers handle the multi-media threat that resulted when a submarine target fired an airborne missile against a surface ship? There clearly would be no time for manually assisted methods by NTDS operators in the event that known Soviet capabilities materialized in a wartime scenario of coordinated missile and torpedo barrages.[27]

Although it will not solve all the Navy's data-handling problems, the Aegis concept is usually described as a quantum leap from anything that went before. Billed as a cruiser, the ship nevertheless has a hull designed largely along the lines of the Spruance-class destroyer. Its principal feature is the large, AN/SPY-1A phased-array radar that can search and track hundreds of air and surface targets. Also equipped with a state-of-the-art sonar suite, the Aegis is for the Navy what the AWACS is for the Air Force: an all-seeing eye. But while the sole function of the AWACS is to acquire and transmit data to ground control stations, Aegis is an independent weapons platform as well. Computers link the radar to the ship's weapons systems, automatically identifying and tracking incoming targets. The system has another feature whose significance should not be overlooked: if set in the automatic special mode, the computer can select and fire the appropriate weapon from the ship's arsenal—SM-2 antiaircraft missiles, antisubmarine rockets and torpedoes, Harpoon antiship missiles, five-inch guns, or the Phalanx point defense gun.[28]

In the aftermath of the Iranian airliner shoot-down in July 1988 (when *Vincennes* mistook an A-300 airbus for a much smaller F-14), it was inevitable that questions about Aegis would be raised: Were its capabilities all that had been promised in light of the billion dollars invested in each ship? If they were, had too much control been taken away from human beings and given to the computer? There were allegations almost immediately following the incident that operational tests of the Aegis system had been unrealistic and had not confirmed the system's effectiveness.[29] Those charges contradicted a 1985 report by Vice Adm. H. C. Mustin, who, as commander of the Second Fleet, tested the ships in a series of exercises designed to replicate Soviet doctrine and capabilities. His conclusion: "*Aegis* has brought clarity to the air battle. . . . the importance of our new ability to put the surface-to-air-missile ships in the outer defense zone, where they can shoot approaching bombers *before* they reach missile launch range, cannot be overstated. . . . with *Aegis,* we can win the air battle against all comers. Without *Aegis,* we cannot win."[30] In the aftermath of the airbus tragedy, the chief of naval operations, Adm. Carlisle H. Trost, argued that operational testing of the Aegis system amounted to a "moral imperative" that the Navy had lived up to by making "exhaustive tests" involving some thirty thousand hours of operational evaluation and the expenditure of more than $900 million. He concluded, "Seldom has a system received this level of confirmation prior to its introduction to the fleet."[31]

The public report that followed the formal military investigation of the *Vincennes* incident provided additional evidence of both the capabilities of the Aegis system and its limitations. On the one hand, "the AEGIS Combat System's performance was excellent—it functioned as designed." On the other, even such a sophisticated system could not offset the effects on the crew of time compression (three minutes and forty seconds from the time of first sighting until the instant the captain had to make the decision to launch missiles), confusion, fear (the ship had just repelled an attack by Iranian gunboats), and even the ghost of the USS *Stark* tragedy the year before. "The fog of war and those human elements which affect each individual differently . . . are factors which must be considered."[32] Although the investigation revealed the need for some refinements in the "human engineering" of the Aegis battle display system, Adm. William Crowe, chairman of the Joint Chiefs of Staff, summed up the lessons learned from the system's first exposure to combat: "AEGIS' major advantages are the extended range of its sensors, its fast reaction time, the capacity to track many targets at once, its ability to send this information automatically to other units, and its data display. . . . Operating close-in to a land-based airfield, however, these advantages can be severely eroded. That problem is not the fault of the system but geography."[33]

Because of their metaphysical character, questions about the control exercised by the computer versus "the man in the loop" could not be resolved by the easy reply that the system had worked as designed. This aspect of the Iranian airbus tragedy highlights the third basic concern of naval command and control: increasing the ability of naval commanders and their staffs to deal with a data stream that is rapidly becoming a torrent. Until recently, the shore-based Fleet Command Center was the lowest level at which operational and intelligence data from a wide variety of sources could be manipulated and "fused." Now, however, an extension of this system has been deployed in Navy flagships. Known as the Tactical Flag Command Center (TFCC), these centers are compact versions (four hundred square feet or less) of their counterparts ashore, providing task force and battle group commanders at sea with an organic capability to collect, process, analyze, display, and disseminate tactical data. Current plans call for TFCCs to be placed aboard the Navy's principal surface combatants, the latest versions featuring state-of-the-art color monitors, large-screen video displays, and automatic status boards. All of this equipment is intended to give the commander at sea a "God's-eye view" of the tactical situation which would have seemed unimaginable only a decade ago.[34]

The TFCC concept originally grew out of the same dissatisfaction with the NTDS that gave rise to Aegis. The great digital data increases that resulted from the introduction of new modular information systems for airborne early warning and antisubmarine warfare in the late 1960s and early 1970s imposed additional burdens on control centers. Hard-pressed to keep up with the torrential data flows, fleet commanders reacted to local needs as best they could, usually by introducing program changes in NTDS subsystems. As one Navy study noted, this practice "inevitably led to differences in performance capabilities of identical ship classes as well as incompatibilities between . . . programs that adversely affected interoperability when units from one fleet joined another."[35]

The TFCC was thus seen as an approach that would help standardize, consolidate, and decentralize naval command and control at sea. The fitting together of various modules of otherwise autonomous data systems also represented a recognition by the Navy that, though responsibilities of command at sea may not have changed, certain of its methods had been transformed.[36] Even more significant is the fact that the TFCC represents a technological response to the realization that the Navy's Composite Warfare Concept stresses the unity of combat at sea, regardless of the specific medium from which threats may be generated. This is a powerful idea in a service whose three major constituent communities—surface warfare officers, aviators, and submariners—have tended to have a strong sense of their individual identities.

In each of the three aspects discussed here—the extension of shore-based information systems, the deployment of advanced command and control systems at sea, and the parallel improvement of sea-going command post technology—naval command and control can be seen as a global system that has retained its "macro" orientation while permitting modernization to proceed from the strategic to the tactical level. In doing this efficiently, Navy planners have been aided considerably by their modular approach to command and control, permitting the gradual development of systems geared to the dynamics of controlling general classes of naval platforms. Because most of these platforms are deployed around carrier-centered battle groups and task forces, and because the Navy seems to have confined itself to a realistic appraisal of technical capabilities, the job of designing interoperable command and control systems has been easier. The Navy also appears to have benefited from its determination to make these modernization efforts fit into its existing structure of command. That the Navy has dealt resolutely with known quantities, from the microprocessor gateway to required shipboard spaces, suggests a capability for organizational and engineering discipline that has led to a successful modernization strategy.

This is not to say there are not problems, the most important of which may be the questions of doctrine and leadership posed by more modern, and therefore more intrusive, systems of command and control. In a 1983 lecture to the students of the Naval Postgraduate School and the Naval War College, Dr. Eberhardt Rechtin neatly summarized this dilemma:

> The difficulty of designing a naval communications architecture is compounded by the Navy's own traditions of command, an important element of which is the meaning of "special trust and confidence." Every naval officer's commission includes those words, and they have come to mean to him that he is trusted to carry out missions with the minimum possible instruction, i.e., the *less* communication from above, the better. The tradition is reinforced by the almost absolute authority vested in ships' captains at sea, an authority originally granted in a time of communications delays of days to months. Commanders at every level, however, insist on knowing what is going on within their commands, i.e., the *more* communications to and from below, the better.[37]

Increased connectivity to shore-based command and control and the improved local processing capabilities represented by the TFCC clearly are refinements of the use of naval forces in potential crisis management scenarios. There is a similar benefit in wartime scenarios when the fleet could operate in a "receive only" mode of radio silence without losing sight of the tactical situation. But as Rechtin's words imply, it is not at all clear whether these improved capabilities will be used to grant greater freedom of action to the embarked commander or will result in a further erosion of tactical autonomy.

Perhaps the most troubling questions raised by this new dimension of tactical-strategic connectivity are those asking if constant access to an elaborate communications apparatus is the best way to prepare naval officers for the shock of transition to combat. Few who raise such questions are prepared to argue that the system is so destructive of martial virtue as to require its abandonment. But critics are probably correct in pointing out that in the event of general hostilities, communications terminals and relay points would be among the first targets hit by an aggressive adversary. Should electronic warfare or physical attack result in a complete or partial disruption of the system—a tactic frequently discussed in the literature as "Command-Control-Communications Countermeasures"—the burden on the shoulders of naval commanders would be heavy. A retired Navy captain expressed the dilemma well in pointing out that under such conditions, "the commander at sea will be much more on his own than he is now. Although the present close linkage between the shore and sea commanders may have certain advantages, it does not do anything to develop the exercise of independent judgment in our naval commanders—a quality they will have to use in wartime."[38]

Although there is no simple answer to this problem, training and technology suggest two possible pathways. The classic Navy response to the problem of attenuated control in the age of sail was to select and train sea captains who had the ability to reach sound independent decisions, a quality that does not appear to have vanished from the modern naval officer corps. Developing and testing personal qualities, however, is one of the main reasons training under simulated combat conditions is such a vital part of peacetime readiness: there simply is no other way to prepare for the eventuality of the officer's having to decide, "What do you do when communications are knocked out?" Partial technological solutions to the problem, however, are of acute concern to planners. Indeed, two of the naval command and control system's future objectives are to guarantee its survivability "through redundancy, hardness, dispersion, or reconstitution of the system," and to provide "an assured flow of minimum essential command, operational, intelligence, surveillance, environmental, and logistics data to the tactical commander." Details of how that may be accomplished are not within the scope of this book nor are they in the public domain: but the stakes are so high that there appears to be little doubt that survivability is the next evolutionary step in the development of naval command and control.[39]

The final point to be made here is something of a paradox. On the one hand, the Navy's system is effective precisely because it is a global entity, in which the critical constituencies have been brought to heel and basic decisions reached to ensure the efficiency of the organization as a whole. In this respect, the Navy is indeed a unified service, all of whose elements are designed to be interoperable to the extent required by the full range of maritime operations. Rechtin even elevates this concept to the highest plane of naval thought: "What might Mahan say today? I believe he would be one of the first to recognize that the new technologies of command make possible coordinated operations over vast distances. He would recognize his concentration of force now means coordination and integration of force, not necessarily close proximity, especially in the age of nuclear weapons. He would, as before, discount small, isolated independent forces as a foundation of strategy. He would . . . recognize as in the tradition of his great fleet . . . the concept of a battle group tied together by an integrated information network."[40]

On the other hand, this level of integration, so powerful when applied to the Navy's internal organization, can become almost a closed universe when other services are concerned. Navy planners, for understandable reasons, must look primarily to the needs of their own service when faced with fiscal constraints. Command and control dollars, which tend to be harder to come by than some others, have to be carefully husbanded just to meet the emerging requirements. Small wonder, then, that the interoperability of command and control systems for joint or interservice use comes off as a secondary set of priorities. As a frustrated Pentagon action officer put it, "When the Navy is talking about joint command and control, they usually mean interoperability between themselves and the Marine Corps!"

Command, Control, and the Airland Battle

In turning from an examination of Navy command and control to that of the Army and the Air Force, the relevance of General Gorman's observations concerning their underlying differences is particularly striking. From a coherent global system with a comparatively small number of movable subordinate entities, one enters a realm in which tens of thousands of such entities must be controlled, manipulated, and tied together. Making the matter more difficult is the fact that the physical environment of land warfare, including its adjacent airspace, presents its own challenges for command and control. The physical problems of an environment that is opaque at best are compounded by the difficulties of integrating the functions of two command structures. Although the Army and the Air Force are, of course, both subject to the authority of the unified commands to which they are respectively assigned as components, that authority often confronts fundamental differences when questions of command and command prerogatives arise.

Those are the questions that have emerged since the inception of the Army's new doctrine for fighting and winning mid-to-high-intensity wars into the twenty-first century. Successively known as Airland Battle, Airland Battle 2000, and Army 21 (reflecting longer-range planning), the new doctrine has been the centerpiece of Army operational thinking since it became official in 1982. The implications of Airland Battle create doubt as to which service would control the "extended battlefield" envisioned by its precepts. This question reflects one of the themes of this book: that the tight integration offered by emerging command and control technologies—seemingly demanded by modern warfare—often runs afoul of existing command structures and the theories of warfare those structures embody.

A corollary to this point is that technology, by itself, does not solve the problem and may in fact exacerbate it. As noted in the previous chapter, in the 1970s the Army and the Air Force groped for solutions to the new technological challenges of electronic warfare, precision-guided munitions, battlefield automation, and intelligence. Like the Navy, the Army and the Air Force returned to the fundamental military task of extending the commander's range of vision, both to create additional operational depth and to buy time for tactical decision making. To this end, as noted earlier, the Army fielded the CEWI organization and the Air Force deployed AWACS. The quest for depth, however, was bound to bring about organizational conflict. By seeking to cover areas far beyond the front-line range of its organic weapons and sensor systems, the Army was intruding on Air Force turf, which traditionally had included the responsibility for all territory from the front lines back to the enemy's homeland. Clearly, the delicate balance of service autonomy was once again in some danger of being upset.

As was described in chapters 4 and 5, that balance had been maintained since World War II through the coordinative structure of the Joint Chiefs of Staff and the placement of service components within the structure of the unified and specified commands. The National Security Act of 1947 (and its subsequent amendments), the Key West and Newport agreements, and JCS procedures (most notably, JCS Pub. 2, *Unified Action Armed Forces*) were all carefully crafted compromises between service autonomy and the demands of integrated land, sea, and air combat.[41] Consequently, the structure of the U.S. European Command—where the Airland Battle doctrine has the most relevance—is a unified command; either an Army or an Air Force four-star general can serve as commander in chief (CINC), but this officer is expected to exercise his authority through the separate service components. Until the passage of the Goldwater-Nichols Act in 1986, the CINC had broad control over operations, but little say in the internal organization of the component commands or their application of service doctrine to theater requirements.

For the Air Force, that doctrine continued to rest on the strategic paradigms of Douhet and Mitchell, as well as on the lessons learned from World War II aerial combat, a heritage that was somewhat contradictory. Bernard Brodie provided a classic summation of this paradox:

Airpower had a mighty vindication in World War II. But it was Mitchell's conception of it . . . rather than Douhet's that was vindicated. It was in tactical employment that success was most spectacular and that the air forces won the unqualified respect and admiration of the older services. By contrast, the purely strategic successes, however far-reaching in particular instances, were never entirely convincing to un-

committed observers. . . . If airmen were like laboratory animals running a maze, they would seek to repeat successes and to recoil from
frustrations. They would now be all in favor of tactical as against
strategic uses of air power. But being instead very human, and knowing
also the power of nuclear weapons, they have remained intensely loyal
to their original strategic ideas.[42]

The tactical success of which Brodie wrote was gained at some cost in the
North African desert during the early days of American entry into combat,
the experiences there and elsewhere suggesting that tactical success rested on
the concentration of scarce air assets in order to gain superiority over the
opposing air force. These successive concentrations of force ultimately resulted in air superiority and unhindered close air support of ground operations. Nowhere better highlighted than in the Normandy invasion and the
ensuing campaign for northern Europe, these few simple principles of tactical
air operations provided the doctrinal backdrop for the air-ground teamwork
that was so devastatingly effective throughout the rest of the war.[43]

The Korean and Vietnam conflicts taught additional lessons that further
contributed to the evolution of the air-ground operations system. That system
allowed for the use of both preplanned and immediate requests for air support
to be routed back through the parallel chains of command that now existed for
air and ground units. An important feature was the presence of forward air
controllers in light observation planes above the battlefield who communi-
cated directly with the air liaison officers and tactical air control parties
attached to the ground forces at every echelon down to battalion level. The
system did not provide an answer to the problem of a proliferation of air
forces, which in Vietnam included Navy, Marines, U.S., and South Vietnamese Air Force planes, as well as Army helicopters; however, it was
flexible enough to work well in an atmosphere in which air superiority was
assured.[44]

The system underwent more substantial challenges during the air war over
North Vietnam, where American pilots acquired a great respect for the
capabilities of Soviet-supplied air defenses. All too often, pilots and their
commanders on the way to attack targets were denied precious information on
incoming flights of MIGs or the imminent launch of Russian SAMs. The primary reason for these failures was not the absence of information but the
inability of covering ground control and surveillance stations to transmit the
data using the strike force's overloaded UHF radio frequencies. As one Air
Force general later recalled, "The communications systems could not handle
the traffic. If voice transmissions arrived, they were often ambiguous or

misunderstood. . . . Enemy interception of unencrypted voice transmissions often permitted these countermeasures to evade or defeat planned action. These troubles happened in an environment that was essentially free from enemy jamming, whereas in Europe, we would expect massive jamming."[45]

In the post-Vietnam era, the problems of the NATO Central Front have been the focus of much attention from Air Force commanders at all echelons who have been concerned about the viability and integrity of the tactical air control system should war with the Warsaw Pact ever come about. They worry that such a sophisticated, determined adversary would target command and control centers for massive electronic jamming and for physical destruction—and this at the very time that NATO ground commanders would be counting most heavily on air force support to help counter the numerical preponderance of Warsaw Pact armies. Two key improvements in the system have been the AWACS and the Airborne Battlefield Command and Control Center, a C-130 Hercules aircraft equipped for surveillance and control operations.

The linchpin of that system is the Tactical Air Control Center (TACC), which is responsible for centralized command and control of the numbered air force assigned to its area of operations. The TACC is at the head of a control network that manages airspace over the battle area and processes requests from the ground forces for close air support and longer-range interdiction. Direct support of the ground forces is represented by the Air Support Operations Centers colocated with the Army's corps-level tactical headquarters. Subordinate control parties are deployed with forward ground force elements for immediate processing of close air support requests. Each of these elements of the tactical air control system is thus a critical link in what is essentially a theater-level view of the air war. Moreover, the system is remarkable for being controlled *from the ground and not the air*—this despite the extensive use within the system of the AWACS and other surveillance aircraft. Critical data obtained from those and other sensors are down-linked to ground stations where decisions are made on aircraft utilization. This is an important doctrinal point which explains why the AWACS is not primarily configured for controlling fighter-to-fighter engagements. Similarly, the tactical air liaison officers with the Army ground forces are not independent control centers but primarily information conduits. Decisions on aircraft allocation, in keeping with Air Force paradigms, history, experience, and doctrine, are made at the central ground-based nodes of the tactical air control system.[46]

The Army–Air Force partnership might have remained relatively undisturbed had it not been for the challenge posed by the growth of Soviet military might, a challenge that continues to the present, despite the very real potential of the recent Gorbachev initiatives and the rhetoric that has often accompanied them. Beginning in the aftermath of the 1973 Yom Kippur War, the modernization of the Soviet forces arrayed against NATO represented a steady expansion of Russian capabilities that led to a rigorous self-examination by American military leaders. The Air Force was convinced that the trends evident in Vietnam and the Yom Kippur War would continue apace as Soviet air defenses grew ever more numerous and sophisticated. The 1986 edition of *Soviet Military Power,* for example, noted that more than "4,600 tactical SAM launchers and 12,000 AAA [antiaircraft artillery] pieces are deployed with Air Defense units at regimental through front level," together with 25,000 shoulder-fired SAMs at battalion and company levels. The varied ranges, deployments, and guidance mechanisms employed in these systems combined to make Soviet tactical air defenses a hedgehog designed to blunt the effect of opposing air operations.[47]

The same publication also documented the growth of Soviet frontal aviation, which has since the mid-1970s almost quadrupled the bombing capabilities of its front-line tactical aircraft. Some 5,440 fighters, interceptors, fighter-bombers, and reconnaissance aircraft were deployed in the 140 regiments and squadrons available to Soviet front commanders as their "Tactical Air Armies." This figure, moreover, was in addition to the 2,300 combat aircraft of the non-Soviet Warsaw Pact countries. More worrying still were the qualitative changes evident in newer models, such as the SU-27/29 and MIG-29, which, with look-down, shoot-down radar, long-range air-to-air missiles, improved avionics, and greater operational ranges, were comparable to the newest aircraft in Western inventories.[48]

The Soviet ground forces, traditionally large and well equipped, also had benefited greatly from more than a decade of modernization. Although there is no easy way to summarize the results of that process, figures supplied by the U.S. Defense Department show that in 1988 the 1.9-million-man Soviet ground forces deployed some 53,000 main battle tanks (a third of which were the newest models with production runs continuing), 60,000 armored personnel carriers and infantry fighting vehicles, and 48,000 artillery pieces. The 213 divisions of the Soviet Army, organized around tank and motorized rifle regiments with organic combat support units, thus constitute a force of unprecedented mobility. Probably the most dramatic development of recent years, however, has been the addition to the Soviet inventory of a family of tactical helicopters used for mobility and fire support. Two of its latest models, the MI-24 HIND and the MI-28 HAVOC, are at least the equal of their U.S. counterparts, and the latest Soviet attack helicopter, code-named HOKUM, is of an advanced design that presently has no Western counterpart.[49] And finally, as if these improvements were not enough, the Pentagon stated, "An ambitious force development program is underway involving expansion, equipment modernization, training improvements, innovative tactics and operational concepts, and enhancement of command and control capabilities."[50]

The pace, the extent, and the meaning of the Soviet buildup are topics that have attracted wide attention and debate by the defense analytical community in the wake of perestroika and the announced intentions of Soviet leaders to reduce military expenditures and trim force structures. This brief retrospective look at Soviet military developments, however, sets the stage for the emergence of the doctrine of Airland Battle, a process that began in the mid-1970s as many of these developments were being studied by Western analysts for the first time. The evolution of Airland Battle doctrine has undergone three phases, the first of which began in 1976 with the publication of FM 100-5, *Operations*. Under the leadership of Gen. William E. DePuy, commander of the Army's Training and Doctrine Command (TRADOC), use of the new manual was the first step in coming to terms with the deadly effectiveness of PGMs seen in the Yom Kippur War. Those technologies appeared to give important advantages to the defender, especially if he was well-prepared and equipped for their use. The "active defense" of FM 100-5 therefore rested on the assumptions that the Army had to be prepared to "win the first battle of the next war" and to do so while fighting outnumbered. The manual explicitly called for these imbalances to be redressed by the skillful concentration and application of firepower: "Whether on the offense or the defense, U.S. Army forces must exploit to the maximum the mobility of our weapons systems. Swiftly massed field artillery, totally mobile tank and mechanized infantry battalions, airmobile antiarmor weapons, attack helicopters, close air support aircraft, and, in some circumstances, tactical employment of nuclear weapons offer us the means to concentrate overwhelming combat power and to decisively alter force ratios when and where we choose."[51]

The new doctrine was equally explicit in stating that a defending force, by employing these weapons systems with full terrain advantage, should be able to defeat an attacking force three times its size; therefore any attacking force should seek a superiority at the point of concentration of 6 : 1.[52] Since U.S. Army forces were unlikely to enjoy such a numerical advantage in any conflict with the Warsaw Pact countries, a commander "should attack only if he expects the eventual outcome to result in decisively greater losses than his own, or result in the capture of objectives crucial to the outcome of the larger battle."[53] Both offensive and defensive operations depended on the commander's ability to "see the battlefield," both to take maximum advantage of his own weapons systems and to provide time to concentrate his forces against the weight of the enemy's main thrust.[54]

It was not surprising that a doctrine for "winning the land battle" through the use of the "active defense" was criticized for its defensive orientation, and FM 100-5 became a highly controversial manual. As a subsequent critique put it: "There is nothing subtle about the doctrine—it advocates meeting the strength of the Soviet attack head-on and destroying it through massed firepower. The combat techniques described in the manual stress almost mechanical methods for fighting or applying fire power. Systems analysis terms . . . are used to describe the dynamics of combat. . . . Follow-on interpretations of FM 100-5 use explanations couched in terms such as "the calculus of battle" and in mathematical notions expressed by Lanchester Laws and gaming theory to discuss the modern battlefield."[55]

This second stage in the evolution of Airland Battle doctrine was characterized by the critiques of those who fell roughly into the "military reform/maneuver" school of thought. The maneuver warriors saw in FM 100-5 nothing more than a latter-day restatement of classical American attrition warfare, now adapted to the demands of high-cost, high-technology weapons that were certain to fail in combat. John Boyd's O-O-D-A model was even cited by James Fallows as an intellectual alternative to this style of warfare in a widely read book, *National Defense,* which gave the reformers their first real public exposure.[56] The internal debate over FM 100-5 continued to be featured in the pages of the military's leading professional journals, and gradually the outlines of the maneuver critique became clearer. Rejecting the firepower attrition models in favor of movement to gain tactical leverage, maneuver theorists argued that enemy forces should not be met head-on, but should be allowed to penetrate and engage infantry defenses. At the same time, friendly armor-heavy forces would circle into the enemy's rear to attack his vulnerable supply trains, lines of communications, and command and control centers. Thus, while the enemy's main-force units were being encouraged to extend themselves deep into the defended zone, his support and decision-making lifelines were being cut, and the O-O-D-A cycle of his command structure was being smashed. This use of territory could consequently be seen as one of the main points of departure between the two schools: attrition strategists viewing it as something to be held and organized into progressively more lethal "kill zones," and maneuver advocates offering a more dynamic view—as something to be gained or traded for tactical advantage.[57]

The maneuver critique paced the continuing refinement of Army doctrine, by then the responsibility of Gen. Donn A. Starry. The new TRADOC commander presided over the third stage of the evolutionary pattern, which would ultimately lead to the publication of a revised FM 100-5 in 1982 and the enshrinement of Airland Battle as its centerpiece. By late 1978, Army doctrinal thinking had coalesced into a battlefield development plan which broke combat down into two main functions: a central battle fought largely along the lines of the attrition model, and a force generation effort, which involved the higher-level preparation for the organization and commitment of reserves and other formations needed to turn the tide of battle.[58] Equally noteworthy was the increased focus on the widening range of options now available to Soviet commanders as that country's modernization efforts came to fruition. British defense analyst Christopher Donnelly was the most influential voice calling attention to the fact that the unprecedented speed and mobility of Soviet motorized rifle and tank divisions were allowing the Russians to experiment with operational maneuver groups—combined-arms task forces designed for independent breakthrough and slashing operations in NATO rear areas.[59] Fresh from command of a U.S. corps in West Germany, General Starry was in a position to appreciate that fact, as well as the gains made by the Soviets in strategic and logistical mobility. Those capabilities meant that American forces would have to defeat both the committed elements of Soviet first-echelon armies on the NATO central front and the second-echelon Soviet and Warsaw Pact armies which could now be expected to arrive from the East quickly enough to play a critical reinforcing role.

Airland Battle was to provide the conceptual basis for U.S. forces to engage both the Soviet front-line and the follow-on focus. The new version of FM 100-5 released in August 1982 called for the aggressive use of maneuver and counterattack in order to gain the offensive as rapidly as possible: "The offense is the decisive form of war, the commander's only means of attaining a positive goal or of completely destroying an enemy force. . . . The attacker concentrates quickly and strikes hard at an unexpected place or time to throw the defender off balance. Once the attack is underway, the attacker must move fast, press every advantage aggressively, and capitalize on each opportunity to destroy either the enemy's forces or the overall coherence of his defense."[60] The new manual stressed that the operational concepts of Airland Battle depended upon initiative, depth, agility, and synchronization of all arms at the tactical, operational, and strategic levels of warfare. It was also clear, however, that the doctrine was a synthesis of old and new, emphasizing both firepower and maneuver as vital ingredients of combat power.[61] As one study summarized what had happened, "What had emerged from the 1976 manual and subsequent discussions was the idea of a battlefield that included precision-guided missiles, anti-tank weapons, laser-guided artillery shells,

Figure 6.4   Operational Concept of the Airland Battle
Source: U.S. Army

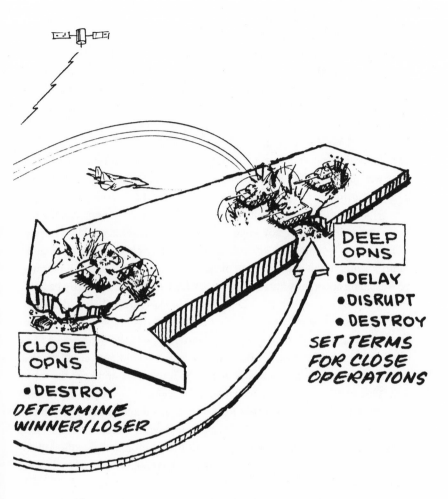

DEEP OPNS
• DELAY
• DISRUPT
• DESTROY
SET TERMS FOR CLOSE OPERATIONS

CLOSE OPNS
• DESTROY
DETERMINE WINNER/LOSER

and cruise missiles to attack the follow-on echelons of Soviet forces and to allow for a counterattack with a favorable U.S. force ratio."[62]

The new doctrine received high marks from many observers for its re-emphasis of the offensive, but no single aspect of Airland Battle has attracted more attention than its concept of the Deep Strike (also called Deep Attack and, more recently, Follow-On Forces Attack) which envisions attacks against Soviet second-echelon forces at strategic depths. This precept flowed logically enough from the perceived threat posed by those forces, but the idea that corps commanders were now responsible for seeing and influencing a deep battlefield that might extend more than a hundred miles behind enemy lines was startling. This extended battlefield was described by General Starry in a 1981 *Military Review* article. In it, he argued that "deep attack is not a luxury, it is an absolute necessity to winning." By coordinating "scarce acquisition and strike assets," key targets in the second echelon could be selected and hit which would play a key role in the "decisive close-in battle." Significantly, "without this coordination, many expensive and scarce resources may be wasted on apparently attractive targets whose destruction actually has little payoff in the close-in battle."[63] Deep attack tools—primarily interdiction by aircraft, long-range artillery, and missiles, but also including electronic warfare and deception—would be used to deny follow-on Soviet forces a "free ride" into the battle area. Similarly, deep strikes would help create tactical opportunities which in turn would help U.S. forces gain and keep the initiative: "Interdiction is the key to battlefield success. . . . [It] is the method whereby we achieve the leverage to slow him down and ultimately stop him from achieving his objectives."[64] It can be argued, therefore, that the Deep Strike concept represented the relegation of the attrition model to the follow-on Soviet forces, even as the maneuver model was being employed to fight the central battle.[65] (See figure 6.4.)

The Airland Battle concept has continued to provide the Army with a doctrinal structure that has not only led to a synthesis between maneuver and attrition but also paced a renascence of strategic thinking. The 1986 version of FM 100-5, for example, stressed four cardinal tenets of the doctrine: initiative ("an offensive spirit in the conduct of all operations"), agility ("the ability of friendly forces to act faster than the enemy"), depth ("the extension of operations in space, time, and resources"), and synchronization ("the arrangement of battlefield activities in time, space and purpose to produce maximum relative combat power at the decisive point"). The concepts of initiative and agility signaled a return to the aggressive warrior spirit, as well as the need to capitalize on the superior fighting qualities of the new generation of Army weaponry: for example, the M-1 Abrams tank, the Bradley Fighting Vehicle, and the AH-64 Apache attack helicopter. But by stressing the need for its commanders to consider combat operations in relation to the need for depth and synchronization, the Army was reemphasizing the importance of the "operational art of war—the employment of [joint] military forces to attain strategic goals in a theater of war [or] operations." Those concepts in turn implied two things that are important for this analysis: a reliance on high-technology command and control systems, and a new order of integration in the combat operations of the Army and the Air Force.[66]

Whatever the respective merits of the attrition and the maneuver models of warfare, there was little question at the start of the debate that the Army's tactical command and control system was ill equipped to handle either of them. Most of its tactical radios, for example, were 1950s FM-voice models, which were not secure against the threats of enemy interception or jamming. Higher-level communications were handled by a network of multichannel radio and cable links tying together both fixed and mobile message centers in the principal tactical commands. The administrative overhead of this system was huge. In a typical corps, whose area of responsibility could encompass a territory almost twice the size of the state of New Jersey, more than five thousand personnel were required just to man the corps signal brigade.[67] Signal installations were primarily equipped with switching devices that were bulky, cumbersome, and hard to move. These features made them unsuitable for the dynamic pace of combat envisioned by FM 100-5; signal centers would have to displace rapidly to keep pace with maneuver units and to ensure their own survival in the face of Soviet attacks.

Because the existing message center equipment used antiquated analog switching devices, the communications network was also unable to handle the rivers of data that were about to be generated by battlefield automation. By 1980, there were some seventy battlefield systems and subsystems in various stages of conversion to automation.[68] But with the revised FM 100-5 intended as a guide for modernization, the Army was eventually able to conceptualize a tactical command and control architecture with five major functions: maneuver control, for supporting battlefield decisions by commanders and staffs; fire support control, for automating the use of indirect fire by artillery, missiles, and aircraft; intelligence and electronic warfare, for the automation of all-source tactical intelligence and the control of electronic warfare; air defense control, for automated management of the Army component of air defense; and combat service support control system, for computer control of logistical data.[69]

Linking these diverse subsystems and components together would be three major new communications systems:

- *SINCGARS:* The Single-Channel Ground/Airborne Radio System is the Army's new family of tactical VHF radios. With embedded electronic countermeasures, SINCGARS radios will be able to transmit either voice or data in a frequency-hopping mode that defeats jamming. Later versions will incorporate secure voice and data transmission capabilities.[70]
- *MSE:* Mobile Subscriber Equipment will allow field commanders in corps and division areas to communicate by voice very much like a commercial radiotelephone network. Also secure and with embedded countermeasures, MSE is an inherently mobile system which can link command posts to each other and to the primary users of the SINCGARS radios. (Interestingly, there have been press reports that these two systems can cause electronic interference with one another when they are operated simultaneously!)[71]
- *The Army Data Distribution System:* This program now consists of the Enhanced Position Locating and Reporting System and the Joint Tactical Information Distribution System. It is an interim system that will be used for high-density data transfer in the tactical environment, primarily for maneuver control and air defense. (This system and its evolution is the subject of the following chapter.)[72]

All these systems represent a heavy investment of time, personnel, and money, and each represents an aspect of the Army's response to the challenge of Airland Battle as it appeared from 1982 onward.

And yet, the marshaling of these forces of technology, important and extensive though it was, was only one aspect of the Army's response. At least as significant was the challenge that Airland Battle posed, in its turn, to the norms of the Air Force, a conflict that continues to the present. The Army investment in its command and control infrastructure was meant to purchase the means to achieve the synchronization called for by its doctrine. This term had a deeper meaning, however. It implied the need for much greater unity between ground and air forces committed to a theater and that notion raised again the troublesome issue of subordination and interservice relationships. The resulting debate on the Army–Air Force role in Airland Battle has been only marginally less acrimonious than that which attended the publication of the original FM 100-5. And, as Air Force proponents are quick to point out, to date it is only an Army doctrine, *not* a joint doctrine.

Air Force objections to Airland Battle fall into three major categories that are distinct but closely related: command structure, doctrine, and resources. Interestingly, most of the questions center around the historical paradigm of the inherently flexible and offensive use of air power. The theories of Douhet

and Mitchell as well as the practical lessons of the North African and Normandy campaigns continue to exert a powerful influence on the present debate,
with Air Force proponents stressing that these lessons show that air power
should not be parceled out like artillery to ground force commanders. Rather,
it should be concentrated and successively applied to targets that will allow it
to establish superiority over the defending air force; air superiority, once
achieved, is the key to all other uses of air power, including close support of
the ground forces. Above all, paradigms and history show that it is still
necessary to view the air war in its totality from a theater-level perspective. It
is precisely on these grounds that Airland Battle, with its emphasis on corps-
level operations, is suspect. As Maj. James Machos has written, "To allow
each theater commander the luxury of 'calling his own shots' with air interdiction would fragment the theater air integration effort. The theater perspective
would be replaced by several narrow, possibly competing, corps perspectives. . . . In at least some ways, such a situation constitutes a return to
practices that proved unworkable during the North African campaign. The
result? TACAIR's ability to mass forces to meet and defeat the enemy at the
critical time and place would be eroded."[73]

Not only would such a concept be a throwback, according to this argument,
it would also disrupt the present air-ground operations system so carefully
crafted in the light of lessons learned from Korea and Vietnam. That system
depended for its effectiveness on parallel structures within the unified commands that placed air and ground component commanders on an equal footing
in both rank and authority. And yet, since 1973, the Army had not recognized
any echelon above that of the corps, doing away with the "theater army" that
had always doubled as the ground component command in favor of a less top-
heavy system in order to conserve scarce manpower spaces. Among other
things, this restructuring implied that the Tactical Air Control Center, normally colocated with the Army and Air Force components, would have to deal
instead with the representatives of one or more corps, rather than a single
counterpart. With the coming of Airland Battle, therefore, the previous
breach was widened still further.[74]

Linked to the imbalance of command structure was a fundamental tenet of
modern aerospace doctrine: centralized command and decentralized execution. As the capstone Air Force manual set forth this concept: "Centralized
control is essential to positive control of aerospace power. Centralized control
is established under a single air commander who directs the employment of
forces at a level of command from which the overall air situation can best be
judged. This level of authority and responsibility rests with the commander in
chief in specified commands and with the air component commander in

unified or combined commands. Under this concept, aerospace operations are exercised at the most effective level. This is decentralized execution."[75] Airland Battle, with its corps emphasis, clearly threatened both the command structure and the doctrine it exemplified. Acknowledging that fact, one Air Force commentator pointed out with admirable candor that "the extended battlefield requires the Army to look deep and control assets out further in time than had been envisioned before. The Air Force controls assets in the area where the Army wants to control assets. Thus, the conflict."[76]

The idea of assets and who controls them introduces the third area of Army–Air Force disagreement: resource allocation. One of the touchier issues between the services has always been the trade-off in the number of missions devoted to close air support of the ground forces versus those considered essential by the Air Force in achieving air superiority. In a 1984 article, Assistant Secretary of the Air Force Tidal McCoy addressed this issue, emphasizing the continuing commitment to close air support but pointing out that "air superiority has mission priority because USAF believes that without control of the air, neither it nor the ground forces can succeed." Further, the principle of centralized command and decentralized execution is the mechanism that "best applies force to the battlefield and to parcel out that force and dedicate it to ground commanders does not provide the strongest defense."[77] In a similar vein, the Air University awarded a prize to a 1985 essay whose author wrote that Airland Battle doctrine was misconceived: Deep Strike would siphon off scarce surveillance and intelligence collection capabilities from the Air Force because of range limitations of organic Army sensors. Equally pernicious were the additional intratheater lift requirements that would logically follow from the increased mobility envisioned by the doctrine.[78]

In the midst of this free-swinging doctrinal debate, there came a welcome reminder that American military leaders have generally been reasonable, well-intentioned men who have tried to put the nation's interests ahead of any lesser concerns. Two of these officers, Gen. John A. Wickham, Jr., chief of staff of the Army, and Gen. Charles A. Gabriel, chief of staff of the Air Force, found themselves united by a long-standing personal friendship and remarkably similar viewpoints on the need for closer cooperation between the services they led. Beginning in mid-1983 (months before the invasion of Grenada would thrust the issue of interservice relationships back into the headlines) both generals quietly put their staffs to work on a cooperative project to rationalize the planning and development of joint combat forces centered around the Airland Battle model. On May 22, 1984, the two service chiefs appeared at a Pentagon press conference to announce that this effort had yielded Army–Air Force agreement on thirty-one separate initiatives, including some that were fundamental to Airland Battle operations—for example, air defense, suppression of enemy air defenses, and fusion of combat information. This was clearly a major step forward, and over the next several years the progress made in these areas would result in closer coordination between the services, the cancellation of several duplicative programs, and the reprogramming of over $1 billion in associated savings.[79]

These were no mean achievements, and they were cited in 1986 by Generals Wickham and Gabriel as examples of why fundamental JCS reforms were not needed. As the official Air Force history notes, however, the pace of change soon slowed. "Cynics might point out that change imposed from the top has a half-life closely related to the job tenure of its advocates."[80] Another explanation, however, is that the process of joint doctrine development has now been institutionalized within the Joint Staff with the reforms mandated by the Goldwater-Nichols Act. Consequently, it can be argued that this process is no longer dependent on ad hoc working groups and good intentions. It is also fair to note, however, that the cooperative process has essentially solved most of the easy problems and that far tougher issues lie ahead in the 1990s. Among them are the following:

■ How adaptable is the Air-Ground Operations Systems—with its parallel chains of command and hierarchical structures—to the chaotic, decentralized melee characteristic of Airland Battle combat?
■ How will the close air support mission and the selection of the next-generation close air support aircraft play out?
■ To this point, the Army and the Air Force have cooperated on plans for the next generation of long-range reconnaissance and surveillance aircraft: the TR-1/Precision Location Strike System and the E-8/Joint Surveillance Target Attack Radar System (JSTARS). With flat or declining defense budgets, there is an inherent potential for developmental problems, procurement stretch-outs, and, inevitably, mission trade-offs. Therefore, can the joint air-ground surveillance orientation of these systems be maintained through the process of development and procurement?[81]

This discussion of Airland Battle would be incomplete, however, were it not to include a final caveat by Steven L. Canby. In a free-ranging critique of the doctrine presented at the Wilson Center in 1984, Canby, one of the more prominent military reformers, argued that "the new technologies for implementing the Deep Attack concept have been undercosted by an order of magnitude, the concept proceeds from a false syllogism, and the concept itself is not feasible. . . . The vulnerabilities Deep Attack presumes in the opposing force array do not exist; its automated command and control leads to deception and inflexibility; and its submunitions can be easily countered."[82]

Canby's thesis reflects the familiar distrust of the military reformers for overreliance on elaborate technology, especially when applied in pursuit of the illusory goal of offsetting numerical imbalances. A detailed analysis of his argument is beyond the scope of this book, but it should be noted that Canby provides an important counterpoint in considering the command and control technologies of the Airland battlefield. Essentially, his point is that there are two dangers to the modernized command and control systems now being fielded: the first is that these systems won't work, and the second is that they will. The technology needed to acquire the Very Intelligent Surveillance and Target Acquisition (VISTA) Technologies and their associated automation systems is, according to the first line of reasoning, easily offset by standard Soviet countermeasures, including direct attack, deception, and electronic warfare. Both the sensor and its processor can be easily deceived or removed entirely by such stratagems; without them, Deep Strike simply will not work.

Second, if the systems *are* allowed to continue working, especially those intelligence and electronic warfare systems that acquire large amounts of data and fuse them according to predetermined algorithms, there is an even greater threat from strategic deception, or spoofing. A conceptual dependence upon automation not only invites such enemy action but encourages him to engage in countermeasures that will cause our own decision mechanisms to break down from information overloads. "The point is simply stated: *Automaticity implies extreme inflexibility whenever the enemy can discover—and operate outside of—the bounds of the predictable*" (emphasis added).[83]

There are no easy answers to such objections. There are few technologies in the history of warfare that have not been either neutralized or nullified by creative countermeasures applied in the manner that Canby describes. One suspects, however, that "predetermined algorithms" and "inflexible automaticity" are terms that may have more to do with theoretical perspectives of these systems rather than with their likely uses in the field. To the extent that they reflect real-world preferences, however, they are more accurate descriptions of Soviet, rather than Western, ideas about troop control. For good or ill, American armed forces are more likely than most others to use any hitech system with a great degree of ingenuity and individuality whenever possible—or to simply pull the plug whenever it is not. Although the soldier, the sailor, the airman, and the marine provide this built-in "sanity check," it is important to remember that they are also the ultimate consumers of the advanced systems now being contemplated. They are consequently the ones with the most to lose if those systems are not designed with one eye on the technology and the other on Murphy's Law.

Conclusion: A Theater Perspective

This chapter has shown the interplay between the highly integrative technology of the information age and the service command structures that seek to exploit it in meeting a variety of challenges, some of which are related to technology and some of which are not. The conceptual models of the command and control process presented by Boyd and Lawson are illustrative of the holistic nature of that process, while the differing service perspectives suggested by Gorman are an important counterpoint, since they highlight the effects of differing operational environments. These differences are accompanied by great variations in the structure, leadership styles, and organizational strategies among Army, Navy, and Air Force units, only some of which are fully appreciated in the usual bureaucratic calculus.

These characteristics, grounded as they are in the everyday practicalities of military life, account for subtle but important differences in the way the services approach command and control. One can compare, for example, the Navy's modular approach with the centralized command–decentralized execution formula that is the centerpiece of Air Force doctrine. Although there are differences between these two philosophies, both are located at one end of the spectrum of "movable subordinate entities," while the Army is at the other. Nowhere is that difference more apparent than in a recent doctrinal publication by the Army Command and General Staff College on the command and control process. Conceptualizing command as a "directive process" for infusing the "will and intent of the commander" among his subordinates, the manual notes that the premise of command rests upon the assumption of "reliable subordinate behavior." Control, however, is an entirely different matter: "Control is a process by which subordinate behavior inconsistent with the will and intent of the commander is identified and corrected. This process is regulatory: its premise is unreliable subordinate behavior. Unreliable behavior in this context . . . will normally be inadvertent, resulting from different perspectives of the battlefield, inattention, a lack of understanding of the mission or the commander's intent—or the fog of battle."[84] Both the Navy and the Air Force might find themselves in some agreement with parts of that approach, but it clearly defines the unique perspective of an Army that must coordinate hundreds of thousands of "entities" to ensure tactical and strategic coherence on the battlefield.

The Army's control problem, therefore, is much more difficult than that of either the Navy or the Air Force. It has no choice other than decentralization, with a distribution of power down to the lowest levels; very junior members of its command hierarchy (corporals or sergeants in charge of rifle squads, for example) will therefore exercise great discretion within certain well-defined limits. Those limits are inherent to a command and control regime in which the premise of unreliable subordinate behavior compels decentralization to be tempered by measures that permit on-the-spot intervention by any member of the chain of command. At least in concept, both the Army and the Air Force would appear to agree on the philosophy of centralized command and decentralized execution—however much they might differ on the operational meaning of that principle. By contrast, the Navy centralizes command at a much lower level—either the individual ship or the task force. Although subordination of naval forces is no less assured than their land or air counterparts, the idea of lower-level centralization necessitates the more modular, or federal, approach characteristic of naval command and control. It is also consistent with the idea of a global system whose parts are interchangeable, allowing innumerable combinations of its modular components.

Although it is tempting to think otherwise, a holistic view of command and control has to be tempered by these operational differences in the service environments. As the Army–Air Force conflict over Airland Battle demonstrates, it is equally important to consider the fact that the services are very human institutions. Organizations of people tend to reflect certain norms, values, and beliefs; not surprisingly, these characteristics combine to provide common perceptions about many matters, technological adaptation being one of the more critical ones in any military organization.[85] Command and control systems are a central feature of the modernization process, but, as the Navy's experience with Aegis has demonstrated, they are expensive and usually accompanied by some degree of technological risk. These hard choices about dollars and uncertainty become even more difficult when command and control systems are considered in the context of their relationship to the larger picture of interservice and multinational operations. As the following chapter demonstrates, these decisions may involve significant cost escalations in order to achieve interoperability—or even a head-on, life-or-death competition with a system developed by another service.

The task of reconciling these competing perspectives is clearly one of the more difficult problems faced by the American defense establishment. It is a responsibility made more difficult by the organizational structure bequeathed by the National Security Act of 1947 and its amendments, which placed the services in the role of "providers" of American fighting forces and the commanders in chief of the unified and specified commands as the "users" of those forces.[86] More than most other weapons, modern command and control systems fall somewhere in between those distinctions, if for no other reasons than the personal styles of the local commander and the unique requirements of the theater mission. This was a point made most strongly in 1978 by a special task force of the Department of Defense Science Board. Among other things, the panel concluded that the major military commands lacked the manpower, expertise, and financial resources to adapt service-developed command and control systems for theater requirements; moreover, the commands lacked the resources to exercise and evaluate their systems. Consequently, the CINCS lacked the most rudimentary means to influence the development of one of the key instruments used in carrying out their wartime missions.[87]

The issue of this structural inadequacy would require lengthier treatment here were it not for retired Lt. Gen. John H. Cushman, who in 1985 explored that topic in *Command and Control of Theater Forces: Adequacy*. Written from the perspective of a former corps commander, General Cushman viewed the theater commander as the focal point of a "vibrant, living web" of interlocking command and control systems which he uses "for perceiving and understanding challenge and for fashioning and producing response."[88] Although commanders at every echelon share only a part of the larger system, which extends all the way through the National Command Authorities in Washington, the theater commander is at a particular disadvantage in understanding, using, and developing his organic command and control systems, for precisely the reasons noted by the Defense Science Board task force. But General Cushman goes further in assessing the impact of a number of technical and institutional factors that contribute to this problem. For present purposes, his four major bureaucratic causes of failure in theater command and control are most important. They include "service failures to view CINC requirements holistically; structural failure in the procurement and acquisition process to give sufficient weight to the CINC's command and control requirements; institutional failure by the Joint Chiefs of Staff to enforce a joint perspective in the development of command and control systems; and finally, a general failure to 'evaluate command and control systems against operational mission performance under conditions of stark reality.'"[89]

General Cushman's arguments are couched in strong terms, befitting the authoritative personal knowledge he brings to the subject. Nevertheless, he goes further than any other student of these matters in assessing the adverse impact of service autonomy on command and control. But a full acceptance of his view is not required to appreciate the point made in this chapter: namely, that the services impose organizational, structural, and operational barriers that would not seem obvious, given the integrative properties of modern and emerging command and control technologies. As has been seen, these barriers are partly the result of operational necessity, partly the product of differing organizational values, and partly the result of fundamentally different ideas about the nature of warfare. Although the Goldwater-Nichols Act greatly strengthened the hand of the unified and specified commanders in correcting some of the failures noted by Cushman, these more fundamental service differences are unlikely to be eliminated by the stroke of a pen. For that reason, the following chapter focuses on how the services approach the problem of joint command and control, especially when hi-tech systems and high-dollar values are on the line.

Building Joint Approaches
Of JINTACCS and JTIDS

The previous chapter demonstrated the conflicting pressures faced by the services as they modernized their command and control structures in response to revolutionary developments in weapons accuracy, electronic warfare, and battlefield automation. Two major cross-currents were identified: the integrative potential of the new command and control systems—whose capabilities for sensing, processing, and fusing data dwarfed anything that had gone before—and the institutional resistance observable whenever this integrative potential threatened existing relationships among the services. This seems paradoxical, since the services were acting as the principal agencies of change even as they imposed barriers to certain implications of those changes. The answer to this seeming contradiction is surely that the services are human institutions, made up of individuals who have strongly identified with the norms, values, and beliefs composing the respective cultures of the Army, Navy, and Air Force. Equally important to an appreciation of these opposing influences, as has been shown, are the very real differences between the land, sea, and aerospace environments, differences that are reflected as well in the services' organizational structures. Perhaps the best way of summing up the paradox is by a simple conceptual metaphor: the services are conduits of change even as an electrical cable is a conduit of power—both, however, offer varying degrees of resistance. These characteristics of change and resistance are equally present in the case study that is the focus of this chapter: the Joint Tactical Information Distribution System (JTIDS, pronounced "jay-tids").

There is no question that every step taken by the services on the road to modernization led to greater and greater pressures for integration. A 1977 study noted the progress being made in each of the services' command and control arenas but also pointed to a glaring deficiency: "Efforts are underway within each Service and command organization to construct a framework for the development of support systems and their interfaces for tactical C2 that will maximize the potential capabilities of U.S. tactical weapons systems and combat forces. However, we still do not have a joint Service plan that integrates, at the tactical level, the interacting organizations, functions, and systems within and across major tactical mission areas."[1] Since those words were written, the development of common or joint approaches to command and control has become one of the most important but least understood aspects of American defense policy.

Three basic factors have been responsible:

1. *Shifting geopolitical requirements:* In the early 1980s, the steady expansion of Soviet military capabilities and rising third world tensions led to the direct involvement of the USSR in Angola, Ethiopia, Afghanistan, Nicaragua, and Grenada, to cite some of the more celebrated examples. The Iranian Revolution, the seizure of the U.S. embassy in Tehran, the failure of the joint mission mounted to rescue the American hostages seized during that takeover, and the potential for instability that accompanied the Iran-Iraq War through much of the 1980s were even more troubling. In American military circles, the talk was of a "requirements-capabilities mismatch" whenever existing resources were compared to possible engagement scenarios in these or other regional conflicts. More worrying still was the prospect of having to fight in several of these far-flung theaters simultaneously. These pressures gave new life to Eisenhower's dictum of a generation before that joint warfare had replaced service separatism; now, however, it seemed that fast-developing command and control technologies might assist this integration, acting as a "force multiplier" that could link hard-pressed American land, sea, and air forces. For example, the U.S. Central Command (CENTCOM)—formed as a unified command in 1983 as the successor to the Rapid Deployment Joint Task Force—had as its main mission the control of American forces moving to any emergency in the Persian Gulf or Southwest Asia, a distance of over seven thousand miles from their home bases. According to its commander at that time, Lt. Gen. Robert Kingston, the success of the CENTCOM mission depended upon "our capability to quickly deploy a sizable force; to promptly receive, process and use intelligence from national, strategic, and tactical sources [and] to exercise effective command and control over forces deployed across a large geographical area." The effectiveness of command and control in turn depended upon the ability of service command and control systems to be interoperable—that is, to communicate effectively with one another.[2]

2. *Key investment decisions:* Beginning at the end of the Carter presidency and reaching a peak during the first six years of the Reagan administration, the increased dollars made available for defense spending represent one of the central events of American security policy in the last quarter of the twentieth

century. The relevance of that event for our purposes lies in the fact that money was at long last becoming available for the modernization of American command and control systems. This trend was nowhere more in evidence than in the attention given to strategic command and control by the incoming Reagan administration, which quickly earmarked more than $18 billion for improvements in the "connectivity and survivability" of the information systems supporting the U.S. nuclear triad.[3] Inevitably, the visibility accorded nuclear command and control helped focus attention on conventional command and control problems as well. With major weapons systems purchases now at hand, with maturing technologies now ready to be applied to pressing military problems, and, most important, with enough money available, major investment decisions on both tactical and strategic command and control systems were about to be made. In consequence, these formerly arcane issues began to receive some public attention.

3. *Public perception of the problem:* At least part of this attention was attributable to the aftermaths of a series of military failures. The special staff report prepared by James R. Locher III, *Defense Organization: The Need for Change,* which served as the backdrop for the Senate Armed Services Committee's deliberations on Pentagon reform in 1985–86, singled out examples of such operations as evidence of problems in defense organization. Two of these failures were the capture of the USS *Pueblo* in 1968 and the aborted Iranian hostage rescue mission in 1980, both of which involved confusion in the chain of command set up during those operations. The confrontation between Defense Secretary Weinberger and Senator Nunn noted in chapter 1 may have been predestined by the Locher Report's characterization of the 1983 invasion of Grenada as an example of an operation whose success obscured lessons that were vitally important for the future: "Probably the largest single problem was the inability of some units to communicate. . . . For example, the Army elements initially on the ground were unable to speak to the Navy ships offshore to request and coordinate naval gunfire. . . . The root cause of this inability to communicate is that each Service continues to purchase its own communications equipment, which all too frequently isn't compatible with the equipment of the other Services."[4] With the publication of this report, the stage was set for Congress to take the most far-reaching look at the way the American defense establishment prepared itself for war since the 1958 amendments to the National Security Act.

Command and control was, of course, only one aspect of this fundamental structural reform, and the revelation of problems in the Grenada operation was merely the latest stroke in the continuing efforts to ensure a high level of interservice teamwork in combat operations. Retired Army Col. Harry Summers, an advocate of defense reform, found some of the criticism of Grenada overblown, especially the question of Army-Navy radio compatibility. His major premise was that "if all military radios were on the same channel, the result would not be better communications. It would be a total lack of communications"—the channel would be rapidly clogged by overuse. Instead, the sine qua non of military communications is the rational allocation of the available electromagnetic spectrum, with different radios using different frequencies for different purposes in support of different missions. Commonality, when required, is achieved by setting up functional networks for higher commanders, for fire support, or, in the case of Grenada, for interservice coordination. Although that procedure may have gone awry during the invasion, he said, "the system itself is sound. And it is a system that most definitely does not depend on every radio being able to communicate with every other radio."[5]

Colonel Summers made an important point here, since he was voicing the orthodox view of how interservice command and control has been achieved ever since World War II on the basis of the lessons learned during that conflict. Many of those procedures are simple, commonsense measures, such as the establishment of the Air Naval Gunfire Liaison radio nets which are common features of joint operations. When more complicated exchanges are necessary, it is not unusual to see service components simply exchange liaison officers equipped with the necessary communications gear. For example, Air Force liaison officers, who operate with front-line Army units, typically carry two sets of radios, one for communication with the ground unit with which they are working and one for controlling the air strikes that unit has been allocated. A routine but important part of the joint planning process, therefore, is the allocation of frequencies and networks that will allow each of the force components to operate without mutual interference; second only to that priority is the establishment of the common channels that will link the components together as required.

This is the system Colonel Summers correctly described as having guided the command and control of joint operations for the last forty years. Although elements of that system will undoubtedly continue for the foreseeable future, the first appearance of tactical automation challenged the established patterns. As one Army general summarized those changes, "Traditional combat tasks were relatively straightforward. These were accomplished with manual procedures, using people as the hub of interoperability. In the mid-1960s, the use of automation in the performance of tactical tasks increased greatly. Today the services are actively pursuing automation across the tactical equipment spectrum; *consequently, joint and combined operations no longer can rely on manual procedures to provide interoperability*" (emphasis added).[6]

If the appearance of the computer on the battlefield did nothing else, it highlighted differing service norms on command and control that had always been present but had lain largely dormant since the Key West Agreement. The residual powers that gave the services the right to organize, train, and equip their forces virtually guaranteed that each service would procure a different computer hardware and software system, oriented primarily toward the requirements of its operational environment and its preferred weapons systems. If there was nothing inherently wrong with this evolutionary pattern—which, after all, had endured in one form or another since the founding of the Republic—it made joint planning even more challenging than before. Although the free market provided handsome rewards to inventive entrepreneurs who could devise hardware or software adaptations that allowed the electronic mating of diverse computer species, the defense establishment itself provided no such system of natural incentives.

Before turning to a brief review of the measures that ultimately gave birth to JTIDS, I will delineate two critical terms, *interoperability* and *commonality,* as set out in the indicated directives:

> *Interoperability:* The condition achieved among communications-electronics systems or . . . equipment when information or services can be exchanged directly and satisfactorily between them and/or their users. The degree of interoperability should be defined when referring to specific cases. (JCS Pub. 1)

> *Commonality:* Tactical command and control systems are common when the systems have the quality of one entity possessing like and interchangeable characteristics with another. Tactical communications equipments and systems are common when: they are compatible; each can be operated and maintained by personnel trained on the others without additional specialized training; repair parts are interchangeable; and consumable items are interchangeable between them. (DOD Directive 4630.5)

It should be noted that there is an ascending order of congruence from interoperability to commonality. As will be shown, however, this progression is somewhat easier to define than to achieve.

Players and Programs

Since the mid-1970s, a command and control "community" has taken on discernible outlines at the highest levels of the government; its membership is not limited to the Defense Department (DOD) but extends to other executive agencies and even to Capitol Hill. The emergence of this community can be traced at least as far back as the early years of the Carter administration, which came into office in 1977 with something of a perceived mandate to accomplish basic organizational changes at the seat of government. One of the first of those changes, made partly in response to congressional pressures, was the naming of Dr. Gerald P. Dinneen to the dual positions of deputy under secretary of defense for research and engineering and assistant secretary of defense for communications, command, control, and intelligence. The twin titles reflected the growing prominence of command and control issues and foreshadowed greater involvement by the top civilian management of the Defense Department in coordinating those responsibilities. In particular, Dr. Dinneen's tenure would be notable for the beginnings of a "general systems approach" to command and control management (a phrase he used repeatedly in speeches and articles on the subject) and for the influence he wielded on the promulgation of DOD Directive 5000.2, which recognized the special, evolutionary nature of command and control systems.[7]

Another evolutionary step in the DOD command and control management structure was taken in 1978, when the Defense Science Board completed a study requested by Dinneen's boss, Dr. William J. Perry, the under secretary of defense for research and engineering. Among Perry's questions were the following: "To what extent should procurement of C3I systems require multiservice cooperation as contrasted with the present procedure of separate procurement in each service?" "To what extent have existing procedures and organizations proven their effectiveness in the procurement of joint systems?"[8] The board's answers to these questions were blunt: "The nation is failing to deploy command and control systems commensurate with the nature of likely future warfare, with modern weapons systems, or with our available technological and industrial base. Consequently, a much stronger focus within DOD on command and control is needed to assure that improved command and control systems will evolve in a timely fashion to meet our national needs."[9] As indicated in the previous chapter, several of the board's recommendations concerned the need to strengthen the role of the unified and specified commanders in the development of their organic systems for command and control.[10] But the panel also called for stronger, more centralized management of command and control within the DOD, either by creating a new defense command and control systems support agency or by amending the charter of the Defense Communications Agency (DCA), which had handled DOD strategic communications since the 1960s.[11]

This recommendation was by far the most controversial proposal of a report that otherwise received general acceptance. It was, of course, consistent with the predominant postwar pattern of defense organization that sought to solve almost every emerging problem by carving out a new office or agency within the civilian management levels of the Defense Department. Almost immediately, it was realized that of the two alternatives the only practical one was the amendment of the DCA charter, and Dr. Dinneen asked the director of that agency, Vice Adm. Samuel L. Gravely, to draft the document. Gravely did so, and by February 1979, he had proposed a charter that gave the DCA effective control over communications integration efforts associated with the Strategic Air Command, as well as "general program guidance" over many service command and control programs. When they were asked for their views on the proposed charter, the Joint Chiefs displayed impressive agreement. According to Dinneen's account, they "were unanimous in their recommendation that such an expanded agency not be created. . . . The primary objection of the services and the Joint Chiefs of Staff . . . was that service prioritization of command and control systems among other programs in the Planning, Programming and Budgeting System would be lost if statutory control of them was given to an agency. What was needed was stronger operational influence on the planning and programming of inter-service command and control systems."[12]

As an alternative, the Joint Chiefs set up in May 1979 the Command, Control, and Communications Systems Directorate within the Joint Staff structure, and gave it the following missions: "to develop policies, plans and programs for the Joint Chiefs of Staff to insure adequate support for the commanders of unified and specified commands and the National Command Authorities for joint and combined military operations; to conceptualize future C3 systems designs; and to provide direction to improve command and control."[13] Of course, no agency of the Joint Chiefs could ever be given directive authority over programs and funds without imperiling the nature of the system set in place by the National Security Act of 1947. So the C3 Systems Directorate was not allowed to be the final arbiter over the command and control systems that continued to be developed by the services. It was, however, well placed to become the leading military spokesman for joint command and control matters and to assume an increasingly influential role as an "honest broker" in reconciling divergent service interests.[14]

By the time the Reagan administration took office in 1981, the evolution of the command and control community had progressed to the point that more agencies than ever were involved in some aspect of the process, so that the chief characteristic of high-level command and control management appeared to be the very fractionation and dispersion of power criticized by the Defense Science Board. For that reason, the following overview is limited to a brief discussion of the principal actors who have an impact on the problem of joint command and control.

Executive Agencies. The lines of command and control merge at the White House, where the president, with his constitutionally mandated powers as commander in chief of the armed forces, sits as the national command authority (NCA). He and the secretary of defense are the ultimate "users" of the system, with direct lines of authority extending from them to the CINCs of the unified and specified commands, in which are vested the combatant forces of the United States. The president and the secretary of defense can therefore have an important role in the development of command and control systems. As was shown in chapter 5, the establishment of the WWMCCS system was in part spurred by President Kennedy's unhappiness over what he saw as communications shortfalls during the Cuban missile crisis; subsequent crises have all generated lessons learned that have led to renewed efforts for even more precise presidential control.[15] Of more day-to-day concern, however, is the role played by the Office of Management and Budget; its impact is significant simply because of the expense of high-technology equipment—a factor that inevitably leads to hard decisions in the preparation of the defense budget. Finally, the intelligence community plays a vital role in command and control, both as producers of intelligence and as developers of the systems that collect, process, and disseminate data.

Congress. Acting under its constitutional mandate to authorize and appropriate the monies to be used for raising armies and maintaining navies, Congress has in recent years exerted a far tighter degree of control over defense spending than ever before. Beginning with the Defense Authorization Act of 1972, Congress has imposed restrictions on the appropriation of research and development funds that allow it to review the progress of major programs annually to determine if the results justify additional spending. With this leverage, the Armed Services committees of both the Senate and the House have exercised close supervision over command and control issues, especially the House committee which has played a particularly influential part in advocating joint approaches to these issues.[16]

Congress has also found it necessary to have an independent base of information in order to compete effectively with the resources available to the executive branch. Three agencies directly responsible to Congress have often been used in recent years to provide the lawmakers with independent analyses of defense programs: the Congressional Budget Office, the General Accounting Office, and the Congressional Research Service of the Library of Congress. Each of these agencies has acquired a staff of defense specialists and, with them, an increasing ability to perform in-depth policy analyses. Armed with the power of the purse and these information resources, Congress can be a formidable player on command and control issues.[17]

DOD: Office of the Secretary of Defense (OSD). As has been noted throughout the previous two chapters, the growth of OSD functions has been one of the constants of postwar defense organization. There are three agencies within the OSD as presently constituted that have the greatest impact upon the command and control process. The Office of the Assistant Secretary for Program Analysis and Evaluation is the lineal descendant of the Enthoven-Hitch systems analysis office brought to the Pentagon by Robert McNamara. Like other budgetary elements throughout the government, this agency can and does have a major impact on proposed programs, since it is responsible for advising the secretary on the cost-effectiveness and financial impact of future expenditures. Historically, the most important OSD agency on command and control matters has been that of the Under Secretary of Defense for Research and Engineering. Originally created in 1958, its powers were significantly increased as the result of DOD Directive 5000.1, promulgated in 1971 by David Packard, then deputy secretary of defense. Its terms left the basic responsibility for systems development in the hands of the services, while OSD's functions included initial acquisition approval and program reviews at key developmental stages as well as when problems reached "pre-determined danger points."[18] That directive gave this agency great authority over defense acquisition, and when command and control issues assumed greater importance in the mid-1970s, this was the office in which the first assistant secretary for C3I was located.

Dr. Dinneen was succeeded in that position by Donald C. Latham, who took office as part of a Reagan administration determined to decentralize much of defense management. In line with the spirit of a memorandum written by Deputy Secretary of Defense Frank Carlucci in 1981, there was a conscious effort to shift the responsibility for command and control developments back to the services.[19] This trend, however, not only ran counter to the recommendations of the Defense Science Board but was difficult to square with the burden of managing the increased funding and program proliferation of this rapidly growing mission area. By 1984, Latham's responsibilities had grown far beyond those of his predecessor with the addition of intelligence oversight responsibilities (long held to be the missing "I" in "C3I"); by 1985, these additional duties had led to his redesignation as an assistant secretary of defense for C3I directly under the secretary of defense. The primacy of this new status was further marked by the republication of DOD Directive 4230.5, which stated the following: "It is DOD policy to develop, acquire and deploy tactical C3I systems and equipment that effectively meet the essential operational needs of the U.S. tactical forces, and that are compatible and interoperable where required with other U.S. tactical C3I systems and equipment. . . . The Assistant Secretary of Defense for Command, Control, Communications, and Intelligence, as the principal assistant to the Secretary of Defense for all C3I matters, shall ensure that all DOD components comply with this policy."[20]

The Joint Chiefs of Staff (JCS). The creation of the C3 Systems Directorate of the Joint Staff has been mentioned, but there are three other aspects of JCS involvement with joint command and control that should be noted here. The first is that the Carlucci memorandum also granted the chairman of the Joint Chiefs permanent membership on the Defense Resources Board, the top management body established in 1979 to review service programs. Set up in 1979 under the chairmanship of the deputy secretary of defense, the board is composed of the service secretaries, the under secretaries of defense, and seven of the principal assistant secretaries of defense. As the only military member of the board, the chairman is thus well positioned to play a strong role in the promotion of joint matters, especially those pertaining to interoperability.[21]

The second notable development of recent years has been the establishment in 1984 of the Joint Tactical Command, Control, and Communications Agency, whose principal mission is to "ensure the interoperability of tactical command, control, and communications systems for joint or combined operations."[22] Set up under the dual control of the OSD and the JCS, the agency is not only a major player representing the interests of interoperability; it also brings together in a single organization the technical resources necessary to work out the practical solutions required when different command and control systems are brought together.

Finally, perhaps the most telling indicator of JCS involvement in the problem of joint command and control came with publication of a new "memorandum of procedure" which set forth the policies to be followed by the services in implementing the revised DOD directive on interoperability. In this document, the Chiefs went further than ever before in stating what was required: "All requirements for tactical C3I systems are of interest to the Joint Chiefs of Staff regardless of whether those requirements are to meet joint, combined, single-Service or defense agency needs. The Joint Chiefs of Staff require that compatibility and interoperability, once established during the requirements validation process, be maintained during acquisition, deployment, and employment of a system throughout its operational life."[23]

The Services and Military Departments. The Joint Chiefs who approved this memorandum, of course, are the same ones who head their respective services; each of these officers consequently plays a critical role in the development of the command and control systems which that service feels are required to carry out its particular mission. That being the case, it might be hard to understand why interoperability has been a problem at all, or, if it has now been identified as such, why it cannot be solved largely on the strength of the memorandum cited above. The answer to this dilemma is suggested by Gen. John Cushman, whose book *Command and Control of Theater Forces: Adequacy* illustrates that there are a multitude of service agencies that develop command and control systems. And not only are there a great many of these agencies, but most of them represent important internal service constituencies, none of them indifferent to questions of bureaucratic self-interest. Because each is a quasi-autonomous power center with its own set of agendas and issues, it is difficult enough for a service to maintain coherence and discipline within its own ranks. Imposing external pressures from the alien world of joint or combined operations is a problem of even greater magnitude. This is specifically not a problem whose solution is achieved with the stroke of a pen; instead it represents a basic organizational and even political problem that has already been the subject of a certain amount of trial and error.[24]

Two of the major approaches toward joint command and control that have been attempted in this process need to be summarized here as a prelude to the JTIDS case study. These approaches are represented by the TRI-TAC and JINTACCS programs—or, respectively, the Joint Tactical Communications Project and the program for Joint Interoperability of Tactical Command and Control Systems. Both programs are still in existence, their organizations and personnel now having been absorbed by the new Joint Tactical C3 Agency. Both programs have made a clear contribution to interoperability, despite the fact that they have represented less than optimal solutions. One major difference between them was their leadership structures. The TRI-TAC program was set up in May 1971 under the OSD office that eventually was reorganized and headed by Dinneen as the assistant secretary of defense for communications, command, control, and intelligence, whereas JINTACCS grew out of a JCS-sponsored project during the Vietnam War and in 1977 was accorded full program status as a JCS activity. The chief difference between JINTACCS and TRI-TAC, however, lay in their basic approach: TRI-TAC was an effort to achieve interoperability from the ground up, that is, by incorporating interservice perspectives at the design and engineering stages. In contrast, JINTACCS attempted to reconcile the differences in the operating characteristics of existing command and control systems in order to achieve at least a minimal level of interoperability. To put it in terms of the definitions advanced earlier in this chapter, TRI-TAC was an effort to achieve complete interoperability through commonality, while JINTACCS set out to achieve a lesser degree of interoperability.[25]

This contrast becomes even clearer with a closer look at TRI-TAC. In accordance with its charter, original TRI-TAC objectives were to achieve interoperability among tactical command and control systems, develop and deploy in a timely manner interoperable telecommunications equipment for the combatant commands, and eliminate duplication of effort in the development and procurement of telecommunications equipment by the uniformed services.[26] The management system set up to achieve these purposes involved TRI-TAC acting as the executive agent for OSD in refining service communications requirements, validating them, and then assigning a single service to act as project manager for the development of specific systems. It was hoped that by coordinating the tasking at the inception of each major telecommunications system, a common family of tactical command and control systems could be developed and procured. By gradually putting together a common architecture for these systems, the services could achieve operational flexibility, reduce logistical overhead, and, it was thought, save procurement dollars.

With such hopes, some disappointment was perhaps inevitable. For one thing, the project managers were handicapped by having to build hybrid systems that not only spanned differing service requirements but also incorporated aspects of previous-generation analog communications together with next-generation digital data equipment. Not surprisingly, research and development became a seemingly endless process. The master switch of the tactical communications system, the AN-TTC-39, experienced prolonged delays in development, seriously lengthening the time required to deploy it and several of its major subsystems. These delays suggested deeper problems. Reviewing the program's progress in 1977, the House Armed Services Committee said, "The Panel has a very uneasy feeling about the entire TRI-TAC program. . . . There is some suggestion that this so-called 'joint' service effort is joint in name alone. Without the full support and cooperation of all the military services, it appears that the program is doomed to continue to stumble along as it has to date. It is a fundamental law of physics that a multicomponent system, left to itself, will continually move to an increasing state of chaos. While not suggesting that the TRI-TAC program is in a chaotic state, it certainly does not appear to be in an orderly state at present."[27] It was against this backdrop of criticism that Dinneen came into office and redoubled the emphasis on interoperability within the OSD.

Progress was made, but the pace continued to be slow. "TRI-TAC is late and expensive," said one DOD official during the Carter administration, "but there are no good alternatives. . . . There will be a lot of Congressional scrutiny, but eliminating TRI-TAC at this point would be an absolute disaster."[28] This point of view seemed to represent a consensus, since the program continued with all deliberate speed and Congress did not allow its earlier criticism to interfere with research and development expenditures year after year. By 1983, the first of the major TRI-TAC end items had reached the procurement stage, the AN/TTC-39 circuit switch proving to have been at least worth the wait.[29] But as TRI-TAC was subsumed in that same year into the new Joint Tactical C3 Agency, its legacy seemed to suggest that the undeniable progress brought by the program had been purchased at what was perhaps a disproportionate cost in time, money, and opportunity. This was an especially compelling notion in view of the fact that the ponderous pace of the program contrasted strongly with a commercial world that had raced to produce and market at least one full generation of digital telecommunications equipment in the same time span. Finally, there was a feeling that the requirements process still had not been well disciplined and that the equipment eventually produced was too big, too bulky, too heavy, and too costly because TRI-TAC was "all things to all men."[30]

The JINTACCS program has from the beginning been less ambitious in scope, since it was set up as a method to link command and control systems that already existed. Its problems, however, have been no less difficult than those of TRI-TAC, because interoperability cuts across service and doctrinal lines at least as much with current equipment as it does with future systems. Adding to this dilemma is the inherent difficulty of integrating systems designed for separate service use. Consequently, any effort to achieve interoperability has to take account of four basic characteristics: computer hardware, which places physical limits on the adaptability of major systems; computer software, which often involves different programs and computer languages; military standards, which affect the meanings and formats of basic messages; and system interfaces, which are the electronic means of exchange between physically remote systems. When JINTACCS was set up, therefore, it was hoped that evolution would lead in two directions: the reconcilation of diverse existing systems and the refinement of an architecture of design standards that would allow interoperability to be built into future systems—all without disturbing the traditional functions of the service acquisition process. The mission of the JINTACCS program—approved by the secretary of defense on August 2, 1977—reflected this: it was to "insure that inter-service and joint plans are developed to achieve technical compatibility, and that tests and demonstrations are conducted to exhibit the compatibility, inter-operability and operational effectiveness of those tactical command and control systems used in support of ground and amphibious military operations."[31]

The JINTACCS program has tackled computer hardware and software problems, but it has been directed primarily at establishing jointly acceptable protocols and message formats between different digital data systems in such areas as air operations, intelligence, fire support, operational control, and amphibious warfare. Although the design of technical interface standards might not appear to be an area of red-hot interservice rivalry, the process itself has turned up some arresting examples of the different cultures now being integrated. At one level, language itself is a problem since the same term can have different meanings in different services. As one JINTACCS action officer described the problem, "You send out a message to all units of a joint force to *secure* their operations. An Army outfit will double the guard force and put out barbed wire, the Air Force will energize their crypto systems, and the Navy will simply pack up and go home!" A similar problem cropped up during the design of a standard message format, when only three characters were available to abbreviate the Navy's Supporting Arms Coordination Center. Naturally, the Navy suggested calling it "SAC," but the Air Force objected that "SAC" already was the official acronym for the Strategic Air Command. The Navy retorted that its SACC had been in existence long before the Strategic Air Command, and that if anyone had to change, it should be the Air Force. A lengthy argument then ensued over a simple acronym until a compromise was reached that satisfied the demands of both automation and service honor: "I think they decided to call the damned thing the SCC!"[32]

It is through such disputes, however ridiculous they may appear, that the infrastructure of interoperability is painstakingly hammered out. More serious problems occur when embedded terms, procedures, or even doctrinal issues arise that cannot be easily compromised. In the instance cited above, for example, the Navy's opposition might easily have been due to the existence of the term SACC in the software of a number of different systems; going into a computer program and changing every instance in which such a term appears can be an expensive and difficult proposition. Small wonder, then, that these disputes do occur. It should be noted, however, that JINTACCS, like the JCS itself, is an interservice body that is not capable of imposing unilateral decisions to resolve problems. Indeed, as one service's briefing guide to the work of the various JINTACCS committees notes, "Decisions are by majority vote, unless one of the permanent members objects, in which case unanimity shall prevail"—exactly the voting procedure followed in the Security Council of the United Nations.[33] In the event of a serious dispute, the matter would have to be referred in succession from the JINTACCS program director to the Joint Standards Group for Tactical C3 Systems to the Joint Tactical C3 Systems Council and ultimately to the Joint Chiefs themselves.

The record to date, however, has not included any such serious conflict within the JINTACCS structure, other than the time taken to work out some of its major projects. And JINTACCS participants can point to some clear examples of success. It played a key role in the development of standard message formats on the tactical digital information links (TADIL) that are part of the new Joint Tactical Air Operations system. Its progress in producing interservice agreements on character-oriented messages means that different components will be able to share computer data base information in joint operations. Finally, JINTACCS is the lead developer in the TADIL which will by 1989 provide the common link in the operations of the JTIDS system to be described below.[34]

If there is a criticism to be made of JINTACCS, it would concern its lack of scope; its limited purposes have, of course, limited its achievements. One example is a JINTACCS program that brought together the data requirements of the Army's TACFIRE artillery system and the Marine Integrated Fire and Air Support System, or MIFASS, a newer and more ambitious fire-control system which (perhaps in the nature of things) the Marines ultimately canceled. Despite similarities in the functions of the two systems, there were basic design differences in the transmission media used (netted FM voice radios for TACFIRE versus a switched digital network for MIFASS) as well as the data rate and the choice of message formats. Eventually JINTACCS succeeded in designing common formats, protocols, and modems between the two systems which—had MIFASS been procured—would have allowed them to communicate, although at the much slower data rate associated with the Army system.[35]

The basic question, however, is why two such systems—three, if the common modems and multiplexers are counted—had to be developed in the first place to perform a single function: indirect fire support for ground units. Considering that Marine and Army units have historically found themselves fighting side by side on numerous occasions (Grenada being merely the latest example), why would it have been necessary to make technical sacrifices just so they could communicate? The answer depends on outlook. The JINTACCS approach suggests that building a series of least common denominators between functionally similar but organizationally discrete systems reflects an acceptance of reality. The TRI-TAC approach would suggest a basic engineering solution, trading off requirements in order to allow the construction of a single system that would satisfy both the Army and the Marines. A cynic might add that the TRI-TAC system would take fifteen years to be developed or even that it would add a statistically significant percentage to the gross national debt. Some middle ground between the TRI-TAC and JINTACCS philosophies might provide the best of both worlds, especially if the services found themselves with problems that seemingly demanded a single solution to be provided by a seductive new technology. This search for a hybrid approach to the problem of interoperability leads naturally to the case study of the system called JTIDS.

JTIDS: Concepts, Applications, and Developments to 1981

All the progress on interoperability charted thus far was very much in the future when the JTIDS program had its inception in the early to mid-1970s. Like TRI-TAC and JINTACCS, this program represented a fundamental development strategy midway between the all-embracing commonality of the TRI-TAC approach and the more limited interoperability envisioned under JINTACCS. As shown, these strategies were responses to the new technological advances represented by the advent of precision-guided munitions and the need for increased mobility of land, sea, and air forces—all of which demanded increased efficiency in command and control. Consequently, a new set of requirements was generated for a communications infrastructure capable of supporting the weight of the data to be passed between remote sensor platforms, widely dispersed weapons systems, and the intelligence-operations fusion centers needed to keep track of it all.

In constructing such an infrastructure, the services were mostly starting from a common baseline, even though their current communications gear varied so much in design and operating characteristics as to be largely unsuitable for interservice use. Despite the Navy's experience with digital data, the bulk of service tactical communications rested on a structure of high-frequency radio nets, in which soldiers, sailors, airmen, or marines simply pushed a button or lifted a receiver in order to talk to one another. Convenient and familiar as these practices were, they simply would not do in an environment in which such signals could be jammed, intercepted for intelligence analysis, or tracked with sufficient speed and accuracy as to permit the sending station to be targeted and destroyed by enemy fire.

The problem was that voice radio systems were carried by analog communications relays—that is, the voice of the sender was broken down into electronic pulses that were transmitted to a receiver which reversed the process for the listener. The process was roughly five thousand times slower than the speeds achievable by digital information systems, which used computers to send thousands of bits of information per second along electronic pathways from machine to machine. Digital data had chiefly been used for long-haul strategic communications between fixed-site message centers, the computers used for this purpose being too large and bulky to permit easy movement. With the advent of the silicon chip revolution and printed microcircuit boards, computers grew smaller and less expensive—leading to new horizons in the marriage of automation and communications.

For communications engineers, the possibilities seemed endless because of two principal developments. First, one of the major problems they had wrestled with had been the "man-in-the-loop problem": the humans on both ends of the communications links that had characterized the earlier analog era and had been one of its least efficient aspects. Now, the smaller and more powerful mini- and microcomputers suggested that it would be possible to design whole systems that would use digital data pathways to "interrogate" sensors continuously, the information then being relayed in nanoseconds back to a command post or fire control center where it would be displayed on a cathode ray tube, or CRT. Human intervention would thus be limited to the decision process itself. This was a powerful concept and led to several service programs, the Air Force AWACS and the Navy Aegis being two of the better-known examples. The second development was the application of the computer to data transmission and distribution techniques. The speed of computer processing allowed a signal to be broken down, packed with data, and transmitted simultaneously over an entire frequency band. This technique—called "frequency hopping"—could defeat enemy jamming and voice interception, permitting the receiving computers to reconstitute the signal, extract the information from the "data bus," and automatically dispatch it to a number of different addressees. Frequency hopping and distributed data techniques represented the same sort of improvement over existing tactical communications as the machine gun had over the bolt-action rifle.

In the early 1970s, the Navy and Air Force separately began work on several programs that addressed their most critical needs in the post-Vietnam era. The Navy's programs were the Integrated Tactical Air Control Program and the Integrated Tactical Navigation System, twin concepts that sought to harness digital data techniques to the problems of coordinating the movements of ships and carrier-based aircraft. The Air Force had similar efforts underway in two programs of its own: Position Location Reporting and Control of Tactical Aircraft and Integrated Communications, Navigation, and Identification. The test results from all four programs were sufficiently encouraging that by 1973 both services were ready to request formal OSD project funding and approval. The Air Force programs had been organized under the leadership of the Mitre Corporation, a privately organized but publicly funded think tank in Bedford, Massachusetts. Experts there quickly noticed the impressive similarities between the Air Force and Navy programs, a coincidence that might eventually lead to a joint project involving the kind of decentralized computer-to-computer communications that had been pioneered by Mitre.

The development of the classic JTIDS concept is most closely identified with Gordon Welchman, a transplanted Englishman whose remarkable career included World War II service with the team at Bletchley Park that cracked the German high command code. His early exposure to the Ultra Secret led to a lifelong fascination with military communications and a number of important contributions during his many years at Mitre. Whatever the deficiencies of German codes, Welchman's study of the North African campaign convinced him that one of the keys to Rommel's victories had been the flexible system of tactical communications that allowed the Desert Fox to command from any point on the battlefield. Similarly, the presence of radios in all German tanks—considered heretical when introduced in the 1930s—not only allowed Rommel and his subordinate commanders to have great connectivity but also gave junior officers the wide latitude for independent action characteristic of decentralized operations. But in Welchman's view these lessons had not been well applied: "After World War Two, the planning of battlefield communications gradually deteriorated into little more than methods of applying telephone system thinking and switchboard technology to provide a rigid structure of point-to-point linkages. . . . The flexible inter-element connectivity that the Germans provided for their blitzkrieg by using interlocking common-user radio nets could have served as a model for our own future planning, but it was forgotten."[36]

To Welchman, and to other Mitre engineers whom he proselytized, JTIDS represented nothing less than a revolutionary attempt to rediscover those forgotten lessons; with the help of modern technology, they could be applied to future battlefields which would demand greater connectivity between different combat elements in order to coordinate otherwise decentralized operations. It is interesting that these ideas were being developed in parallel with much of the thinking that characterized the maneuver school of thought associated with the military reform movement. Yet, while the reformers were— and are—deeply suspicious of technological solutions to command and control problems, Welchman and his followers saw JTIDS as an antidote to the dominant hierarchical pattern of military communications that so troubled the maneuver warriors.

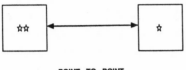

POINT - TO - POINT

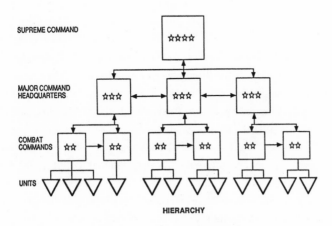

HIERARCHY

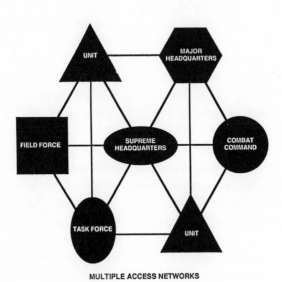

MULTIPLE ACCESS NETWORKS

Figure 7.1   Models Of Communications Networks

Source: Author

The point becomes clearer in the three diagrams shown in figure 7.1. Model I is the simple point-to-point pattern of "telephone-system thinking" disparaged by Welchman, which also characterizes the hierarchical system of top-down linkages shown in Model II. The essence of this system is that it depends on sender-oriented communications—information flows up and down hierarchical lines as a result of single actions taken by the senders of that information. In Model III, a distributed data network is shown, characterized as much by lateral linkages as hierarchical ones and by a common pool of information each member draws upon—and contributes to—depending on its own requirements and abilities. Like borrowers from a library, each member of a distributed data network decides for himself what information he requires and, in the best scholarly tradition, enriches the system with his own contributions to the common store of information. It is this wide pattern of lateral and hierarchical connectivity geared toward individual data decisions that characterizes receiver-oriented communications.[37]

Ideally, JTIDS would be a mobile, decentralized, receiver-oriented communications system characterized by wide-ranging connectivity between combat elements with different functions, command lines, parent services, and even native languages—the latter necessary because of the obvious applications of the system to the NATO environment.[38] In more practical terms, Mitre engineers saw that it might be possible to construct such a system using decentralized computer-to-computer communications, especially given the rapidly growing power of microprocessors. Advances in silicon chip technology promised that these terminals would be smaller, smarter, and cheaper than ever before. They could thus be programmed for use in a wide variety of service applications, beginning with the needs of the Air Force and the Navy for secure, jam-proof digital communications utilizing both voice and data. Consequently, Secretary of Defense James R. Schlesinger directed in September 1974 that the program go forward in a way that would exploit its benefits for all three services. This directive led to the establishment of the JTIDS Joint Program Office under a formal charter by the Deputy Secretary of Defense for Research and Engineering. The Army, Navy, and Air Force were all to be represented, but, in a move that would have lasting significance, the Air Force was chosen to be the executive agent for the program—probably because of the Mitre connection and because it would buy the greatest number of aircraft terminals.[39]

In at least some respects, the choice of the Air Force as lead service in a billion-dollar joint project where important interests were at stake recalled the FTX/F-111 case of the 1960s.[40] Both cases were predicated on an overarching technological solution to separate service requirements. But while Robert

McNamara had enforced commonality largely because of a personal ideological commitment, the Ford and Carter administrations leaned toward the joint approach out of the necessities imposed by the reduced defense expenditures of the post-Vietnam era. Any misgivings the services may have had about another commonality-induced shotgun marriage were far from apparent, however, as the program got underway. By the mid-1970s, it had begun to take on the outlines that would characterize its fundamental technological approach.

The primary concept was that JTIDS terminals would allow aircraft, and ultimately other users as well, to communicate with one another without the involvement of their pilots or crews. A flight of F-15 jet fighters equipped with JTIDS, for example, would exchange information several times per second concerning their heading, altitude, speed, and so on. The data would be sent automatically to every other aircraft, appearing on a CRT on the pilot's console with an alphanumeric display that some likened to the video game "Space Invaders."[41] Any other member of the JTIDS net—a ground control station, an orbiting AWACS aircraft, or other members of the same flight— would both receive these reports and contribute the results of their own sensor suites. The result would be a comprehensive situation display, so comprehensive that the pilot might well be swamped with all the data held by the system. For that reason, JTIDS would also allow the pilot or any other user to select only those categories of data relevant to his assigned mission. The pilot of an F-15 approaching an enemy air defense zone, for example, could select only those data showing his own position relative to enemy interceptors and air defense systems picked up by his own sensors or by those of any other member of the JTIDS network. Another pilot on an air superiority mission could just as easily suppress the data on low-level air defenses and call up instead the system's holdings on opposing enemy fighters and high-altitude SAMs.[42]

Thus, JTIDS technology embodied the classic concepts of both receiver-oriented communications and selective retrieval of information from a larger data pool.[43] Both facets of the system were made possible by the physics embodied in JTIDS, which featured a kind of computer-sharing technique known as "time-division multiple access," or TDMA. Like other computer time-sharing techniques, TDMA allows many users to have access to a shared network; unlike them, however, JTIDS was to be built not around a central processing unit of a single computer but around a number of small computers constantly communicating with one another. The coordination of the JTIDS system would be achieved by a timing device organic to each terminal which would synchronize its transmissions to fit in with the other users, thus avoiding

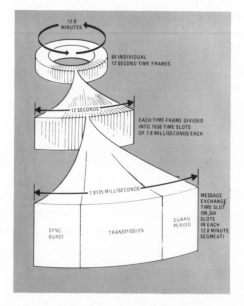

Timeslot Structure of a Single JTIDS Net

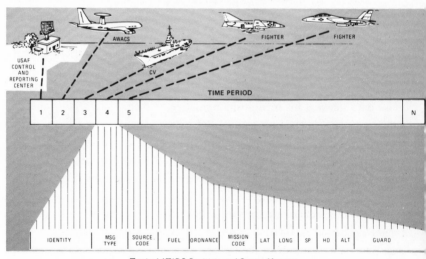

Typical JTIDS Position and Status Message

The basic idea of JTIDS technology is to use small, synchronized computers to place unprecedented amounts of information on a radio signal. The signal is broken down into time slots of 7.8 milliseconds (top), with slots assigned to each member of the net. The bottom illustration shows the large amounts of data that can be packed into each of these time slots and displayed graphically on the JTIDS terminal.

Figure 7.2   JTIDS Message Technology

Source: JTIDS Joint Program Office

interference and expediting message processing. Indeed, the effective synchronization of "time division" permitted the "multiple access" under TDMA.[44]

The essential workings of the system are illustrated in figure 7.2. In the first illustration, the internal timing device divides slots for message transmission into "epochs" of 12.8 minutes, consisting of 64 individual 12-second time frames. Each time frame is further subdivided into 1,536 time slots of 7.8125 milliseconds each—meaning that 98,304 time slots are available in each JTIDS epoch. Each one of these 7.8 millisecond messages contains synchronization periods on either end that help to maintain system alignment. The fantastic speeds and information densities possible with digital data flows are shown graphically in the second illustration, which depicts the information content possible in just one of these bursts. In routine position and status reports by a single aircraft on the JTIDS net, data on all the categories shown would be transmitted automatically. And, as shown in the illustration, potential users might well include the aircraft, ships, and ground stations of different services.[45]

The technological choices that framed the initial development of JTIDS thus had the following characteristics:

- The JTIDS system would be self-regulating, without the inherent necessity for central communication centers or nodes which would be easy to target and destroy in combat.
- The nodeless character of the system was also a function of the fact that each JTIDS terminal would act as an inherent repeating station, allowing the typical network to be spread across an area of three hundred to five hundred miles. Similarly, the destruction of any one terminal would not affect the integrity of the network as a whole.
- The JTIDS architecture lent itself particularly well to the use of multiple nets accommodating the needs of a wide variety of users. The digital data flow, for example, could also handle voice transmissions, although it was true that "a little bit of voice would eat up a lot of data."
- Each JTIDS terminal would provide embedded positive identification of every other terminal in the system, as well as their precise distances from one another; it thus automatically provided for relative navigation as well as the distinguishing of enemy and friendly units.[46]
- The terminals would feature an encryption device allowing secure communications to be transmitted automatically. The technology of frequency hopping across a "spread-spectrum" also constituted an embedded improvement in signal security practices, since it would be difficult for en-

emy jammers to block an entire frequency band. Enemy interception and exploitation of JTIDS signals would be made far more difficult not only because its mobile terminals would be hard to pinpoint but also because critical command nets would be hidden within the mass of data being passed over the net each microsecond.[47] Together, these improvements would mean a quantum jump in all phases of communications security.

The capabilities of the JTIDS technology thus offered the services a common baseline from which to derive solutions to some of their most pressing problems. What follows is a summary of service objectives as they approached the first phase of the program.

Air Force. The potential represented by JTIDS appeared to be especially rich for the Air Force, and not only because it was the lead service in developing the program. By 1978 the AWACS aircraft was coming into initial operational use, and JTIDS could be an efficient tool for distributing its data to ground control stations. The long-range surveillance capabilities of the AWACS promised a new era in the precise control of high-performance aircraft such as the F-15, which, no less than land forces, would have to fight outnumbered and win in any confrontation with the air forces of the Warsaw Pact. A better system of tactical information distribution among surveillance planes, fighter aircraft, and ground control stations would help provide the needed edge. As a Mitre report summarized it in 1977, with JTIDS "command and control support to fighters is going to be a great deal better. Controllers won't be saturated. Pilots will have the information they need soon enough to fly their own maneuvers. JTIDS will plot MIG locations relative to the pilot. . . . If part of the command and control system is lost, full connectivity with the remainder provides survivability. . . . Fighter mutual support can be coordinated much more easily when information comes in advance and does not come as a surprise."[48] Above all, JTIDS would provide secure, jam-resistant communications, without which the tactical air control system would not be able to survive known Soviet capabilities.

If there were any reasons for reservations about the Air Force approach, they lay in the fact that JTIDS appeared to affect three important service norms, primarily those associated with the "Fighter Mafia" whose opinions would have a dominant influence on system development. First, the Air Force mostly relied upon voice communications in its operations, both for ground control and cockpit-to-cockpit exchanges. Switching to data would be a big adjustment under any circumstances. Second, JTIDS terminals represented another increment in the steadily growing problem of cockpit complexity, if they were actually deployed in fighters. The reasons for this problem are many, but most come down to the fact that the Air Force remains firmly wedded to the idea of single-seat fighters. Whatever its benefits, the JTIDS terminal would be yet another system competing for the attention of an already overworked pilot. Finally, if JTIDS terminals were installed in individual strike aircraft, the resulting information flow would give new life to the traditional doctrine of decentralized execution. Indeed, it could even be argued that receiver-oriented communications in fighter cockpits might call into question the whole notion of command centralized and exercised from the ground.

Navy. The Navy, as mentioned earlier, had been using digital data for naval air operations for more than a decade at the start of the JTIDS program, so it did not need to be convinced of the potential value of the system. Nor did adding a terminal in the cockpit of the fighter present a problem. Navy fighters had flown with Naval Tactical Data System terminals for years, the problem of cockpit complexity having been largely solved by the "guy in back"—the standard two-seat configuration of Navy fighters. Consequently, the Navy looked upon the surveillance, navigation, and control potential of JTIDS much the same as the Air Force did, but with fewer reservations. The Navy's version of AWACS was the E2C Hawkeye; with JTIDS it would be even more capable of extending the umbrella of air defense coverage around the carrier battle group because of the embedded relay characteristics of the system's terminals. And, though always suspicious of Air Force involvement in maritime operations, the Navy coveted the potential of AWACS for extending that umbrella still farther if a way could be found to provide its data to surface ships. Another advantage in the Navy's eyes was JTIDS' potential for becoming the single system that could tie together the diverse Navy networks responsible for air, surface, and submarine warfare. Amphibious operations would similarly be enhanced if the Marines and the Army were part of the JTIDS network.

Tactical applications of JTIDS seemed equally promising, among them dropping JTIDS-equipped sonar buoys in an area of suspected submarine contacts to provide a continuous readout of their position, heading, and depth; dropping JTIDS-equipped beacons off hostile beachheads to guide landing craft into cleared channels and to create corridors for close air support; and using JTIDS aircraft terminals to extend air-to-air missile guidance ranges. In one technique called "Forward Pass," for example, an F-14 that had expended all its missiles would engage an attacking aircraft. Meanwhile, another F-14 in the vicinity would fire one of its missiles without having a radar lock on the intruder. The JTIDS link would allow the unarmed F-14 to acquire the missile and guide it to the target. To the Navy, therefore, JTIDS represented the next generation of the digital data revolution of which the service was already an active proponent.[49]

Army and Marine Corps. At the inception of the JTIDS program, Army interest was largely theoretical, although it also wanted to share in the data the AWACS could provide to ground stations responsible for air defense. But another near-term gain suggested itself by the late 1970s because of the embedded identification and navigation capabilities of the system. Both the Army and the Marines have had to grapple with the difficult problems of land navigation in the tactical environment, where one of the standard challenges has always been to know where one's own troops are located. The standard tools for accomplishing that task have always been the map, the compass, and the second lieutenant, a combination with an unusual capacity for illustrating the workings of Murphy's Law. But even when things were going well, it was common military practice to send most unit position reports to higher head-quarters by unencrypted radio voice transmissions. The Vietnam War had shown that even a technologically unsophisticated adversary could be sur-prisingly adept at intercepting and exploiting such messages. Thus, the ground force contingent was eager for a method of securely tracking and reporting the location of maneuver units on the battlefield.

Giving that requirement additional urgency was the proliferation of highly accurate air defense weapons among Army and Marine units. The most so-phisticated of these weapons, such as the Hawk and Chaparral missiles and the Vulcan air defense gun, had always been tied into Air Force nets, but the Redeye and Stinger air defense systems were shoulder-fired, heat-seeking missiles, designed to be used by individual soldiers with the forward maneu-ver units. Knowing the deadly effect these missiles could have on low-flying aircraft and fearing the infantryman's historic indifference to the finer points of distinguishing hostile from friendly aircraft ("Shoot 'em all down and sort 'em out on the ground!"), Army, Marine, and especially Air Force leaders were properly concerned about the potential for "fratricidal" aircraft losses due to "friendly fire." Therefore, something had to be done to improve the connectivity between air defense and close air support.

The JTIDS technology could provide the answer to both air defense and land navigation problems. Terminals small enough to be mounted in aircraft were also small enough to be transportable in tactical vehicles; the connectivity of these terminals meant that a few of them could cover a wide area and link both JTIDS and non-JTIDS units. This was the principal idea behind what unfortu-nately became known as the PLRS/JTIDS Hybrid, a jaw-crunching acronym, the first part of which (pronounced "plarz") stood for the Position Location Reporting System. Under this concept, Net Control Units (NCU) were to be set up, consisting of a JTIDS terminal and a display console deployed in a shelter on the back of a standard Army/Marine two-and-a-half-ton truck. The NCU terminal would be linked to aircraft, ground control centers, and any other member of the network with a JTIDS terminal. Its principal linkage with forward troops, air defense teams, and fire support coordinators would be through the "enhanced PLRS user units" deployed with those forces. These user units were little more than manpack radios tied to a data entry device that closely resembled a hand-held calculator. Not only would the NCU be linked to both aircraft and air defenders; it would also display automatically the position of all user units on the map grid of the console. A division commander could then know from a single glance at the NCU display the actual positions of his maneuver units. Those units could also use the system to determine their own position by interrogating the NCU and could exchange limited "free text" messages with other user units. To both the Army and the Marines, these were revolutionary capabilities, well worth the effort of participation in the JTIDS Joint Project Office.[50]

The identification of these service applications was one of the major features of the JTIDS program during the formative years of 1975–80. That same period, however, was marked by a mixed pattern of conflict and cooperation that ended with a series of important decisions in the final year of the Carter administration. Before turning to a discussion of those developments, I will summarize the agreements reached on the direction of the JTIDS program by the end of the decade. Essentially, it focused on the development and production of three classes of terminals:

- *Class I Terminals:* The Class I terminals were to be the answer to the most immediate concern of the Air Force, which was the near-term deployment of a data distribution system on the AWACS aircraft. The airborne version of the terminal weighed six hundred pounds and filled an entire equipment rack in the KC-135/Boeing 707 aircraft used for AWACS. Its primary role was to be the "data down-link" of JTIDS messages from the AWACS to ground control stations, which would receive those signals via an Adaptable Surface Interface Terminal (ASIT) that would also translate JTIDS data into the existing tactical air control nets. The Air Force planned to buy eighty-six development and full production models of the terminals, with initial deployments in 1983.
- *Class II Terminals:* In concept, the Class II terminals represented the full flowering of JTIDS technology. As many as five thousand of these terminals

might be purchased, as the Navy and Air Force deployed them on aircraft and ships and the Army and Marines made them the linchpin of the PLRS/JTIDS Hybrid. Possessing the same capabilities as the Class I terminals, but far smaller and lighter (1.6 cubic feet and 125 pounds), the Class II terminals were to be developed and purchased beginning in the mid-1980s.

■ *Class III Terminals:* Although they would never ultimately come into existence, Class III terminals were something of a gleam in the eyes of early JTIDS planners as they anticipated the 1990s bringing further advances in miniaturization, increased computer power, and decreased costs. In particular, it was thought that JTIDS might well represent a "candidate capability" for the application of a DOD-sponsored program called Very High Speed Integrated Circuitry (VHSIC), which would help usher in the fourth generation of computer technology.[51]

Although the services were able to agree on an overall plan for JTIDS, they disagreed about some aspects of the program. The most serious of these disagreements involved the message standards to be used in implementing JTIDS and, even more profound, the technological architecture of the system itself. Little more than a year into the program, the Navy and the Air Force got into serious difficulty over the configuration of the tactical data link (TADIL) to be used in the Class I terminals. The argument centered on whether it was necessary to create an Interim JTIDS Message Standard for these terminals until an entirely new standard—TADIL J—was developed around the operations of the Class II terminals by the mid-1980s. The Navy argued that the existing TADILs for joint operations could serve as an interim standard and questioned the costs and difficulties of developing new software that was seemingly programmed for early obsolescence. The Air Force countered that the old TADILs were inappropriate, that they hoped the interim standard would be the basis for interoperability of the AWACS in NATO, and that they had to give the AWACS contractor (Boeing) an early decision on whatever standard was to be applied if aircraft deliveries were to proceed on time.[52]

The Navy began to feel that it was being steam-rollered by the Air Force as the lead service. As Brock Robertson's account put it, "The main point made by the Navy was that the new message specification did not meet its requirements. The Navy wanted a system that would interface with its existing TADILs and hence keep its expense down to the absolute minimum. . . . The root reason was again economics."[53] The dispute simmered along until late 1976, when the issue was raised all the way to the Air Staff. A compromise of sorts was reached: the interim standard would be put in place for AWACS, but the TADIL J standards would be designed under the auspices of a joint working group formed under the new JINTACCS charter. The Navy had clearly lost a battle. Consequently, the compromise did not entirely settle the issue of message standards and the relative costs of having to adapt to new systems.

The disagreement over message forms cropped up again in 1978, but now in a more serious context because it was linked to a schism—no other word is appropriate here—that had developed between the Navy and the Air Force over the technological architecture. The original TDMA architecture envisioned multiple nets, but all as part of a single system. The Navy's concept was an alternative to TDMA, known as Distributed Time Division Multiple Access, or DTDMA. The technical differences between the "T" and the "D" architectures are varied, complex, and not especially relevant to this analysis: suffice it to say that the message forms were fundamentally different and it was not at all clear they could even be made compatible. The conceptual divergence came principally from the differences in the way the Air Force and the Navy envisioned JTIDS in the first place, a divergence that only grew wider as the project wore on. Figure 7.3 illustrates the difference. As shown in the top drawing, TDMA envisioned the use of multiple nets, but all as part of a single system. Below is DTDMA, which was far more easily adapted to the Navy's long-standing preference for federal, quasi-autonomous organizational structures and their corresponding electronic networks. Another reason for the Navy's preference may have been the fact that the prototype DTDMA message structure and characteristics closely paralleled the TADIL A and TADIL C links the Navy had used extensively for years. For whatever reason, the DTDMA architecture was to be the Navy's technology of choice for the next seven years.[54]

By 1978, the differences were becoming more evident. Progress on TADIL J was excruciatingly slow, so much so that several issues had been raised to the level of the Joint Tactical C3 Council before being resolved. The Navy was building hardware to demonstrate the DTDMA architecture and was not mollified when the Air Force proposed in March an "advanced" form of TDMA, which, after the linguistic fashion of these matters, was termed Advanced TDMA, or ATDMA. The system was identical to TDMA except that it claimed to double the data rate of the system—an issue that had been a Navy concern. Navy suspicions of Air Force intentions were further heightened when the Air Force began to seek funds for an "interim" anti-jam radio voice system called "SEEK TALK." The Navy was, of course, looking to JTIDS as the integrated radio and data distribution system of the future; it now appeared that the Air Force saw JTIDS only in terms of data distribution and that it might be prepared to go off on its own to acquire the anti-jam radio capability that was so consistent with its practices and known preferences.[55]

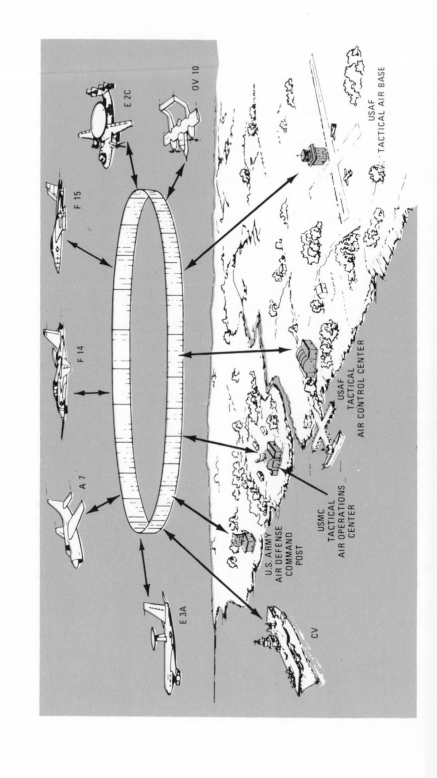

E 2C

OV 10

F 15

F 14

A 7

E 3A

CV

USAF
TACTICAL AIR BASE

USAF
TACTICAL
AIR CONTROL CENTER

USMC
TACTICAL
AIR OPERATIONS
CENTER

U.S. ARMY
AIR DEFENSE
COMMAND
POST

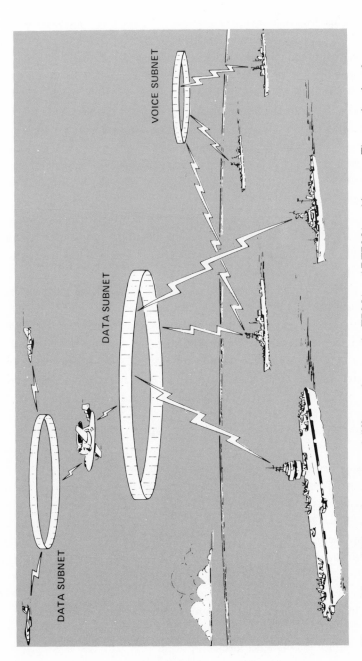

These two figures illustrate the conceptual difference between the TDMA and DTDMA architectures. The top drawing shows JTIDS operating with multiple users of a single common structure, the approach favored by the Air Force in developing its TDMA architecture. The use of multiple data subnets in a more decentralized overall structure (bottom) was characteristic of the DTDMA approach favored by the Navy.

Figure 7.3   JTIDS Net Structures

Source: JTIDS Joint Program Office

It was against this backdrop that Gerald P. Dinneen took a series of actions that sealed his personal commitment to the JTIDS program as a symbol of interoperability and joint development of command and control systems. On September 5, 1978, he issued a memorandum directing that the effort toward Class II terminals be pursued "based upon the Advanced TDMA technical approach. To insure maximum interoperability . . . the Navy is to join and support [that] effort." Now DTDMA was to be relegated to a "technical contingency" only.[56] In November, Dinneen prevailed on the secretary of defense to sign a directive declaring JTIDS a major acquisition system subject to OSD management scrutiny (that is, by Dinneen) under the provisions of DOD Directives 5000.1 and 5000.2.[57] And in March 1979, he chided the services again on their slow progress in designing JTIDS message standards. Not only did he urge them to do better, but he announced the formation of a JTIDS Executive Committee under his chairmanship.[58] This was top-management intervention with a vengeance.

The Navy saw the situation as one in which its critical interests were threatened not only by the Air Force but also by an OSD staff increasingly prone to sacrifice operational interests for conformity with the wishes of the lead service. Throughout 1979 and 1980, therefore, the Navy waged a skillful rear-guard action designed to preserve its options without flouting Dinneen's authority, a strategy that recalled its behavior during the TFX case. The tactics employed can be discerned in an internal Navy memorandum written by D. E. Mann, the assistant secretary of the navy for research and engineering, which documented his meeting with Deputy Secretary of Defense Charles Duncan to discuss JTIDS. After presenting the rationale for DTDMA, Mann recounted for Duncan's benefit his recollection of the first meeting of Dinneen's JTIDS Executive Committee: "I set the record straight on pressing and unrelieved Navy concerns over the course OSD has directed the JTIDS program to follow despite Navy objections. Specifically, I indicated that I could not comprehend the justification for Dinneen's directive [of September 5, 1978] instructing the Navy to abandon its approach in favor of the Air Force proposal, the plan to send forth in the very near future an RFP [contract proposal on Class II terminals] framed in terms which may result in a design that precludes the Navy from satisfying its future requirements and ignores already developed, more flexible Navy technology, and finally, that I intended to pursue the matter further and to higher levels, if possible."[59]

There is no record that Mann's candid luncheon meeting with the deputy secretary of defense resulted in specific directives to Dinneen to back off. Nevertheless, the OSD position was softened somewhat in an August 1979 memo which reestablished TDMA as the JTIDS baseline, but directed the Navy to continue (!) its DTDMA evaluation activities.[60] Pressures continued to build when, in late January 1980, the General Accounting Office (GAO) issued a formal report to Congress entitled "The Joint Tactical Information Distribution System—How Important Is It?" Although the GAO had made a low-key inquiry about JTIDS management the year before, this was an attack from an unexpected quarter, since Congress had largely been supportive of JTIDS; indeed, the 1977 House Armed Services Committee Report that had criticized TRI-TAC had singled out JTIDS for praise.[61] Now, however, the investigating arm of Congress had formally reached out to question DOD management of the program and its ability to resolve interservice conflicts in the development process.[62] In preparing its rebuttal, OSD followed the usual practice of soliciting service reactions to and comments on the GAO report. The Air Force response amounted to a stirring defense of its stewardship as the lead service. The Navy response said flatly, "The Department of the Navy concurs in general with the findings and recommendations stated in the report" in a memo signed by none other than D. E. Mann. There is no evidence whatever that Mann had thus made good on his threat to appeal to higher authority, and any inference to that effect ought to be dismissed out of hand. But given the Navy's well-known ability to make its views known on Capitol Hill, it is probable that OSD viewed the GAO report as a "shot across the bow."[63] That interpretation would seem to be confirmed by the pleading tone adopted by Dinneen in his letter responding to the GAO on behalf of the Defense Department: "In summary, let me note that we share most of the same concerns for JTIDS as the GAO. We and the Services are all agreed that the operational requirement is urgent. Even so, the determination of optimal solutions is an interactive process. I think we have 'turned the corner' as far as management issues are concerned and our planning will put the JTIDS program firmly onto the normal milestone and accountability tracks of any other major program. By this time next year, the results should speak for themselves."[64]

It could hardly have come as a surprise, then, that on July 18, 1980, Dinneen signed a memorandum reversing his 1978 decision. Although TDMA would be the baseline architecture for Class I and Class II terminals—the latter now approaching a contract decision point—he said he had decided that the development of higher capacity terminals would proceed based on DTDMA. In practical terms, this meant that the Army, Air Force, and (presumably) Marine terminals would be Class II TDMA systems. The Navy would not be required to purchase them, since it would be developing its own Class II terminals using the DTDMA technology. Dinneen further specified that the architecture of the overall system should be maintained "so that all JTIDS equipment will be interoperable for joint and combined operations."[65]

This decision clearly represented a major fork in the road, one that arguably affected all subsequent action on the program. In making it, Dinneen had been converted—or pressured—to the view espoused by the Navy for the preceding five years; he had also accepted the argument made by the Navy at least since 1978, which was that DTDMA and TDMA could be made "backwards compatible"—some slots in both architectures could be reserved for joint use. Nevertheless, a major step had been taken away from the common direction that had been the hallmark of the JTIDS program since its inception. More fallout was not long in coming, as the Air Force continued to express both reservations about JTIDS terminals in fighter cockpits and enthusiasm concerning ever-newer and more elaborate "interim systems" for anti-jam radio systems: in the bizarre terminology so commonly encountered in these matters, SEEK TALK had given way to HAVE QUICK. In the final days of the Carter administration, the dissatisfaction surfaced in the press with an article in *Defense Week* entitled "Dinneen's Legacy: The Million Dollar Radio." The article charged that JTIDS was so ineffective and expensive that it would have been canceled outright had Dinneen not manipulated the procurement process so that a contractor would be chosen for the Class II TDMA terminals just one week prior to the inauguration of President Reagan.[66]

These charges were at least overdrawn and certainly unfair to a man whose personal integrity and intentions were universally considered to be above reproach. It is nevertheless a fact that on January 16, 1981, the Air Force, as the executive service for JTIDS, was given approval to proceed with full-scale development of the Class II TDMA terminals. Later, the team of Singer Kearfott/Rockwell Collins was chosen to provide some forty of these "development" terminals which would provide the basis for a full production decision to be made by 1986 on further proliferation of the system. As Gerald P. Dinneen left office, therefore, what legacy did he leave behind? Clearly, he had much more to show for his efforts than the "million-dollar radio" deplored by the anonymous subordinates who floated that story. In his close personal involvement with JTIDS, like that of Robert McNamara with the TFX a decade before, Dinneen had exercised the full range of central management powers inherent in his office. Like McNamara as well, Dinneen had ultimately been forced to compromise with Service norms, none more important than the definition of their unique mission requirements. But while the TFX did not long survive after McNamara's incumbency, JTIDS remained a contentious issue within the Defense Department for years after Dinneen's departure.

JTIDS **Developments 1981–1985: Divergence and Denouement**

It was somewhat ironic that the Reagan administration, though determined to avoid what it saw as the overcentralized management of the Carter Defense Department, appointed to the job of supervising its command and control programs a man whose qualifications, talents, and personality would make him every bit as formidable as Gerald Dinneen. Donald C. Latham would emerge from the shadows of the Office of the Under Secretary of Defense for Research and Engineering to become an assistant secretary of defense for command, control, communications, and intelligence, developing the powers of that position to an unprecedented extent. Yet neither Latham nor Dinneen could have predicted the strange outcome of the JTIDS program during the half-decade between 1981 and 1985:

- The Air Force, despite its status as the lead service for the JTIDS program, actually wound up buying the fewest terminals as it ended its plan for putting Class II terminals in fighter cockpits.
- The Navy, having won recognition of its need for a separate architecture, eventually gave up on DTDMA and, after much bitterness, reevaluated its need for JTIDS under the TDMA architecture it had spurned for so many years.
- The Army, the service that had watched most of the JTIDS controversy from the sidelines, was the only one to gain from the JTIDS program a result that approximated its original objective.
- The Marines, because of the above developments, were spared the embarrassment of being the only service to have two sets of terminals—TDMA for use in conjunction with the Army's PLRS/JTIDS Hybrid and DTDMA for all other operations with the Navy.

By any reckoning, this was a remarkable turn of events, the Navy's DTDMA failure in particular giving an entirely new meaning to the concept of "backwards compatibility." And yet, the roots of these unintended consequences can be found in the Carlucci memorandum of March 27, 1981, which set the tone for the decentralized management style of the Defense Department and sent a strong signal that service interests were in the ascendant. This directive followed by less than a year the "Great Schism" between the DTDMA and TDMA technologies. The effects of both decisions were already evident by May of 1981, when John C. Cittadino (OSD director for Theater and Tactical C2 Systems and an important source of institutional memory) stated in a cover brief written for Latham's acting deputy that "despite Congressional direction and OSD efforts, the JTIDS program is proceeding more as a confederation of two programs than (ideally) as a single fully integrated one." Not only that, but the Navy had moved out of the JTIDS Joint Program Office at Hanscom Air Force Base, Massachusetts, its representative now ensconced with the rest of the Naval Electronic Systems Command in Crystal City, Virginia.[67]

By now, GAO inquiries on JTIDS, if not exactly routine, had at least become an accepted part of the cost of doing business in the Defense Department. So no one was startled when, on April 2, 1982, the familiar GAO letterhead appeared at the top of a four-page document that once again raised questions about DOD management of the JTIDS program. The primary thrust of the GAO inquiry was directed at what it saw as a detectable softening of the respective service commitments to JTIDS: fewer terminals were planned for acquisition; funding levels for the program had been reduced; there was an absence of provisions for JTIDS in new aircraft or ancillary systems. The letter also questioned the split over TDMA/DTDMA technology and, like the previous GAO report, leaned discernibly toward the Navy position: "We are concerned that the use of two different technologies with the associated increased development costs and interoperability problems may not be appropriate. We understand that the Navy's Distributed Time Division Multiple Access has greater growth potential [than TDMA] which would appear to be desirable for the Air Force as well."[68]

The DOD reply came on May 24, 1982. As expected, it rebutted most of the GAO's concerns but was candid in asserting that any developmental program such as JTIDS was subject to uncertainty. It also pointed out that the Air Force anti-jam voice requirements meant that this service wanted "a demonstration of JTIDS Class 2's operational utility in a realistic tactical environment before making its major resource commitments to a new concept for fighter operations."[69] One of the most interesting aspects of the DOD reply, however, was the revelation of its basic management philosophy about JTIDS: "Although it is treated programmatically as a major system, JTIDS is really a sub-system program. Different terminal types and ancillary equipment must be tailored to Service platform and mission needs. . . . For the near term, the urgency of Service mission needs determines whether a terminal will be retrofitted into one platform rather than incorporated into a lesser-priority user during production. . . . In the meantime . . . the dual-technology approach of the several Service programs will both give us a healthy production base and assure a long-term competitive situation."[70] This approach was, of course, consistent with administration philosophy, which stressed the regulative mechanisms of the free market and the importance of rebuilding American defenses rather than restructuring the defense establishment. Yet the decentralized management style foreshadowed by the Carlucci memorandum would often be at loggerheads with the need to maintain coherence in a command and control budget that was at last experiencing real growth.[71]

In turning to the various service interests as they appeared in the early 1980s, it is appropriate to begin with the Army, simply because its JTIDS applications presented the fewest conflicts with the interests of the other services and, perhaps for that reason, its program was proceeding with some success. The Net Control Stations of the PLRS/JTIDS Hybrid (which became known as PJH before being rechristened the "Army Data Distribution System") were set up as the linchpins of the system, linking Army fire and maneuver units as well as other compatible service and allied users. The system was to be primarily dependent on the Class II TDMA terminals being manufactured by Singer Kearfott, full-scale development having been approved in 1980. No significant problems appear to have been encountered in that contract during this time; initial deliveries began in 1983, and the process of field testing and evaluation commenced.[72] Each Army division was eventually expected to have over eight hundred users of the system, the great majority being connected through the austere PLRS user unit described above. The direct costs of this equipment were estimated by the Army at just over $33 million for each of the nineteen divisions (or their equivalents) in its force structure, for a total procurement outlay of some $627 million.[73] This figure, though hardly insignificant, was not an unreasonable investment in light of the great improvement the system represented for a wide range of Army tactical operations. Assuming that the program remained reasonably on time and within budget, there were considerable grounds for optimism as the procurement cycle continued.[74]

Aside from the fact that its requirements did not conflict with those of the Navy and Air Force, what other reasons lay behind the Army's comparatively successful experience with JTIDS? One factor may be that its requirements were well understood by the service's top leadership—both the problem and its solution—prior to any commitment to the project. The Army realized that it was in a relative Stone Age insofar as its ability to move perishable data around the battlefield was concerned. The JTIDS system represented a way to solve that problem and to connect with the larger, joint world that was essential to Airland Battle and a host of lesser initiatives.[75] Another reason was that the Army's concept for employment of JTIDS modified the classic "many-to-many" principle of JTIDS connectivity to fit its own circumstances. Each of the PLRS user units was required to go through the Net Control Stations to reach any other user, although the system for all practical purposes would be "transparent" to these subscribers. These control stations therefore were nodes, whereas the original JTIDS concept had stressed nodeless connectivity. This concession to traditional hierarchy reflected a strong sense of reality: mainly the fact that the great number of "movable subordinate entities" in the Army environment would quickly swamp the capacity of the fastest computer that could be fielded. The solution was to recognize that an infantryman did not need the same level of connectivity and situation awareness demanded by a jet pilot. Therefore, rather cheap and simple PLRS user units could accommodate the soldier's normal requirements and still put him in effective contact with the pilot if the tactical situation so demanded.

The situation between the other two services, the Air Force and the Navy, was far more complex. Five major areas of divergence—all separate but inextricably linked—can be extracted from the record of their interaction.

- *Different operational environments:* As simplistic as it may sound, the different operational environments of the Navy and Air Force lay at the heart of their dispute over JTIDS, especially in relation to the anti-jamming capabilities they sought.
- *Data versus voice:* The preference of the Navy for data and the equally strong Air Force belief in voice control were products of both their operational environments and their histories. That difference over JTIDS persisted throughout the program.
- *Differing commitment levels:* As the lead service, the Air Force was seen by the Navy to be in a clear position of dominance; yet its waning enthusiasm for JTIDS led to further bad feelings, especially in the area of efforts to make two increasingly diverse architectures compatible.
- *DTDMA versus TDMA:* The two fundamentally different architectural approaches were never resolved until cancelation of the Navy's program in 1985. Here again, the divergence reflected underlying functional differences.
- *Technological risk:* The Navy DTDMA architecture carried an inherent degree of technological risk as it pushed the state of the art in electronics. The Air Force TDMA was high technology, but considerably more doable.

Probably the best indicator of where the services stood on these five issues can be gleaned from their annual appearances before the Research and Development Subcommittee of the House Armed Services Committee (HASC). Their testimony during the authorization process for the years 1982 through 1985 shows their preferences on these issues as well as the evolution of the program as a whole. It is important to realize that the record was far from being one of unalleviated failure. The Air Force Class I TDMA terminals became operational on the AWACS in 1983, and both services made important progress in pioneering ways to share that data and to provide for better integration of Navy and Air Force operations. Also, the interim JTIDS message standard went forward, even as TADIL J was being readied for fielding by the end of the decade. The issues at the heart of this case were the placement of JTIDS Class II terminals in the tactical aircraft of the respective services and the extent to which those subsystems required interoperability. The evolution of those issues can readily be seen between 1982, when the HASC was persuaded of the necessity for compatibility of the parallel systems, and 1985, when its patience with the arguments over that question came to an end. To demonstrate the effect of the five issues outlined above on this outcome, I will examine each in turn.

Different Operational Environments. The respective operational environments of the Navy and Air Force represent differences so profound as to seem obvious to the most casual observer. And yet, the implications of those differences were not at all obvious during the HASC hearings, which generated a series of exchanges among witnesses, congressmen, and professional committee staff members, notably Anthony R. Battista, one of the Hill's most expert observers of defense technology and a relentless inquisitor. The environmental differences centered around the anti-jam capabilities of JTIDS versus other systems that the Air Force was pushing as either complementary to JTIDS or, ultimately, as a substitute for it. The Air Force premise was that the JTIDS anti-jam margin was insufficient to break through known Soviet capabilities on the European battlefield. That point led to questioning by Battista and others to the effect that, if the threat was so great for the Air Force, why was it any different for the Navy? Was the threat indeed different or were these purported differences just examples of interservice rivalry? Their skepticism reached a high point during the 1984 hearings when the Air Force, after having progressively named its preferred anti-jam voice system SEEK TALK and HAVE CLEAR, went all-out for funding by rechristening it Enhanced JTIDS, or EJS. It was doubtful that this system had anything in common with the "real" JTIDS, and sharp questioning was the order of the day throughout the hearings.

Near the end of these sessions the commander of the Tactical Air Command, Gen. Wilbur L. Creech, appeared before the subcommittee to argue for EJS. He explained the Navy and Air Force differences as follows:

> First of all, we operate in different ways against different missions. Let's take a central European war, for example. . . .
> Now the threat that we [USAF] face are jammers that are distributed along the FEBA [Forward Edge of the Battle Area], ground based. Very

powerful because you can package high power in a ground system. Plus there are airborne jammers behind the FEBA. So, you have both ground and airborne jammers, and we must operate in the teeth of those jammers. The Navy, on the other hand, is back here [at sea] where if somebody is coming to them and going to jam them, they have to bring it in airborne jammers. Now of course the Navy has force projection aircraft that carry the fight to the shore. In a carrier battle group, there are 24 to 30, sometimes as many as 36. . . . That is a little over one squadron of Air Force air to surface aircraft.

In contrast, we the Air Force . . . are going to take 89 squadrons to Europe. And with our Allies we are going to be operating 200 squadrons in that area which is the size of Oregon. Clearly, the scale, the need, the missions are different.[76]

General Creech went on to explain another critical difference. An Air Force base was a fixed point, whereas a carrier was constantly moving; therefore the relative navigation characteristic of JTIDS was more useful to the Navy than to the Air Force. This was well-crafted and powerful testimony, and, though the Air Force eventually lost on EJS, General Creech's delineation of the differences in service perspectives was unmatched by any other witness.

Data versus Voice. The issue of whether it was better to control tactical aircraft by voice or data was familiar to everyone even remotely associated with the JTIDS program, for it had been a bone of contention between the Air Force and the Navy from the beginning. As the program evolved after 1980, however, the stakes rose as the Air Force became more concerned about jammers and their disruptive effects on air operations. The relationship of jamming to the data-voice controversy was technologically driven: there was a trade-off between the computer power invested in the *content* of a message (either data or voice) and its protective anti-jam *margin* (or "sheath"). Although questioners such as Anthony Battista raised the point again and again, the Air Force repeatedly claimed that it made far more sense to make that investment in ways that considered the fundamental differences between a pure voice system, which was what the Air Force wanted, and JTIDS Class II, which was at the most a data-voice hybrid.[77]

Apart from the technological questions, there were equally important doctrinal issues at stake, the term *doctrine* being used here to connote the services' historical reactions to their roles and missions in their respective operational environments. The Navy, with its longer experience in digital data, came to a different set of conclusions from that of the Air Force, even when those services were describing their reactions to a common threat. Some of the most interesting contrasts between the two service doctrines became apparent during a colloquy on April 20, 1983, among Congressman William L. Dickinson, the ranking Republican on the committee, Gen. Robert D. Eaglet of the U.S. Air Force Systems Command, and Rear Adm. Robert E. Kirksey of the Office of the Chief of Naval Operations:

GENERAL EAGLET: In the Air Force, it is clear to us that, whereas we can use a lot of data link communications, there are a number of missions, particularly those in a high-threat environment, for which voice communications are absolutely imperative, such as a flight penetrating well into enemy territory and one member needing to call a wingman's attention to the fact that a SAM has been launched from his right wing and is approaching him. We don't believe the way to get that data to him is to format it and communicate it to a monitor display. We think the way to do it is for the wingman to be able to push a button and say: "Joe, break left. There's a SAM." . . .

MR. DICKINSON: I don't mean to be argumentative. It is my recollection that the Navy flew missions in Vietnam over land, and that they were subject to SAMS. . . . How is your threat different?

ADMIRAL KIRKSEY: . . . One of the problems that exists in the strictly voice system and during the large strikes in Vietnam where you have 45 to 60 aircraft involved in a relatively small restricted area was that everyone would be on the voice circuits at the same time. On one occasion we had 35 surface-to-air missiles that were launched around the city of Hanoi, and of course directions were being called: "Hey, there is a missile coming at 030," and so forth. A lot of them were relative [position] calls and people's heads were going around on a swivel trying to find out, "Is that missile actually after me?" So there are a lot of problems involved . . . in flying combat operating only with voice circuits.[78]

Interestingly, in this discussion no one ever brought up the fundamental difference between the single-seat fighters of the Air Force versus the two-seat configuration of Navy planes. In any case, the matter was not likely to be resolved in a congressional hearing. Therefore, the data-versus-voice controversy, as both an important doctrinal problem and an obstacle to joint interoperability, simmered throughout the JTIDS program and persists to this day.

Differing Commitment Levels. The anti-jam and voice-versus-data issues were almost reverse sides of the same coin, and there was a similar linkage between the differing levels of commitment to the JTIDS program and the whole question of system architecture. This was due to Navy perceptions concerning the choice of the Air Force as the executive service for JTIDS, a choice ostensibly driven by expectations that the Air Force would eventually purchase more than five thousand JTIDS terminals. That position of dominance enabled the Air Force to have its own way on the TDMA architecture (and joint message standards) needed most urgently for the AWACS. Once those requirements were met, it was the Navy view that the Air Force had backed away from the program. This meant that the Navy—though at least free to develop DTDMA—incurred additional costs in remaining compatible with an architecture for which it had no use. Vice Adm. Gordon R. Nagler, the director of naval command and control, summed up the Navy outlook:

> On JTIDS . . . 10 years ago the decision was made by the Secretary of Defense to go with a basic system. . . . That was to be the basic Air Force system. The Navy, after several years of discussion . . . was told to go to the systems with D that gave you more capability. But the Navy was told you must be backward compatible with T. We said, "Roger," because at that time, the Air Force was buying 5,000 T sets. Now they're going to buy 5,000 EJS. But at that time they were going to buy 5,000 T's. They've [now] got 144 programmed. We're still backward compatible. We have in our budget approved by the Secretary of the Navy . . . [funds so] that by 1988 D's [will all be] built to be backward compatible with T's so we can interoperate with the Air Force.[79]

Apart from the trouble and expense involved, it was the Navy position that it had received the worst of both worlds: project dominance by another service which sacrificed Navy requirements and the proliferation of yet another system with which it was required to maintain compatibility. These grievances help explain the pained attitudes that often lay just under the surface of JTIDS issues.

DTDMA versus TDMA. The DTDMA/TDMA controversy continued to simmer, even though it had seemingly been resolved with the 1980 agreement to explore the two architectures. In 1982, it was evident that Congress largely agreed with that decision—or at least found no serious grounds on which to question it. Indeed, part of their acceptance may well have been due to the distraction of having to keep track of two architectures and the arcane reasons they existed. As difficult as this was, the nomenclature was at least consistent compared to the bewildering array of Air Force anti-jam radio designations that seemed to change yearly. Witness the following exchange during the 1982 hearings between committee staffer Dr. Thomas Cooper (who subsequently became the assistant secretary of the air force for research, development, and logistics) and Donald Latham:

DR. COOPER: It appears we have this proliferation of equipment that seems to address basically the same requirements, and I just want to ask you your personal opinion. In your opinion, do we need Seek Talk, JTIDS with DTDMA and JTIDS with TDMA, given that Have Quick is here? That is a good thing to do . . . but do we need all three?

MR. LATHAM: In my personal opinion we do not, but if I have to opt for something, I will opt for the JTIDS program if I must be forced into a personal view on it. Within the JTIDS program, I would be willing to live, and I think we can live adequately with the D and the T. . . . So, I would keep the two JTIDS programs.[80]

The more serious question always was the interoperability of the two systems as they grew increasingly more distinct. By 1983, for example, the Navy had a plan that aped that of the TDMA terminals: large Class I DTDMA terminals were to be outfitted in carriers and cruisers, smaller Class IA DTDMA terminals in E2C surveillance aircraft, and Class II DTDMA terminals in fighter-bombers.[81] Admiral Nagler pointed out in the 1983 hearings that the costs of maintaining interoperability were not insignificant, but that they would be less were the DTDMA architecture to be adopted as the interoperable standard:

ADMIRAL NAGLER: If we adopted DTDMA in AWACS and throughout the Navy, we would be interoperable through AWACS. We could save $250 million in our program in JTIDS. We would not have to add the T version and be backwards compatible if we would work through the AWACS and the aircraft carriers, cruisers and AAW destroyers. . . . [The Air Force has its] own problems, but to have a joint program that's interoperable, I want us to be interoperable at the AWACS level and at the U.S. carrier and cruiser level. Not every airplane that flies over central Europe has to talk to every airplane flying over the ocean, if they talk through AWACS. That's my version. I'm sure the Air Force has a different version.

MR. DICKINSON: General Eaglet, do you want to respond?

GENERAL EAGLET: . . . We believe . . . that we should look at the alternative solution—that is the one which is currently directed since 1980 to continue TDMA as the common interservice interoperable mode. We suggest that [each] one should be studied at the same time. This would enable us to make a wiser selection between the two approaches and converge on the one which is most cost effective for the taxpayer. Now that's our view on that issue.[82]

This disagreement would persist until technical difficulties with DTDMA provided a "convergence" that few would have imagined.

Technological Risk. The open record of the HASC hearings between 1982 and 1984 fails to provide much, if any, indication that the Navy's DTDMA development program was in trouble. And yet, it was clear from the outset that the Navy had accepted a much higher degree of technical risk in the design of its architecture. The growth potential cited in the 1982 GAO report and the multinet design of DTDMA depended principally on the packaging of printed microcircuitry and silicon chips in a box that would fit into the ships and aircraft it would serve: weight, size, shape, cooling, and power requirements were all potential problem areas. The same challenge faced the TDMA terminals as well; but this architecture was one whose design had been crafted in the mid-1970s, stabilized at the contract award in 1980, and further refined as deliveries began to take place in 1983. The DTDMA approach was far more ambitious and pushed the state of the art. One indication of problems was that development milestones and initial operational capability dates slid gradually toward the end of the decade. Then, in November 1984, Secretary of the Navy John Lehman abruptly canceled the DTDMA contract with TADCOM, a joint venture subsidiary of ITT and Hughes Aircraft.[83] Although the contract was renegotiated to minimize the risk to the government, the Navy's problems with DTDMA were now out in the open.

As the 1985 hearings began, committee staffer Anthony R. Battista made this point clear to the members in his overview of the Defense Department's research and development efforts:

> DTDMA is a very attractive feature for the Navy to have except the program again has been in trouble. It was terminated by the Navy last year. They reinstated the contractor and put a cap on the program, and I can tell you right now that the Navy will sign up to a 9-month delay in the program. I will tell you it is closer to 12 months, and I believe that right now, even though it costs you a little capability, the Navy could go with TDMA. . . . accordingly, I would recommend that you consider terminating that program because there is an alternative to it.[84]

With that sort of introduction, it was inevitable that tough questioning would follow. Congressman Dennis Hertel, normally soft-spoken, bluntly asked Donald Latham why both architectures were necessary: "Why should we pay the price for them to do their own thing? We are on the same side."

Latham responded politely that the duality was based on need, and he added that the services "could show you in spades why that is so." The following exchange then ensued:

MR. HERTEL: No, they cannot show us that. We have had them in here and they cannot show us that at all. And they cannot show us the different threat. They can make up reasons.

MR. LATHAM: Not the threat, not the threat. It is the way that you use the system.

MR. HERTEL: They have tried that too. We mandated that they have the same system. This is several years now. In law, it was mandated that they have the same system.

MR. LATHAM: Well, you can argue that you have one JTIDS program that uses two different signal wave forms that are fully interoperable.

MR. HERTEL: It costs more. That is what it does.

MR. BATTISTA: That is like saying, I have got an AM radio and you have got an FM radio, and we are interoperable because we welded the receivers together. That is all they have done here.[85]

Equally severe questions greeted Navy representatives later in the hearings.[86] What this reception made clear was that Congress had been long-suffering in its willingness to go along with different architectures, despite its occasional misgivings that these systems might be tending toward less, rather than greater, interoperability in the long run. When the Navy program ran into trouble, then, it was ripe for cancelation. This was, after all, a Congress whose willingness to fund the Reagan defense buildup was fast running out of steam. The stage was thus set for the final act.

It came when, as expected, the House of Representatives recommended termination of the DTDMA program in favor of the TDMA architecture. The Senate, however, recommended continuation of DTDMA, a position reflecting the traditional support the Navy had enjoyed in that body, as well as the fact that the Republican Senate tended to favor the official administration position. The best account yet published of what happened next was a 1986 article by writer John Englund: "With their patience wearing thin, the members of the House committee decided to hold back money for both programs, giving OSD an ultimatum: Choose one JTIDS program for all the Services or forget about JTIDS altogether. . . . The House-Senate conference eventually reached a delicate compromise. Rather than resolving the issue, the legislators asked for several outside studies of the JTIDS issue. In the meantime, the conferees accepted the House argument that the money should not be released."[87]

Different stories are told to explain the ultimate effects of the studies and the personalities involved. Englund's version is that Anthony Battista exerted further pressure against DTDMA, aided by his knowledge of the TADCOM contract difficulties. Donald Latham states that an OSD-sponsored study of the Navy program in the summer of 1985 provided the basis for final action.[88] In any case, on October 22, 1985, Secretary of the Navy John Lehman announced the cancelation of the DTDMA program. According to the *Washington Post,* "Navy Secretary John F. Lehman decided that the time for solving the problems had passed and that joining the Army and Air Force on a similar project being developed by a rival contracting team is more practical."[89] What was not immediately explained, of course, was how the Navy proposed to reconcile its future requirements with an architecture whose inadequacy it had so steadfastly criticized for a decade or more.

Perhaps the best summation of the case came from Donald Latham, who objected, among other things, to Englund's characterization of the JTIDS program as a "$600 Million Pentagon Fiasco": "In summary, the choice is not always clear as to whether or not it is more cost-effective to compromise requirements to have one system for all services or more than one, optimized to service-peculiar requirements. We learned from the TFX program in the mid-1960's that it is counterproductive to state a firm policy that all services must always buy and use the same equipment. We will continue to work hard to make the right decisions without abdicating our responsibility to ensure that our services have highly capable, cost-effective interoperable equipment. In the meantime, JTIDS, a vitally needed capability, is on the right track, and we intend to keep it there."[90]

JTIDS: Epilogue and Implications

Latham's comments on this occasion were exactly the kind of spirited defense one would expect from a man who had fought hard for the JTIDS program, effectively using the force of his office and personality to promote the goal of interoperability despite the pressures of competing interests. After leaving government late in the Reagan administration, he could occasionally be coaxed into more candid reminiscences about the difficulties of maintaining that focus in the face of "end runs to Congress by the services." He even went so far in one interview with me as to describe JTIDS as "a joint program that has become progressively more disjointed." Although understandable, that judgment is probably too harsh. Certainly the costs in time, money, and levels of effort were far greater than JTIDS advocates anticipated at the program's inception, but the same thing can be said for many ambitious undertakings, especially those involving high-technology defense programs. There is little doubt, however, that the basic JTIDS concept has provided a relatively constant benchmark for almost fifteen years. The continuity of this program has thereby become one of its principal assets, providing an element of certainty in the often uncertain technical and bureaucratic worlds in which command and control systems are developed.

The JTIDS program has naturally been subject to this same evolutionary process, spawning a family of related technological offspring:

- The first-generation JTIDS Class I terminals were successfully deployed on the E-3 AWACS and they now provide the basic air-ground linkage for the NATO air defense community.
- The marriage of the Army's PLRS-JTIDS Hybrid eventually ended in divorce—or at least annulment; PLRS emerged from the experience with an even more unlikely name, EPLRS (the "E" standing for "enhanced"). Although the new acronym was every bit as unimaginative as the old, expectations for the "enhanced" system were remarkably similar to what the Army had been hoping for since the early 1980s.[91]
- The other half of this marriage was eventually rechristened as ADDS (Army Data Distribution System). Although it was primarily earmarked for air defense functions, its uses were eventually to be extended to all areas of the Army command and control system. A variation of the Class II terminal—an "M"-series adapted for use in the field but with the high data rates characteristic of the basic JTIDS system—was being developed for this task.[92]
- Two versions of the basic Class II airborne terminal were planned. The one in full-scale development was intended for surveillance aircraft (such as the AWACS) and larger fighters (F-14 and F-15) as well as their "downlinks" on ships or ground stations. The other terminal (now in "concept definition," a term synonymous with "gleam in the eye") is a smaller version called MIDS, which is intended for smaller fighters, such as the U.S. F-16 and F/A-18 and possibly the European Tornado and Rafale as well.[93]
- Its suspicion of digital data in the fighter cockpit intact, the Air Force, the lead service in the development of JTIDS, still planned to buy the fewest number (200) Class II terminals—all but 20 of which were destined for its tactical air control and surveillance elements. However, planned procurement by Army, Navy, Marine, and NATO users would bring the total purchase of Class II terminals to more than 1,800 at a total cost of $4.3 billion. As such, JTIDS would become the backbone of joint and combined interoperability by the 1990s.[94]

What then, are the appropriate lessons to be learned from the JTIDS experience? The first is surely that this is a cautionary tale for those who wonder why defense acquisition is such a tortuous process and who long to slash through its red tape with a stroke of either pen or sword. Neither implement is likely to solve that problem quickly enough to satisfy most defense critics, if for no other reason than that none of the principal players from the executive or legislative branches of the government seems inclined to leave the field. Given the number of actors involved and a procurement system seemingly designed around the motto "Never steal anything small," it is no wonder that JTIDS could be conceived in the 1960s, developed in the seventies, developed some more in the eighties, and (maybe) procured in the nineties. The parallels with the TFX case are equally striking, most of them suggesting that here, as in so many other issues, defense decisions are almost an incidental by-product of the political process. Another reminder is that there are clear limits in the ability of OSD to intervene and impose rationality on the system. Although the legal and constitutional role of OSD is vital, there are practical limits faced by any political appointee who attempts to compel military institutions to do things they find fundamentally obnoxious. Over any significant length of time, the pluralistic nature of the American civil-military system is more likely to favor the institution than the individual.

A second implication that can be drawn from the record of JTIDS is a healthy skepticism about commonality—which is not to say that commonality is necessarily a bad thing. Rather, like the attainment of perfect grace, it is a worthwhile end that is seldom achieved on earth. Like the TFX, JTIDS was an experiment in commonality that achieved some worthwhile ends, most of which were not clearly envisioned at the program's inception. It has been suggested from time to time that the TFX case might have turned out better had Robert McNamara been willing to accept a lesser degree of commonality between the Navy and Air Force versions of the plane. The JTIDS program began as an attempt to achieve 100 percent commonality, aided by an all-embracing technology that, it was thought, would be universally applicable to all service environments. Service requirements—some real and others less so—quickly proved otherwise. Had DTDMA actually been built and performed to expectations, the commonality level between it and TDMA would have been no more than the 10 percent required to maintain the minimum level of interoperability. It is difficult for a layman to judge, but somewhere between the 10 percent of bare-bones connectivity and the 100 percent of complete commonality might have been a better objective for OSD's top management. Had that middle ground been diligently sought in the initial stages of JTIDS, the subsequent schisms might have been avoided. (In fact, the "family" of JTIDS terminals now being developed suggests that one size doesn't fit all—and that it may not have to.)

A third and related point is that it is absolutely essential for the top civilian and military leaders of the defense establishment to take whatever actions are required to ensure that the long-term *strategic* planning of command and control systems architecture is being attended to. Part of the problem with JTIDS was that it started years before this aspect of defense management was being adequately addressed. The TRI-TAC program, JINTACCS, the Joint Tactical C3 Agency, and even JTIDS itself represented important steps along the learning curve in bringing together separate organizations and procedures in pursuit of a larger goal. One of the great benefits of this kind of architectural development is that it reduces the pain associated with sudden and disruptive changes in areas that are often critical to service missions, requirements, doctrines, and even careers. The JTIDS case showed how very real that pain could become, even when the time line in question involved programs that were five to ten years from realization. Indeed, the pain was so great that programs like DTDMA and TADIL J occasionally seemed to *stay* five to ten years from realization—the point here being that the essence of strategic planning is that it is done so as to permit effective choices, not to postpone them indefinitely.

A fourth observation that can be drawn from the JTIDS experience is consistent with the general theme of this study. It is that the service paradigms and the human institutions that carry them out are primarily focused on their respective operational environments and the preferred weapons systems that enable them to carry out their missions. This was seen particularly clearly in the quarrels over the anti-jam margin of the system—a technical characteristic that was a surrogate for different Navy and Air Force roles, missions, and operational environments. The major implication of this finding for command and control is that the American military establishment does not naturally create the institutions necessary to evolve the "system of systems" (to borrow Cushman's phrase) demanded by warfare in the information age. When it has done so—as with JINTACCS and the other examples cited in this chapter—it has usually been at the express or implicit bidding of its civilian masters and always with some reluctance. There is, again, nothing inherently wrong in this aspect of the civil-military partnership. The only drawback, in fact, is that the military all too often ends up abdicating responsibility for matters on which its collective professional judgment ought to be solicited, considered, and respected by the civilian leadership. As an example, Representative William L. Dickinson, one of the most consistently effective participants in the five years of JTIDS hearings examined here, complained during the 1984 session that the committee was being put in the position "of having to make the technical assessment and technical decisions when we have neither the information nor the expertise to do this. This really should be done within the Department of Defense."[95] In that assessment, he was undoubtedly correct.

Finally, it would be inappropriate to close this discussion without offering at least some speculative thoughts on the future of JTIDS technology, if not the system itself. A future historian of command and control at the dawn of the information age may well observe that JTIDS was an attempt by the American armed forces to lift themselves up by their bootstraps using a primitive, immature technology. That, at least, is the impression an observer gets from reading the testimony by defense officials who complained that the system was too big, too expensive, and too disruptive of contemporary practices. The technology is already in sight that will satisfy two of these objections. A Defense Department project for the creation of Very High Speed Integrated Circuitry (VHSIC) involves the production of microcircuits capable of performing over a million operations per second, all of it on a wafer-thin ceramic base slightly smaller than a telephone push button. The military applications of this technology were illustrated some years ago in an *Aviation Week* magazine article that showed several generations of aircraft radar equipment. With the application of VHSIC, the twenty-one-inch portable TV-sized radar set of the 1960s is reduced to a device of about the same dimensions as a pack of chewing gum.[96] Interestingly, the twenty-one-inch TV set approximates the size of the JTIDS Class II terminal. The VHSIC technology of the 1990s may well answer many of the physical problems experienced in the mounting of the current generation of JTIDS equipment, although one naturally hesitates to make any similarly optimistic predictions regarding cost.

The conceptual aspect of what these systems may portend is not as easy to predict, for many of the reasons shown in this study. Distributed data systems like JTIDS offer potential solutions to a wide variety of battlefield problems, many of which are linked to a hierarchical pattern of communication. For that reason, their continued development is a virtual certainty. The concepts of receiver-oriented communication and selective retrieval of data are essential parts of that evolution, with the potential for fostering greater situational awareness at progressively lower levels in the military hierarchy. Nor is the perspective of these systems likely to be limited to the three-hundred-nautical-mile range of the JTIDS system. By the late 1970s, for example, the Air Force had already demonstrated the feasibility of LASERSATCOM, a relay system using laser beams as the data channel and a geosynchronous satellite as its communications relay. The expected data rate of this system was such that it

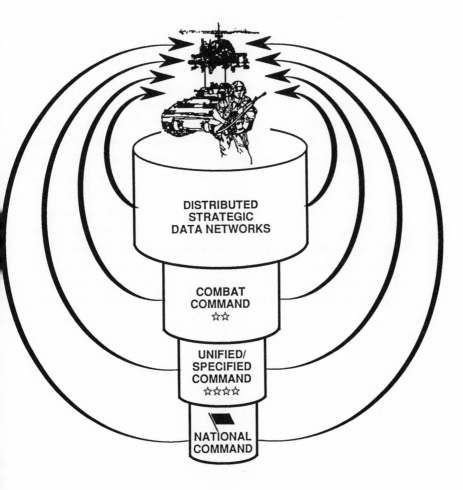

The strategic use of distributed data networks may be one of the ways in which decision-makers at higher echelons of command may eventually be able to use a modern equivalent of "Napoleon's Telescope." The potential advantages of such a receiver-oriented system include real-time sharing of crisis or combat data and common situation awareness, as well as the elimination of both information filters and information overload.

Figure 7.4   Linkages For The Future?

Source: Author

would permit the intercontinental transmission of the entire thirty volumes of the *Encyclopaedia Britannica* in about one second.[97]

There is no reason, therefore, to expect that distributed data networks such as JTIDS will be limited in their potential contribution to the military forces that are bold enough in their science and creative enough in their organizational structures to make the most effective use of these technologies. A hypothetical example is portrayed in figure 7.4 to show how distributed data networks could be used for both strategic and tactical connectivity, given relay techniques like LASERSATCOM. Selected nets and advanced relays could provide situation awareness independent of the limitations of standard hierarchical information flows. Ultimately, the proliferation of these distributed data systems could even involve considerable organizational stresses should command and information lines, once firmly welded together, begin to diverge. All this is, of course, highly speculative, despite the reality of the wide range of technological choices confronting the American military establishment. If JTIDS gives that establishment some ideas on how to make those choices, the system may ultimately provide an intellectual legacy as important as the increased operational efficiency it promises to bring to the armed forces of the United States.

8 Historical Linkages and Future Implications

One of the central points made by this book is that the problems of modern command and control did not spring full-grown from the minds of technocrats and that they cannot be properly understood in isolation from the human institutions—governmental and military—that actually do the commanding and controlling. Command and control can thus be seen as the apex of a pyramid (see figure 8.1) whose connected layers include in ascending order national values, operational environments, strategic paradigms, service organizational norms, technological choices, patterns of interservice organization, national command, and finally, the command and control environment itself. In essence, this represents an organic view of command and control, one that seeks causes by examining the observable record of the historical-political, conceptual, and organizational choices that shape the circumstances in which specific technological decisions are made. Similarly, this approach rejects the idea that technology somehow has a mind of its own, despite the frequent statements in discussions of command and control issues to the effect, "Well, the technology is driving us in this direction." Of course, the technology is doing nothing of the sort: it is inherently neutral, a kind of level playing field on which human beings (either on their own or as members of a team) make choices that produce certain outcomes. This, of course, is one of the classic assumptions of the social sciences: that men and women shape their institutions and are in turn shaped by them. It assumes as well that technology cannot be well understood if one insists upon looking at it as a kind of deus ex IBM machina.

This approach also permits an interdisciplinary outlook in seeking root causes. At the heart of the argument is the idea that history can teach something about modern conditions, both in laying bare the record of previous choices and making explicit the assumptions and rationales on which those choices were based. Figure 8.1 thus shows the concept of a basic building block labeled national values:

241

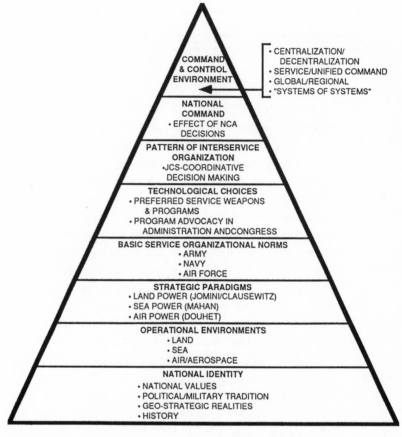

Figure 8.1 Key Determinants of Command and Control
Source: Author

this broad category consists of those historically significant factors that have helped determine the character of the American approach to command and control. For that reason, the lines of this category could be drawn widely enough to embrace a wide range of other disciplines. For example, a sociologist might suggest the importance of including such characteristics as population, character, and national will. An economist could make an equally strong case for considering such elements as gross national product, industrial base, and state of technological sophistication. I have chosen to concentrate instead on the strategic conditions and assumptions that framed the American approach to its military establishment and the civil-military tradition that arose from that assessment.

In chapter 2 I pointed out that the strategic consensus reached by the new Republic emphasized the importance of providing and maintaining a navy as the first line of defense for a maritime nation—to be supplemented by the raising and supporting of armies only as the occasion demanded. This fundamental division of labor was matched by pragmatic concerns: the Navy would contribute to the commercial expansion and economic integration of the new nation, while the very small Regular Army would occupy itself in peacetime with constabular duties on the frontier. The American civil-military tradition was founded on the separation of powers and an absolute requirement for the subordination of the military to the civil authority. These norms, as well as the Hamiltonian strain of administrative rationalism, led by the start of the nineteenth century to two cabinet-level services linked to each other primarily through the president as their common commander in chief. The "subjective" control of both services was further assured by their common subordination to a Congress determined to use its power of the purse to ensure that decisions on the structure and employment of these forces took place in an atmosphere of considerable political intimacy—especially when naval construction and procurement were at issue. These differing constitutional, legal, and practical differences gave rise to the tradition of service autonomy, which became the dominant factor in defense organization for at least the next century and a half.

This autonomy is further reflected by the second level of the diagram, which symbolizes the differing operational environments confronted by the Army and Navy from the nineteenth century onward—then being joined by the Air Force in the mid-twentieth century. The physical differences between land, sea, and air operations are far more obvious than the ideological, organizational, and practical consequences that flow from them. The water's edge, for example, served not only as the physical embodiment of the division of labor between the Army and the Navy but also as the standard for interservice relations until the airplane obliterated that long-standing benchmark. Similar discrepancies, rooted in fundamental environmental differences but carrying equally important philosophical and ideological overtones, can be seen as well in the wartime dispute between the Army and its then-organic Air Force. Should scarce air assets be concentrated at the theater level, as the airmen argued, or should those aircraft be dispersed to the control of individual division and corps commanders, according to the more traditional notions of support for committed ground forces? As shown in chapter 6, that basic conceptual anomaly has its modern expression in the contemporary debate over Airland Battle. Most important, however, the respective operational environments directly influence the numbers of ships, aircraft, and troops required to cope successfully with sea, air, and land combat: these "movable subordinate entities" constitute a fundamental but usually overlooked facet of comparative command and control.

The conditions required to bring about victory in each of the three operational environments lead to the next level: that of strategic paradigms. The ideas of Jomini and Clausewitz on land warfare, Mahan on control of the sea, and Douhet on command of the air are not just prescriptive theories about the measures and primary weapons required to meet and defeat one's enemies in these particular environments; they are also arguments for the decisive impact of those respective operational environments on the nation's destiny. Jomini, Clausewitz, Mahan, Douhet, and Mitchell were all persuaded that the conditions of victory they prescribed were also the keys to national survival, and current arguments for the decisive effect of Landpower, the Maritime Strategy, or the B-1 and B-2 bombers are all, in a sense, their modern descendants. The inherent competitiveness of these paradigms cannot therefore be overstated: indeed, in their purest form, each represents the negative of the other two. Each one also represents the embodiment of the most profound truths that experience and insight can reveal to the practitioners of these individual forms of warfare, somewhat to the exclusion of all others. As such, the strategic paradigms represent the ideological component of service autonomy. As many analysts have pointed out, it is a small step from these internal belief systems to the public rationales expressed in the competition for budget resources necessary to provide armies, warships, and bombers.[1]

The strategic paradigms exercise a powerful internal influence in each of the services, because, as prescriptions for victory, they carry with them formulas for the organization of the forces required to execute them. The most obvious differences in these organizational norms (the next level in figure 8.1) can be seen in the contrasting levels of centralization employed by the Army and the Navy. Two of the fundamental requirements of land warfare involve the concentration of forces and the combination of arms. The numbers and diversity of these forces necessitated decentralized operations at the lowest levels; staff development from the eighteenth century onward was an effort to balance this decentralization by concentrating power at the top and extending the commander's span of control throughout an increasingly complex hierarchical structure. Even with the fleet concentrations advocated by Mahan, the smaller numbers and physical isolation of ocean warfare meant that the Navy would consistently centralize authority at the lowest possible level: the ship's quarterdeck. The Navy approached top management in a noticeably more decentralized, linear, and federal manner than did its sister service, the evolutionary pattern of naval administration being epitomized by semi-autonomous bureaus (described as "watertight compartments") and a reluctance to adopt the cross-cutting general staff model favored by both Army and Navy reformers in the early twentieth century.

The influence of strategic paradigms upon service organization was also reflected in the internal distribution of power within the individual services, because the emergence of those paradigms went hand-in-hand with the rise of service professionalism in the Army and Navy of the late nineteenth and early twentieth centuries. In the Air Force, the paradigm of air power predated the existence of that service by more than twenty years, but, nevertheless, cleared the pathway to power for the "bomber generals" who won de facto autonomy during World War II and exercised a dominant influence within its ranks after 1947. The paradigms of land and sea warfare provide a longer evolutionary history, with a much richer pattern of shifting professional elites over time. The mechanization of land warfare, however, and the supplanting of the battleship by the aircraft carrier—though they have been linked to the emergence of dominant career groups within each service—have largely consisted of technological reinterpretations of the respective paradigms. For that reason, it is difficult to separate service organizational norms from the next level depicted in the diagram, that of technological choice. Precisely because warfighting doctrines must be constantly reevaluated, one of the key functions of any service organization is its control over the development of future weapons and equipment. Not only is this a matter of choosing the weapons that will produce the necessary combat power to win on land, at sea, or in the air (important as that task is for the nation's security); it is also the embodiment of the professionalism and expertise of the military officer. The National Security Act of 1947 preserved the ability of the Army, Navy, and Air Force to make fundamental technological choices, including those relating to command and control systems. What is subsumed here as well is the fact that, having made these technological choices, the services also play the predominant role in advocating them in terms of specific programs not only within the Defense Department and elsewhere in the executive branch but before Congress as well. This fact also helps explain why, in the JTIDS case, two services, having different preferences regarding digital or voice control of aircraft, could exert competing influences in what was supposed to be a joint program.

The JTIDS program, of course, was a notable example of a rare opportunity for the application of technological choice to the problem of joint, or interoperable, command and control. The difficulties that case study documented are a function of the next two levels shown in figure 8.1: the pattern of interservice organization and national command. These two concepts are linked in important ways, inasmuch as they constitute the levels meant to yoke together the respective service organizations to the common defense. Interservice organization has been shown throughout this book to be a consideration secondary to the primary service structures. In the nineteenth century, there was no interservice organization per se, Army-Navy relations resting on the simple and familiar doctrine of "mutual cooperation." The demands of twentieth-century warfare brought about the quest for unity of command, most notably by the development during World War II of the Joint Chiefs of Staff and the system of unified and specified commands.

Codified by the National Security Act of 1947, this structure was to provide the basic framework for interservice relations: as such, it represented a balance between the requirements for centralized direction of the national defense and the legacy of service autonomy. The services were to continue to perform their traditional roles of training, equipping, and providing forces and the JCS was to be a collaborative body whose chief function was allocating forces to the commanders in chief of the unified and specified commands, who were themselves expected to exercise their combatant authority through the service components assigned to them. The level of national command depicted here represents the constant of military subordination to civilian control, adjusted by the National Security Act to the present outline of a single Department of Defense that replaced the separate cabinet-level departments of War and Navy. In the context of command and control, this level represents not only the dramatic effects that presidential directives and other decisions can have (the creation of WWMCCS in the aftermath of the Cuban missile crisis, for example) but also the day-to-day interactions by the OSD staff that implement administration policies and, as shown in the JTIDS case, can become strong influences in their own right.

How do these varied and dynamic influences affect the command and control environment, with its complex pressures for centralization and decentralization, regional versus global priorities, and interacting "systems of systems"? The record of TRI-TAC, JINTACCS, and most of all, JTIDS suggests a mixed pattern of cooperation and conflict. In each case, the services endorsed the idea of interoperability, a goal universally acknowledged to be in the interest of all. Equal measures of cooperative conduct can also be seen in the interservice agencies, such as the C3 Systems Directorate of the Joint Staff and the Joint Tactical C3 Agency, that were chartered with the specific objective of providing an institutional focus for joint command and control. The conflicts that were so obvious in the JTIDS study provide the counterpoint to cooperation. It is important to note that these difficulties do not arise out of service knavery or any failings of individuals, but rather as the inescapable result of the legacy of service autonomy, especially when the services, in their institutional role of military experts, make the key technological choices. The results of those choices can have a determinative effect on joint command and control because they usually take place in a setting or a preexisting time frame that emphasizes unique service perspectives, not joint priorities. Thus, the choices the Air Force made for voice control resulted in aircraft configurations, organizational structures, and communications doctrine that preceded JTIDS by many years and ultimately contributed to the outcome of that case. The ability of the Air Force to take those actions, thereby exerting a direct impact upon the command and control environment, is itself an example of the legacy of service autonomy.

This is not to suggest that this legacy is without some considerable merits. It is difficult, for example, to imagine how the American defense establishment would look without the distinctive coloration of the services, inasmuch as they continue to embody certain fundamental roles and missions. And in a society that enshrines progress so aggressively that Civil War battlefields must constantly be protected from hyperactive commercial development, there is much to be said for organizations encompassing traditions that, in the case of the Army, predate the founding of the Republic. If nothing else, these traditions embody a warrior ethos that serves not only as a repository for the hard-won lessons of combat but also as a generational link between past and present. Continuity and military expertise are therefore two of the better reasons why separate services exist and why they will continue to do so. A third reason exists as well: a deeply and profoundly pluralistic democracy has little enthusiasm for monoliths, especially military monoliths. The American experience consequently seems well suited to its heritage of diverse service cultures.

Naturally, there is a downside: having separate services simply makes it more difficult to weld their diverse capabilities into a single, well-integrated fighting machine. This problem is the same whether one is talking about individual weapons, pieces of equipment, command and control systems, or even joint organizations. It is reasonable to observe, however, that this problem has been well understood for a generation or more and that the National Security Act of 1947, or at least its amendments in 1958, rendered service autonomy into an anachronism. A similar argument is that, although the 1958 amendments did not quite finish the job, the provisions of the Goldwater-Nichols Act of 1986 have now diminished service separatism to an irreducible minimum; like Keynesian economists, this line runs, we are all joint warriors now. Further, since this law strengthens the role of the chairman of the JCS and the unified commanders in the defense acquisition process, joint concerns (including interoperable command and control) are certain to receive greater attention. Finally, the heightened emphasis on national strategy—as evidenced by provisions of Goldwater-Nichols as well as the continuing refinement of the defense planning process—ensures that there will be countervailing pressures to whatever narrower, service concerns may occasionally have the temerity to show themselves.

The answer to the first objection is easier to deal with than the second. Certainly the evidence presented in these chapters indicates that service influences—whether or not one is comfortable with the designation of autonomy used here—were pervasive long after the National Security Act of 1947 and its 1958 amendments. Indeed, had the problems of joint planning versus service interests been truly resolved at this point, there would have been no need for further legislative enactments. On the second point, there is no question that Goldwater-Nichols represents a significant evolutionary step away from parochial interests and toward more effective teamwork. It is unlikely, however, to solve every problem where joint and service interests may not coincide. Consider only the fact that the joint military institutions (and especially the staff of the JCS) are not peopled by the representatives of some hitherto unknown "fifth service." They are, instead, serving members of the Army, Navy, Air Force, and Marines whose selection for and standing within the joint community is a function of their primary combat specialties. It is naive to think that these officers will not continue to be strongly influenced by the basic ideas their parent services bring to the problem of war fighting— however much they are engaged during these assignments in the business of joint combat power.

It is equally unrealistic to assume that the unified and specified commanders and their staffs will somehow be isolated from service influences in the future. In fact, part of the intent of Goldwater-Nichols and the larger body of reform it represented was to tie the services and the weapons development process even closer to the joint war-fighting perspectives of the unified commands. Like the members of the Joint Staff, unified commanders, component commanders, and their respective staffs are selected for these positions on the basis of their standing within their parent services. The particular operational characteristics of each theater of operations also tend to dictate the makeup of these commands: the Pacific Command headed by a Navy admiral, the European Command headed by an Army general. None of these arrangements suggests the eclipse of basic service values, however much they may be balanced by joint perspectives.

As before, the services remain the key sources of operational expertise in the making of technological choices, whatever marginal bureaucratic adjustments Goldwater-Nichols may have made to the Defense Department procurement structure. Edward Luttwak, therefore, may be premature in dismissing as "nonstrategies" the ideas of the "naval, air, and nuclear" proponents if those services still have leeway in developing their preferred weapons.[2] Similarly, if the chiefs of those services, wearing their other hats as the Joint Chiefs of Staff, must recommend balancing regional and global requirements against finite budget resources, it is a fair assumption that command and control systems—even joint or interoperable ones—will not be immune to service priorities. What, then, are some reasonable conclusions that can be drawn from our historical experience?

Implications for the Future

There is no question that the management of command and control systems is part of the much larger problem of the management of defense technology. In this realm, technological choice involves taking calculated risks not only in terms of the familiar relationship between costs and benefits but also in terms of larger effects: if we invest a given amount of dollars in a piece of equipment, will it work, and will it be a good thing if it does? Nowhere are these questions more difficult to answer than in the field of command and control, largely because the application of the computer to this age-old problem of war carries so many inherent uncertainties. For all its wonders and promises, the computer is no less susceptible to Murphy's Law than any other human invention, and our ability to understand its military potential is handicapped by its relatively short track record. Only the current generation of computer equipment has been small and durable enough to make it usable in the demanding environments of ship spaces, aircraft compartments, and tactical operations centers. Even so, problems with the reliability and delicacy of this equipment have prompted questions: will these systems add to the already heavy burdens of logistics and maintenance or, even worse, will they fail under the full stress of combat? Those uncertainties are compounded by the difficulties of standardizing military procedures and equipment so that the armed forces can work together in those increasingly frequent instances when joint operations are required by mission and circumstances.

It is somewhat cold comfort to note Brig. Gen. Richard Simpkin's observation of a thirty-to-fifty-year cycle in technological innovation, so that "full acceptance of and integration of computers will have to wait until the computer-literate school children of today become the power generation of the day after tomorrow."[3] If the computer is still a maturing technology in which the best is yet to come, then what complicates life for the present generation of defense decision makers are the ample opportunities for pitfalls in the transition of military communications systems from analog to digital formats, from fixed sites to mobile platforms, from single-service to joint systems, and from information hierarchies to distributed data networks. Naturally, some of these choices inevitably affect established roles, missions, procedures, and careers—what Maj. Gen. Otto Nelson called "pride of place" in his pioneering study of the Army's organizational history.[4] But as difficult as these basic questions of command and control are, there should be no doubt as to the ultimate stakes. Maj. Gen. Clay Buckingham summarized them well: "As we approach the turn of the century, our ability to project power and our ability to fight is going to be increasingly influenced by the command and control factor, that is, by our ability to command and control our own forces, both strategically and tactically in a high-intensity environment; by our ability to deny [the] enemy access to our command and control information; and by our ability to attack and disrupt the enemy's command and control system."[5]

Given these complexities, are there any useful benchmarks to help defense decision makers maintain a consistent focus? One possibility might be to think of command and control as a kind of electronic equivalent of the "directed telescope," the practice of Napoleon and other commanders in which trusted aides or observers were sent to gather critical battlefield information to supplement the regular channels of information about both friendly and enemy forces. The use of these emissaries as the "eyes of the commander" would then permit a situation assessment that did not exclusively depend upon information that had been transmitted up through (and possibly watered down by) the chain of command.[6] Commanders who used this system recognized the existence of a problem that is still present in modern bureaucracies. In the aftermath of the *Challenger* disaster, for example, reporter Charles Peters noted that "the bad news doesn't travel up" in large organizations such as NASA, so that "the executive at or near the top lives in constant danger of not knowing, until he reads it on Page One some morning, that his department is hip-deep in disaster."[7]

With remote decentralized operations, there is a pronounced need for relatively unfiltered information channels that can tie decision makers *at every level* to operational realities. Naturally, every command and control system that is developed and procured cannot function primarily as a "directed telescope": *but at the very least they should not interfere with this function.* The interoperability of otherwise diverse command and control systems ought to be the sine qua non in any development and acquisition decisions made by top leaders in the Department of Defense, both uniformed and civilian. Effective two-way information flows are a common concern of leaders in either crisis management or actual combat. To return to Murphy's Law for a moment, it should be a foregone conclusion that the forces needed to deal with an incipient crisis or a particular combat mission will probably *not* be the ones that are on the scene or even closest to it. If by good luck they are, it is a virtual certainty that they will have to be supported and reinforced by units hastily committed as the situation develops. And beyond any question, these forces will be drawn from more than one service.

Interoperability must be the key if the unexpected is to be treated as an everyday occurrence, but the record to date does not demonstrate the practicality or even the wisdom of a universal family of computers and linkages in which everything is compatible with everything else. Recognizing that reality, a more realistic goal for commanders and defense policymakers may be what I call the *baseline of interoperability*. This concept springs from two related propositions. The first is that, though every electronic system does not necessarily have to be compatible with every other system, it is important for commanders to ensure that compatible linkages are maintained between those elements that must be in communication with one another. The second is that, in establishing such a *baseline of interoperability,* it is important to distinguish carefully between the requirements, capabilities, and limitations of both organizations and technical systems. Common to both propositions is the assumption that there can be no substitute for the direct involvement of the commander in establishing both the requirements for interoperability and the organizational or technical means for achieving them. More specifically, the key leadership tasks involve finding precise answers to three related sets of questions:

▪ What is the *primary* mission? What are the other important missions that the unit is also called upon to perform?
▪ What are the units (or who are the individuals) that *must* communicate with one another in order to perform a unit's primary and other missions? What kinds of information are needed from them, and what kinds of information do they need in return? How fast and how often does this information need to be exchanged?
▪ What are the *means* required to achieve interoperability with the units that *must* be in communication? Are these means primarily technical (hardware, software, data bases, protocols, networks) or can the same ends be accomplished by specific organizational strategies (leadership, followership, management, teamwork, cohesion, procedures, training)? Finally, how can these technical and organizational choices best reinforce one another?

There is nothing especially startling about these questions, except for the fact that they often tend to be overlooked by the leaders of organizations pressured by deadlines and bottom lines. The result is that what is thought to be a command and control problem can actually be an organizational or leadership problem, a basic misperception that can have perverse effects in two ways. First, the investment of time, money, and effort to set up a command and control system will probably not solve an underlying organizational problem and may even make it worse—witness, for example, the Navy–Air Force rivalry over the architecture of JTIDS. Second, it is equally unlikely for any command and control system to be effective if it does not enjoy the confidence of both the leaders it is primarily intended to serve and the operators who must make that system work—the clear example here being the institutional reluctance of the Air Force to embrace any system of digital control in the cockpits of its fighters. Consequently, one of the fundamental tasks for organizational leaders in the information age is to set the terms of reference by which those organizations manage their internal and external communications. Implicit in that responsibility as well is the need to use the *baseline of interoperability* as the essential balance between the diverse operational environments of the services and the requirements for effective joint teamwork.

The declaratory policy of the Defense Department, as we have seen, is firmly on the side of interoperability, but the actual spending of scarce acquisition dollars to achieve that objective in practice is a continuing test of its management and resolve. With the services making the fundamental technological choices in systems development, interoperability can often become a budgetary "option," like the air conditioning added on to the sticker price of an automobile; of course, this is normal practice for an establishment in which "dollars equal policy." What may be the key to future developments in this matter will be the newly strengthened voices of the unified and specified commanders in defense resource decisions. Equally significant will be the ability over time of the JCS chairman to represent joint concerns before the Defense Resources Board (newly rechristened as the Defense Planning and Resources Board under the Pentagon management initiatives put forward by Secretary of Defense Richard Cheney in July 1989) when service programs are being evaluated. Both will give added weight to the infrastructure for interoperability that is already established within OSD and the Joint Staff. The most critical contribution of bodies such as the Joint Tactical C3 Agency and the Joint Staff J-6 (which succeeded the C3 Systems Directorate) is likely to be made within the incremental process that eventually will allow future systems to be engineered in consonance with joint requirements. A common

Defense Department software language, known as ADA, has been developed, for example, even as the JINTACCS program has made steady progress toward common data links, such as TADIL J.

A far more difficult question to address is the proliferation of service command and control systems that in some cases have parallel functions, such as the Army's TACFIRE and the ill-fated MIFASS system that was eventually canceled by the Marines. This was precisely the issue the House Armed Services Committee was concerned with during the deliberations on JTIDS, when the members became impatient with the twin architectures of that program juxtaposed against the steady progression of different Air Force programs for anti-jam voice communications. The JTIDS case shows, however paradoxically, that interoperability can be an elusive goal and that Congress, OSD, and the services are often loath to choose between competing systems— especially when sunk costs are involved and no one wishes to be blamed for having "wasted" those dollars. One answer, originally proposed by the 1978 Defense Science Board task force, called for the creation of a defense command and control agency that would have the primary task of developing common or modular systems for use by the services. Such systems would then be available for the services to order for their own use—a kind of Sears, Roebuck catalog approach to command and control.

To say that the creation of such a superagency is an idea that does not attract universal enthusiasm within the uniformed ranks is to risk serious understatement. The usual arguments against it are numerous: it would be isolated from service inputs and unresponsive to their requirements; it would abrogate military responsibility for their most critical systems; the costs of establishing it would be prohibitive; the addition of yet another defense agency to the line management responsibilities of OSD would be a step in the wrong direction. This assessment seems to square with prevailing sentiments on Capitol Hill, which no longer regards the defense agencies as an unmixed blessing, especially in the era of Gramm-Rudman-Hollings deficit reduction.[8] Consequently, the creation of another such agency, for command and control supervision or any other purpose, is an idea seriously out of step with the times.

Another potential solution to the problem of choosing among competing command and control systems may involve greater use of the Joint Staff, particularly the J-6, which has specific responsibility for joint communications matters. As with any other activity of the Joint Staff, this directorate is limited in the scope of what it can accomplish because it has only an indirect role in the systems acquisition process. To date, that role has largely consisted of good-faith efforts to build bridges with the command and control system developers in each of the services in an attempt to promote interoperability concerns when future systems are still on the drawing boards. Winning friends and influencing programs in this way undoubtedly represent the maximum use of the tools now in the hands of the JCS. But what more might be done? One strategy would be to give the J-6 more authority over the development of command and control systems that have the greatest potential for use in the joint environment. This could be accomplished either by using "fenced money"—specifically earmarked funds—or by ensuring an authoritative voice for the directorate in the top management reviews of key command and control systems under development.

The JCS chairman, for example, sits in as a regular member at meetings of the Defense Resources Board which makes those critical management decisions. Both the former chairman, Gen. John Vessey, and his successor, Adm. William Crowe, have reportedly made extensive use of J-6 reviews of command and control systems in their recommendations to the board. The continuance of that practice, perhaps accompanied by greater use of the directorate to monitor board decisions, would be a positive step for the future. It is important to note as well that the gradual acquisition of more power in the hands of the JCS chairman—one of the measures consistently advocated in JCS reform studies and a central feature of Goldwater-Nichols—implies the grant of additional authority to the Joint Staff. The effective use of that authority to affect key management decisions on command and control suggests a greater reliance on military professionalism to achieve better interoperability—itself a task that can hardly be achieved in any other way. The objective of any such effort has to be ensuring that, while the services continue to make the basic technological choices with respect to their unique operational requirements, the interests of the larger, joint environment are considered as well.

But though it is easy to say that military professionals should be primarily responsible for ensuring better interoperability and solving a host of other problems in the joint world, there is still another basic problem to be confronted. In the modern era of command and control, what, exactly, does "joint" or, even worse, "jointness" really consist of? The standard definition for more than a century has simply been "more than one service." The movement toward JCS reform was accompanied in the 1980s by assertions that better teamwork was needed, as well as an improved integration of combat power from all available forces. In this regard it is even possible to distinguish a "minimalist" approach, which views joint matters as a kind of limited liability partnership, and a "maximalist" viewpoint, which suggests a synergy of joint forces wherein the whole is more than the sum of its parts. The reason these and other fundamental concepts of this larger strategic realm remain vague and contentious may be that no prophet of the joint operational art of war has yet stepped forward to tie its theories or suppositions together in a systematic and comprehensive way. In this book I have taken a somewhat unusual approach toward the problems of command and control by examining the strategic paradigms that constitute the ideological and doctrinal basis for the services in coping with the challenges of the land, sea, and air environments. In the previous chapters I summarized the effects of those paradigms in promoting the separate identities of the services, reinforcing their individual autonomy, and ultimately helping to shape the environment of command and control. But though Clausewitz, Mahan, and Douhet all contain valuable insights into the problems of single-service combat, there is no single overarching strategic paradigm that similarly encompasses the modern relationship between land, sea, and air combat at those varied levels of conflict short of general thermonuclear war.

This observation echoes those made some twenty years ago by Adm. J. C. Wylie, whose book *Military Strategy: A General Theory of Power Control* remains as timely today as when it was written. As I pointed out in chapter 1, Wylie's work is an eloquent statement of the need for both scholars and military professionals to understand the underlying strategic theorems that shape the everyday realities of force design and overall response to the challenges of the international environment. He is explicit in defining the limits to these theorems, however: "There is as yet no accepted and recognized general theory of strategy. Such a general theory would have to meet very stringent requirements. It would have to be applicable to any conflict situation, any time, any place. It would have to be applicable under any restrictions that might actually exist or might be placed upon it. It would have to absorb within its conceptual framework the realities of the existing specific concepts of war strategy, the continental, the maritime, and the air theories."[9] Wylie also points out that a further difficulty is that any such general theory would have to be sufficiently elastic to embrace these criteria, but specific enough to yield practical guidance. By any standard, the definition of such a "general theory of strategy" or (as it has been referred to here) a joint strategic paradigm is a future intellectual task of the first magnitude.

For the present, however, the obvious question is: does the absence of either prophet or paradigm matter at all? Equally obvious is the fact that no final answer to that question is possible and none is attempted here. One must nevertheless be impressed at the extraordinary staying power of the paradigms I have considered in this book, especially in their ability to serve as relatively constant reference points for the services during periods of pronounced technological changes over the course of many generations. Those reference points have lent stability to the institutions of the services as they redefined

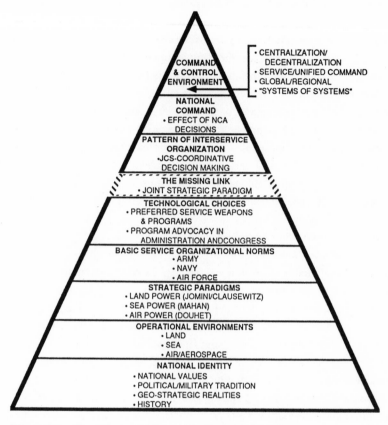

Figure 8.2   The Missing Link: A Joint Strategic Paradigm
Source: Author

their paradigms in light of new developments in warfare, a process largely accomplished through the cyclical refining of operational doctrine. Mahan's prescriptions, for example, originally provided the rationale for fleets of battleships. Yet his theories were equally relevant to the carrier task force when that weapon superseded the dreadnought during World War II, and it can be argued that they continue to provide the underpinnings for the Navy's maritime strategy of the 1980s. Perhaps the key element these paradigms provide is an objective that defines the context for the continuing choices (technological and organizational) that are made to secure each operational environment.

As useful as such precepts have been for the services, the absence of a more general strategic paradigm also helps explain why interservice organization has been such a persistent problem in the postwar world. As depicted in figure

8.2, the lack of a higher-level paradigm makes the problem of interservice organization more difficult. As we have seen, service organizational norms represent the institutional embodiment of the beliefs surrounding each set of unique paradigms. The overarching joint paradigm or "general theory" is, in an important sense, a kind of missing link. Its absence means that interservice organizational norms are cast not in terms of a higher plane of strategy but rather in terms of their impact upon service autonomy and everything it represents. Seen from this perspective, the pattern of interservice organization as it currently exists makes perfect sense. How better to account for the ponderous, coordinative style and committee-laden approach that characterizes the Joint Chiefs of Staff other than to say that it is an organization in search of a paradigm?

Wylie is certainly correct in his estimation of the difficulties involved in coming to grips with this theoretical impasse. Indeed, a skeptic might well argue that the whole is no more than the sum of the parts and that the search for any higher reality is not only futile but a case of "the tail wagging the dog." But the main reason for seeking to improve the larger body of joint force theory is to sharpen the mechanism of choice that a coherent strategy always provides. If one conceives of land, sea, and air forces as members of the nation's combined arms team elevated to the level of grand strategy, then the framing of choices among those forces would be one of the most useful contributions a new paradigm might make. It is not particularly surprising that such a paradigm does not now exist. Samuel P. Huntington noted the existence of "technicism" in the American military tradition from its earliest days, capable enough in dealing with specific military skills, but reluctant to organize and subordinate them into a "distinctive military science . . . directed to the exclusively military purpose of war."[10] Although certainly modified by the rise of military professionalism in the nineteenth century, the technicist influence did not entirely disappear. What paradigms and professionalism may have produced is a kind of "service technicism," which is similarly reluctant to accept subordination to a higher plane of theory beyond the scope of specific service instruments.

From a less theoretical standpoint, the absence of a joint paradigm can also be attributed to the fact that the "joint age" represents little more than a single generation's experience, with budget levels and responses to specific security problems shaping real-world choices between service programs. Each year, those choices are defended before Congress in annual reports of the secretary of defense and posture statements by the service chiefs, all of which are couched in terms emphasizing their contribution to the overall American strategy of deterrence. In reality, however, these pragmatic responses to problems represent the tentative linkages between service capabilities and emerging joint perspectives; they also represent the raw material from which a true overarching strategic paradigm may ultimately be refined.

The precise nature of such a paradigm clearly awaits further investigation, yet it may not be unduly speculative to suggest what it might look like. Once again, it is appropriate to use Wylie as a baseline. The objective of such a paradigm must be "to provide a common and basic frame of reference for the special talents of the soldier, the sailor, the airman, the politician, the economist, and the philosopher in their common efforts toward a common aim."[11] His assumptions are that war, while not inevitable, at least cannot be precluded; "that the aim of war is some measure of control; that the pattern of war is not predictable; and that the ultimate tool of control in war is the man on the scene with a gun."[12] The application of this strategy is set forth by Wylie in terms that vividly recall Jomini: "The primary aim of the strategist in the conduct of war is some selected degree of control of the enemy for the strategist's own purpose; this is achieved by control of the pattern of war; and this control of the pattern of war is had by the manipulation of the center of gravity in a war to the advantage of the strategist and the disadvantage of the opponent."[13] Finally, this control is achieved by the varied capabilities of the services; by the airman, who delivers destruction from the skies; by the sailor, who uses control of the seas to facilitate control of the land; and by the soldier, whose unchallenged physical presence is the ultimate form of control in warfare.[14]

Wylie's view is thus consistent with the findings of this book: a general strategic paradigm must clearly be capable of unifying the individual perspectives of the operational environments. That theoretical finding is of more than passing interest to American military audiences because, more than any other country, the military power of the United States ultimately depends upon a combination of land power, sea power, air power, and, increasingly, space power. As the record of service autonomy presented here has amply demonstrated, each of their respective paradigms becomes an argument for the decisive effect of that particular operational environment on the nation's security and, implicitly, a rationale for Army, Navy, or Air Force programs. A truly useful set of principles, therefore, has to be broad enough to accept the merits of the service paradigms to the extent that they are effective prescriptions for victory in their respective operational environments. But it must also be narrow enough to reject the ideological overtones of those paradigms in favor of a prescription that produces the most synergistic combination of these forces—the set of norms that allows the contribution of each arm of the services to be maximized for the common good. The philosophical underpinning here recalls that passage in which Clausewitz describes military genius as "not one single quality bearing upon War" but rather a "harmonious associa- tion of powers, in which one or the other may predominate, but none must be in opposition."[15] The conduct of American defense policy over the past forty years has been an attempt to achieve that end with respect to the nation's land, sea, and air forces; yet practice has not thus far yielded paradigm.

Implicit in this philosophical underpinning is the assumption that each of the services is competent to organize, train, and equip forces for combat in its respective operational environment, however much the matter of specific roles and missions may be subject to continuing debate. As I have shown throughout this book, the principle of the combined arms came to be accepted as a fundamental organizing principle in each of the services, as various components grew to maturity (for example, armored forces, naval aviation) and were integrated into the war-fighting apparatus of their respective forces. In much the same way, looking at the services as components of a larger whole requires both an acceptance of the primary purpose of their individual forces and a need to look long and hard at where they fit together at the margins. These are difficult decisions to make in the abstract, but they are even more painful when service doctrinal preferences (which are linked to their paradigms) come into conflict with certain unique requirements of the unified commanders: close air support over a landing beach, for example. Precisely for this reason, Title II of Goldwater-Nichols enhanced the power of the unified and specified commanders over their service components, espe- cially in the streamlining of internal command lines.[16] That important evolu- tionary step is certain to produce the kind of adjustments by trial and error that will answer the all-important questions: what is "service," what is "joint," and how do we tell the difference? The record of those marginal, incremental, but vital developments may eventually yield valuable clues about the outline of a new paradigm.

If one looks to the margins of interservice relationships for a future para- digm, then one of its dimensions is almost certain to include the qualitatively new factor of modern command and control. Any new and largely untested capability ought to be approached with a fair amount of skepticism, but there is little doubt of the great potential that exists in the application of information-age technologies to the fundamental problem of combat com- mand. Nowhere is this potential greater than in the ability of command and control systems to link remote and physically dissimilar things, such as ar- mies, airplanes, and ships. When one recalls Wylie's assumption that the pattern of warfare cannot be predicted, the importance of using command and control to link these dissimilar elements becomes obvious. Precisely because the next crisis—or an even more fundamental military challenge—will almost certainly require a combination of unique forces that no one had anticipated, it ought to be axiomatic that the interoperability of diverse command and control systems is the one element that cannot be left to chance. There are a number of methods to ensure interoperability, some more painful and expensive than others. But whatever method is followed, command and control can provide the vital ingredient of an effective linkage to the margins of the services. As such, it can be a fundamentally unifying influence, both in operations and, possibly, in paradigm as well.

On logical grounds alone, there is always the possibility that a joint strategic paradigm may never be reduced to a well-understood set of principles, either because joint warfare really is nothing more than the successive application of land, sea, and air power or perhaps because the organization of joint forces into unified commands at the theater level prevents the derivation of a useful series of principles at the global level. The development, however, of joint *doctrine*—as distinct from *paradigm*—was one of the significant additions to the responsibilities of the chairman of the Joint Chiefs of Staff mandated by Goldwater-Nichols.[17] The bulk of those duties is now entrusted to the new J-7 Directorate of the Joint Staff, which in 1987 developed a "joint doctrine master plan" in order to begin the herculean task of comparing service doctrines across a wide range of subject areas—for example, command and control countermeasures, airspace control, fire support, special operations, suppression of enemy air defenses, sea-air rescue, and so on. The Joint Staff, the services, and the unified commands share the responsibility for generating consensus on the joint principles to be followed in each of these subject areas, and it is hoped that eventually those specific functional agreements can be linked to the more general categories of joint operations: intelligence, planning, logistics, communications, combat support, and, most critical, combat operations. Out of this hierarchy, a body of theory or "joint doctrine capstone" is finally to emerge.[18]

The experience with JINTACCS and JTIDS strongly suggests that the launching of new bureaucratic entities and the imposition of new processes do not necessarily represent final victories in and of themselves. The JCS system is above all a consensual one, and the real merits of the joint doctrinal refinement process will be seen when that quest confronts the hurdles of established procedures and institutional interests—as it inevitably must. It is equally important to ensure that the evolution of joint doctrine occurs as the result of a conscious effort to distill the lessons of field experience. Figure 8.3 is a schematic representation of how that process might work. At the left-hand scale is the joint system much as it is now, with joint operations the result of an

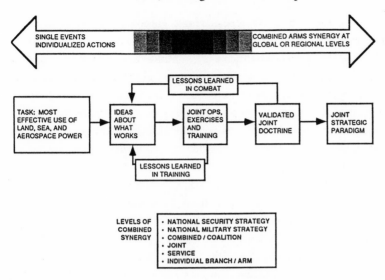

Figure 8.3   The Evolution of Joint Doctrine and Strategy
Source: Author

infinitely varied set of unique circumstances, each one of which requires an equally unique, handcrafted kind of response. The trick is in moving away from what some Joint Staff officers refer to as the "perpetual All-Star game." This is done by moving toward the right side of the schematic: an organized effort is set in motion to plan joint exercises, training, readiness tests, and actual operations around the notion of testing prospective concepts about what will work in the field. The lessons learned from those experiences drive the doctrine refinement and formation process—which itself can generate tentative hypotheses that can be plugged back into the field evaluation process.

Whether this process ever yields a joint paradigm may be considerably less significant than the fact that it incorporates a disciplined means for generating, testing, and evaluating those operational concepts that will eventually form the body of joint doctrine. Thus far, the formation of this doctrine has largely been confined to the gathering of service ideas on specific warfighting functions—for example, air defense, landing force operations, and low-intensity conflict. As this process goes further, it will be increasingly important that these areas of tentative interservice agreement are validated by exposure to the rigors of field testing. There is ample historical precedent for such efforts by a national-level military staff because, as I. B. Holley points out, this is just the sort of problem that challenged the elder Von Moltke as he drove the Prussian General Staff to perfect its mobilization planning: "Just promulgating appropriate doctrine was not enough. Moltke understood that staffs have to be exercised by repeated trials. He conducted test mobilizations which revealed imperfections in the plans and less than gratifying performances by inexperienced officers. . . . Moltke's genius lay in applying Scharnhorst's emphasis on a careful recording of experience, which he then analyzed with utter objectivity to produce viable doctrine."[19] Similarly, the formulation of a body of doctrine for the joint employment of American combat power cannot be just a "paper drill"; it must result from a deliberate effort to subject ideas about joint warfare to realistic operational testing and rigorous analytical evaluation.

The focal point for the refinement of joint doctrine is, of course, the JCS, but an important part of the work must be accomplished by the military educational establishment, including the service war colleges as well as the National Defense University system. Their placement in this process is important for three reasons. First, they are the only institutions capable of providing the shared academic and operational perspectives that can help produce the intellectual underpinnings of the larger body of joint doctrine. Second, their twin missions of research and training make the war colleges ideal places to study the larger strategic implications of joint doctrine and to inculcate those perspectives into a student population from which our future generals and admirals are ultimately selected. The incorporation of such a common ideal was something strongly hoped for by those who enacted Goldwater-Nichols; however, it does not appear that there was always a full understanding of the fact that the absence of an effective body of joint doctrine has made far more difficult the task of training officers for joint service—in the war colleges or anywhere else. It was similarly unclear how joint education, rather than simply joint training, was to take place without the benefit of a higher plane of theory to guide it. All the more reason, then, to set the creation of doctrine and theory as a basic goal, to put an ordered process in motion to achieve it, and to use the military educational establishment as the main engine of intellectual development.[20]

The schematic depicted in figure 8.3 ultimately arrives at the realm of applied operational strategy suggested by the synergy of the joint paradigm. This, of course, is speculative for the reasons outlined above. But regardless of whether such a unity of thought can ever be discerned and captured by the words of a latter-day Clausewitz or some modern apostle of the joint art, there is much to be said for any systematic effort to codify the results of the American military experiment with its unique balance of disparate forces. In particular, those who study strategy need to better understand that these forces are developed, procured, and employed in ways that reflect in no small measure the peculiar geopolitical circumstances that confront the United

States. It is the beginning of wisdom to understand both the capabilities and the limitations those strategic choices entail.

The problem of coherent strategic choice is a matter hardly less demanding than the difficulties of reconciling the many issues of command and control in the armed forces of the United States: ultimately both involve a crosscurrent of conflicting organizational and individual values—all juxtaposed against the backdrop of a "big, lumbering, pluralistic, affluent, liberal, democratic, individualistic, materialistic [and] technologically supremely sophisticated society." Samuel P. Huntington is undoubtedly correct in this formulation, as he is in saying that the character of that society makes it difficult for any military strategy to be followed with Machiavellian precision.[21] Added to this is the fact that the American military institution itself is a peculiarly pluralistic one, a basic character trait that makes it extraordinarily difficult to achieve the tight standardization seemingly demanded by warfare in the information age. And yet this kind of warfare is precisely the type at which the "technologically supremely sophisticated society" must excel if it is to prevail and survive, should its essential interests be threatened. These are depressing thoughts, which foster still another: is it all worth it?

The answer is: probably yes. Although the promise of modern command and control stops well short of completely dissipating the fog of war, it has the potential to turn night into day, to achieve spans of control that can be measured in global terms, and to mass collective combat power without massing forces. One needs only to consider the demonstrated effects of the present generation of battlefield reconnaissance systems fielded by the services to understand the veracity of the lesson the Army learned from the 1973 Yom Kippur War: what can be seen can be hit; what can be hit can be killed. The function of "seeing" now entails a wide range of electronic, optical, and acoustic sensors that are increasingly linked in real-time to computer-controlled firing systems, such as the Aegis-class cruisers. The ranges and discrimination of cruise missiles, laser-guided artillery, and other "smart" munitions similarly suggest the possibility for coordinated attacks from diverse and dispersed platforms and weapons systems. All this suggests a level of lethality comparable to some of the great technological advances in military history: the archers at Agincourt, the rifled musketry of the American Civil War, and the machine gun in World War I.[22]

This is not to suggest that the action-reaction cycle of measure and countermeasure is likely to be repealed—in fact it is more intense than ever. What is suggested, however, is that the ultimate winner in this contest will not necessarily be the side with the latest piece of electronic gadgetry. Rather, the armed forces that can gather and exploit the most critical information are likely to have the decisive advantage. In writing about the comparative differences between the British and German development of radar prior to World War II, the always thoughtful I. B. Holley again captures the essence of this point: "It was not the basic electronic theory that gave the British such a decided edge over the enemy. After all, the Germans also had radar which they were developing more or less in parallel with the RAF. The big difference came from the fact that the British pushed further. They not only deployed radar as a weapons system but also devised sound tactical doctrine to guide its use and provided the operational training to insure that the system actually functioned in practice."[23] Command, control, organization, and joint doctrine ultimately come together at this point, because no technology could possibly overcome the corrosive effects of a top-heavy, inefficient bureaucracy. If, for example, the computer is used to reinforce hierarchical information flows—and thus continues the now-familiar pattern of information overloads and bottlenecks—this is the fault of humans, not technology, because the electron simply does not care.

The great potential of distributed data systems like JTIDS is that they can bring a democratic influence to the flow of battlefield information. Data can be shared and selected, for example, by commanders and operators who may not even be members of the same tactical organizations but who are transient members of the same computer network. The Stinger gunner and the F-15 pilot linked by JTIDS may have no closer relationship to each other than two researchers browsing through the same stack at a university library; both pairs, however, are effectively using nonhierarchical information regimes that reconcile their individual needs within an overall cooperative framework. The drawback, of course, is that such information sharing can be utterly subversive of the notion of military hierarchy, which, for all practical purposes, considers command and information lines to be identical. In the end, it may well be that the command and information lines may diverge, especially if, God forbid, the reality of the Army's Airland Battle ever matches the decentralized combat model called for in its doctrine. In the interim, compromises and intelligence planning will be required to exploit JTIDS-style technologies in ways that favor decentralized operations but do not sacrifice overall coherence. What good planning may ultimately produce is an ability to move information so quickly it will extend the commander's span of control in ways that may revolutionize military organization itself. The answer lies neither in a blind overreliance on high technology nor in a Luddite rejection of new methods but in the making of wise technological choices and tough organizational decisions. If that course is followed, command and control may yet make its greatest contribution to the common defense.

Notes

Chapter 1 Paradigms and Perspectives

1 U.S. Congress, *Defense Organization: The Need for Change,* by James R. Locher III, Staff
   Report to the Committee on Armed Services, S. Rpt. 99–86, Oct. 16, 1985 (Washington:
   GPO, 1985), p. 365; hereafter, Locher Report.
2 George C. Wilson, "Weinberger Questioned on Grenada Reform Plan," *Washington Post,*
   Nov. 15, 1985, p. A11. The complete transcript of Weinberger's testimony is printed in U.S.
   Congress, Senate, *Reorganization of the Department of Defense: Hearings before the Com-*
   mittee on Armed Services, United States Senate, S. Hrg. 99–1083, 99th Cong., 1st Sess.,
   1985 (Washington: GPO, 1987), pp. 67–145.
3 U.S. Congress, House, *Goldwater-Nichols Department of Defense Reorganization Act of*
   1986, Conf. Rpt. 99-824 to accompany HR 3622, 99th Cong., 2nd Sess., 1986, pp. 88, 91–
   98. The most recent account of the passage of the Goldwater-Nichols Act is by Mark Perry,
   Four Stars (Boston: Houghton Mifflin, 1989), pp. 328–340. Former senator Barry Goldwater recounted in characteristically vivid language his recollection of those same event in his
   memoir, *Goldwater,* with Jack Casserly (New York: Doubleday, 1988), pp. 334–361.
4 Locher Report, p. 365.
5 John H. Cushman, *Command and Control of Theater Forces: Adequacy* (Washington:
   AFCEA Press, 1986), and Verl R. Stanley and Phillip L. Noggle, "Command and Control
   Warfare: Seizing the Initiative," *Signal* 38:8 (Apr. 1984), pp. 23–26.
6 "Navy Scraps Communications System," *Washington Post,* Oct. 23, 1985, p. 4.
7 For example, see John Englund, "JTIDS: Diary of a $600 Million Pentagon Fiasco," *Wash-*
   ington Post, May 11, 1986, p. D1, and letter to the editor from Assistant Secretary of
   Defense Donald C. Latham, "Navy and Air Force Pilots *Can* Talk!" *Washington Post,* May
   26, 1986, p. A20.
8 Englund, op. cit.
9 See Joseph Weizenbaum, *Computer Power and Human Reason* (San Francisco: W. M.
   Freeman, 1976), esp. pp. 8–16, 23–38.
10 "What Loyalty Can Mean to the Top Marine," *Washington Post,* July 3, 1986, p. A21. For a
   more thoughtful if no less contrarian approach to the problem of integrated combat power,
   see former secretary of the navy John Lehman's account of the invasion of Grenada in
   Command of the Seas (New York: Scribner's, 1988), pp. 291–305. In a chapter titled "What
   Price Jointness?" Lehman goes so far as to argue that "the current defense ideology of
   'jointness' hobbles our military effectiveness terribly, and in the event of a major war with
   the Soviet Union could well lead to defeat" (p. 300).
11 For a succinct discussion of the span-of-control problem in military history, see Irving B.
   Holley, Jr., "Command, Control, and Technology," *Defense Analysis* (special issue on
   command and control) 4:3 (November 1988), p. 268.
12 *Webster's New World Dictionary of the American Language,* 2nd coll. ed. (New York:
   World, 1974), p. 95.
13 Arthur T. Hadley, *The Straw Giant* (New York: Random House, 1986), p. 67.

266 ■ Notes to Pages 9–15

14 Ibid., p. 68.
15 Ibid., p. 70.
16 Arthur T. Hadley, "The Split Military Psyche," *New York Times Magazine*, July 13, 1986, p. 26.
17 Col. William G. Hanne, "A Separatist Case," U.S. Naval Institute *Proceedings*, 111/7/989 (July 1985), pp. 88–96.
18 Comdr. T. R. Fedyszyn, "A Maritime Perspective," U.S. Naval Institute *Proceedings*, 111/7/989 (July 1985), p. 82.
19 Ibid., p. 89.
20 Ibid., p. 82.
21 See Samuel P. Huntington, *The Soldier and the State* (Cambridge: Harvard Univ. Press, 1981), p. 193.
22 Ibid., chaps. 8–10, pp. 193–283, et passim. Huntington, *The Common Defense* (New York: Columbia Univ. Press, 1961).
23 Rear Adm. J. C. Wylie, *Military Strategy: A General Theory of Power Control* (New Brunswick, N.J.: Rutgers Univ. Press, 1966), pp. 37–56. Wylie actually asserts four major theories. The final one, guerrilla warfare, is not relevant here, because it has not been as dominating an influence in the evolution of service command structures as the theories of land, sea, and air power.
24 Ibid., pp. 65–76.
25 Thomas S. Kuhn, *The Structure of Scientific Revolutions*, 2nd ed. (Chicago: Univ. of Chicago Press, 1970), esp. pp. 35–65. See also Kuhn, *The Fundamental Tension* (Chicago: Univ. of Chicago Press, 1977), esp. pp. 293–319 and n. 4, p. 295.
26 Arnold Kanter, *Defense Politics: A Budgetary Perspective* (Chicago: Univ. of Chicago Press, 1979), pp. 17, 28–29.
27 Carl H. Builder, *The Army in the Strategic Planning Process: Who Shall Bell the Cat?* (Santa Monica, Calif.: Rand Corp., 1987), pp. 22–27.
28 Ibid., pp. 50–71.
29 Ibid., p. 71.
30 Ibid., p. 73.
31 Ibid., pp. 78–86, 90–91. It is a measure of the superficiality with which these issues are often considered that Builder's failure to address the classical roots of Army doctrine went unremarked in a report primarily intended for Army audiences. Regrettably, the same flaw persists in the slightly expanded version of this report, published commercially as *The Masks of War* (Baltimore: Johns Hopkins Univ. Press, 1989).
32 Edward N. Luttwak, *Strategy: The Logic of War and Peace* (Cambridge: Harvard Univ. Press, Belknap Press, 1987).
33 Ibid., p. 113. See also chaps. 8–10.
34 Ibid., pp. 158–159.
35 Ibid., pp. 161–168.
36 Ibid., pp. 171–174.
37 Philip A. Crowl, "Alfred Thayer Mahan: The Naval Historian," in Peter Paret, ed., *Makers of Modern Strategy from Machiavelli to the Nuclear Age* (Princeton: Princeton Univ. Press,1986), p. 477. The same thought was more recently echoed by another Newport colleague:"Our students read more Mao Zedong than Alfred Thayer Mahan; they study the

deadlock on the Western Front in World War I but hear barely five minutes on the Battle of Jutland; they discuss Airland Battle as well as the Maritime Strategy" (Alvin H. Bernstein, "Naval War College Took a Bum Rap," *Armed Forces Journal International* 126:1 [Aug. 1988], p. 71).

38 Peter Paret, "Napoleon," in Paret, ed., op. cit., p. 141.

39 See Steven M. Walt, "The Search for a Science of Strategy," *International Security* 12:1 (Summer 1987), pp. 154–155.

40 U.S. Joint Chiefs of Staff, *JCS Pub. 1: Department of Defense Dictionary of Military and Associated Terms* (Washington, OJCS, Jan. 1986), p. 74.

41 I am indebted to Prof. Frank Snyder of the Naval War College, who has imparted the importance of command style to a generation of students, for emphasizing this point to me. His more general comments have been equally helpful throughout this chapter.

42 This is not to suggest, however, that the requirements for effective, redundant communications linking the chain of command from top to bottom are anything less than absolute. See the brief discussion that follows in this chapter on strategic command and control, as well as the more comprehensive description in chapter 5.

43 Frank M. Snyder, *Command and Control: Readings and Commentary,* Publication of the Harvard Univ. Program on Information Resources Policy, Cambridge, April 1989, p. 39.

44 Ibid., p. 62.

45 James M. Rockwell, ed., *Tactical C3 for the Ground Forces* (Washington: AFCEA Press, 1986), and Gordon R. Nagler, ed., *Naval Tactical Command Control* (Washington: AFCEA Press, 1985).

46 Cushman, op. cit.

47 Paul Bracken, *The Command and Control of Nuclear Forces* (New Haven, Conn.: Yale Univ. Press, 1983), and Bruce G. Blair, *Strategic Command and Control* (Washington: Brookings Institution, 1985).

48 Martin Van Creveld, *Command in War* (Cambridge: Harvard Univ. Press, 1985).

49 Ibid., p. 261.

50 Martin Van Creveld, *Technology and War* (New York: Free Press, 1989), pp. 228–229, hereafter *Technology;* see also pp. 217–232, 235–257, 267–282, et passim. See also former senator Goldwater's account of the legislation that now bears his name in *Goldwater,* pp. 334–361. Mark Perry also writes of the passage of the Goldwater-Nichols bill in *Four Stars,* pp. 312–340.

51 The classic treatment of the levels-of-analysis problem is contained in Graham T. Allison, *The Essence of Decision* (Boston: Little, Brown, 1971), pp. 245–263.

52 A sampling of the topical literature on DOD structural reform would include Locher Report; Archie D. Barrett, *Re-Appraising Defense Organization* (Washington: National Defense Univ. Press, 1983); Robert J. Art, Vincent Davis, and Samuel P. Huntington, eds., *Reorganizing America's Defense* (Washington: Pergamon-Brassey's, 1985); Asa R. Clark et al., eds., *The Defense Reform Debate* (Baltimore: Johns Hopkins Univ. Press, 1984); John M. Collins, *U.S. Defense Planning: A Critique* (Boulder, Colo.: Westview Press, 1982); and Barry M. Blechman and William J. Lynn, eds., *Toward a More Effective Defense* (Cambridge: Ballinger, 1985). (See also n. 3 above.)

Chapter 2   The Roots of Service Autonomy

1 Samuel P. Huntington, *The Soldier and the State* (Cambridge: Harvard University Press, 1957), p. 168.
2 U.S., The Constitution. Congressional powers are enumerated in Article I, Section 8, and those of the president in Article II, Section 2.
3 Huntington, op. cit., p. 84.
4 Ibid., p. 80.
5 Ibid., pp. 163–169.
6 One military scholar recently argued that Huntington "does little more than place the Uptonian premise in an ideological context"—that is, that American society is "liberal," and the military institution is "conservative." See Major Andrew J. Bacevich, Jr., "Emory Upton: A Centennial Assessment," *Military Review* 61:12 (December 1981), pp. 21–28.
7 Alexander Hamilton ("Publius"), No. 24, *The Federalist Papers,* Mentor ed. (New York: New American Library, 1961), pp. 161–162.
8 Ibid., Nos. 25 and 26, pp. 162–174.
9 Ibid., p. 162.
10 Ibid., Nos. 41 and 42, pp. 255–271.
11 Ibid.
12 See Charles A. Beard, *The Economic Basis of Politics* (New York: Vintage Books, 1957).
13 Harold and Margaret Sprout, *The Rise of American Naval Power* (Princeton: Princeton Univ. Press, 1967), p. 23.
14 For some recent constitutional perspectives on defense, see the special issue of *Armed Forces & Society* 14:1 (Fall 1987), which contains a compendium of articles on this topic.
15 Lloyd M. Short, *The Development of National Administration in the United States* (Baltimore: Johns Hopkins Univ. Press, 1923), pp. 78–118.
16 Vice Adm. Edwin B. Hooper, *The Navy Department: Evolution and Fragmentation* (Washington: Naval Historical Foundation, 1978), p. 2.
17 Huntington, op. cit., pp. 193–199.
18 J. D. Hittle, *The Military Staff: Its History and Development,* 3rd ed. (Harrisburg, Pa.: Stackpole Press, 1961), p. 1.
19 Ibid., p. 3.
20 Numbers 31:1–54. Interestingly, his officers did not carry out Moses' orders regarding the taking of prisoners (capturing not only the virgins called for by their instructions but the rest of the women as well) and were required to do penance.
21 For a succinct example, see the discussion of the command structure of ancient Greece set forth by Virgil Ney, *The Evolution of Military Unit Control,* Combat Operations Research Group Memorandum M-217 (Washington: U.S. Army Combat Developments Command, Sept. 10, 1965), pp. 8–15.
22 Ibid., pp. 13–16. Hittle, op. cit., pp. 22–26. See also Van Creveld, *Technology,* pp. 81–97.
23 Hittle, op. cit., pp. 13–22.
24 See Martin Van Creveld, *Supplying War: Logistics from Wallenstein to Patton* (Cambridge: Cambridge Univ. Press, 1980), pp. 5–39.
25 Hittle, op. cit., pp. 39–47, 52–60; Ney, op. cit., pp. 32–36.
26 Ney, op. cit., p. 33.
27 Hittle, op. cit., pp. 178, 180.

28 George Washington, Letter to Secretary of War James McHenry, July 4, 1798. Cited in *Legislative History of the Army of the United States, 1775–1901*, Senate Doc. No. 229, 56th Cong., 2nd Sess. (Washington: GPO, 1904), p. 4.

29 Ernest F. Fisher, Jr., "Weapons and Equipment Evolution and Its Influence upon Organization and Tactics in the American Army from 1775–1963," report (Washington: U.S. Army, Office of the Chief of Military History, n.d.), pp. 10–11. Fisher states that the idea for a legion concept came directly from von Steuben, who proposed the plan for the postwar organization of the Continental Army. See also Russell F. Weigley, *History of the United States Army*, rev. ed. (Bloomington: Indiana Univ. Press, 1984), pp. 92–94.

30 Sprout and Sprout, op. cit., p. 86.

31 Charles O. Paullin, *History of Naval Administration, 1775–1911* (Annapolis: U.S. Naval Institute Press, 1968), p. 452. Probably the most authoritative source on the Navy's organizational history during this period, Paullin points out that the U.S. Navy also had "flotillas," but that they were deployed as harbor defenses and usually consisted of barges, useless Jefferson-vintage gunboats, and whatever else would float. For a succinct discussion of naval developments that led up to this historical period, see Van Creveld, *Technology*, pp. 125–136.

32 Alfred Thayer Mahan, *Naval Administration and Warfare* (Boston: Little, Brown, 1908), p. 32.

33 Emory Upton, *The Military Policy of the United States* (Washington: GPO, 1904), pp. 95–96.

34 Ibid., pp. 126–133; see also T. Harry Williams, *Americans at War* (Baton Rouge: Louisiana State University Press, 1960), pp. 25–27, and John K. Mahon, *The War of 1812* (Gainesville: Univ. of Florida Press, 1972), pp. 295–300.

35 Short, op. cit., pp. 127–128.

36 Weigley, op. cit., p. 135.

37 Williams, op. cit., pp. 31–32.

38 Sprout and Sprout, op. cit., p. 92.

39 Huntington, op. cit., p. 201. See also Henry P. Beers, "The Development of the Office of the Chief of Naval Operations: Part I," *Military Affairs* 10 (Spring 1946), pp. 41–42.

40 Charles M. Wiltse, *John C. Calhoun, Nationalist, 1782–1828*, p. 297; cited by Williams, op. cit., p. 34.

41 Capt. John H. Rodgers to Secretary of the Navy John Branch, U.S. Congress, House Doc. no. 2 (Ser. no. 195), November 23, 1829. Cited by Hooper, op. cit., p. 5.

42 Abel P. Upshur, *Annual Report of the Secretary of the Navy* (Washington: Dept. of the Navy, 1841), p. 378. Cited by Paullin, op. cit., 209.

43 Paullin, op. cit., p. 210. See also Short, op. cit., p. 167.

44 Sprout and Sprout, op. cit., p. 123.

45 Ibid., p. 93.

46 This is also what Martin Van Creveld refers to as the "Stone Age" of command and control. See his *Command in War* (Cambridge: Harvard Univ. Press, 1985), pp. 17–57.

47 Historical Evaluation and Research Organization, *A Preliminary, Interpretive Survey of the History of Command and Control* (Albuquerque, N. Mex.: Sandia Corp., 1963), p. 23; hereafter, HERO.

48 David L. Woods, *A History of Tactical Communications Techniques* (Orlando, Fla.: Martin Marietta Corp., 1965), p. 6. See also Van Creveld, *Technology*, pp. 114–123. In his

discussion of warfare in the eighteenth and early nineteenth centuries, Van Creveld noted the important contributions to battlefield control made by maps and clocks. Both technologies were undergoing a slow but steady improvement during this period.

49 Ibid., pp. 1–12.

50 Ibid., pp. 33–34.

51 D. A. Paolucci, Norman Polmar, and John Patrick, *A Guide to U.S. Naval Command and Control,* NOSC Technical Document no. 247 (San Diego, Calif.: U.S. Naval Ocean Systems Center, July 1, 1979), p. 9.

52 Rear Adm. Julius A. Furer, *Administration of the Navy Department in World War II* (Washington: U.S. Naval Historical Division, 1959), p. 4.

53 Ibid.

54 Fisher, op. cit., p. 13.

55 Maurice Matloff, ed., *American Military History* (Washington: U.S. Army, Office of the Chief of Military History, 1973), p. 127.

56 Woods, op. cit., p. 52.

57 Matloff, op. cit., pp. 144–147.

58 Upton, op. cit., pp. 145–147.

59 Cited figures are from Weigley, op. cit., pp. 566–567, and Matloff, op. cit., p. 154.

60 HERO, p. 32.

61 Alfred Thayer Mahan, *The Influence of Sea Power upon History* (Boston: Little, Brown, 1918), p. 108.

62 Leonard D. White, *The Jacksonians,* p. 65; cited by Williams, op. cit., p. 41.

63 Williams, op. cit., p. 39. See also Allen R. Millett and Peter Maslowski, *For the Common Defense* (New York: Free Press, 1984), pp. 137–150.

64 Alfred H. Bill, *Rehearsal for Conflict: The War with Mexico, 1846–1848,* p. 186; cited by Lawrence H. Legere, "Unification of the Armed Forces," manuscript (Washington: U.S. Army, Office of the Chief of Military History, n.d.), p. 23.

65 Weigley, op. cit., p. 175.

66 T. Harry Williams, *The History of American Wars* (New York: Alfred A. Knopf, 1981), p. 180; Matloff, op. cit., pp. 174–175; Legere, op. cit., pp. 23–24.

67 Williams, *The History of American Wars* (New York: Alfred A. Knopf, 1981), p. 175.

68 Legere, op. cit., p. 25. See also Edward L. Beach, *The United States Navy* (New York: Holt, 1986), pp. 159–160.

Chapter 3   Paradigms on Land and Sea

1 Antoine Henri Jomini, *Précis de l'art de la guerre,* I:158. Originally published as *The Art of War,* trans. G. H. Mendell and W. P. Craighill (Philadelphia: J. P. Lippincott Co., 1862. Reprint. Westport, Conn.: Greenwood Press, 1971), p. 70. See also Crane Brinton, Gordon A. Craig, and Felix Gilbert, "Jomini," in Edward Mead Earle, ed., *Makers of Modern Strategy,* rev. ed. (Princeton: Princeton Univ. Press, 1973), pp. 77–92. The sequel to Earle's classic work appeared in 1986 with the publication of *Makers of Modern Strategy from Machiavelli to the Nuclear Age,* ed. Peter Paret (Princeton: Princeton Univ. Press, 1986). See in particular John Shy's excellent chapter, "Jomini," pp. 143–185.

2 Col. John I. Alger, "Jomini," Lecture to the National War College, Washington, D.C., September 6, 1985. See also Alger, *The Quest for Victory* (Westport, Conn.: Greenwood Press, 1982), esp. pp. 16–50.

3   Brinton, Craig, and Gilbert, op. cit., p. 89.

4   Henry W. Halleck, *Elements of Military Art and Science*, 3rd ed. (New York: D. Appleton, 1862), pp. 39–40. Cited by Weigley, op. cit., p. 84. See also his chapter on Mahan and Halleck, pp. 77–91. On Jomini's influence on the U.S. Army, see T. Harry Williams, *The History of American Wars* (New York: Knopf, 1981), pp. 194–197.

5   Martin Van Creveld, *Command in War* (Cambridge: Harvard Univ. Press, 1985), pp. 65–66. See also J. D. Hittle, *The Military Staff: Its History and Development* (Harrisburg, Pa.: Stackpole Press, 1961), pp. 86–128.

6   Daniel L. Woods, *A History of Tactical Communications Techniques* (Orlando, Fla.: Martin-Marietta Corp., 1965), pp. 105–108. See also Van Creveld, *Technology*, pp. 154–158.

7   Dr. Ernest F. Fisher, Jr., "Weapons and Equipment Evolution and Its Influence upon Organization and Tactics in the American Army from 1775–1963," manuscript (Washington: U.S. Army, Office of the Chief of Military History, n.d.), p. 29. More generally, see Martin Van Creveld, *Supplying War: Logistics from Wallenstein to Patton* (Cambridge: Cambridge Univ. Press, 1980).

8   See Thomas Weber, *The Northern Railroads in the Civil War* (New York: Columbia Univ. Press, 1962), esp. pp. 220–232. See also Van Creveld, *Technology*, pp. 158–162, 167–170.

9   Harold and Margaret Sprout, *The Rise of American Naval Power* (Princeton: Princeton Univ. Press, 1967), p. 152.

10 Packet vessels had not, of course, been unknown during the Age of Sail. See Adm. S. S. Robinson, *A History of Naval Tactics* (Annapolis: U.S. Naval Institute Press, 1942), pp. 542–557.

11 Ibid., pp. 591–597.

12 Fisher, op. cit., pp. 30–34. See also Maurice Matloff, ed., *American Military History*, Army Historical Series (Washington: U.S. Army, Office of the Chief of Military History, 1973), pp. 181–183, and Van Creveld, *Technology*, pp. 170–172.

13 Trevor N. Dupuy, *A Genius for War* (New York: Prentice-Hall, 1977), pp. 24–25.

14 Ibid. Naturally, Dupuy's admiration for the Prussian General Staff is not inconsistent with either his scholarly writings or his long experience as an officer in the U.S. Army.

15 Cited by Hittle, op. cit., p. 189.

16 Colmar van der Golz, *The Nation in Arms* (London, 1913), p. 1. Cited by Michael Howard, "The Influence of Clausewitz," in Karl von Clausewitz, *On War*, ed. and trans. Michael Howard and Peter Paret (Princeton: Princeton Univ. Press, 1976), p. 31.

17 Clausewitz, op. cit., Book I, p. 87.

18 Ibid., p. 87.

19 Ibid., Book III, p. 204.

20 Ibid., Book V, p. 285.

21 Ibid., Book V, p. 294.

22 Roger A. Leonard, ed., *A Short Guide to Clausewitz on War* (New York: Capricorn Books, 1967), p. 71. Cited version is an extract of the standard 1874 translation by Graham and Maude which in this quotation reads better than more current translations. Trevor Dupuy uses the same quote in this version for obvious reasons in his *Genius for War*.

23 Russell F. Weigley, *History of the United States Army* (New York: Macmillan, 1967), p. 227; hereafter, *History*.

24 Lloyd M. Short, *The Development of National Administrative Organization in the United States* (Baltimore: Johns Hopkins Univ. Press, 1923), p. 236.

25 Charles O. Paullin, *History of Naval Administration, 1775–1911* (Annapolis: U.S. Naval Institute Press, 1968), p. 250.

26 Ibid., p. 260.

27 Alfred Thayer Mahan, *Naval Administration and Warfare* (Boston: Little, Brown, 1908), pp. 73–74.

28 T. Harry Williams, *Americans at War* (Baton Rouge: Louisiana State Univ. Press, 1960), p. 76; hereafter *Americans*. See also Williams, *Lincoln and His Generals* (New York: Knopf, 1952).

29 Ibid., p. 81.

30 Hittle, op. cit., p. 190.

31 Virgil Ney, *The Evolution of Military Unit Control*, Combat Operations Research Group Memorandum M-217 (Washington: U.S. Army Combat Developments Command, 1965), p. 55.

32 Weigley, *History*, p. 241.

33 Hittle, op. cit., pp. 191–192.

34 Fisher, op. cit., pp. 30–34. See also Weigley, *History*, pp. 234–237. The definitive work on unit command problems in the Civil War at the tactical level is Kenneth P. Williams, *Lincoln Finds a General: A Military Study of the Civil War*, 5 vols. (New York: Macmillan, 1949–59).

35 Fisher, op. cit., p. 33. See also Van Creveld, *Technology*, pp. 169–178.

36 Woods, op. cit., pp. 80–85. See also J. W. Brown, *The Signal Corps in the War of the Rebellion* (Boston: Wilkins Press, 1896), pp. 115–139.

37 Ibid., p. 86.

38 Brown, op. cit., pp. 170–181.

39 Woods, op. cit., p. 114.

40 U. S. Grant, *Personal Memoirs of U. S. Grant*, vol. 2 (New York: Webster, 1886), pp. 205–207.

41 Woods, op. cit., p. 87.

42 Grant, op. cit., 1:461.

43 Ibid., p. 574.

44 Williams, *Americans*, p. 67. See also Allen R. Millett and Peter Maslowski, *For the Common Defense* (New York: Free Press, 1984), pp. 160–164.

45 Rowena Reed, *Combined Operations in the Civil War* (Annapolis: U.S. Naval Institute Press, 1978), p. xxiii. Her theory is developed in pp. 34–40, 384–387, et passim.

46 *Legislative History of the General Staff of the United States, 1775–1901*, Senate Doc. no. 229, 56th Cong., 2nd Sess. (Washington: GPO, 1904), p. 5.

47 Alger, op. cit., p. 88.

48 Sprout and Sprout, op. cit., p. 205.

49 Alfred Thayer Mahan, *The Influence of Sea Power upon History, 1660–1783*, 12th ed. (Boston: Little, Brown, 1918), p. 25.

50 Ibid., pp. 26–29.

51 Ibid., p. 85.

52 Col. James L. Abrahamson, *America Arms for a New Century* (New York: Free Press, 1981), p. 2.

53 See Margaret Tuttle Sprout, "Mahan: Evangelist of Sea Power," in Edward M. Earle, ed., *Makers of Modern Strategy* (Princeton: Princeton Univ. Press, 1973), pp. 415–445. See also Sprout and Sprout, op. cit., pp. 202–228.

54 Mahan, *Sea Power,* p. 138.

55 See Philip A. Crowl, "Alfred Thayer Mahan: Naval Historian," in Peter Paret, ed., op. cit., pp. 456–460.

56 Herbert Rosinski, *The Development of Naval Thought* (Newport, R.I.: Naval War College Press, 1977), pp. 23–24. This book is a collection of essays published between 1939 and 1947.

57 Rosinski's work naturally draws from that of another eminent naval scholar, Sir Julian Corbett. See in particular Corbett's treatment of "Inherent Differences in the Conditions of Warfare on Land and on Sea," in *Some Principles of Maritime Strategy,* new ed. (Annapolis: U.S. Naval Institute Press, 1972), pp. 157–164.

58 Karl Lautenschlager, "Technology and the Evolution of Naval Warfare," *International Security* 8:2 (Fall 1983), pp. 16–19. See also Van Creveld, *Technology,* pp. 199–216.

59 Lautenschlager, op. cit., p. 19.

60 Mahan, *Naval Administration and Warfare,* p. 73.

61 Paullin, op. cit., p. 440.

62 See, for example, Abrahamson, op. cit., p. 47.

63 See Edward L. Beach, *The United States Navy: 200 Years* (New York: Holt, 1986), pp. 407–417.

64 Henry P. Beers, "The Development of the Office of the Chief of Naval Operations," *Military Affairs,* part 1, 10 (Spring 1946), pp. 40–68; part 2, 10 (Fall 1946), pp. 10–38.

65 Paullin, op. cit., pp. 407–408.

66 Ibid., pp. 439–440.

67 Ibid., p. 437.

68 Otto L. Nelson, Jr., *National Security and the General Staff* (Washington: Infantry Journal Press, 1946), pp. 18–21.

69 See Emory Upton, *The Military Policy of the United States* (Washington: GPO, 1904); Upton, *The Armies of Asia and Europe* (New York: Appleton, 1878). The standard biography of Upton is Stephen A. Ambrose, *Upton and the Army* (Baton Rouge: Louisiana State Univ. Press, 1964). See also Millett and Maslowski, op. cit., pp. 256–258.

70 Maj. Gen. William Harding Carter, *Creation of the American General Staff,* U.S. Senate Doc. No. 119, 65th Cong., 1st Sess. (Washington: GPO, 1924), p. 17.

71 A good account of these difficulties is covered by Weigley, *History,* pp. 295–312.

72 Cited by Legere, op. cit., p. 49.

73 Ibid., pp. 52–53.

74 Ibid.

75 See Spenser Wilkinson, *The Brain of an Army: A Popular Account of the German General Staff* (London: Constable, 1895). Less influential was a shorter companion essay by Wilkinson which was also published at the same time: *The Brain of the Navy* (London: Constable, 1895). For a current appraisal, see Col. Michael D. Krause's review of *The Brain of an Army* in *Defense Analysis* 4:3 (September 1988), pp. 321–326.

76 Letter from the secretary of war to the chairman, Senate Committee on Military Affairs, March 3, 1902. Cited by Carter, op. cit., p. 47.

77 Cited by Carter, op. cit., p. 43.

78 Ibid. See also Weigley, *History*, pp. 319–321, and Richard W. Leopold, *Elihu Root and the Conservative Tradition* (Boston: Little, Brown, 1954), pp. 32–43.

79 Carter, op. cit., p. 43.

80 Leopold, op. cit., p. 43.

81 Sprout and Sprout, op. cit., p. 353.

82 Vincent Davis, *The Admiral's Lobby* (Chapel Hill: Univ. of North Carolina Press, 1967), p. 30.

83 Beers, op. cit., pp. 22–25.

84 D. A. Paolucci, Norman Polmar, and John Patrick, *A Guide to U.S. Navy Command, Control and Communications* (San Diego, Calif.: U.S. Naval Ocean Systems Center, July 1979), p. 17.

85 Nelson, op. cit., p. 299.

86 Ibid., pp. 230–236.

87 James G. Harbord, *The American Army in France* (Boston: Little, Brown, 1936), p. 111. Cited by Nelson, op. cit., p. 258.

88 Nelson, op. cit., p. 258.

89 James G. Harbord, *The American Expeditionary Force: Its Organization and Accomplishments* (Evanston, Ill.: Evanston Publishing Co., 1929), p. 64.

90 *Historical Sketch of the Signal Corps, 1860–1928* (Ft. Monmouth, N.J.: U.S. Army Signal School, 1929), pp. 89–90.

91 See Mario de Arcangelis, *Electronic Warfare* (New York: Sterling Press, 1985), esp. pp. 11–26. Properly speaking, as de Arcangelis points out, both the Russians and the Japanese tried to exploit each other's naval signals during their war of 1904–05, most notably at the Battle of Tsushima Straits.

Chapter 4 The Quest for Unity of Command

1 William Mitchell, *Memoirs of World War I: From Start to Finish of Our Greatest War* (New York: Random House, 1960), pp. 630–632; cited by Russell F. Weigley, *The American Way of War* (New York: Macmillan, 1973), p. 224.

2 William Mitchell, *Our Air Force: The Keystone of National Defense* (New York: Dutton, 1921), and *Winged Defense: The Development and Possibilities of Modern Air Power, Economic and Military* (New York: Putnam, 1925). See also Weigley, op. cit., pp. 223–241.

3 Giulio Douhet, *The Command of the Air*, trans. Dino Ferrari (Reprint, Office of Air Force History; Washington: GPO, 1983), p. 9. See also Van Creveld, *Technology*, pp. 183–197.

4 See Edward Warner, "Douhet, Mitchell, Seversky: Theories of Air Warfare," in Edward Mead Earle, ed., *Makers of Modern Strategy*, 2nd ed. (Princeton: Princeton Univ. Press, 1973), pp. 485–503. A current appraisal of Warner's contribution appears in the sequel to this book. See David MacIsaac, "Voices from the Central Blue: The Air Power Theorists," in Peter Paret, ed., *Makers of Modern Strategy from Machiavelli to the Nuclear Age* (Princeton: Princeton Univ. Press, 1986), pp. 624–647.

5 Warner, op. cit., p. 490. These five points are paraphrased from Warner's summary.

6 Douhet, op. cit., p. 23.

7 Perry M. Smith, *The Air Force Plans for Peace, 1943–1945* (Baltimore: Johns Hopkins Univ. Press, 1970), p. 36.

8   Major Horace M. Hickam, Testimony in *Aircraft, Hearings before the President's Aircraft Board* (Washington: GPO, 1925), pp. 389, 410. Cited by Lawrence J. Legere, Jr., "Unification of the Armed Forces," manuscript (Washington: U.S. Army, Office of the Chief of Military History, n.d.), pp. 125–126.

9   Robin Higham, *Air Power* (New York: St. Martin's Press, 1972), p. 62.

10 Ibid. See also Van Creveld, *Technology,* pp. 199–216.

11 Legere, op. cit., p. 153. See also Louis Morton, "War Plan ORANGE: Evolution of a Strategy," *World Politics* 11 (Jan. 1959), pp. 221–250. For a more recent treatment, see Michael K. Doyle, "The United States Navy and War Plan ORANGE: Making Necessity a Virtue," *Naval War College Review* 32:3 (May-June 1980), pp. 49–63.

12 Joint Board Serial no. 19, "Joint Operations of the Army, Navy and Marine Corps," Oct. 22, 1919. Cited by Legere, op. cit., p. 76.

13 Ibid., pp. 155–156. See also Allan R. Millett and Peter Maslowski, *For the Common Defense* (New York: Free Press, 1984), pp. 374–377.

14 Council of National Defense, *Hearings before the Committee on Military Affairs, 69th Cong., 1st Sess., on H.R. 10248, H.R. 10982 and H.R. 10985* (Washington: GPO, 1926), pp. 35–36. Cited by Legere, op. cit., p. 133.

15 Vincent Davis, *The Admirals' Lobby* (Chapel Hill: Univ. of North Carolina Press, 1967), p. 100.

16 See Roberta Wohlstetter, *Pearl Harbor: Warning and Decision* (Stanford, Calif.: Stanford Univ. Press, 1962), and Gordon W. Prange, *At Dawn We Slept* (New York: Penguin, 1982). These works have recently been joined by a controversial volume written by a retired rear admiral, Edwin T. Layton, *"And I Was There"* (New York: William Morrow, 1985). Layton, who was Admiral Kimmel's intelligence officer at the time of the Pearl Harbor attack, argues that bureaucratic in-fighting and personal jealousies at the Navy Department prevented critical information from being sent to Hawaii in time to make a difference.

17 J. F. C. Fuller, *Generalship: Its Diseases and Their Cure* (Harrisburg, Pa.: Military Services Publishing Co., 1936), pp. 66–67.

18 Otto L. Nelson, Jr., *National Security and the General Staff* (Washington: Infantry Journal Press, 1947), pp. 325–328.

19 Cited by Ray S. Cline, *Washington Command Post: The Operations Division,* Official History of the U.S. Army in World War II (Washington: U.S. Army, Office of the Chief of Military History, 1951), p. 73.

20 Nelson, op. cit., p. 333.

21 Details of the reorganization effort are covered in Nelson, op. cit., pp. 335–396. For a more recent treatment, see James E. Hewes, Jr., *From Root to McNamara: Army Organization and Administration, 1900–1963* (Washington: U.S. Army, Office of the Chief of Military History, 1975), pp. 66–76. See also Cline, op. cit., pp. 90–95. Information on Nelson's contribution to the reorganization effort was obtained in several telephone interviews with him from January to June 1982.

22 Memo from Gen. H. H. Arnold to the chief of staff, Nov. 14, 1941; subject: Organization of the armed forces for war. Cited by Nelson, op. cit., pp. 337–341.

23 Cline, op. cit., p. 95.

24 Nelson, op. cit., p. 335.

25 Hewes, op. cit., p. 76.

26 Cline, op. cit., p. 93.

27 Rear Adm. Julius A. Furer, *Administration of the Navy Department in World War II* (Washington: GPO, 1959), pp. 125–126.

28 Ibid., pp. 113–114.

29 Ibid., pp. 163–167.

30 The most comprehensive account of the JCS committee structure is by Vernon E. Davis, *Development of the JCS Committee Structure,* vol. 2 of *The History of the Joint Chiefs in World War II* (Washington: Historical Office, OJCS, 1972).

31 Demetrios Caraley, *The Politics of Military Unification* (New York: Columbia Univ. Press, 1966), p. 18.

32 Paul Y. Hammond, *Organizing for Defense* (Princeton: Princeton Univ. Press, 1961), p. 163.

33 Ibid., p. 164.

34 U.S. National Archives, Records of the War Department General and Special Staffs, ABC 370.62, "Unity of Command File" (Sec. 1-B, RG 165), memo, "General Harmon's Command Responsibilities in the South Pacific under 'Unity of Command,'" n.d.

35 Gen. Henry H. Arnold, *Global Mission* (New York: Harper Bros., 1949), p. 349.

36 Gen. William M. Momyer, *Airpower in Three Wars* (Washington: GPO, 1978), p. 349.

37 Ibid., p. 41. See also Sherry, op. cit., pp. 147–176.

38 U.S. Army FM 100-20, Field Service Regulations, *Command and Employment of Air Power* (Washington: War Dept., July 21, 1943); reprinted as appendix to *Air Superiority in World War II and Korea,* U.S.A.F. Warrior Studies (Washington: U.S.A.F. Office of Air Force History, 1983).

39 Cited in *The Effectiveness of Third Phase Tactical Air Operations in the European Theater,* Report of the Army Air Forces Evaluation Board in the European Theater of Operations (Orlando, Fla.: Orlando Army Air Force Base, August 20, 1945), p. 73. See also R. H. Kohn and J. P. Hanrahan, eds., *Condensed Analysis of the Ninth Air Force in the European Theater of Operations,* U.S.A.F. Warrior Studies, Rev. ed. (Washington: U.S.A.F. Office of Air Force History, 1984).

40 Cited by Forrest C. Pogue, *The Supreme Command,* Official History of the U.S. Army in World War II (Washington: U.S. Army, Office of the Chief of Military History, 1954), p. 53.

41 Walter Millis, *Arms and Men,* Paperback ed. (New York: Capricorn Books, 1967), p. 283.

42 *The Army Lineage Book,* vol. 2 (Washington: U.S. Army, 1953), p. 57. Cited by Virgil Ney, *Evolution of Military Unit Control,* Combat Operations Research Group Memorandum M-217 (Washington: U.S. Army Combat Developments Command, 1965), p. 283.

43 Ney, op. cit., p. 117. See also pp. 97–117.

44 Karl Lautenschlager, "Technology and the Evolution of Naval Warfare," *International Security* 8:2 (Fall 1983), p. 31.

45 Ibid.

46 D. A. Paolucci, Norman Polmar, and John Patrick, *A Guide to U.S. Navy Command, Control and Communications,* NOSC Technical Doc. 247 (San Diego, Calif.: U.S. Navy Ocean Systems Center, July 1979), p. 26.

47 Ibid.

48 Vice Adm. Sir Arthur Hezlet, *Electronics and Sea Power* (New York: Stein and Day, 1975), p. 263.

49 Samuel Eliot Morison, *The Two-Ocean War* (Boston: Little, Brown, 1963), pp. 129–130. See also Elting E. Morison's interesting essay on this incident in *Men, Machines and Modern Times* (Cambridge: MIT Press, 1976), pp. 45–74. For the Army Air Force perspective, see W. F. Craven and J. L. Cate, eds., *The Army Air Forces in World War II*, 7 vols. (Chicago: Univ. of Chicago Press, 1948–58), vol. 2, esp. chaps. 8 and 12.

50 The act was promulgated by the Eightieth Congress as P.L. 253. It is reprinted in its original and amended versions in Rudolph A. Winnacker et al., eds., *The Department of Defense Documents on Establishment and Organization, 1944–1978* (Washington: OSD Historical Office, 1978), pp. 35–50.

51 Harry Howe Ransom, "Department of Defense: Unity or Confederation?" in *American Defense Policy*, eds., The Associates in Political Science, U.S. Air Force Academy (Baltimore: Johns Hopkins Univ. Press, 1965), p. 180.

52 Legere, op. cit., pp. 276–277; Caraley, op. cit., pp. 23–24.

53 Caraley, op. cit., pp. 23–34; Winnacker, op. cit., pp. 3–4; Hammond, op. cit., pp. 192–196.

54 Caraley, op. cit., p. 58.

55 Mark S. Watson, *Chief of Staff: Prewar Plans and Policies,* Official History of the U.S. Army in World War II (Washington: U.S. Army Historical Division, 1950), p. 15.

56 Testimony of the Hon. Robert P. Patterson, Secretary of War, *Hearings before the Committee on Military Affairs, U.S. Senate, 79th Cong., 1st Sess., on S. 84 and S. 1482* (Washington: GPO, 1945). Testimony taken before these hearings hereafter referred to as *Senate, 1945.*

57 John C. Ries, *The Management of Defense* (Baltimore: Johns Hopkins Univ. Press, 1964), pp. 10–15.

58 Caraley, op. cit., p. 63.

59 Hammond, op. cit., pp. 228–229.

60 Testimony of Adm. Ernest J. King, *Senate, 1945*, p. 121.

61 Caraley, op. cit., p. 87.

62 Ibid., pp. 87–109.

63 Testimony of Fleet Adm. William F. Halsey, *Senate, 1945*, p. 543.

64 *Report to the Hon. James Forrestal, Secretary of the Navy, on Unification of the War and Navy Departments and Postwar Organization for National Security* (Eberstadt Report), Senate Comm. Print, 79th Cong., 1st Sess. (Washington: GPO, 1945), pp. 6–14.

65 See also Hammond, op. cit., pp. 205–213.

66 Testimony of Lt. Gen. James Doolittle, *Senate, 1945*, pp. 290 and 308.

67 Testimony of Fleet Adm. William F. Halsey, *Senate, 1945*, pp. 537–538.

68 Testimony of General of the Army Dwight D. Eisenhower, *Senate, 1945*, pp. 361–363.

69 Cited by Caraley, op. cit., p. 151. See also Perry, *Four Stars*, pp. 3–11.

70 Ibid., p. 238.

71 U.S. National Archives, Records of the War Department General and Special Staffs. ABC File 370.26, "Unity of Command" (Sec. 1-b), "Memorandum for General Norstad," October 17, 1946.

72 James F. Schnabel, *The Joint Chiefs of Staff and National Policy, 1945–1947*, vol. 1 of *The History of the Joint Chiefs of Staff* (Wilmington, Del.: Glazier, 1979), pp. 171–186.

73 Caraley, op. cit., pp. 251–256; see also Hammond, op. cit., pp. 220–221, and Winnacker, op. cit., pp. 17–21.

74 Steven L. Rearden, *The Formative Years, 1947–1950*, vol. 1 of *The History of the Office of the Secretary of Defense* (Washington: OSD Historical Office, 1984), pp. 16–23. See also Gordon W. Keiser, *The U.S. Marine Corps and Defense Unification, 1944–1947* (Washington: National Defense Univ. Press, 1982), pp. 67–80.

75 Rearden, op. cit., p. 25.

76 Winnacker, op. cit., pp. 35–50.

77 Henry L. Stimson and McGeorge Bundy, *On Active Service in Peace and War* (New York: Harper Bros., 1948), p. 506.

Chapter 5 Setting the Scene

1 Julius A. Furer, *Administration of the Navy Department in World War II* (Washington: GPO, 1959), pp. 26–28.

2 Paul Y. Hammond, *Organizing for Defense* (Princeton: Princeton Univ. Press, 1961), pp. 23–24, 59–62. See also Samuel P. Huntington, *The Soldier and the State* (Cambridge: Harvard Univ. Press, 1981), pp. 193–203.

3 Testimony of former secretary of the navy Josephus Daniels, *Hearings before the Committee on Military Affairs, U.S. Senate, 79th Cong., 1st Sess., on S. 84 and S. 1482* (Washington: GPO, 1945), p. 205.

4 Ray S. Cline, *Washington Command Post: The Operations Division*, Official History of the U.S. Army in World War II (Washington: GPO, 1951), pp. 352–361.

5 For a discussion of the Key West and Newport conferences, see Steven L. Rearden, *The Formative Years, 1947–1950*, Vol. I of *The History of the Office of the Secretary of Defense* (Washington: OSD Historical Office, 1984), pp. 385–401. See also Perry, *Four Stars*, pp. 12–16.

6 *Unified Action Armed Forces* is published as JCS Pub. 2 (Washington: OJCS, December, 1986). The current version was written in the aftermath of the Goldwater-Nichols Act. While it still makes careful distinctions among the roles and missions of the services, the unified and specified commands, and their service components, it nevertheless goes further than any of its predecessors in addressing the need for "maximum integration," "full utilization of forces," and "interoperability" as key elements of joint action.

7 The statutory basis for the current organization of OSD is contained in the Goldwater-Nichols Act. See *Conference Report, Goldwater-Nichols Department of Defense Reorganization Act of 1986, House of Representatives, 99th Cong., 2nd Sess.*, Report No. 99–824, September 12, 1986. One of the directives of this act required the services to study the size and configuration of OSD and the defense agencies, a subject of some controversy and uncertainty throughout the defense reform effort. The Army's report listed some 96,578 military and civilian personnel employed by the ten major defense agencies and eight "field activities" supervised by OSD. Over half of these, however, were assigned to a single organization, the Defense Logistics Agency. See *Army Study of Defense Agencies and DOD Field Activities: Report to the Secretary of Defense*, vol. 1 (Washington: Department of the Army, August 31, 1987), pp. 18–19.

8 1949 Amendments: P.L. 81-36, 63 Stat. 30 (April 2, 1949); 1953 Amendments: P.L. 83-15, 67 Stat. 19 (April 4, 1953); 1958 Amendments: P.L. 85-599, 72 Stat. 514 (August 6, 1958).

9 See Perry, *Four Stars*, especially chapters 4–6. Perry's account of the stormy relationship between the service chiefs and OSD during the McNamara years is one of the highlights of this excellent history of the JCS.

10 The standard work on the budgetary innovations of the McNarama era is Alain C. Enthoven and K. Wayne Smith, *How Much Is Enough? Shaping the Defense Program, 1961–1969* (New York: Harper & Row, 1969). See also Charles J. Hitch, *Decision-Making for Defense* (Berkeley: Univ. of California Press, 1965). A more recent treatment is by Lawrence J. Korb, "The Budget Process in the Department of Defense, 1944–77: The Strengths and Weaknesses of Three Systems," *Public Administration Review* 37:4 (July-August 1977), pp. 334–345. For a more general treatment of McNamara's tenure at DOD, see Douglas Kinnard, *The Secretary of Defense* (Lexington: Univ. of Kentucky Press, 1980), pp. 72–112.

11 See Arthur M. Schlesinger, Jr., *A Thousand Days: John F. Kennedy in the White House* (Boston: Houghton Mifflin, 1965), pp. 298–319.

12 Ibid., p. 319.

13 Kennedy School of Government, *TFX: The Commonality Decision,* Case Study 9-375-035 (Cambridge: Intercollegiate Case Clearing House, 1978), pp. 1–12; hereafter, *TFX Case,* and Richard A. Smith, "The Seven Billion Dollar Contract That Changed the Rules," *Fortune* 67:2 (April 1963), pp. 110–111, 191–192, 199–200.

14 *TFX Case,* pp. 14–20, and Robert J. Art, *The TFX Decision: McNamara and the Military* (Boston: Little, Brown, 1968), pp. 157–166.

15 Robert F. Coulam, *The Illusions of Choice: The F-111 and the Problem of Weapons Acquisition* (Princeton: Princeton Univ. Press, 1977), p. 31.

16 Graham T. Allison, *The Essence of Decision* (Boston: Little, Brown, 1971), pp. 127–128.

17 Letter, Adm. Thomas J. Moorer to Lt. Gen. Victor H. Krulak, Aug. 16, 1982, cited by Krulak in *Organization for National Security* (Washington: U.S. Strategic Institute, 1983), pp. 86–87.

18 The most comprehensive treatments of the development of strategic command and control are by Paul Bracken, *The Command and Control of Nuclear Forces* (New Haven: Yale Univ. Press, 1983), and, in a somewhat more controversial vein, Bruce Blair, *Strategic Command and Control* (Washington: Brookings Institution, 1985).

19 Anthony G. Oettinger, "Information Resources: Knowledge and Power in the 21st Century," *Science* 209 (July 4, 1980), pp. 191–198.

20 Blair, op. cit., pp. 51–65.

21 *WWMCCS History,* TRW Defense and Space Systems Support Group, McLean, Va., WWMCCS System Spec. WSS-78, Annex J (UNCLAS), September 30, 1977, pp. 3–4.

22 U.S. Congress, House, *Review of DOD Worldwide Communications. Phase I. Report of the Armed Services Investigating Subcommittee of the Committee on Armed Services* (Mollohan Report), 92nd Cong., 1st Sess. (Washington: GPO, 1971), p. 6.

23 Ibid., p. 18.

24 This incident was variously described by a number of sources interviewed for this project, but the only documented account appears in James Ray and Ted Schroeder, *The Revolution in Command and Control Technology and the Civilian-Military Chain of Command* (Maxwell Air Force Base, Ala.: Air Univ. Press, 1977), p. iii. Ray and Schroeder's version is that Rumsfeld spoke with a lieutenant commander on the scene, "while the JCS watched on the sidelines."

25 U.S. General Accounting Office, *The Worldwide Military Command and Control System— Major Changes Needed in Its Automated Data Processing Management and Direction* (Washington: GPO, 1979), pp. 5–6.

26 The Jonestown incident was documented by the GAO's follow-up report on WWMCCS, which also contained an analysis of the DOD rebuttal. See *Worldwide Military Command and Control System—Evaluation of Vendor and Department of Defense Comments* (Washington: GPO, 1980). The Jonestown incident, the exercise problem, and the Dinneen comment were reported by William J. Broad, "Computers and the U.S. Military Don't Mix," *Science* 207 (Mar. 14, 1980), p. 1184. Further criticism of WWMCCS appeared in two articles reprinted by the U.S. Army War College journal: James North, " 'Hello, Central, Get Me NATO': The Computer That Can't," and Frank Greve, "Pentagon Calls Super Computer a Disaster," *Parameters* 10:1 (March 1980), pp. 91–97. A rebuttal by Col. Perry R. Nuhn (then the WWMCCS system manager) appeared as "WWMCCS and the Computer That Can," *Parameters* 10:3 (Sept. 1980), pp. 16–21.

27 Cited by John Fialka, "The Pentagon's Exercise 'Proud Spirit': Little Cause for Pride," *Parameters* 11:1 (March 1981), p. 40.

28 Interestingly, the requirements of strategic connectivity in this instance apparently extended to the use of unsecured radio-telephone links between Defense Secretary Weinberger and President Reagan, who were flying in separate military aircraft while they discussed the proposed operation. See Bill Keller, "U.S. Plans Were Made on Open Line," *New York Times*, Oct. 15, 1985, p. 15.

29 James Digby, *Precision Guided Weapons*, Adelphi Paper no. 118 (London: IISS, 1975), p. 2. See also Richard K. Betts, *Cruise Missiles: Technology, Strategy, Politics* (Washington: Brookings Institution, 1981). For a discussion of the Tomahawk cruise missile, see John Lehman, *Command of the Seas* (New York: Scribner's, 1988), pp. 164–170.

30 Karl Lautenschlager, "Naval Warfare Technology," *International Security* 8:2 (Fall 1982), p. 44.

31 Lehman, op. cit., p. 170.

32 For a comprehensive treatment of electronic warfare in World War II, see R. V. Jones, *The Wizard War* (New York: Coward, McCann and Geoghegan, 1978), and Alfred Price, *Instruments of Darkness: The History of Electronic Warfare* (New York: Scribner's, 1978).

33 Gen. William M. Momyer, *Air Power in Three Wars* (Washington: GPO, 1978), p. 123.

34 Ray Bonds, ed., *The U.S. War Machine* (New York: Crown Press, 1978), p. 156. On the general topic of modern air combat, see Lon O. Nordeen, Jr., *Air Warfare in the Missile Age* (Washington: Smithsonian Institution, 1985).

35 Parts of the following section have been adapted from C. Kenneth Allard, "Re-Shaping American Military Intelligence: Decisions for the 1980s," published as an incidental paper in *Seminar on Command, Control, Communications and Intelligence*, Harvard Univ. Program on Information Resources Policy, Cambridge: Harvard Univ., 1980, pp. 159–205.

36 Omar Bradley, *A Soldier's Story* (New York: Holt, 1951), p. 33.

37 F. W. Winterbotham, *The Ultra Secret* (London: Weidenfeld and Nicolson, 1974). More recent information on Ultra has emerged with the official publication of the declassified British archives from World War II. See F. H. Hinsley et al., eds., *British Intelligence in the Second World War: Its Influence on Strategy and Operations* (London: HMSO, 1979).

38 Lt. Gen. Harry W. O. Kinnard, "Narrowing the Combat Intelligence Gap," *Army* 19:8 (August 1969), p. 23; cited by M. B. Powe and E. E. Wilson, *The Evolution of American Military Intelligence* (Ft. Huachuca, Ariz.: U.S. Army Intelligence Center, 1973), p. 120.

39 Ibid., pp. 107–123.

40 See Chaim Herzog, *The War of Atonement* (Boston: Little, Brown, 1975), and the Insight Team of the London *Sunday Times, The Yom Kippur War* (New York: Doubleday, 1974).

41 U.S. Army Field Manual 100-5, *Operations* (Washington: Dept. of the Army, 1976), p. 2-2; hereafter, FM 100-5.

42 Ibid., p. 2-6.

43 Ibid., pp. 7-2, 7-3.

44 As summarized by the U.S. Army Intelligence Center, Ft. Huachuca, Ariz., "Draft Operational and Organizational Concept: CEWI Group," Feb. 27, 1980, p. 8.

45 A. N. Stubblebine III, "C3I for Automated Focus on the Battlefield," *Army* 20:3 (March 1979), pp. 33–34. See also Don E. Gordon, *Electronic Warfare: Element of Strategy and Multiplier of Combat Power* (New York: Pergamon Press, 1981), pp. 65–73.

Chapter 6   Tactical Command and Control of American Armed Forces

1 Gerald P. Dinneen, "A Systems Approach to Communications, Command, Control, and Intelligence," *Signal* 34:5 (Feb. 1980), p. 8.

2 Cited by Lt. Col. Frederick W. Timmerman, "Yes, Sir! General Machine, Sir!" *Army* 32:1 (Jan. 1982), p. 30.

3 One of the most comprehensive discussions of this issue is by Col. Richard J. DeBastiani, *Computers on the Battlefield: Can They Survive?* (Washington: National Defense Univ. Press, 1983).

4 Irving B. Holley, Jr., "Command, Control, and Technology," *Defense Analysis* (special issue on command and control) 4:3 (November 1988), pp. 268–269.

5 For an overview of the maneuver school of thought by one of its most ardent advocates, see William S. Lind, *Maneuver Warfare Handbook* (Boulder, Colo.: Westview Press, 1985).

6 John R. Boyd, "Organic Design for Command and Control," briefing paper (mimeograph), March 1984, pp. 5, 32–35. Col. Boyd's contribution to the defense reform movement rests largely on the strength of his personal briefings and presentations rather than on published writings. Many of these themes are also contained in an earlier briefing, "Patterns of Conflict" (May 1981), which is also unpublished. I have relied on both, as well as on a series of interviews and other discussions with Col. Boyd from 1982 to the present.

7 Maj. George E. Orr, *Combat Operations C3I: Fundamentals and Interactions* (Maxwell Air Force Base, Ala.: Air Univ. Press, 1983), pp. 23–27.

8 Dr. Joel S. Lawson, Jr., "Naval Tactical C3 Architecture, 1985–1995," *Signal* 33:10 (Aug. 1979), pp. 71–72.

9 Ibid. For a more comprehensive treatment of this subject by the same author, see Lawson, "State Variables of a C2 System," in John Hwang et al., eds., *Selected Analytical Concepts in Command and Control* (New York: Gordon and Breach Science Publishers, 1982), pp. 61–84.

10 Ibid., p. 63. See Gregory D. Foster's discussion of several command and control models, including those of Boyd and Lawson, in "Contemporary C2 Theory and Research: The Failed Quest for a Philosophy of Command," *Defense Analysis* 4:3 (September 1988), pp. 201–228. In the same issue, see also Philip S. Kronenberg, "Command and Control as a Theory of Interorganizational Design," pp. 229–252. The most comprehensive treatment of command and control models and organizational designs to date appears in Stuart E. Johnson and Alexander H. Levis, *Science of Command and Control*, 2 vols. (Washington: AFCEA Press, 1988, 1989).

11 Gen. Paul F. Gorman, "Toward a Stronger Defense Establishment," in Asa A. Clark IV et al., eds., *The Defense Reform Debate* (Baltimore: Johns Hopkins Univ. Press, 1984), p. 291. Now retired from the Army, General Gorman formerly served as assistant to the chairman of the JCS and as commander in chief, U.S. Southern Command. He most recently served as a member of the Packard Commission. Interestingly, Van Creveld has also noted recently the differing obstacles to control presented by the operational environments of land, sea, and air. See his discussion in *Technology*, pp. 228–232, 265–284.

12 Rear Adm. Frederick C. Johnson, "Naval Surveillance and Target Acquisition," *Signal* 34:2 (Oct. 1979), p. 13.

13 Karl Lautenschlager, "Technology and the Evolution of Naval Warfare," *International Security* 8:2 (Fall 1983), p. 37.

14 Barry M. Blechman and Steven Kaplan, *Force without War: U.S. Armed Forces as a Political Instrument* (Washington: Brookings Institution, 1978). More recently, see former secretary of the navy John Lehman's comments concerning U.S. operations in the Mediterranean Sea and the Persian Gulf, 1986–1988, in *Command of the Sea*, pp. 363–401.

15 Raymond T. Tate, "The U.S. Navy in Transition," *Signal* 34:7 (April 1980), p. 35.

16 See Seymour J. Deitchman, *Military Power and the Advance of Technology*, rev. ed. (Boulder, Colo.: Westview Press, 1983), pp. 91–104.

17 Lautenschlager, op. cit., p. 44.

18 Ibid. See also Louise Hodgden, "Satellites at Sea: Space and Naval Warfare," *Naval War College Review* 32:4 (July-Aug. 1984), pp. 31–45, and Franklin W. Diederich, "Architectural Considerations for the C3 Aspects of a Space-Based Naval Ocean Surveillance System," in Gordon R. Nagler, ed., *Naval Tactical Command and Control* (Washington: AFCEA Press, 1985), pp. 192–203.

19 Lautenschlager, op. cit., p. 48.

20 Deitchman, op. cit., pp. 97–98.

21 Scott C. Truver, "To Get the Drop on Soviet Archers, U.S. Navy Needs Bows, Arrows and Bucks," *Armed Forces Journal International* 123:10 (Apr. 1986), p. 51.

22 U.S. Dept. of Defense, *Soviet Military Power* (Washington: GPO, 1986), pp. 82–88; hereafter, *SMP86*. On the growth of the Soviet navy, the literature has expanded almost as dramatically as the subject. See, in particular, Bradford Dismukes and James M. McConnell, eds., *Soviet Naval Diplomacy* (New York: Pergamon Press, 1979); Michael McGwire and John McDonnell, eds., *Soviet Naval Influence: Domestic and Foreign Dimensions* (New York: Praeger, 1977); George Hudson, *The Soviet Navy Enters the Nuclear Age: The Development of Soviet Naval Doctrine, 1953–1973* (Ann Arbor, Mich.: University Microfilms, 1980); Steve F. King, *Soviet Naval Strategy for the Eighties* (Washington: NDU Press, 1978); and Bruce W. Watson and Susan M. Watson, eds., *The Soviet Navy: Its Strengths and Liabilities* (Boulder, Colo.: Westview Press, 1986).

23 Rear Adm. Frederick C. Johnson, "Command and Control Overview," *Signal* 34:10 (Aug. 1980), p. 62.

24 William D. O'Neill, "Naval Anti-Air Warfare," *National Defense* 65:365 (Feb. 1981), p. 27.

25 U.S. Navy, "Navy Command and Control Systems Ashore," study, U.S. Navy Electronic Systems Command, Washington, D.C., n.d.; hereafter, NCCS paper. See also W. J. Holmes, *Double-Edged Secrets* (Annapolis: U.S. Naval Institute Press, 1979), and, more recently, the book that, although controversial, is the best eyewitness account to date of naval

intelligence in the Pacific, Rear Adm. Edwin T. Layton with Capt. Roger Pineau and John Costello, *"And I Was There"* (New York: William Morrow, 1985).

26 Truver, op. cit., p. 51. On the lessons for naval warfare suggested by the Falkland Islands War, see Charles W. Koburger, *Sea Power in the Falklands* (New York: Praeger, 1984), and David Brown, *The Royal Navy and the Falklands War* (London: L. Cooper, 1987).

27 Paolucci, op. cit., p. 87. Probably the most graphic demonstration of such a scenario occurs in popular fiction. See Tom Clancy, *Red Storm Rising* (New York: G. P. Putnam, 1986), esp. pp. 210–234.

28 Deborah G. Meyer, "The Aegis Factor: Does John Lehman Still Need or Want a 600-Ship Navy?" *Armed Forces Journal International* 123:10 (Apr. 1986), pp. 60–62.

29 See Tony Capaccio and Anne Rumsey, "Congress Not Told Full Details of Aegis Tests," *Defense Week,* July 18, 1988, p. 1. Coverage of the Iranian airbus disaster was widely covered by the media in the days following the July 3, 1988, incident. See, for example, the extended coverage in the July 18, 1988, issue of *Time* magazine, pp. 14–20.

30 Cited by Truver, op. cit., p. 50.

31 Adm. Carlisle H. Trost, "The Navy Is Living Up to Its Moral Imperative," *Washington Post,* August 20, 1988, p. A21.

32 U.S. Dept. of Defense, *Investigation Report: Formal Investigation into the Circumstances Surrounding the Downing of Iranian Air Flight 655 on 3 July 1988,* Washington, D.C., July 28, 1988, p. 43.

33 Ibid., Letter, 2nd endorsement. From the chairman of the Joint Chiefs of Staff to the secretary of defense, August 18, 1988, pp. 7–8.

34 See Lt. Lowell F. Eggert, "Navy Command Control System—Tactical Fleet Command," *Signal* 34:10 (Aug. 1980), pp. 64–65, and Lt. Comdr. John G. Robinson, "Tactical Flag Command Center," *Surface Warfare,* Headquarters, Dept. of the Navy, publication (January 1981), pp. 8–9; OP-094 briefing, "TFCC Restructured Program," August 3, 1989.

35 U.S. Navy, "U.S. Navy Tactical Command and Control Plan for Allied Interoperability," study (Washington: Office of the Chief of Naval Operations, OP-094, September 1980), pp. 2–3. See also, Lt. Christopher W. Maillefert, *Command and Control: A Contemporary Perspective* (Newport, R.I.: U.S. Naval War College, July 1974), p. 57.

36 Vice Adm. Robert E. Kirksey, "Tactical Command and Control: The Battle Group Commander's Perspective," in Nagler, op. cit., pp. 110–114.

37 Dr. Eberhardt Rechtin, *The Technology of Command* (Washington: National Academy Press, 1983), pp. 23–24.

38 William Outerson, "Peacetime Admirals–Wartime Admirals," *Proceedings of the US Naval Institute* 107:4 (Apr. 1981), p. 35.

39 NCCS Paper, p. 1.

40 Rechtin, op. cit., p. 30.

41 See discussion in chap. 4 of this book. See also U.S. Joint Chiefs of Staff, *Unified Action Armed Forces,* JCS Pub. 2 (Washington: Office of the Joint Chiefs of Staff, Dec. 1986).

42 Bernard Brodie, *Strategy in the Missile Age* (Princeton: Princeton Univ. Press, 1971), p. 107.

43 See discussion in chap. 4 of this book.

44 Riley Sunderland, *Evolution of Command and Control for Close Air Support* (Washington: Office of U.S.A.F. History, March 1973), pp. 42–60. For an example of more recent

scholarship on Air Force operations over North Vietnam, see Mark Clodfelter, *The Limits of Air Power* (New York: Free Press, 1989).

45 Lt. Gen. Robert T. March, "Tactical C3: The Modern Challenge," *Signal* 32:11 (Sept. 1978), p. 16.

46 See Dr. Fred A. Diamond, "A Structure for Tactical C3," *Signal* 33:10 (Aug. 1979), pp. 77–81, from which this discussion of the Air Force tactical command architecture is drawn. See also U.S. Army Field Manual, FM 100-25, *The Air-Ground Operations System* (Washington: HQDA, March 30, 1973). Although the basic outline of the Air-Ground Operations System has remained unchanged for more than twenty years, a more recent reference is a pamphlet, "General Operating Procedures for Joint Attack of the Second Echelon," jointly published by the Army Training and Doctrine Command as TRADOC Pam. 525-45 (Ft. Monroe, Virginia) and the Air Force Tactical Air Command as TACP 50-29 (Langley AFB, Virginia), dated December 31, 1984.

47 *SMP* 86, op. cit., pp. 80–81.

48 Ibid., pp. 76–79. On the development of Soviet airpower, see the annual edition of the "Soviet Aerospace Almanac" published in *Air Force Magazine* 69:3 (March 1986), pp. 40–93; 70:3 (March 1987), pp. 46–100; 71:3 (March 1988), pp. 45–90; and 72:3 (March 1989), pp. 40–102.

49 *SMP* 88, pp. 64–75; see also *SMP* 86, pp. 64–72.

50 *SMP* 86, p. 64. The literature on the development of Soviet conventional theater forces is extensive. In addition to the six editions of the *SMP* series, see Joseph D. Douglass, *Soviet Military Strategy in Europe* (New York: Pergamon Press, 1980); William J. Lewis, *The Warsaw Pact: Arms, Doctrine and Strategy* (New York: McGraw-Hill, 1982); Harriet F. Scott and William F. Scott, *The Armed Forces of the USSR* (Boulder, Colo.: Westview Press, 1979); and Christopher N. Donnelly, *Red Banner: The Soviet Military System in Peace and War* (Alexandria, Va.: Jane's, 1988).

51 U.S. Army, Field Manual 100-5, *Operations* (Washington: Headquarters, Dept. of the Army, July 1, 1976), pp: 3–4.

52 Ibid.

53 Ibid., p. 4-3.

54 See also the TRADOC official history by John L. Romjue, *From Active Defense to Airland Battle: The Development of Army Doctrine 1973–1982* (Ft. Monroe, Va.: Headquarters, TRADOC, June 1984), pp. 3–12. For the earlier period in the evolution of the Army's new doctrine, see Maj. Paul H. Herbert, *Deciding What Has to Be Done: General William E. DePuy and the 1976 Edition of FM 100-5*, Leavenworth Papers no. 16 (Washington: GPO, 1988).

55 Col. Wayne A. Downing, "U.S. Army Operations Doctrine: A Challenge for the 1980s and Beyond," *Military Review* 61:1 (January 1981), p. 66.

56 James Fallows, *National Defense* (New York: Random House, 1981), pp. 26–31.

57 See Downing, op. cit., and David P. Porreca, "New Tactics and Beyond," *Military Review* 59:5 (May 1979), pp. 21–29. See also Lind, op. cit.

58 Romjue, op. cit., pp. 23–26.

59 See Christopher N. Donnelly, "Soviet Operational Concepts in the 1980's," in *Strengthening Conventional Defense in Europe*, Report of the European Security Study (London: St. Martin's Press, 1983), pp. 105–136.

60 U.S. Army, Field Manual 100-5, *Operations* (Washington: Headquarters, Dept. of the Army, August 20, 1982), p. 8-1.

61 Ibid., pp. 2-1, 2-4.

62 Herbert I. London, *Military Doctrine and the American Character* (New Brunswick, N.J.: Transaction Books, 1984), p. 24.

63 Gen. Donn A. Starry, "Extending the Battlefield," *Military Review* 61:3 (Mar. 1981), pp. 32–33.

64 Ibid., p. 45. For a good journalistic account contrasting the attrition and Airland Battle approaches, see Deborah Shapley, "The Army's New Fighting Doctrine," *New York Times Magazine*, November 28, 1982, pp. 36–42, 47–52, 56.

65 Although not specifically related to Airland Battle, Richard E. Simpkin makes the sensible point that maneuver and attrition are mirror images of each other and are complementary in combat. See his *Race to the Swift* (New York: Pergamon-Brassey's, 1985), pp. 19–23.

66 U.S. Army, Field Manual 100-5, *Operations* (Washington: Headquarters, Dept. of the Army, May 1986), pp. 10–17. See also Raoul Henri Alcala, "The United States Army and the Future of Land Warfare: The Airland Battle," in Robert L. Pfaltzgraff, Jr., et al., eds., *Emerging Doctrines and Technologies* (Lexington, Mass.: D. C. Heath, 1988), pp. 173–187, for a succinct and exceptionally well-informed account of the Army's thinking on this subject.

67 U.S. Army, Field Manual 11-92, *Combat Communications within the Corps* (Washington: Headquarters, Dept. of the Army, Nov. 1, 1978), p. 3-1.

68 See William M. Mannel, "Army Tactical C3 Architecture," *Signal* 30:10 (Aug. 1979).

69 Headquarters, Dept. of the Army (DAMO-FDQ), briefing memorandum, "Tactical Army C2 Systems," July 16, 1984. See also Lt. Gen. James W. Rockwell, ed., *Tactical C3 for the Ground Forces* (Washington: AFCEA Press, 1985), especially the chapters by William R. Richardson, "The Army Command and Control Master Plan," pp. 66–72, and Loren D. Diedrichson, "Evolution and Integration of Army Tactical C3 Systems," pp. 205–215.

70 SINCGARS briefing by Lt. Col. Walter Oleson, SINCGARS Project Manager's Office, U.S. Military Academy, March 21, 1985; Magnavox Electronic Systems Co., "Executive Summary on SINCGARS Combat Net Radios," Ft. Wayne, Ind., Nov. 23, 1987; U.S. Army, *1989 Weapons Systems* (Washington: Headquarters, Dept. of the Army, Jan. 15, 1989), p. 133, hereafter *Weapons '89*.

71 See Don Schaum et al., "MSE, the Operational Concept," in Rockwell, op. cit., pp. 157–170; GTE Tactical Systems Division, "MSE: The U.S. Army's Choice," Needham Heights, Mass., n.d.; *Weapons '89*, p. 129. On the question of SINCGARS/MSE mutual interference, see Neil Munro, "$10 Billion Radio Systems Can't Cooperate," *Army Times*, July 31, 1989, p. 24.

72 Norman E. Wells, "A View from the Joint Program Office: JTIDS," in Rockwell, op. cit., pp. 225–230; *Weapons '89*, p. 123.

73 Maj. James A. Machos, "TACAIR Support for the Airland Battle," *Air University Review* 35:4 (May-June 1984), p. 21. See also Col. Thomas A. Cardwell, "Airland Battle Revisited," *Military Review* 65:9 (Sept. 1985), p. 11, for a discussion of the structural imbalance with respect to "synchronization."

74 U.S. Air Force (XOXID), "The Air Force Role in the Airland Battle, 1984," Doctrine Information Publication no. 13 (mimeograph) (Washington: Headquarters, U.S.A.F., n.d.), pp. 2–5.

75 U.S. Air Force, Air Force Manual 1-1, *Basic Aerospace Doctrine of the United States Air Force* (Washington: Headquarters, U.S.A.F., Mar. 16, 1984), pp. 4-2 and 4-3.

76 Col. Thomas A. Cardwell, "One Step Beyond: Airland Battle, Doctrine, Not Dogma," *Military Review* 64:4 (Apr. 1984), p. 48. By the same author, see *Command Structure for Theater Warfare: The Quest for Unity of Command* (Maxwell Air Force Base, Ala.: Air Univ. Press, 1984). This study is a detailed analysis of service doctrinal differences as they affect control of component forces and command arrangements in joint theater warfare, especially control over organic air assets.

77 Tidal W. McCoy, "'Full Strike': The Myths and Realities of Airland Battle," *Armed Forces Journal International* 212:11 (June 1984), p. 83.

78 Maj. Jon S. Powell, "Airland Battle: The Wrong Doctrine for the Wrong Reason," *Air University Review* 35:4 (May-June 1985), pp. 15–22.

79 Richard G. Davis, *The 31 Initiatives* (Washington: Office of Air Force History, 1987), pp. 35–47.

80 Ibid., p. 86.

81 See U.S. Congress, Office of Technology Assessment, *New Technology for NATO: Implementing Follow-On Forces Attack,* OTA-ISC-309 (Washington: GPO, 1987), pp. 143–167.

82 Steven L. Canby, "The Conventional Defense of Europe: The Operational Limits of Emerging Technology," Working Paper no. 55, Wilson Center (Washington: Smithsonian Institution, April 1984), p. 1.

83 Ibid., p. 23.

84 U.S. Army, Field Circular 101-55, *Corps and Division Command and Control* (Ft. Leavenworth, Kans.: U.S. Army Command and General Staff College, Feb. 28, 1985), pp. 3-1 and 3-2.

85 For a standard text on the relationship of large organizations to sociological theory, see John M. Ivancevich et al., *Organizational Behavior and Performance* (Santa Monica, Calif.: Goodyear Publishing Co., 1977), esp. chaps. 11, 12, 16, and 17.

86 See chap. 4, this book.

87 U.S. Dept. of Defense, *Report of the Defense Science Board Task Force on Command and Control Systems Management* (Washington: Office of the Secretary of Defense for Research and Engineering, July 1978), pp. 2–3.

88 Lt. Gen. John H. Cushman, *Command and Control of Theater Forces: Adequacy* (Washington: AFCEA Press, 1985), p. 25.

89 Ibid., p. 198.

Chapter 7 Building Joint Approaches

1 David T. Signori and Harold A. Cheilek, "An Overview of Joint Tactical Command and Control," in John Hwang et al., eds., *Selected Analytical Concepts in Command and Control* (New York: Gordon and Breach Science Publishers, 1982), p. 145.

2 Lt. Gen. Robert A. Kingston, "C3I and the U.S. Central Command," *Signal* 38:3 (Nov. 1983), p. 23. See also Maj. Gen. Vaughn O. Long, "Interoperability: The Key to C3 Systems in Support of USPACOM," *Signal,* 38:6 (Feb. 1984), pp. 25–28.

3 See Bruce Blair, *Strategic Command and Control* (Washington: Brookings Institution, 1985), esp. pp. 182–280.

4 U.S. Congress, Senate, Committee on Armed Services, *Defense Organization: The Need for Change,* by James R. Locher III, Comm. Print 99-86 (Washington: GPO, 1985), p. 365.

5   Harry G. Summers, Jr., "Military Radio Foul-Up Wasn't Like That at All," *Los Angeles Times,* Dec. 11, 1985, p. 7.

6   Maj. Gen. Clay T. Buckingham, "JINTACCS," *Signal* 34:8 (May-June 1980), p. 53.

7   Dr. Gerald P. Dinneen, "A Systems Approach to Communications, Command, Control, and Intelligence," *Signal* 24:5 (Feb. 1980), pp. 8–12.

8   William J. Perry, "Memorandum for the Chairman, Defense Science Board Task Force," September 20, 1977. Reprinted as Appendix A in U.S. Defense Dept., *Report of the Defense Science Board Task Force on Command and Control Systems Management* (Washington: Dept. of Defense, USDRE, July 1978), p. 19; hereafter, DSB.

9   Ibid., p. 1.

10   See chap. 6, this book.

11   DSB, p. 1.

12   Dinneen, op. cit., p. 18. See also Bruce Blair, *Strategic Command and Control* (Washington: Brookings Institution, 1985), pp. 50–65.

13   U.S. Office of the Joint Chiefs of Staff, C3 Systems Division, "C3 Systems Goals and Projects," briefing paper, Mar. 15, 1981, p. I-1.

14   See Lt. Gen. John H. Cushman, *Command and Control of Theater Forces: Adequacy* (Washington: AFCEA Press, 1985), pp. 164–165.

15   See chap. 5, this book.

16   U.S. Congress, House, Committee on Armed Services, *Review of the Department of Defense Command, Control, and Communications Systems and Facilities. Report by the Command, Control and Communications Panel, Sub-Committee on Investigations of the Committee on Armed Services,* 94th Cong., 1st Sess. (HASC 94-72), Feb. 18, 1977 (Washington: GPO, 1977); hereafter, HASC C3I Panel.

17   For a succinct account of research and development issues in the Defense Department and the growing congressional role, see Albert G. Dancy, "Department of Defense Research and Development Management," *Public Administration Review* 37:4 (July-August 1977), pp. 347–356.

18   Ibid., p. 353.

19   Frank J. Carlucci, "Management of the DOD Planning, Programming and Budgeting System," U.S. Defense Dept. memorandum, March 27, 1981; hereafter, Carlucci memorandum.

20   U.S. Defense Dept., *DOD Directive 4230.5, Compatibility and Interoperability of Tactical Command, Control, Communications, and Intelligence Systems* (Washington: Dept. of Defense, ASDC3I, July 5, 1984), p. 1.

21   Carlucci memorandum, p. 6. In 1989 the Bush administration was no better than its predecessors at resisting the temptation to reform defense management. See Secretary of Defense Richard Cheney, *Defense Management Report to the President* (Washington: OSD, July 1989).

22   U.S. Defense Dept. *DOD Directive 5154.28, Joint Tactical Command, Control, and Communications Agency* (Washington: Dept. of Defense, ASD-C, July 5, 1984), p. 1.

23   U.S. Office of the Joint Chiefs of Staff, "Memorandum of Policy No. 160: Compatibility and Interoperability of Tactical Command, Control, Communications and Intelligence Systems," January 7, 1986, pp. 7–8.

24   Cushman, op. cit., pp. 114–141.

25 Buckingham, op. cit., pp. 53–61.

26 U.S. Defense Dept., *TRI-TAC,* briefing pamphlet (Washington: OSD—Joint Tactical Communications Office, September 1979), p. 4.

27 HASC C3I Panel, pp. 27–28.

28 Dr. J. Neil Burch, program director under Dinneen, cited by James Fawcette, "C3: Key Challenges Face Military Planners," *Defense Electronics* (June 1978), p. 58.

29 See Thomas C. Bennett, "What Now, Colonel," *Defense Systems Review* 1:5 (Oct. 1983), pp. 61–64. According to this article, the AN-TTC-39 represents a quantum jump in the handling of record copy transmissions (teletype, fax, photo, etc.) at corps and field army levels.

30 Interview with Col. Donn M. Knisely, commander, TRI-TAC Test Element, Ft. Huachuca, Ariz., January 5, 1984.

31 Buckingham, op. cit., p. 57. Note that the mission order did not specify naval or air operations per se. However, it would be difficult to conceive of "ground or amphibious military operations" that did not involve air or naval forces—which may explain the wording.

32 Both "war stories" recounted in this section emerged during discussions I held with action officers at the Joint Interface Test Force, JTC3A, Ft. Monmouth, N.J., February 8, 1985.

33 U.S. Navy, Office of the Chief of Naval Operations, "U.S. Navy Tactical Command and Control Plan for Allied Interoperability," September 1980, pp. 3–11.

34 U.S. Office of the Joint Chiefs of Staff, *JINTACCS: Command Briefing* (Ft. Monmouth, N.J.: JTC3A, Apr. 30, 1984), p. 13.

35 Information on the problems of TACFIRE-MIFASS interface was extracted from an untitled briefing by the JINTACCS systems engineer, dated September 19, 1978.

36 Gordon Welchman, *The Hut Six Story* (New York: McGraw-Hill, 1982), p. 256.

37 Ibid., pp. 255–283, et passim. Many of these concepts are drawn from Welchman's treatment of this topic. To develop the point further, some analysts prefer to think of receiver-oriented communications in terms of a local TV station which broadcasts over a given area. The residents "interface" with this system through their TV receivers and may or may not choose to receive the telecasts. When they do, it is an example of nonhierarchical communication oriented around the independent receiver of that information.

38 Ibid., esp. pp. 262–278.

39 U.S. Army, "Plan for U.S. Army Participation in the JTIDS Joint Service Program," Army Deputy Program Director, JTIDS Joint Program Office, Hanscom Air Force Base, Mass., July 15, 1981, pp. 3–4; hereafter, Army JTIDS Plan, 1981.

40 See chap. 5, this book.

41 U.S. Air Force, *TDMA JTIDS Overview Description,* ESD-TR-84-183 (Hanscom Air Force Base, Mass.: USAF-ESD, July 1984), pp. 104–105; hereafter, *TDMA Overview.*

42 Ibid. See also Billy Joe Workman, "An Overview of the JTIDS," Mitre Corp. Report no. MTR-3228, Bedford, Mass., Apr. 1976, pp. 47–62.

43 Ibid., p. 11.

44 Billy Joe Workman, "A User's Guide to JTIDS," Mitre Corp. Report no. 3140, Bedford, Mass., Oct. 24, 1975, pp. 15–18.

45 Ibid.

46 N. E. Bolen, "An Introduction to TDMA, ATDMA, and DTDMA," Mitre Corp. Report no. MTR-3864, Bedford, Mass., Nov. 1979, p. 18, et passim.

47 Workman, "Overview," pp. 29–46.

48 D. W. Cullivan, "Combat Applications of the JTIDS," Mitre Corp. Report no. MTR-3513, Bedford, Mass., Dec. 1979, p. 113.

49 Workman, "Overview," pp. 63–82.

50 Army JTIDS Plan, pp. 12–15. Also, Hughes Aircraft Company, "Position Location Reporting System," Ground Systems Group, Fullerton, Calif., July 1980 (contractor briefing).

51 Army JTIDS Plan, p. 5. Also, TDMA Overview, pp. 43–63.

52 Brock L. Robertson, "JTIDS—The Early Years," Tactical Air Forces Interoperability Group Report, Langley Air Force Base, Va., 1983, pp. 22–33.

53 Ibid., p. 27.

54 See Bolen, op. cit., pp. 2–8.

55 Ibid. See also Robertson, op. cit. pp. 39–42.

56 U.S. Defense Dept., Memorandum by Under Secretary of Defense for Research and Engineering Gerald P. Dinneen; Subject: JTIDS; Sept. 5, 1978; p. 1. Subsequent Dinneen JTIDS memoranda under this heading are cited as Dinneen JTIDS Memo, with the corresponding date.

57 Robertson, op. cit., p. 44.

58 Dinneen JTIDS Memo, March 15, 1979.

59 U.S. Navy, Memorandum for the secretary of the navy by the assistant secretary of the navy for research, engineering, and systems; Subject: JTIDS; Apr. 27, 1979; p. 3.

60 Dinneen JTIDS Memo, Aug. 2, 1979.

61 HASC C3I Panel, pp. 24–26.

62 U.S. General Accounting Office, *Report to the Congress by the Comptroller General of the United States: The Joint Tactical Information Distribution System—How Important Is It?* PSAD-80-22 (Washington: GPO, Jan. 30, 1980), pp. iii–v, et passim.

63 U.S. Navy, Memorandum for the under secretary of defense for research and engineering from the assistant secretary of the navy for research, engineering, and systems; Subject: GAO Report, JTIDS, How Important Is It? (OSD Case 5400-17); March 6, 1980. Repeated efforts over a two-year period to elicit further information from Dr. Mann regarding his role in the Navy's JTIDS program were unsuccessful.

64 U.S. Defense Dept., Letter from the under secretary of defense for research and engineering to the comptroller general of the United States, Apr. 7, 1980.

65 Dinneen JTIDS Memo, July 18, 1980, pp. 1–2.

66 Andrew Cockburn, "Dinneen's Legacy: The Million Dollar Radio," *Defense Week*, Jan. 12, 1981, p. 3.

67 U.S. Defense Dept., Memorandum from the director, Theater and Tactical C3, to the acting deputy under secretary of defense (C3I); Subject: JTIDS Program (Cover Brief); May 21, 1981; p. 3.

68 U.S. General Accounting Office, Letter from director, GAO Mission Analysis and Systems Acquisition Div., to the secretary of defense; Subject: Need to Re-examine JTIDS Requirements and Architecture; Apr. 2, 1982.

69 U.S. Defense Dept., Letter from the under secretary of defense for research and engineering to director, GAO Mission Analysis and Systems Acquisition Div.; May 24, 1982. Cited portion is from p. 3 of enclosure to basic correspondence.

70 Ibid., pp. 2–3 (basic correspondence).

71 John C. Cittadino, "Advancing C3: A View from OSD," *Signal* 38:9 (May 1984), pp. 123–129.

72 Col. William S. Jones, "Army Firms Up JTIDS Planning," *Battlefield Electronics* (Aug. 1982), pp. 81–87.

73 Army JTIDS Plan, p. 46. Cited figures are in 1981 dollars.

74 See also U.S. Army, "Revised PLRS/JTIDS Hybrid Operational and Organizational Plan," Combined Arms Center (AZTL-CAC-CC), Ft. Leavenworth, Kans., June 27, 1984, pp. 2-1 to 2-5.

75 Ibid., p. 1-2.

76 U.S. Congress, House, *Department of Defense Authorization of Appropriations for FY 1985 and Previously Authorized Programs,* Committee on Armed Services, 98th Cong., 2nd Sess., 1984 (HASC 98-34), pp. 1300–1301; hereafter HASC 1984.

77 Ibid., pp. 1296–1298.

78 U.S. Congress, House, *Hearings on H.R. 2287, Department of Defense Authorization of Appropriations for FY 1984 and Oversight of Previously Authorized Programs,* Committee on Armed Services, 98th Cong., 1st Sess., 1983 (HASC 98-6), pp. 1233–1234; hereafter, HASC 1983.

79 HASC 1984, pp. 456–457.

80 U.S. Congress, House, *Hearings on Military Posture and H.R. 5968, Department of Defense Authorization of Appropriations for FY 1983,* Committee on Armed Services, 97th Cong., 2nd Sess., 1982 (HASC 97-33), pp. 1150–1151; hereafter, HASC 1982.

81 HASC 1983, pp. 1226–1227.

82 Ibid., pp. 1231–1232.

83 Benjamin F. Schemmer, "OSD/UK Agree on Common JTIDS as U.S. Navy Terminates Its Program," *Armed Forces Journal International* 121:6 (Jan. 1984), p. 19.

84 U.S. Congress, House, *Hearings on H.R. 1872, Department of Defense Authorization of Appropriations for FY 1986 and Oversight of Previously Authorized Programs,* Committee on Armed Services, 99th Cong., 1st Sess., 1985 (HASC 99-2), p. 18.

85 Ibid., p. 233.

86 Ibid., p. 760.

87 John Englund, "JTIDS: Diary of a $600 Million Dollar Fiasco," *Washington Post,* May 11, 1986, p. D1.

88 Letter to the editor from Donald C. Latham, assistant secretary of defense, "Navy and Air Force Pilots *Can* Talk," *Washington Post,* May 26, 1986, p. A20.

89 "Navy Scraps Communication System," *Washington Post,* October 23, 1985, p. 4.

90 Latham, op. cit.

91 Hughes Aircraft Company, "EPLRS Briefing Booklet," Fullerton, Calif., 1989. (Report no. 844280-111/6-2-89.)

92 *Weapons 1989,* p. 123.

93 OSD, "C3I System Review Committee of JTIDS," Briefing packet, Nov. 8, 1988.

94 Ibid.

95 HASC 1984, p. 1306.

96 Philip J. Klass and Benjamin M. Elson, "Broad Technology Gains Made," *Aviation Week and Space Technology* 114:7 (Feb. 16, 1981), pp. 47–82.

97 Benjamin F. Schemmer, "Satellite Arena Twenty Years after Sputnik," *Armed Forces Journal International* (Feb. 1978), p. 29.

Chapter 8   Historical Linkages and Future Implications

1   The strategic paradigms noted here are discussed at length in chapter 3 (Jomini, Clausewitz, and Mahan), and chapter 4 (Douhet). The relationship between service ideologies and competition for defense resources is addressed in chapter 1. Also see Arnold Kanter, *Defense Politics* (Chicago: Univ. of Chicago Press, 1979). Of course, it is also possible to argue that black is a delicate shade of white, and that these doctrines are the subtle underpinnings of a delicately balanced military policy supporting national strategic objectives. See, for example, William T. Pendley, "The U.S. Navy, Forward Defenses, and the Airland Battle," in Robert L. Pfaltzgraff et al., eds., *Emerging Doctrines and Technologies* (Lexington, Mass.: D. C. Heath, 1988), pp. 189–199.

2   Edward N. Luttwak, *Strategy: The Logic of War and Peace* (Cambridge: Harvard Univ. Press, 1987), pp. 156–174.

3   Richard E. Simpkin, *Race to the Swift* (New York: Pergamon-Brassey's, 1985), p. 6.

4   Maj. Gen. Otto L. Nelson, Jr., *National Security and the General Staff* (Washington: Infantry Journal Press, 1946), pp. 578–580.

5   Maj. Gen. Clay T. Buckingham, "The Requirements of Environmental Threat," in James M. Rockwell, ed., *Tactical C3 for the Ground Forces* (Washington: AFCEA Press, 1985), p. 325.

6   A paper prepared at the Army's Combat Studies Institute presents a succinct summary of this practice. See Maj. Gary B. Griffin, "The Directed Telescope: A Traditional Element of Effective Command," U.S. Army Command and General Staff College, Ft. Leavenworth, Kans., May 20, 1985. On the personal intervention of ground commanders as a function of command and control in land warfare, see chaps. 2 and 3 in this book.

7   Charles Peters, "From Ouagadougou to Cape Canaveral: Why the Bad News Doesn't Travel Up," *Washington Monthly* (April 1986), p. 27.

8   During the second session of the Ninety-ninth Congress, Rep. Jim Courter (R-N.J.), a member of the House Armed Services Committee, went so far as to introduce legislation that would have abolished the defense agencies and transferred their functions back to the services.

9   Rear Adm. J. C. Wylie, *Military Strategy: A General Theory of Power Control* (New Brunswick, N.J.: Rutgers Univ. Press, 1966), p. 67.

10 Samuel P. Huntington, *The Soldier and the State* (Cambridge: Harvard Univ. Press, 1981), p. 195.

11 Wylie, op. cit., p. 105.

12 Ibid., p. 87.

13 Ibid., p. 91.

14 Ibid., pp. 103–104.

15 Roger A. Leonard, ed., *A Short Guide to Clausewitz on War* (New York: Capricorn Books, 1967). See also chap. 3 in this book.

16 U.S. Congress, House, *Goldwater-Nichols Department of Defense Reorganization Act of 1986*, Conference Rpt. 99-824 to accompany H.R. 3622, 99th Cong., 2nd Sess., Sept. 12, 1986, pp. 14–29, 104–120.

17 Ibid. (Title II, Sec. 153, [a]5), p. 18.

18 U.S., Organization of the Joint Chiefs of Staff (J-7), "Joint Doctrine Master Plan," briefing, 1987; see also *JCS Pub. 1-01, Joint Publication System, Joint Doctrine, and Joint Tactics, Techniques, and Procedures Development Program* (Washington: OJCS, April 15, 1988).

19 Irving B. Holley, Jr., "Doctrine and Technology of Warfare," in Pfaltzgraff, op. cit., p. 18.

20 Throughout much of 1988, the military educational establishment was the subject of an inquiry by a special panel of the House Armed Services Committee chaired by Representative Ike Skelton of Missouri. The panel's final report addressed itself not only to the strengthening of the joint educational curriculum but also viewed the officer education system as a whole, recommending a number of steps to advance the study of strategy within that system. See, U.S. Congress, House, *Report of the Panel on Military Education of the One Hundredth Congress of the Committee On Armed Services, House of Representatives,* 101st Cong., 1st Sess., Comm. Print No. 4, April 21, 1989 (Washington: GPO, 1989).

21 Samuel P. Huntington, *American Military Strategy,* Policy Papers in International Affairs No. 28 (Berkeley: University of California Institute for International Studies, 1986), p. 13.

22 One of the foremost exponents of this view of C3I is Army Captain Ralph Peters, whose novel *Red Army* (New York: Pocket Books, 1989) is a gripping portrait of a lethal, theaterwide battlefield that develops from a post-INF Soviet invasion of Western Europe. His nonfictional works have also stressed the linkage of information and lethality—for example, "The Age of Fatal Visibility," *Military Review* 68:8 (August 1988), pp. 49–59.

23 Holley, op. cit., p. 30.

Bibliography

I. Books

Abrahamson, James L. *America Arms for a New Century*. New York: Free Press, 1981.

Alger, John A. *The Quest for Victory*. Westport, Conn.: Greenwood Press, 1982.

Allison, Graham T. *The Essence of Decision*. Boston: Little, Brown, 1971.

Ambrose, Stephen A. *Upton and the Army*. Baton Rouge: Louisiana State Univ. Press, 1964.

Arcangelis, Mario De. *Electronic Warfare*. New York: Sterling Bros., 1985.

Arnold, Henry H. *Global Mission*. New York: Harper Bros., 1949.

Art, Robert J. *The TFX Case: McNamara and the Military*. Boston: Little, Brown, 1968.

Art, Robert J.; Davis, Vincent; and Huntington, Samuel P. *Reorganizing America's Defense*. Washington: Pergamon-Brassey's, 1985.

Barrett, Archie D. *Re-Appraising Defense Organization*. Washington: NDU Press, 1983.

Beach, Edward L. *The United States Navy: 200 Years*. New York: Holt, 1986.

Beard, Charles A. *The Economic Basis of Politics*. New York: Vintage Books, 1957.

Betts, Richard K. *Cruise Missiles: Science, Technology, Politics*. Washington: Brookings, 1981.

Blair, Bruce. *Strategic Command and Control*. Washington: Brookings, 1985.

Blechman, Barry M. *Force without War: U.S. Armed Forces as a Political Instrument*. Washington: Brookings, 1978.

Blechman, Barry, M., and Lynn, William J. *Toward a More Effective Defense*. Cambridge: Ballinger, 1985.

Bonds, Ray, ed. *The U.S. War Machine*. New York: Crown Books, 1978.

Bracken, Paul. *The Command and Control of Nuclear Forces*. New Haven: Yale Univ. Press, 1983.

Bradley, Omar. *A Soldier's Story*. New York: Holt and Co., 1951.

Brown, J. W. *The Signal Corps in the War of the Rebellion*. Boston: Wilkins Press, 1896.

Builder, Carl H. *The Masks of War*. Baltimore: Johns Hopkins Univ. Press, 1989.

Caraley, Demetrios. *The Politics of Military Unification*. New York: Columbia Univ. Press, 1966.

Cardwell, Thomas A., III. *Command Structure for Theater Warfare: The Quest for Unity of Command*. Maxwell AFB, Ala.: Air Univ. Press, 1984.

Clark, Asa K., et al., eds. *The Defense Reform Debate*. Baltimore: Johns Hopkins Univ. Press, 1984.

Clausewitz, Carl von. *On War*. Trans. and ed. Michael Howard and Peter Paret. Princeton: Princeton Univ. Press, 1976.

Cline, Ray S. *Washington Command Post: The Operations Division*. Official History of the U.S. Army in World War II. Washington: OCMH, 1951.

Clodfelter, Mark. *The Limits of Air Power*. New York: Free Press, 1989.

Collins, John M. *U.S. Defense Planning: A Critique*. Boulder, Colo.: Westview Press, 1982.

Coulam, Robert F. *The Illusions of Choice: The F-111 and the Problem of Weapons Acquisition*. Princeton: Princeton Univ. Press, 1977.

293

Craven, W. F., and Cate, J. L., eds. *The Army Air Forces in World War II*. 7 vols. Chicago: Univ. of Chicago Press, 1948–58.

Cushman, John H. *Command and Control of Theater Forces: Adequacy*. Washington: AFCEA Press, 1986.

Davis, Richard E. *The 31 Initiatives: A Study in Army–Air Force Cooperation*. Washington: Office of Air Force History, 1987.

Davis, Vernon E. *Development of the JCS Committee Structure*. Vol. 2 of *The History of the Joint Chiefs in World War II*. Washington: OJCS Historical Office, 1972.

Davis, Vincent. *The Admiral's Lobby*. Chapel Hill: Univ. of North Carolina Press, 1967.

De Bastiani, Richard J. *Computers on the Battlefield: Can They Survive?* Washington: NDU Press, 1983.

Deitchman, Seymour. *Military Power and the Advance of Technology*. Rev. ed. Boulder, Colo.: Westview Press, 1983.

Douglass, Joseph D. *Soviet Military Strategy in Europe*. New York: Pergamon Press, 1980.

Douhet, Giulio. *Command of the Air*. Trans. Dino Ferrari. Reprint ed. by USAF Office of History. Washington: GPO, 1983.

Dupuy, Trevor N. *A Genius for War*. New York: Prentice-Hall, 1977.

Earle, Edward Meade, ed. *Makers of Modern Strategy*. Rev. ed. Princeton: Princeton Univ. Press, 1973.

Enthoven, Alain K., and Smith, K. Wayne. *How Much Is Enough: Shaping the Defense Program, 1961–1969*. New York: Harper & Row, 1969.

Fuller, J. F. C. *Generalship: Its Diseases and Their Cure*. Harrisburg, Pa.: Military Service Pub. Co., 1936.

Furer, Julius A. *Administration of the Navy Department in World War II*. Washington: USN Historical Division, 1959.

Goldwater, Barry M., with Jack Casserly. *Goldwater*. New York: Doubleday, 1988.

Gordon, Don E. *Electronic Warfare: Element of Strategy and Multiplier of Combat Power*. New York: Pergamon Press, 1981.

Grant, Ulysses S. *Personal Memoirs of U. S. Grant*. 2 vols. New York: Webster, 1886.

Grechko, A. A. *The Armed Forces of the Soviet State*. USAF trans. Soviet Military Thought Series. Washington: GPO, n.d.

Hadley, Arthur T. *The Straw Giant*. New York: Random House, 1986.

Halleck, Henry W. *Elements of Military Art and Science*. 3rd ed. New York: D. Appleton, 1862.

Hamilton, Alexander. *The Federalist Papers*. Mentor ed. New York: New American Library, 1961.

Hammond, Paul Y. *Organizing for Defense*. Princeton: Princeton Univ. Press, 1971.

Harbord, James G. *The American Expeditionary Force: Its Organization and Accomplishments*. Evanston, Ill.: Evanston Pub. Co., 1929.

———. *The American Army in France*. Boston: Little, Brown, 1936.

Hemsley, John. *Soviet Troop Control*. New York: Pergamon Press, 1982.

Herzog, Chaim. *The War of Atonement*. Boston: Little, Brown, 1975.

Hewes, James E., Jr. *From Root to McNamara: Army Organization and Administration, 1900–1963*. Washington: OCMH, 1975.

Hezlet, Sir Arthur. *Electronics and Sea Power*. New York: Stein and Day, 1975.

Higham, Robin. *Air Power*. New York: St. Martin's Press, 1972.

Hinsley, F. H., et al., eds. *British Intelligence in the Second World War: Its Influence on Strategy and Operations*. London: HMSO, 1979.

Hitch, Charles J. *Decision-Making for Defense*. Berkeley: Univ. of California Press, 1965.

Hittle, James D. *The Military Staff: Its History and Development*. 3rd ed. Harrisburg, Pa.: Stackpole Press, 1961.

Holmes, W. J. *Double-Edged Secrets*. Annapolis, Md.: U.S. Naval Institute Press, 1979.

Hooper, Edwin B. *The Navy Department: Evolution and Fragmentation*. Washington: Naval Historical Foundation, 1978.

Huntington, Samuel P. *The Common Defense*. New York: Columbia Univ. Press, 1961.

_____. *The Soldier and the State*. Cambridge: Harvard Univ. Press, 1981.

Hwang, John, et al., eds. *Selected Analytical Concepts in Command and Control*. New York: Gordon and Breach Science Publishers, 1982.

Ivanov, D. A., et al. *Fundamentals of Tactical Command and Control: A Soviet View*. Trans. USAF. Soviet Military Thought Series. Washington: GPO, n.d.

Johnson, Stuart E., and Levis, Alexander H. *Science of Command and Control*. 2 vols. Washington: AFCEA Press, 1988, 1989.

Jomini, Antoine Henri. *The Art of War*. Trans. G. H. Mendell and W. P. Craighill. Philadelphia: Lippincott Co., 1862. Reprint. Westport, Conn.: Greenwood Press, 1971.

Jones, R. V. *The Wizard War*. New York: Coward, McCann and Geoghegan, 1978.

Kanter, Arnold. *Defense Politics: A Budgetary Perspective*. Chicago: University of Chicago Press, 1979.

Keiser, Gordon W. *The U.S. Marine Corps and Defense Organization, 1944–1947*. Washington: NDU Press, 1982.

Kohn, R. H., and Hanrahan, J. P., eds. *Condensed Analysis of the Ninth Air Force in the European Theater of Operations*. USAF Warrior Studies. Rev. ed. Washington: USAF Historical Office, 1984.

Krulak, Victor H. *Organization for National Security*. Washington: U.S. Strategic Institute, 1983.

Kuhn, Thomas S. *The Structure of Scientific Revolutions*. Chicago: Univ. of Chicago Press, 1970.

_____. *The Fundamental Tension*. Chicago: Univ. of Chicago Press, 1977.

Lane, John J., Jr. *Command and Control and Communications Structures in Southeast Asia*. Maxwell AFB, Ala.: Air Univ. Press, 1981.

Layton, Edward T. . . . *And I Was There*. New York: Wm. Morrow & Co., 1985.

Lehman, John F., Jr. *Command of the Seas*. New York: Charles Scribner's Sons, 1988.

Leonard, Roger A., ed. *A Short Guide to Clausewitz on War*. New York: Capricorn Books, 1967.

Leopold, Richard W. *Elihu Root and the Conservative Tradition*. Boston: Little, Brown, 1954.

Lewis, William J. *The Warsaw Pact: Arms, Doctrine and Strategy*. Cambridge: Institute for Foreign Policy Analysis, 1982.

Lind, William F. *Maneuver Warfare Handbook*. Boulder, Colo.: Westview Press, 1985.

London, Herbert I. *Military Doctrine and the American Character*. New Brunswick, N.J.: Transaction Books, 1984.

Luttwak, Edward N. *Strategy: The Logic of War and Peace*. Cambridge: Harvard Univ. Press, 1987.

Mahan, Alfred Thayer. *The Influence of Sea Power upon History*. 12th ed. Boston: Little, Brown, 1918.

_____. *Naval Administration and Warfare*. Boston: Little, Brown, 1908.

Matloff, Maurice. *American Military History*. Washington: OCMH, 1973.

Millett, Allen R., and Maslowski, Peter. *For the Common Defense.* New York: Free Press, 1984.

Millis, Walter. *Arms and Men: A Study in American Military History.* New Brunswick, N.J.: Rutgers Univ. Press, 1984.

Mitchell, William. *Our Air Force: The Keystone of National Defense.* New York: Dutton, 1921.

————. *Winged Defense: The Development and Possibilities of Modern Air Power, Economic and Military.* New York: Putnam's, 1925.

————. *Memoirs of World War I: From Start to Finish of Our Greatest War.* Rev. ed. New York: Random House, 1960.

Momyer, William W. *Air Power in Three Wars.* Washington: GPO, 1978.

Morison, Elting E. *Admiral Sims and the Birth of the Modern American Navy.* Cambridge: Riverside Press, 1942.

————. *Men, Machines, and Modern Times.* Cambridge: MIT Press, 1976.

Morison, Samuel Eliot. *History of United States Naval Operations in World War II.* 15 vols. Boston: Little, Brown, 1947–62.

————. *The Two-Ocean War.* Boston: Little, Brown, 1963.

Nagler, Gordon R., ed. *Naval Tactical Command Control.* Washington: AFCEA Press, 1986.

Nelson, Otto L., Jr. *National Security and the General Staff.* Washington: Infantry Journal Press, 1946.

Nordeen, Lon O., Jr. *Air Warfare in the Missile Age.* Washington: Smithsonian, 1985.

Orr, George E. *Combat Operations C3I: Fundamentals and Interactions.* Maxwell AFB, Ala.: Air Univ. Press, 1983.

Paret, Peter, ed. *Makers of Modern Strategy from Machiavelli to the Nuclear Age.* Princeton: Princeton Univ. Press, 1986.

Paullin, Charles O. *History of Naval Administration, 1775–1911.* Reprint. Annapolis, Md.: U.S. Naval Institute Press, 1965.

Perry, Mark. *Four Stars.* Boston: Houghton Mifflin, 1989.

Peters, Ralph. *Red Army.* New York: Pocket Books, 1989.

Pfaltzgraff, Robert L. Jr., et al., eds. *Emerging Doctrines and Technologies.* Lexington, Mass.: D. C. Heath, 1988.

Pogue, Forrest C. *The Supreme Command.* Official History of the U.S. Army in World War II. Washington: OCMH, 1954.

Prange, Gordon W. *At Dawn We Slept.* New York: Penguin Books, 1982.

Price, Alfred. *Instruments of Darkness: The History of Electronic Warfare.* New York: Scribner's, 1978.

Radziyevskiy, A. I. *Dictionary of Basic Military Terms: A Soviet View.* Trans. USAF. Soviet Military Thought Series. Washington: GPO, n.d.

Rearden, Steven L. *The Formative Years, 1947–1950.* History of the Office of Secretary of Defense Historical Series. Washington: OSD Historical Office, 1984.

Reed, Rowena. *Combined Operations in the Civil War.* Annapolis, Md.: U.S. Naval Institute Press, 1978.

Robinson, S. S. *A History of Naval Tactics.* Annapolis, Md.: U.S. Naval Institute Press, 1942.

Rockwell, James M., ed. *Tactical C3 for the Ground Forces.* Washington: AFCEA Press, 1986.

Rosinski, Herbert. *The Development of Naval Thought.* Newport, R.I.: U.S. Naval War College Press, 1977.

Schnabel, James F. *The Joint Chiefs of Staff and National Policy, 1945–1947.* History of the JCS Series. Wilmington, Del.: Glazier, 1979.

Scott, Harriet F., and Scott, William F. *The Armed Forces of the USSR*. Boulder, Colo.: Westview Press, 1979.

Short, Lloyd M. *The Development of National Administration in the United States*. Baltimore: Johns Hopkins Univ. Press, 1923.

Simpkin, Richard E. *Race to the Swift*. New York: Pergamon-Brassey's, 1985.

Smith, Perry M. *The Air Force Plans for Peace*. Baltimore: Johns Hopkins Univ. Press, 1970.

Sprout, Harold, and Sprout, Margaret. *The Rise of American Naval Power*. Princeton: Princeton Univ. Press, 1967.

Stimson, Henry L., and Bundy, McGeorge. *On Active Service in Peace and War*. New York: Harper Bros., 1948.

U.S. Air Force. *Air Superiority in World War II and Korea*. USAF Warrior Studies. Washington: USAF Historical Office, 1983.

U.S. Army. *Historical Sketch of the Signal Corps, 1860–1928*. Fort Monmouth, N.J.: U.S. Army Signal School, 1929.

———. *The Army Lineage Book*. Vol. 2. Washington: OCMH, 1953.

U.S. Congress. Office of Technology Assessment. *New Technology for NATO: Implementing Follow-On Forces Attack*. Washington: GPO, 1987.

Upton, Emory. *The Armies of Asia and Europe*. New York: Appleton, 1878.

———. *The Military Policy of the United States*. Washington: GPO, 1904.

Van Creveld, Martin. *Supplying War: Logistics from Wallenstein to Patton*. Cambridge: Cambridge Univ. Press, 1980.

———. *Command in War*. Cambridge: Harvard Univ. Press, 1985.

———. *Technology and War*. New York: Free Press, 1989.

Watson, Mark S. *Chief of Staff: Pre-War Plans and Policies*. Official History of the U.S. Army in World War II. Washington: OCMH, 1950.

Weber, Thomas. *The Northern Railroads in the Civil War*. New York: Columbia Univ. Press, 1982.

Weigley, Russell F. *The American Way of War*. New York: Macmillan, 1973.

———. *History of the United States Army*. Rev. ed. Bloomington: Indiana Univ. Press, 1984.

Weizenbaum, Joseph. *Computer Power and Human Reason*. San Francisco: W. M. Freedman, 1976.

Welchman, Gordon. *The Hut Six Story*. New York: McGraw-Hill, 1982.

Wilkinson, Spenser. *The Brain of an Army: A Popular Account of the German General Staff*. London: Constable, 1895.

———. *The Brain of the Navy*. London: Constable, 1895.

Williams, Kenneth P. *Lincoln Finds a General: A Military Study of the Civil War*. 5 vols. New York: Macmillan, 1948–59.

Williams, T. Harry. *Lincoln and His Generals*. New York: Knopf, 1952.

———. *Americans at War*. Baton Rouge: Louisiana State Univ. Press, 1960.

———. *The History of American Wars*. New York: A. Knopf, 1981.

Winnacker, Rudolph A., et al., eds. *The Department of Defense Documents on Establishment and Organization*. Washington: OSD Historical Office, 1978.

Winterbotham, F. W. *The Ultra Secret*. London: Weidenfeld and Nicolson, 1974.

Wohlstetter, Roberta. *Pearl Harbor: Warning and Decision*. Stanford, Calif.: Stanford Univ. Press, 1962.

Wylie, J. C. *Military Strategy: A General Theory of Power Control*. New Brunswick, N.J.: Rutgers Univ. Press, 1966.

II. Articles

Bacevich, Andrew J., Jr. "Emory Upton: A Centennial Assessment." *Military Review* 61:12 (Dec. 1981), 21–28.

Beers, Henry P. "The Development of the Office of the Chief of Naval Operations." *Military Affairs* 10, Part I (Spring, 1946), 40–68; Part II (Fall, 1946), 10–38.

Broad, William J. "Computers and the U.S. Military Don't Mix." *Science* 207 (March 14, 1980), 1184.

Buckingham, Clay T. "JINTACCS." *Signal* 34:8 (May-June 1980), 53–62.

Cardwell, Thomas A., III. "One Step Beyond: Airland Battle—Doctrine, Not Dogma." *Military Review* 64:4 (Apr. 1984), 45–53.

———. "The Quest for Unity of Command." *Air University Review* 35:4 (May-June 1984), 25–29.

———. "Airland Battle Revisited." *Military Review* 65:9 (Sept. 1985), 4–13.

Cittadino, John C. "Advancing C3: A View from OSD." *Signal* 38:9 (May 1984), 123–129.

Cockburn, Andrew. "Dinneen's Legacy: The Million Dollar Radio." *Defense Week,* Jan. 12, 1981.

Dancy, Albert G. "Department of Defense Research and Development Management." *Public Administration Review* 37:4 (July-Aug. 1977), 347–356.

Diamond, Dr. Fred I. "A Structure for Tactical C3." *Signal* 33:10 (Aug. 1979), 77–81.

Dinneen, Gerald P. "A Systems Approach to Communcations, Command, Control and Intelligence." *Signal* 34:5 (Feb. 1980), 8–12.

Doyle, Michael K. "The United States Navy and War Plan ORANGE: Making Necessity a Virtue." *Naval War College Review* 22:3 (May-June 1980), 49–63.

Englund, John. "JTIDS: Diary of a $600 Million Fiasco." *Washington Post,* May 11, 1986, D1.

Fedyszyn, T. R. "A Maritime Perspective." U.S. Naval Institute *Proceedings,* 14/7/989 (July 1985), 80–87.

Fialka, John. "The Pentagon's Exercise 'Proud Spirit': Little Cause for Pride." *Parameters* 11:1 (March 1981), 40.

Foster, Gregory D. "Missing and Wanted: A U.S. Grand Strategy." *Strategic Review,* Fall, 1985, 13–23.

———. "Contemporary C2 Theory and Research: The Failed Quest for a Philosophy of Command." *Defense Analysis* (special edition on command and control) 4:3 (Nov. 1988), 201–220.

Gooding, Judson. "Protector of the American Fleet." *New York Times Magazine,* Oct. 6, 1985, 34.

Greve, Frank. "Pentagon Calls Super Computer a Disaster." *Parameters* 11:1 (March 1980), 95–97.

Hadley, Arthur T. "The Split Military Psyche." *New York Times Magazine,* July 13, 1986, 26–33.

Hanne, William G. "A Separatist Case." U.S. Naval Institute *Proceedings,* 111/7/989 (July 1985), 88–96.

Hodgden, Louise, "Satellites at Sea: Space and Naval Warfare." *Naval War College Review* 32:4 (July-Aug. 1984), 31–45.

Holley, Irving B., Jr., "Command, Control and Technology." *Defense Analysis* (special edition on command and control) 4:3 (Nov. 1988), 267–286.

Irvine, Dallas D. "The Origin of Capital Staffs." *Journal of Modern History* 10:2 (June 1938), 161–179.

_____. "The French and Prussian Staff Systems before 1870." *Journal of the American History Foundation* 2:4 (Winter, 1938), 192–203.

Johnson, Frederick C. "Naval Surveillance and Target Acquisition." *Signal* 34:2 (Oct. 1979), 13–16.

_____. "Command and Control Overview." *Signal* 34:10 (Aug. 1980), 62–65.

Jones, William S. "Army Firms Up JTIDS Planning." *Battlefield Electronics,* Aug. 1982, 81–87.

Kingston, Robert P. "C3I and the U.S. Central Command." *Signal* 38:3 (Nov. 1983), 23–25.

Komer, Robert W. "The Neglect of Strategy." *Air Force Magazine* 67:3 (March 1984), 51–59.

Korb, Lawrence J. "The Budget Processes in the Department of Defense: The Strengths and Weaknesses of Three Systems." *Public Administration Review* 37:4 (July-Aug. 1977), 334–345.

Kronenberg, Philip S. "Command and Control as a Theory of Interorganizational Design." *Defense Analysis* (special edition on command and control) 4:3 (Nov. 1988), 229–252.

Lautenschlager, Karl. "Technology and the Evolution of Naval Warfare." *International Security* 8:2 (Fall, 1983), 3–51.

Lawson, Joel S., Jr. "Naval Tactical C3 Architecture, 1985–1995." *Signal* 33:10 (Aug. 1979), 71–79.

Long, Vaughn O. "Inter-Operability: The Key to C3 Systems in Support of US PACOM." *Signal* 38:6 (Feb. 1984), 25–28.

Machos, James A. "TACAIR Support for the Airland Battle." *Air University Review* 35:4 (May-June 1984), 21–26.

March, Robert T. "Tactical C3: The Modern Challenge." *Signal* 32:11 (Sept. 1978), 16–19.

McCoy, Tidal W. " 'Full Strike': The Myths and Realities of Airland Battle." *Armed Forces Journal International* 212:11 (June 1984), 78–83.

Meyer, Deborah G. "The Aegis Factor: Does John Lehman Need or Want a 600-Ship Navy?" *Armed Forces Journal International* 123:10 (Apr. 1986).

Morton, Louis. "War Plan ORANGE: Evolution of a Strategy." *World Politics* 11 (Jan. 1959), 221–250.

North, James. " 'Hello, Central, Get Me NATO': The Computer That Can't." *Parameters* 10:1 (March 1980), 91–94.

Nuhn, Perry R. "WWMCCS and the Computer That Can." *Parameters* 10:3 (Sept. 1980), 16–21.

Nutting, Wallace H. "Pulling Together: The Services as Team Players." *Army* 36:5 (May 1986), 22–30.

Oettinger, Anthony G. "Information Resources: Knowledge and Power in the 21st Century." *Science* 209 (July 4, 1980), 191–198.

O'Neill, William D. "Naval Anti-Air Warfare." *National Defense* 65:365 (Feb. 1981), 27.

Powell, Jon S. "Airland Battle: The Wrong Doctrine for the Wrong Reason." *Air University Review* 35:4 (May-June 1985), 15–22.

Shapley, Deborah, "The Army's New Fighting Doctrine." *New York Times Magazine,* Nov. 28, 1982, 36–42, 47–52, 56.

Stanley, Verl R., and Noggle, Phillip L. "Command and Control Warfare: Seizing the Initiative." *Signal* 38:8 (Apr. 1984), 23–26.

Starry, Donn A. "Extending the Battlefield." *Military Review* 61:3 (March 1981), 32–38.

Tate, Raymond T. "The U.S. Navy in Transition." *Signal* 34:7 (Apr. 1980), 33–35.

Truver, Scott C. "To Get the Drop on Soviet Archers, U.S. Navy Needs Bows, Arrows and Bucks." *Armed Forces Journal International* 123:10 (Apr. 1986), 51–58.

Walt, Steven M. "The Search for a Science of Strategy." *International Security* 12:1 (Summer, 1987), 140–165.

Wilson, George C. "Weinberger Questioned on Grenada, Reform Plan." *Washington Post*, Nov. 15, 1985.

III. Reports, Monographs, and Unpublished Sources

Bolen, N. E. "An Introduction to TDMA, DTDMA and DTDMA." MITRE Corp. Report No. 3864. Bedford, Mass.: MITRE Corp, Nov. 1979.

Boyd, John R. "Patterns of Conflict." Briefing paper. Washington, May 1981 (mimeograph).
———. "Organic Design for Command and Control." Briefing paper. Washington, March 1984 (mimeograph).

Canby, Steven L. "The Conventional Defense of Europe: The Operational Limits of Emerging Technology." Working Paper No. 55. Washington: Wilson Center, Smithsonian, Apr. 1984.

Cullivan, D. W. "Combat Applications of the JTIDS." MITRE Corp. Report No. 3513. Bedford, Mass.: MITRE Corp. December 1979.

Digby, James. *Precision Guided Munitions*. Adelphi Paper No. 118. London: International Institute for Strategic Studies, 1975.

Fisher, Ernest F., Jr. "Weapons and Equipment Evolution and Its Influence upon Organization and Tactics in the American Army from 1775–1963." Report. Washington: OCMH, n.d.

Herbert, Paul H. *Deciding What Has to Be Done: General William E. Depuy and the 1976 Edition of FM 100-5*. Leavenworth Papers No. 16. Washington: GPO, 1988.

Historical Evaluation and Research Organization. *A Preliminary Interpretive Survey of the History of Command and Control*. Albuquerque, N. Mex.: Sandia Corp., 1963.

Kennedy School of Government, Harvard University. "TFX: The Commonality Decision." Case Study No. 9-375-035. Cambridge: Intercollegiate Case Clearing House, 1978.

Legere, Lawrence H. "Unification of the Armed Forces." Manuscript. Washington: OCMH, n.d.

Maillefert, Christopher W. "Command and Control: A Contemporary Perspective." Thesis. Newport, R.I.: U.S. Naval War College, 1974.

Ney, Virgil. *The Evolution of Military Unit Control*. Combat Operations Research Group Memorandum M-217. Washington: U.S. Army Combat Developments Command, Sept. 10, 1965.

Oettinger, Anthony G., ed. *Seminar on Command, Control, Communications and Intelligence*. Incidental Paper of the Harvard Univ. Program on Information Resources Policy. Cambridge: Harvard Univ., 1980.

Paolucci, D. A.; Polmar, Norman; and Patrick, John. "A Guide to U.S. Naval Command and Control." NOSC Technical Document No. 247. San Diego, Calif.: U.S. Naval Oceans Systems Center, July 1, 1979.

Powe, Mark B., and Wilson, E. E. "The Evolution of American Military Intelligence." Instructional text. Fort Huachuca, Ariz.: U.S. Army Intelligence Center and School, 1973.

Ray, James, and Schroder, Ted. "The Revolution in Command and Control Technology and the Civilian-Military Chain of Command." Thesis. Maxwell AFB, Ala.: Air University, 1977.

Rechtin, Eberhard. *The Technology of Command*. Washington: Academy Press, 1983.

Robertson, Brock L. "JTIDS—The Early Years." Report of the Tactical Air Forces Interoperability Group. Langley AFB, Va.: Headquarters, USAF Tactical Air Command, 1983.

Romjue, John L. *From Active Defense to Airland Battle: The Evolution of Army Doctrine, 1973–1982*. Fort Monroe, Va.: Headquarters, U.S. Army Training and Doctrine Command, 1984.

Snyder, Frank M. *Command and Control: Readings and Commentary*. Publication of the Harvard University Program on Information Resources Policy. Cambridge, April 1989.

Sunderland, Riley. *The Evolution of Command and Control for Close Air Support*. Washington: USAF Historical Office, 1973.

Thornton, Patrick H. "The C3 Conceptual Architecture and Its Value." Thesis. Newport, R.I.: U.S. Naval War College, 1975.

TRW Corp. *WWMCCS History*. Annex J (unclassified). McLean, Va.: TRW Defense and Space Systems Group, September 30, 1977.

U.S. Air Force. "TDMA JTIDS Overview Description." Technical report #ESD-TR-84-183. Hanscom AFB, Mass.: Headquarters, USAF Electronic Systems Division, July 1984.

——. "The Air Force Role in the Airland Battle." Doctrine Information Publication No. 13. Washington: Headquarters, USAF (XOXID), n.d. (mimeograph).

U.S. Army. "Airland Battle 2000." Study. Fort Monroe, Va.: Headquarters, U.S. Army Training and Doctrine Command, August 10, 1982.

——. Army staff papers on Airland Battle: "Information Paper, Army 21—U.S. Army Concepts for the Future," Apr. 12, 1984; "U.S. Army Airland Battle Doctrine and Future Concepts," June 28, 1984; "Tactical Army C2 Systems," July 16, 1984. Washington: Headquarters, DA (DAMO-FDQ).

——. "Extracts of the JINTACCS Implementation Planning Document." Working paper. Washington, Headquarters, DA (DAMO-C4J), 1984.

——. "Plan for Participation in the JTIDS Joint Service Program." Hanscom AFB, Mass.: JTIDS Joint Program Office, July 15, 1981.

——. *Soviet Army Operations*. Arlington, Va.: U.S.A. Intelligence and Security Command, 1978.

——. *The Effectiveness of Third Phase Tactical Air Operations in the European Theater*. Report of the Army Air Forces Evaluation Board in the European Theater of Operations. Orlando, Fla.: Orlando Army Air Force Base, Aug. 20, 1945.

U.S. Department of Defense. Memorandum by the Deputy Secretary of Defense, Hon. Frank J. Carlucci. Subject: "Management of the DOD Planning, Programming and Budgeting System," Washington, March 27, 1981.

——. OSD Memoranda by the Under Secretary of Defense for Research and Engineering (C3I), Dr. Gerald P. Dinneen. Subject: "JTIDS," Washington. Memos dated Sept. 5, 1978; March 15, 1979; Aug. 2, 1979; and July 18, 1980.

——. OSD Memorandum from the Director, Theater and Tactical C3, to the Acting Deputy Under Secretary of Defense (C3I). Subject: "JTIDS Cover Brief," May 21, 1981.

U.S. Joint Chiefs of Staff. "C3 Systems Goals and Projects." Briefing paper. Washington: OJCS (C3 Systems), March 15, 1981.

——. "Memorandum of Policy No. 160: Compatibility and Interoperability of Tactical Command, Control, Communications and Intelligence Systems." Washington: OJCS, Jan. 7, 1986.

U.S. Navy. JTIDS Memoranda: "Memorandum for the Secretary of the Navy by the Assistant Secretary of the Navy for Research, Engineering and Systems," Washington, Apr. 27, 1979; "Memorandum for the Under Secretary of Defense for Research and Engineering from the Under Secretary of the Navy for Research, Engineering and Systems." Subject: GAO Report–JTIDS, Washington, March 6, 1980.

————. "Navy Command and Control Systems Ashore." Study. Washington: U.S. Naval Electronic Systems Command, n.d.

————. "Navy Tactical Command and Control Plan for Allied Interoperability." Study. Washington: Office of the Chief of Naval Operations (OP-094), Sept. 1980.

Woods, David L. *A History of Tactical Communications Techniques.* Orlando, Fla.: Martin Marietta Corp., 1963.

Workman, Billy Joe. "An Overview of JTIDS." MITRE Corp. Report No. 3228. Bedford, Mass.: MITRE Corp., April 1976.

————. "A User's Guide to JTIDS." MITRE Corp. Report No. 3140. Bedford, Mass.: MITRE Corp, Oct. 24, 1975.

IV. Government Documents

U.S. Air Force. Air Force Manual 1-1. *Basic Aerospace Doctrine of the United States Air Force.* Washington: Headquarters, USAF, Mar. 16, 1984.

U.S. Army. Field Circular 101-55. *Corps and Division Command and Control.* Fort Leavenworth, Kans.: USA Command and General Staff College, Feb. 28, 1985.

————. Field Manual 11-92. *Combat Communications within the Corps.* Washington: Headquarters, DA, Nov. 1, 1978.

————. Field Manual 100-5. *Operations.* Washington: Headquarters, DA, July 1, 1976. (Revised editions August 1982, May 1986).

————. Field Manual 100-20. *Field Service Regulations. Command and Employment of Air Power.* Washington: War Department, July 21, 1943.

————. *Weapons Systems, 1989.* Washington: Headquarters, DA, Jan. 15, 1989.

U.S. Congress. House. *The Goldwater-Nichols Department of Defense Reorganization Act of 1986.* Conf. rpt. 99-824 to accompany H.R. 3622, 99th Cong., 2nd sess., 1986.

————. Committee on Armed Services. *Hearings on Military Posture and H.R. 5968, Department of Defense Authorization of Appropriations for Fiscal Year 1983.* Before the Committee on Armed Services, House of Representatives, 97th Cong., 2nd. sess. HASC 97-33. Washington: GPO, 1982.

————. Committee on Armed Services. *Hearings on H.R. 2287, Department of Defense Authorization of Appropriations for Fiscal Year 1984 and Oversight of Previously Authorized Programs.* Before the Committee on Armed Services, House of Representatives, 98th Cong., 1st sess. HASC 98-6. Washington: GPO, 1983.

————. Committee on Armed Services. *Department of Defense Authorization of Appropriations for Fiscal Year 1985 and Oversight of Previously Authorized Programs.* Before the Committee on Armed Services, House of Representatives, 98th Cong., 2nd sess. HASC 98-34. Washington: GPO, 1984.

————. Committee on Armed Services. *Hearings on H.R. 1872, Department of Defense Authorization of Appropriations for Fiscal Year 1986 and Oversight of Previously Authorized Programs.* Before the Committee on Armed Services, House of Representatives, 99th Cong., 1st sess. HASC 99-2. Washington: GPO, 1985.

————. *Report of the Panel on Military Education of the One Hundredth Congress of the Committee on Armed Services, House of Representatives.* 101st Cong., 1st sess. Comm. Print No. 4, April 21, 1989. Washington: GPO, 1989.

_____. Committee on Armed Services. *Review of DOD Worldwide Communications, Phase I.* (Mollohan Report). Report of the Armed Services Investigations Subcommittee of the Committee on Armed Services, 92nd Cong., 1st sess. Washington: GPO, 1976.

_____. *Review of the Department of Defense Command, Control, and Communications Systems and Facilities.* Report by the Command, Control, and Communications Panel, Sub-Committee on Investigations of the Committee on Armed Services, 94th Cong., 1st Sess. HASC 94-72. Feb. 18, 1977. Washington: GPO, 1977.

U.S. Congress. Senate. *Creation of the American General Staff,* by Major General William Harding Carter. Document No. 119. 65th Cong., 1st sess. Washington: GPO, 1924.

_____. Committee on Armed Services. *Defense Organization: The Need for Change,* by James R. Locher III. Staff Report No. 99-86 to the Committee on Armed Services. October 16, 1985. Washington: GPO, 1985.

_____. *Hearings before the Committee on Military Affairs on S. 84 and S. 1482.* 79th Cong., 1st sess. Washington: GPO, 1945.

_____. *Legislative History of the Army of the United States, 1775–1901.* Document No. 229, 56th Cong., 2nd sess. Washington: GPO, 1904.

_____. *Reorganization of the Department of Defense: Hearings before the Committee on Armed Services, United States Senate.* S. Hrg. 99-1083, 99th Cong., 1st sess., 1985. Washington: GPO, 1987.

_____. *Report to the Hon. James Forrestal, Secretary of the Navy, on Unification of the War and Navy Departments and Postwar Organization for National Security* (Eberstadt Report). Comm. Print. 79th Cong., 1st sess. Washington: GPO, 1945.

U.S. Department of Defense. DOD Directive 4230.5. *Compatibility and Interoperability of Tactical Command, Control, Communications and Intelligence Systems* (ASD-C3I). Washington, July 5, 1984.

_____. DOD Directive 5154.28. *Joint Tactical Command, Control and Communications Agency* (ASD-C). Washington, July 5, 1984.

_____. *Report of the Defense Science Board Task Force on Command and Control Systems Management.* Washington: OSD, July 1978.

_____. *Soviet Military Power.* 5th and 6th eds. Washington: GPO, 1986, 1988.

U.S. General Accounting Office. *Report to the Congress by the Comptroller-General of the United States: The Joint Tactical Information Distribution System—How Important Is It?* PSAD 80-22. Washington: GPO, Jan. 30, 1980.

_____. *The Worldwide Military Command and Control System—Major Changes Needed in Its Automated Data Processing Management and Direction.* Washington: GPO, 1979.

_____. *Worldwide Military Command and Control System—Evaluation of Vendor and Department of Defense Comments.* Washington: GPO, 1980.

U.S. Joint Chiefs of Staff. *JCS Pub. 1: Dictionary of Military and Associated Terms.* Washington: OJCS, Jan. 1986.

_____. *JCS Pub. 2: Unified Action Armed Forces* (for official use only). Washington: OJCS, 1974.

U.S. National Archives. Records of the War Department General and Special Staffs. ABC 370.62. "Unity of Command."

Index

AAA (Antiaircraft artillery), 140
Abrahamson, James L., 66–67
Abrams, Creighton W., 144
Achille Lauro incident, 138
AEF. *See* American Expeditionary Force
Aegis cruiser, 140, 162, 163–64, 205
Aide system, 70–71
Airborne Battlefield Command and Control
  Center, 171
Airborne Warning and Control System
  (AWACS), 141, 205; JTIDS and, 212,
  213–14, 215, 216, 235
Aircraft carrier, 94, 106, 117, 139–40, 158
Air defense: capability of Soviet Union,
  140–41, 143, 170–72; proliferation of
  Army weapons for, 214
Air-ground operations system, 170–71, 181
Airland Battle doctrine, 12–13, 168–85,
  173–79; Army–Air Force conflict over,
  180–83, 186; Army C2 and, 178–80;
  Canby's objections and, 183–85; Deep
  Strike concept in, 178, 182, 183–84;
  ground and air integration problem and,
  149; information lines and, 264; Soviet
  countermeasures and, 184; stages in evolution of, 173–75; tenets of, 178–79; un-
  resolved issues for, 183
Air Naval Gunfire Liaison radio nets, 192
Air power: Army Field Service Regulation
  100-20 and, 107; as component command,
  105–08; controversies over, 97; Douhet's
  influence on, 90–93; early advocacy of,
  88–90; flexibility of, 107; in interwar
  period, 89; service autonomy and, 87;
  summary of theory of, 11; in World War
  I, 87; in World War II, 105–08
Alexander, Edward P., 60
Alexander the Great, 29, 37
Alger, John, 65
Allied Expeditionary Force, 107
American Expeditionary Force (AEF), 84–
  85, 86

Amphibious command ships, 110
Anderson, George W., 134
Antiaircraft artillery (AAA), 140
Antiair warfare (AAW), 162
Anti-jam radio system, 222, 224, 227, 228
Arab-Israeli War (1973), 143, 172, 173, 263
Army Data Distribution System (ADDS),
  180, 235
Army *21. See* Airland Battle doctrine
Army War College, 77
Arnold, Henry H., 101, 102, 104, 106
ATDMA (Advanced TDMA), 217–18
Attrition warfare vs. maneuver warfare, 151,
  174, 178–79. *See also* Airland Battle doc-
  trine
Aufragstaktik, 151–52
Automation: battlefield intelligence and,
  145; danger of conceptual dependence on,
  184; joint combat operations and, 192–93
AWACS. *See* Airborne Warning and Control
  System

Backwards compatibility, 222, 223
Baruch, Bernard, 84
Baseline of interoperability, 251–52
Battista, Anthony R., 228, 232
Battle, as key in war, 55
Battlefield reconnaissance systems, 145, 263
Battle of Bladensburg, 33, 40
Battle of Mobile Bay, 61–62
Battle of New Orleans, 40
Beard, Charles A., 24
Benson, William S., 82
Berthier, Louis-Alexandre, 49–50
Blair, Bruce G., 18
Blechman, Barry M., 158
Boeing E-3A Sentry. *See* Airborne Warning
  and Control System
Boyd, John, 150–52, 154, 174
Bracken, Paul, 18
Bradley, Omar, 141
Brodie, Bernard, 169–70

Buckingham, Clay, 250
Builder, Carl, 12–13, 14
Bundy, McGeorge, 121–22
Bureaucratic proliferation, 128
Bureau of Aeronautics, 93
Bureau system: Army and, 74–75, 78–79;
    Navy and, 70, 94
Butler, Benjamin "Beast," 62

Calhoun, John C., 33–35
Canby, Steven L., 183–84
Caraley, Demetrios, 114, 115, 118
Carlucci, Frank, 197
Carter, Jimmy, 193–94
Carter, William Harding, 74–75, 77, 78, 79,
    80
Central Intelligence Agency (CIA), 112, 138
Centralization: advances in telecommunica-
    tions and, 134–35; of aircraft control,
    107–08; amendment of DCA charter and,
    194–95; electronically enhanced, 134–38;
    postwar rise in, 125–26. See also General
    Staff; Unity of command
Centralization-decentralization balance: Air
    Force doctrine and, 185, 186; Airland
    Battle doctrine and, 181–82; in World
    War II, 99, 108
CEWI (Combat Electronic Warfare and In-
    telligence) battalion, 145
Cheney, Richard, 252
Chief of Naval Operations (CNO), 71, 72,
    82, 102–03
Chief of staff, Army, 30. See also General
    Staff; Military staff
CIA (Central Intelligence Agency), 112, 138
CIC (Combat Information Center), 110
CINCS. See Commanders-in-chief
Citizen-soldier, 22–23. See also Militia sys-
    tem
Cittadino, John C., 223
Civilian control: Army General Staff and,
    79; of Army vs. Navy, 41–42; in Civil
    War, 57–60; as Navy objective, 116; op-
    erational autonomy in 1960s and, 133–34;
    power in Defense Department and, 127–
    28; in Revolutionary War, 40; subjective

vs. objective, 22–23; U.S. Constitution
    and, 21–23
Civil-military partnership, 237–38
Civil War, 47, 50–52, 56–60, 62
Clausewitz, Karl von, 11, 47, 54–56, 244,
    255, 259
Cline, Ray, 102, 125
CNO. See Chief of Naval Operations
CNO-COMINCH, 102–03
Collins, J. Lawton, 117, 118
Combat Electronic Warfare and Intelligence
    (CEWI) battalion, 145
Combat Information Center (CIC), 110
Combined arms concept, 31, 32, 88, 99, 114
COMINCH (Commander-in-Chief, United
    States Fleet), 102–03
Command: controversy over line of, 84–85;
    defined, 16; evolution of, in modern war-
    fare, 18–19; need to extend authority of,
    28–30, 32; personal intervention and, 41–
    42; as process, 150, 185; structure of, as
    internal to services, 2–3; style of, in land
    vs. sea warfare, 123–24. See also General
    command structure; National command
    structure; Unified and specified com-
    manders; Unified commands
Command, Control, Communications, and
    Intelligence (C3I), 197–98
Command and control: approaches to prob-
    lem of, 8–15; bureaucratic causes of fail-
    ure in, 187; classical, 37–42; defined, 16;
    development of joint approaches to, 189–
    240; dual emphasis on organization and
    technology for, 17–20; environment of,
    246–47; failures in 1960s of, 135–36; for-
    mative influences on, 123–47; future di-
    rections for, 15; historical linkages of,
    241–49; in Mexican War, 42–46; in nine-
    teenth century, 41–42; structural anoma-
    lies in, 3–8
Command and control community, 193–96
Command and control system: Airland Battle
    doctrine and, 168–85; combat command
    and, 259–60; competing systems and,
    253–54; conceptual models for, 149–57;
    defined, 16; "directed telescope" function
    and, 250; Grenada as test of, 4–5; inter-

service differences and, 154–55, 168; leadership tasks in choice of, 252; management of defense technology and, 249–50; modularity in, 152, 159, 165; service-related emphasis and, 129–30; superagency proposal and, 253

Command and control warfare, 5, 250

Command centers: on-board systems and, 162–65; shore-based systems and, 162, 164, 166

Commander-in-Chief, United States Fleet (COMINCH), 102–03

Commanders-in-chief (CINCS): Airland Battle doctrine and, 169; Goldwater-Nichols provisions and, 3; influence on weapons development, 187

Command structure. See General command structure; National command structure

Commerce, role of Navy in, 24, 64, 65–66, 111

Commonality: defined, 193; functional networks and, 192; skepticism about, 236; as threat, 133; weapons procurement and, 132–33. See also TRI-TAC program

Communications system: interservice compatibility and, 4; naval command structure and, 38; sender- vs. receiver-orientation of, 208; technological advances in, and power of OSD, 134; in Vietnam air war, 170–71; in World War I, 82–83. See also Telecommunications

Component command: air power as, 105; in unified command structure, 104, 119

Composite warfare doctrine, 140. See also Aegis cruiser

"Compunications," 135

Computer technology: battlefield automation and, 145; in command centers, 136; interservice rivalry and, 7; limitations of, 137, 164, 249–50; in modern naval C2 systems, 157–58, 164; security issues and, 205, 206, 211–12; survivability and, 149, 167

Congress: creation of Army General Staff and, 77–79; creation of defense agencies and, 26; defense reform and, 1–2, 6, 15, 20, 33–36; information resources of, 196–

97; joint C2 systems and, 196; JTIDS and, 221, 226–34; role in defense establishment, 22, 23–24; Senate hearings on defense organization (1985), 1–2, 15; TRI-TAC program and, 200–201; Woodrum committee hearings, 113

Coningham, Arthur, 107

Constituency interests, 79

Continental theory, 11, 13–14

Control: pride of position and, 85; problem of, in nineteenth century, 39–40; as process, 150, 185. See also Command and control

Cooper, Thomas, 230–31

Coordinative authority, 80–81

Cost-analysis: McNamara's use of, 128, 131, 132; prioritization of C2 systems and, 195

Coulam, Robert F., 133

Counterintelligence/human intelligence (HUMINT), 142–43

Creech, Wilbur L., 227–28

Crisis management: politico-military coordination and, 133–34; telecommunications and, 136, 138; use of naval forces in, 166; vs. wartime scenarios, and naval C2 systems, 166–67

Crowe, William, 164

C3I (Command, Control, Communications, and Intelligence), 197–98

C2. See Command and Control

Cuban missile crisis, 133–34

Cushman, John H., 5, 187–88, 199

Dahlgren, John A., 52

Daniels, Josephus, 82, 125

Darling, Charles H., 72

Data-handling issues: Aegis concept and, 163–64; NTDS and, 162–63; TFCC and, 164–65

Data-voice controversy, 212–13, 226, 228–29

DCA (Defense Communications Agency), 135, 194–95

Decentralization. See Bureau system; Centralization-decentralization balance; U.S. Navy: command structure in

Decision-making: human intervention limited to, 205; in JINTACCS, 202–03; by Joint Chiefs of Staff, 116

Defense agencies: creation of, 26–27; reorganization in *1800s* of, 33–36

Defense Authorization Act (1972), 196

Defense budget: bureaucratic proliferation and, 128; Congressional control and, 196–97; development of joint approaches and, 113, 114, 190–91; JTIDS program and, 233–34; services' influence on, 128–30; services' roles and missions and, 125–26; unification debate of *1940s* and, 113, 114

Defense Communications Agency (DCA), 135, 194–95

Defense Electronics (journal), 149–50

Defense Resources Board, 198, 252

Defense Science Board: C2 management study and, 194; superagency proposal and, 253

Delafield, Richard, 54

Department of Defense (DOD): centralization vs. autonomy and, 130–38; civil-military partnership and, 237–38; decentralized management in, 223, 224–25; Directive S-5100.30 (WWMCCS), 135–37; establishment of, 112; integration of planning and, 128–29; under McNamara, 130–34; powers of OSD and, 126–28; summary of Soviet capabilities by, 172–73; technological choices and, 252–53. *See also* Office of the Secretary of Defense

Department of the Navy, 26–27, 32

DePuy, William E., 173

Dickinson, William L., 229, 237–38

Digital data flows, speed of, 205, 211

Dinneen, Gerald P., 137, 148, 194–95, 220–22

"Directed telescope" function, 250

Distributed data techniques, 205, 238, 240

Distributed Time Division Multiple Access (DTDMA), 217–22, 230–32

Doctrine of mutual cooperation: in Civil War, 47, 62; Joint Board and, 95, 96; Pearl Harbor and, 97–98; replacement of, 89

DOD. *See* Department of Defense

Donnelly, Christopher, 175

Doolittle, James, 117

Douhet, Giulio, 11, 90–92, 93, 98, 169–70, 244, 255

DTDMA (Distributed Time Division Multiple Access), 217–22, 230–32

DTDMA/TDMA controversy, 217–22, 230–32

Dupuy, Trevor, 53

Eaglet, Robert D., 229

Eberstadt, Ferdinand, 117, 129

Eberstadt Plan, 117, 118, 120

ECM (Electronic countermeasures), 139–40

Educational establishment, 53, 262, 292n20

Eisenhower, Dwight D.: Defense Department reorganization and, 127; unity of command and, 105, 118, 119

Electronic command and control. *See* Telecommunications

Electronic countermeasures (ECM), 139–40

Electronic warfare (EW), 140–41; in Arab-Israeli War, 143; beginnings of, in World War I, 86; Grenada invasion and, 4–5; modern naval C2 systems and, 166–67; precision-guided munitions and, 139

Encryption, in JTIDS, 211–12

Englund, John, 233, 234

Enhanced JTIDS (EJS), 227, 228

Ericsson, John, 51

EW. *See* Electronic warfare

Executive agencies, 196

Executive Order *9096*, 102–03

Fallows, James, 174

Farragut, David, 61–62

Fedyszyn, T. R., 9–10

Fialka, John, 137

Fisher, Ernest, 51

Fiske, Bradley, 70–71, 80

Flag signal system, 38, 60

Force without War (Blechman and Kaplan), 158

Forrestal, James, 117, 120, 126

Fox, Gustavus V., 57

Frederick the Great, 30

Frémont, John C., 44, 45

Frequency hopping, 205, 211–12
Fuller, J. F. C., 100
Furer, Julius, 123

Gabriel, Charles A., 182–83
General Accounting Office (GAO): JTIDS program and, 221, 224; WWMCCS controversy and, 137
General Board of the Navy, 70, 72, 73
General command structure: air paradigm and, 92–94; Civil war and, 56–57; at component command level, 105; evolution of, 26–36; functional integration of, 99–108; at high command level, 99–104; interservice differences in, 71–73; Mahan's influence on, in Navy, 68–73; operational forces and, 105–08; Spanish-American War and, 73–81; at unified command level, 104–05; World War II and, 99–108. See also specific services
General Dynamics Corporation, 132
General Staff: of the Army, 70, 76–81, 83–84, 100; naval command structure and, 70–73, 79; postwar defense establishment and, 114–15; Prussian, 52–54, 56
General strategic paradigm. See Joint paradigm
Geopolitical requirements, and joint approaches, 190
German U-boat, 82, 110
Global reach, 157–68
Gneisenau, August von, 52–53
Goldwater-Nichols Act (1986), 3, 247–49, 259
Gorman, Paul, 154–57, 168
Grant, Ulysses S., 57, 58, 60, 61, 62
Gravely, Samuel L., 195
Great Britain, General Staff in, 76
Grenada invasion, 1–2, 3–5, 15, 191–92
Grumman Corp., 132
Guderian, Heinz, 109
Guerrilla warfare, 142–43, 266n23
Gustavus Adolphus (Swedish king), 30

Hadley, Arthur T., 8–9
Halleck, Henry Wager, 49
Halsey, William F., 116, 117

Hamilton, Alexander, 23–24, 27
Hammond, Paul Y., 105, 115, 124
Hanne, William G., 9
Harbord, James G., 84–86
HAVE CLEAR, 227
HAVE QUICK, 222
Hertel, Dennis, 232–33
Hezlet, Arthur, 110
Hickam, Horace M., 93
Higham, Robin, 93
Hittle, J. D., 28, 30
Holley, I. B., Jr., 150, 261, 264
Hull, William, 40
HUMINT (Counterintelligence/human intelligence), 142–43
Huntington, Samuel P., 10–11, 21–22, 27, 34, 124, 257, 263

Ideology, 11. See also Strategic paradigms
Indian fighting, 40–41, 64
Information. See Intelligence
Information age, warfare in, 263–64
Information flows, 205, 211, 263–64
Integration: pressures for, 189; service autonomy and, 168–69; of service planning by DOD, 128–29; of World War II forces, 99–108
Intelligence: Army developments in, 141–45; developments in 1970s in, 138, 141–45; guerrilla warfare and, 142–43; in Lawson's model, 152–54; precision-guided munitions and, 139; in World War I, 141. See also Battlefield reconnaissance systems
Intelligence community, and joint C2 systems, 196
Interoperability: baseline of, 251–52; defined, 193; "directed telescope" function and, 250–52; DTDMA-TDMA controversy and, 231–32; infrastructure of, 201–03, 252–53; JINTACCS vs. TRI-TAC approach toward, 199–200; Joint Chiefs of Staff "memorandum of procedure" on, 198–99; JTIDS as backbone of, 235; key leadership tasks for, 251; Navy planning and, 168; problems of, in Grenada invasion, 1–2, 3–5, 6, 15, 191–92; rapid technological change and, 165

Interservice cooperation: interservice agencies and, 246; in Mexican War, 43–45
Interservice organization: lack of joint paradigm and, 256–57; national command structure and, 245–47. *See also* Joint Chiefs of Staff
Interservice relationships: Airland Battle doctrine and, 180–82; in Civil War, 61–63; in interwar years, 94–97; joint paradigm and, 259–60; in Spanish-American War, 75–76
Intraservice loyalties, 19
Iranian airbus tragedy, 162, 163–64
Iranian hostage rescue mission, 191

Jackson, Andrew, 40, 41
Jargon, 148
JCS. *See* Joint Chiefs of Staff
Jefferson, Thomas, 27
JINTACCS program, 199–200, 201–04
Johnson, Frederick C., 157
Joint Action of the Army and the Navy (Joint Boards), 95–96
Joint Board of the Army and Navy, 73, 76, 94–95
Joint Chiefs of Staff: C3 Systems Directorate and, 195; decision-making process in, 116; development of joint doctrine and, 260–62; function of services in, 104; Goldwater-Nichols provisions and; joint C2 systems and, 198–99; operations of WWMCCS and, 136; origin of, 103–04; peacetime unified command structure and, 119; powers of, under National Security Act, 112, 120, 121; proliferation of C2 systems and, 253–54; service autonomy and, 10; service membership of personnel of, 248; technological choice and, 16, 253–54. *See also* Joint Staff J-6
Joint doctrine, development of, 260–62
Joint operation: during Civil War, 61–63; communication and, 192; *Joint Action* and, 96; in World War II, 108, 110–11
Joint paradigm: absence of, 254–58; applied operational strategy and, 262–63; joint doctrinal refinement process and, 260–62; nature of, 258–60

Joint Staff J-6, 252, 253–54
Joint Staff J-7 Directorate, and joint doctrine, 260
Joint Tactical Command, Control, and Communications Agency, 198, 252
Joint Tactical Information Distribution System (JTIDS): agreements on plan for, 215–16; Air Force and Navy divergence on, 226–34; Air Force applications for, 212–13; architecture of, 216, 217–22, 223–24; Army applications for, 214–15, 223, 225–26; battlefield information flow and, 264; capabilities of, 211–12; classes of terminals in, 215–16; concept of, 206–12, 209–11; C2 environment and, 245–47; developments from *1981* to *1985*, 223–34; developments to *1981*, 204–23; DTDMA/TDMA controversy and, 217–22, 230–32; goal of interoperability and, 252, 253; implications of experience of, 236–40; interservice disagreements on, 216–22; Marine Corps applications for, 214–15; Navy applications for, 213–14; Navy vs. Airforce commitment levels, 229–30; tactical applications and, 213–14; technological offspring of, 234–35, 238. *See also* Army Data Distribution System
Jomini, Antoine-Henri, 11, 47–49, 67–68, 244, 258
Jonestown (Guyana) evacuation, 137
JTIDS. *See* Joint Tactical Information Distribution System

Kamikaze suicide bomber, 138
Kanter, Arnold, 12
Kaplan, Steven, 158
Kearfott, Singer, 225
Kearny, Stephen W., 45–46
Kelley, Paul X., 7
Kennedy, John F., 133–34
Kimmel, H. E., 97–98, 102–03
King, Ernest J., 103, 104, 113, 115, 116
Kingston, Robert, 190
Kinney, J. C., 61–62
Kirksey, Robert E., 229
Kluge, Hans von, 108

Knox, Frank, 113
Kriegsakademie, 53
Kuhn, Thomas S., 11–12

Land navigation, problems of, 214–15
Land power theory, 11, 13–14
Land warfare: command style and, 123–24; developments leading to paradigm for, 48–56; evolution of military staff for, 28–31; nineteenth-century technology and, 50–52; unity of command and, 29; visual signals in, 37–38, 41
LASERSATCOM, 238, 240
Latham, Donald C., 197, 223–34
Lawson, Joel S., C2 model of, 152–54, 159
Layton, Edwin T., 275n16
Leahy, William D., 103, 104
Legere, Lawrence J., Jr., 94–95
Lehman, John, 5, 232, 234
Leopold, Richard, 80
Levels-of-analysis problem, 19–20
Lincoln, Abraham, 57, 58
Locher, James R., III, 4, 191
Luttwak, Edward N., 13–14, 249

MacArthur, Douglas, 85
McClellan, George B., 54, 58–59, 63
McCoy, Tidal, 182
Machos, James, 181
McNamara, Robert, 128, 129; DOD management and, 130–35; TFX case and, 132–33, 222, 236
McNarney, Joseph T., 101, 113
McNarney Plan, 113
Madison, James, 23, 24
Mahan, Alfred Thayer, 11, 32–33, 42, 47, 57, 244, 255, 256; Douhet's doctrines and, 91–92; *Influence of Sea Power upon History*, 65–69; Navy strategy and, 64–69
Mahan, Dennis Hart, 49, 67
"Maneuver warfare school," 150-51
"Man-in-the-loop" problem, 205
Mann, D. E., 220–21
March, Peyton C., 83–84
Marconi, Marchese, 66
Maritime strategy, 11, 12, 14–15

Marshall, George C., 100–101, 104, 112–13
Mason, John, 43
Meade, George G., 58, 59, 60
Message standards, and JTIDS, 216, 220, 227
Mexican War (1846–48), 42–46
Meyer, E. C., 137
Meyer, G. V. L., 70
Miles, Nelson A., 75, 78–79
Military education, 74, 77, 167, 262, 292n20
Military failures, and joint approaches, 191
Military force: components of, in modern Navy, 159–60; concentration of, 67, 68; functional complexity of, 29–30; operational characteristics of, 29; size of, 28–29
Military history, themes in, 19
Military organization: absence of joint paradigm and, 256–57; in Army vs. Navy, 244–45; autonomy and, 10; evolution of, 27–36; general command structure and, 245; pride of position in, 85; Prussian system of, 52–54; service differences in, 123–24; strategic paradigms and, 244–45
Military staff: in Army, 85–86, 124; in Army Air Corps, 92–93; in Civil War, 58–59; evolution of, 28–36; functional groupings in, 85–86, 92–93; as method for command and control, 28–30; of Napoleon, 49–50; in nineteenth century, 49–50. *See also* General command structure; Military organization
Military tradition, 10, 257
Militia system, 33, 74
Millis, Walter, 109
Mitchell, William ("Billy"), 11, 89, 89–90, 98, 169–70, 244
Mitre Corporation, 206, 208
Mobile Subscriber Equipment (MSE), 180
Modernization: pace in *1970s* of, 148; problems of, 148–88; service differences in strategies for, 158; of Soviet forces, 172–73, 175
Modularity, in C2 system, 152, 159, 165
Moffett, William A., 93–94

Moltke, Helmuth von, 261–62
Momyer, William, 106
Moorer, Thomas, 134
Morison, Samuel Eliot, 111
Morse, Samuel F. B., 50
Moses, 29, 268*n*20
MSE (Mobile Subscriber Equipment), 180
Mustin, H. C., 163
Myer, Albert James, 60, 61

Nagler, Gordon R., 230, 231–32
Napoleon, 48–50
National command authority (NCA), 196
National command structure: autonomy and, 10; in Civil War, 57–60; emergence of Joint Chiefs of Staff and, 103–04; interservice organization and, 245–47; in Mexican War, 42–43; in modern age, 129; National Security Act and, 246; in World War I, 84–85; in World War II, 104–08
National Defense Act (1916), 80
National Defense University (NDU), 17
National Security Act (1947), 111–12, 247–48; amendments to (1958), 127, 130, 247, 248; competing perspectives on C2 and, 186–87; language of, 126; provisions of, 112; technological choice and, 245; unity of command and, 246
National Security Council, 112, 128
National security strategy report, 3
National strategy, and service autonomy, 14, 248
National values, and character of C2, 241–43
NATO. *See* North Atlantic Treaty Organization
Naval Tactical Data System (NTDS), 139–40, 158, 162–63
Naval War Board, 70
Navy EC-121 reconnaissance aircraft incident, 136
NDU (National Defense University), 17
Nelson, Otto L., Jr., 85, 101, 250
Net Control Units (NCU), 215, 225
Ney, Virgil, 30

Normandy invasion, and service integration, 108
North Atlantic Treaty Organization (NATO): interoperability issues, 19; JTIDS concept and, 208; Soviet forces and, 171, 172–75; tactical air control system and, 171
NTDS. *See* Naval Tactical Data System
Nuclear weapons: air power paradigm and, 114; Defense Department management and, 131; integrated C2 and, 134; service strategies and, 14; strategic C2 and, 18
Nutting, Wallace H., 4

Ocean area tactical integration, 160
Offensive, as key to victory, 49
Office of Management and Budget (OMB), 196
Office of the Chief of Naval Operations (CNO), 71, 72, 82, 102–03
Office of the Secretary of Defense (OSD): amendments of *1958* to National Security Act and, 130–31; C3I and, 136, 197–98; growth of, 126–29; joint C2 systems and, 197–98; JTIDS program and, 220–22; in national command structure, 246; organization of, 278*n*7; Program Analysis and Evaluation Office, 128, 197; Research and Engineering Office, 197; service autonomy and, 133. *See also* Department of Defense
OMB. *See* Office of Management and Budget
O-O-D-A (Observation, orientation, decision, and action) model, 150–52, 174
Operational environment: command style and, 123–24; C2 problems of land warfare and, 168; electronic surveillance and, 139; general strategic paradigm and, 258–59; JTIDS and, 226, 227–28; military organization and, 8–9; modern C2 and, 155, 157; service autonomy and, 45, 243–44; service differences in, 8–9, 19, 185–86; technological superiority and, 19
Orr, George E., 152
OSCAR submarine (U.S.S.R.), 161
OSD. *See* Office of the Secretary of Defense

Packard, David, 136, 197

Panama canal, and naval policy, 66, 67

Paradigms. *See* Strategic paradigms

Parallel systems, and JINTACCS vs. TRI-TAC approaches, 203–04

Paret, Peter, 15

Patterson, Robert P., 114, 120

Paullin, Charles O., 70, 72

Pearl Harbor, 97–98, 275n16

Perry, Matthew C., 44, 51

Pershing, John J., 84, 85, 130

Personal intervention by commanders, 41–42

Peters, Charles, 250

Peters, Ralph, 292n22

Planning, Programming, and Budgeting System. *See* Cost-analysis

PLRS-JTIDS Hybrid, 214–15, 216, 225–26, 235

Polk, James K., 43, 45

Popularism, in military tradition, 10

Porter, David, 62

Position Location Reporting System. *See* PLRS-JTIDS Hybrid

Power projection, as naval mission, 158–59

Prange, Gordon W., 97–98

Precision-guided munitions (PGM), 138–40; demands for C2 efficiency and, 204; modern naval C2 and, 59, 157–58; as threat to naval force, 160–62

President: Army-Navy differences and, 27; role in defense establishment, 22. *See also* Executive agencies; *and individual presidents*

Procurement process: army service bureaus and, 83; cost-analysis and, 132; JTIDS experience and, 236; service autonomy and, 146–47; services' role in, 15–16; systems for joint environment, 130; unified commands and, 129

Professionalism: citizen-soldier and, 22; interoperability and, 254; in military tradition, 10; "service technicism" and, 257; strategic paradigms and, 245; of von Steuben, 30

Prussian military organization, 52–54, 74

Public perception, and joint approaches, 191

Quartermaster-general's office, 30

Quesada, Elwood, 108

Railroad, 51, 53

Range extension: modern naval C2 systems and, 160–62; Soviet threat and, 160–61, 162–63. *See also* Global reach

Ransom, Harry Howe, 112

Reagan, Ronald: C2 management and, 195–96; defense buildup under, 2, 191; defense centralization and, 137–38; use of seapower by, 158

Receiver-oriented communications, 208, 209, 213, 238, 288n37

Rechtin, Eberhardt, 166, 167

Reed, Rowena, 63–64

Resource allocation: Airland Battle doctrine and, 182; centralization and, 99; World War II interservice bargaining and, 105. *See also* Defense budget; Procurement process

Revolutionary War, 38–40

Rhetoric, of unification debate, 117–18

Richardson, James O., 113

Richardson committee report, 116–17

Ries, John C., 114–15

Rifled projectile, 52

Robertson, Brock, 216

Rockwell Collins, 222

Roosevelt, Franklin D., 103, 104

Roosevelt, Theodore, 67

Root, Elihu, 76–79, 98

Rosinski, Herbert, 68

Rumsfeld, Donald, 136

Sampson, William, 75

Scharnhorst, Gerhard von, 52–53

Schlesinger, James R., 208

Scott, Winfield, 44

Sea power strategy, 11, 12, 14–15

Sea warfare: paradigm for, 64–73; visual signals in, 38

Security of telecommunications system, 205, 206, 211–12

SEEK TALK, 222, 227

Senate Bill *2044*, 120

Sender- vs. receiver-oriented communications, 208. *See also* Joint Tactical Information Distribution System

Service agencies, joint C2 systems and, 199–204

Service autonomy: air power and, 88–89; electronic C2 and, 110–11; ideology and, 244; intellectual underpinnings of, 10–12; interoperability and, 17; legacy of, and C2 conflict, 246–47; merits of, 247; Mexican War C2 and, 45–46; national concerns and, 247–49; under National Security Act, 120–21; need for unity of command and, 7–8; objective and subjective civilian control and, 23; operational environment and, 243–44; postwar commitment to, 124–26; postwar defense budget and, 129; procurement process and, 146–47; roots of, 21–46, 243; state of, in mid-*1920s*, 97; U.S. Constitution and, 21–26; World War I perspectives on, 81–87; World War II combat and, 104–05

Service command structure. *See* General command structure

Service organization. *See* Military organization

Service paradigms. *See* Strategic paradigms

Shafter, William R., 75

Sherman, William Tecumseh, 74, 77

Short, Walter C., 97–98

Signal (journal), 18, 149–50

Signal communications, 38, 60, 61–62

Simpkin, Richard, 249

SINCGARS. *See* Single-Channel Ground/Airborne Radio System

Singer Kearfott, 222

Single-Channel Ground/Airborne Radio System (SINCGARS), 180

Single Integrated Operations Plan (SIOP), 131

SIOP. *See* Single Integrated Operations Plan

Skelton, Ike, 292*n*20

"Skip-echeloning," 136–37

Smith, Perry M., 91–92

Snyder, Frank, 17

Soviet Military Power (Department of Defense), 172

Soviet Union: air defense capability of, 140–41, 143, 170–72; military buildup by, 171–73; modern naval threats from, 160–61, 162–63

Spanish-American War, 67, 73–81

Sprout, H., 36

Sprout, M., 36

Staff action cycle, 28

Stanton, Edwin M., 56, 61

Starry, Donn A., 174–75, 178

States, Constitutional role of, 22

Steam propulsion, 64

Steamship, 51

Stimson, Henry L., 121–22

Stockton, Robert F., 44–45, 46

Strategic command and control, 18

Strategic connectivity, 135, 138, 166–67

Strategic paradigms: Air Force doctrine and, 169–70; Air Force views on Airland Battle doctrine and, 180–81; air power doctrine and, 91–92; competitiveness of, 244; data-voice controversy and, 228–29; joint paradigm and, 254–63; Jominian legacy and, 48–49; modern C2 and, 155; Naval paradigm and, 115–16; postwar unification debate and, 112–22; service autonomy and, 244; service differences and, 11; service organizations and, 244–45; stability provided by, 255–56; in World War II combat, 105

Strategic planning, and defense leadership, 237

Subordination: cooperation and, 62; Naval separation and, 26–27; operational characteristics of forces and, 29; organizational strategies of services and, 27–36

Summers, Harry, 192

Superagency for C2 systems, 253

Surface-to-air missiles (SAM), 140

Survivability of computer technology, 149, 167

Tactical Air Control Center (TACC), 171

Tactical control: in Civil War, 52; Indian fighting and, 41; maps and clocks and, 270n48; in Navy, 42; telecommunications and, 108–11; World War I Army communications and, 86. See also Automation

Tactical digital information link (TADIL), 203, 216–17

Tactical fighter, experimental (TFX), 131–33

Tactical Flag Command Center (TFCC), 164–65

TADIL (Tactical digital information link), 203, 216–17

TADIL J standards, 216, 227

TDMA. See Time Division Multiple Access

Technical interface standards, 202, 203

Technicism, 10, 257

Technological choice: conflict in C2 environment and, 247–49; ideology and, 69; interoperability and, 245–47; role of services in, with developments of 1970s, 146; service organization and, 245; uncertainties of computer equipment and, 249–50

Technological risk, 226, 232–34

Technology: advances in, and competitive advantage, 263–64; Airland Battle doctrine and, 178; of Industrial Revolution, 50–52; from JTIDS, 234–35, 238; modern naval wartime scenarios, 167; need for standardization in, 17; neutrality of, 241; nineteenth-century military operation and, 50–52, 59–60, 68–69; role of, in C2 developments, 138–47; service autonomy and, 168–69. See also Computer technology; Telecommunications; Weapons technology

Tedder, Arthur, 107

Telecommunications: centralization and, 134–35, 136; security issues for, 205, 206, 211–12; systems for, as combat target, 166–67; World War II C2 and, 99, 108–11

Telegraph: Civil War use of, 60–61; impact of, 50–51, 53; naval threat and, 66; in World War II, 86

Telephone, 86

Telephone-system thinking, 208

Territory, emphasis on control of, 49, 55, 58

Theater perspective, 185–88

Time Division Multiple Access (TDMA), 209–11, 217–22, 230–32

Training, for modern naval wartime scenarios, 167

TRI-TAC program, 199–201, 203–04. See also Commonality

Trost, Carlisle H., 163–64

Truman, Harry, 118, 119–20, 121

Unification debate, 112–22

Unified Action Armed Forces (Joint Chiefs of Staff), 126

Unified and specified commanders: joint vs. service concerns and, 247–48; in national command structure, 246–47; OSD and, 128–29; power over service components, 259; role of, in system development, 194

Unified Command Plan, 119

Unified commands: peacetime structure of, 118–19; in World War II, 104

U.S. Air Force: Airland Battle doctrine and, 180–82; Army-Navy rivalry and, 106; creation of, 92, 112; combat technologies of 1970s and, 138, 139, 140–41; JTIDS applications for, 212–13; JTIDS architecture and, 217–22; JTIDS Class I terminals and, 215; JTIDS Class II terminals and, 223, 235; as lead service for JTIDS program, 208–09, 221, 223, 230; modern C2 systems and, 170–71; operational environment for, 9; TFX episode and, 131; unification debate of 1940s and, 113–15; War Department reforms of 1942 and, 102

U.S. Army: Air Corps, 92–93, 96, 102; air power and, 87; battlefield technologies of 1970s and, 141–45; in Civil War, 56–57, 64; command structure in, 73–81; Constitutional perspectives on, 24–26; evolution of organization in, 28–31, 33–34; Field Service Regulation 100-20, 107; FM 100-5, 143–44, 173–74; FM 100-5, revised, 175, 178–79; ground force control of aircraft and, 106; JTIDS and, 223, 225–26; nineteenth-century C2 in, 39–41;

U.S. Army (*continued*)
  operational environment for, 9; premodern
  communications in, 179; service bureaus
  in, 73–74, 83; Spanish American War
  and, 73–81; strategic paradigm of, 12–13;
  World War I battle staff in, 85–86; World
  War II telecommunications in, 109; unification debate of *1940s* and, 113–15. *See
  also* War Department
U.S. Army Signal Corps, 60, 86
U.S. Constitution, service autonomy and,
  21–26
U.S. Marine Corps: JTIDS and, 223; unification debate and, 120
U.S. Navy: air power and, 87, 93–94; in
  Civil War, 57, 64; combat technologies of
  1970s and, 139–40; command structure
  in, 10, 68–73, 82–83, 102–03, 115; commerce and, 24, 64, 65–66, 111; Constitutional perspectives on, 23, 24–26; C2
  systems in, 157–68; evolution of organization in, 28, 31–33, 34–36; intraservice
  loyalties in, 19–20; JTIDS and, 5–7,
  213–14, 217–22, 223; Mahan's influence
  on, 64–73; modern combat technology
  and, 160; modern C2 systems in, 154,
  157–68; Navy Department and,26–27;
  operational environment for, 9; strategic
  paradigm of, 12, 67–68, 158–59; TFX
  episode and, 131–33; unification debate
  of *1940s* and, 113, 114; in World War I,
  82–83; in World War II, 102–03,
  109–10
Unity of command: advent of air power and,
  93, 96–97; Army General Staff and, 80;
  Clausewitz and, 55; Frederick the Great
  and, 30; Joint Board of the Army and the
  Navy and, 94–95; land warfare and, 29;
  in Navy, 32; under Polk, 43, 45; precedent set by Washington, 31; pressure for,
  in modern warfare, 29–30; quest for, 246;
  War Department reorganization and, 101–
  02; World War II and, 89, 98–111. *See
  also* National command structure
Upshar, Abel P., 35–36
Upton, Emory, 74

USS *Liberty*, 135–36
USS *Pueblo*, 136, 191
USSR. *See* Soviet Union

Van Creveld, Martin, 18–19
Very High Speed Integrated Circuitry
  (VHSIC), 216, 238
Vietnam conflict, 139, 140, 142–43, 170–
  71
Vincennes incident, 162, 163–64
Visual signals, 37–38, 41
Voice: drawbacks of radio systems and,
  204–05, 214; in JTIDS architecture, 211,
  228. *See also* Data-voice controversy
Von Steuben, Friedrich, 30

War Department: creation of, 26; organiza-
  tion of staff, 31; reorganization in, 83–84,
  100–102, 113; in unification debate of
  1940s, 113–15
War Industries Board, 84
War of *1812*, 32–36, 38–40
War Plan ORANGE, 94, 95
Washington, George, 30–31
Watson, Mark S., 114
Wayne, Anthony, 31
Weapons technology: developments of *1970s*
  in, 138–47; in late-nineteenth-century
  Navy, 68–69; modern naval C2 and, 157–
  58; in World War I, 81–82
Weinberger, Caspar W., 1–2
Weizenbaum, Joseph, 7
Welchman, Gordon, 206
Wickham, John A., Jr., 182–83
"Wig-wag" system, 60
Wilkinson, Spenser, 76
Williams, T. Harry, 58, 63
Wilson, Woodrow, 82
Winterbotham, F. W., 142
Wireless radio, 47, 66, 68, 82–83, 86. *See
  also* Electronic warfare
Wohlstetter, Roberta, 97–98
Woodrum, Clifton A., 113
Woodrum committee, 113
World War I, 81–87

World War II, 98–111
Worldwide Military Command and Control
    System (WWMCCS), 135–37
Wylie, J. C., 11, 255, 257, 258, 259–60

Yom Kippur War, 143, 172, 173, 263
Young, S. B. M., 78